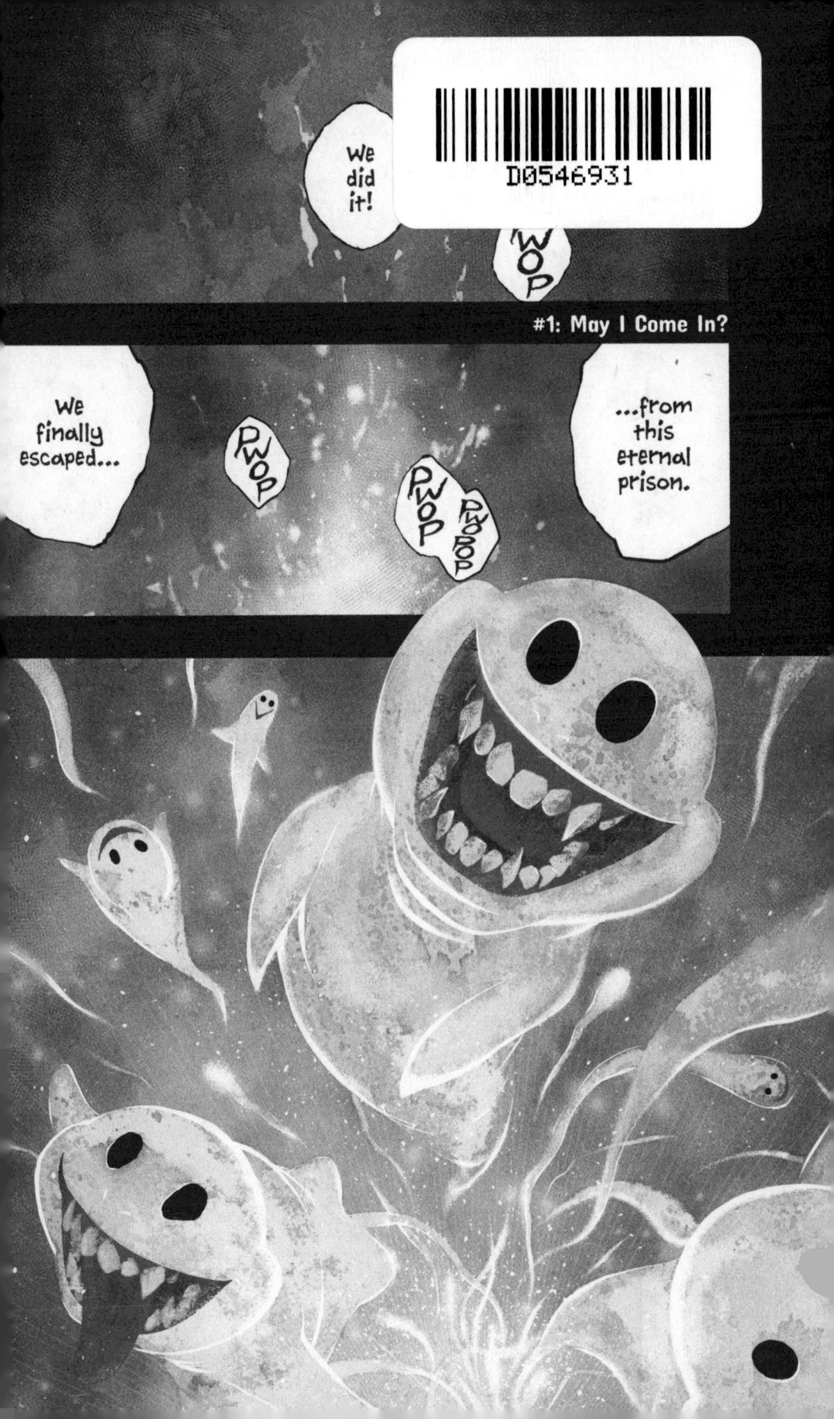
We did it!
PWOP
#1: May I Come In?
We finally escaped...
PWOP
PWOP
PWOPOP
...from this eternal prison.

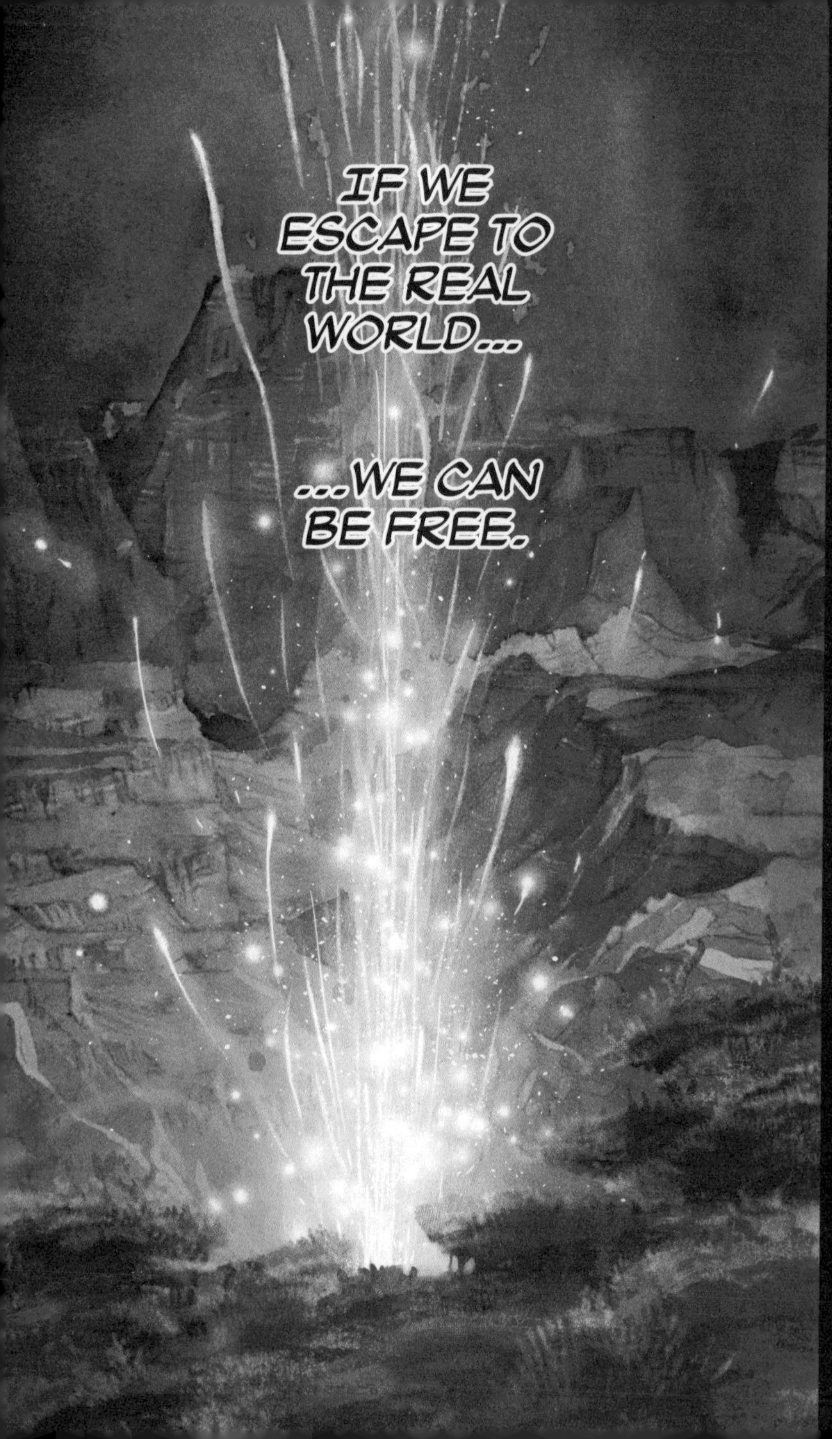
IF WE ESCAPE TO THE REAL WORLD...
...WE CAN BE FREE.

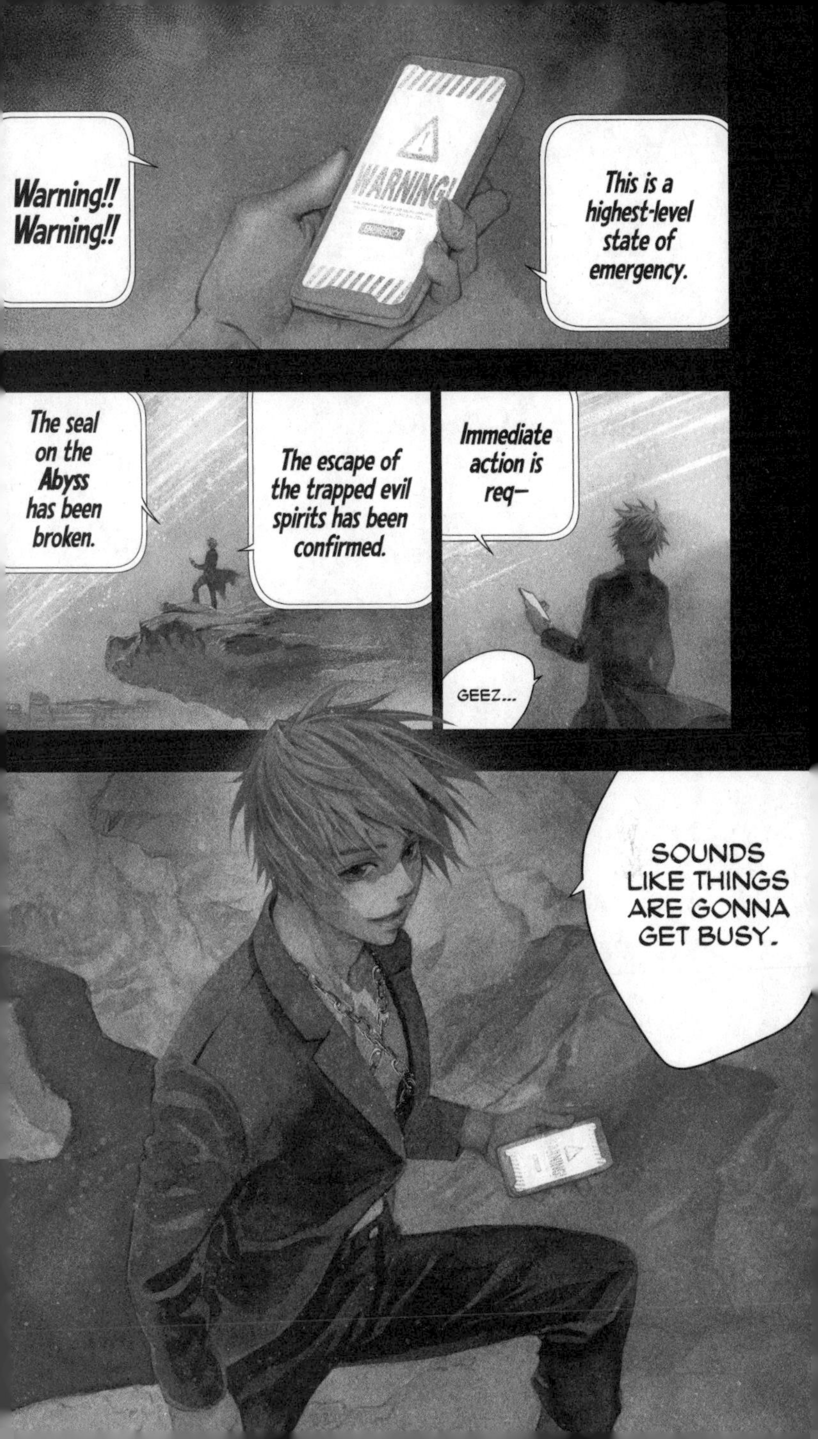
Warning!! Warning!!
WARNING!
This is a highest-level state of emergency.
The seal on the Abyss has been broken.
The escape of the trapped evil spirits has been confirmed.
Immediate action is req—
GEEZ...
SOUNDS LIKE THINGS ARE GONNA GET BUSY.

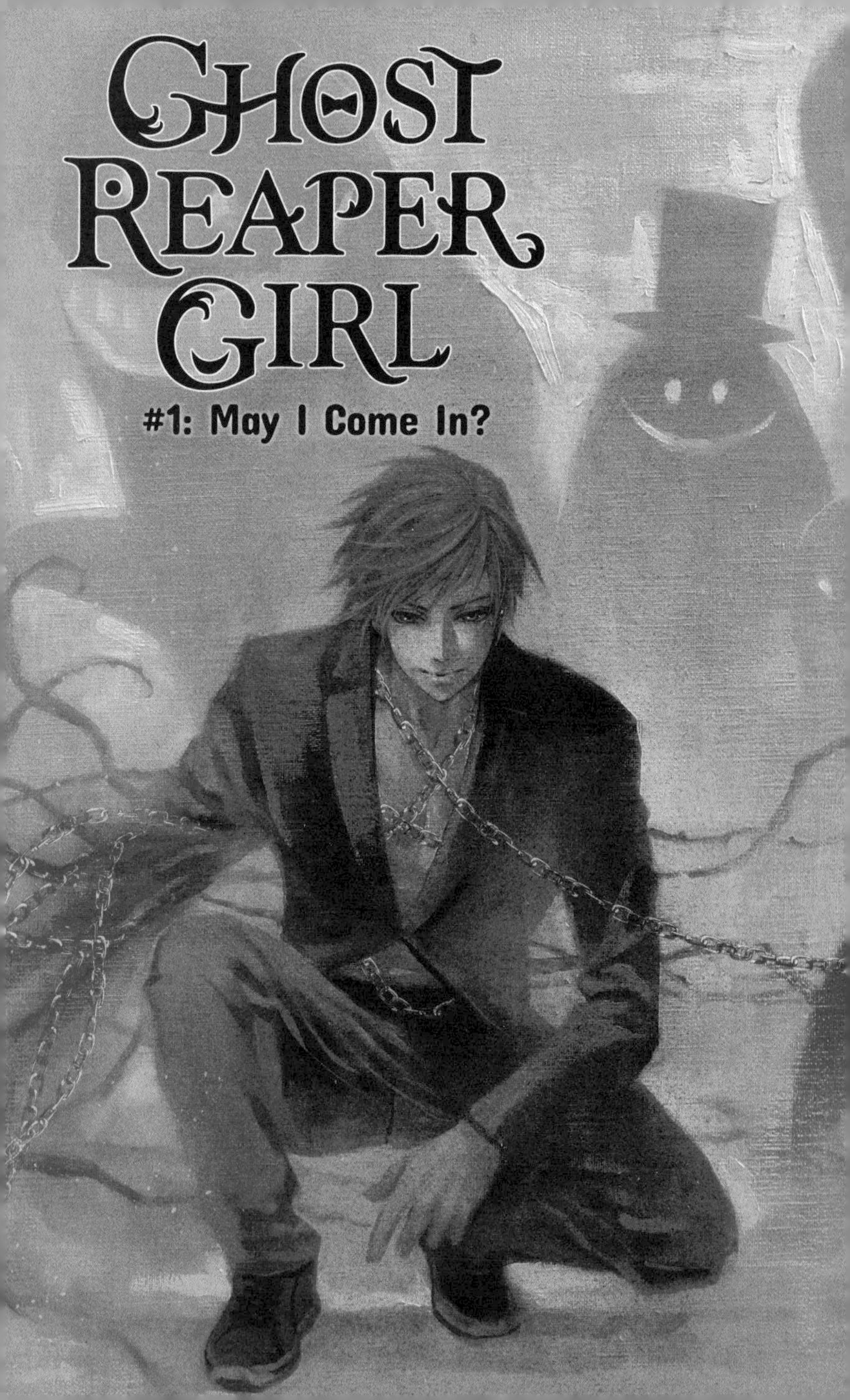
GHOST REAPER GIRL
#1: May I Come In?

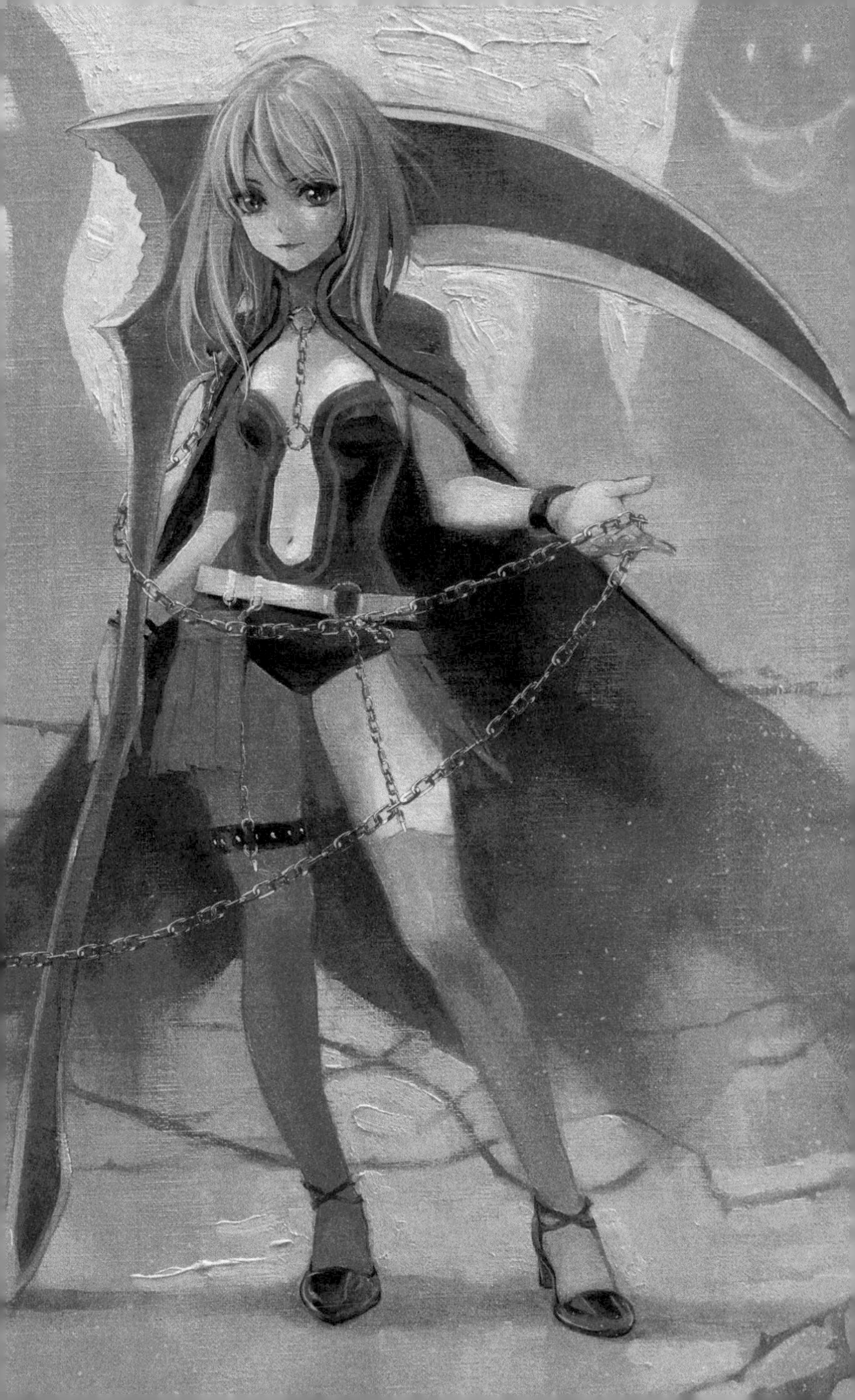

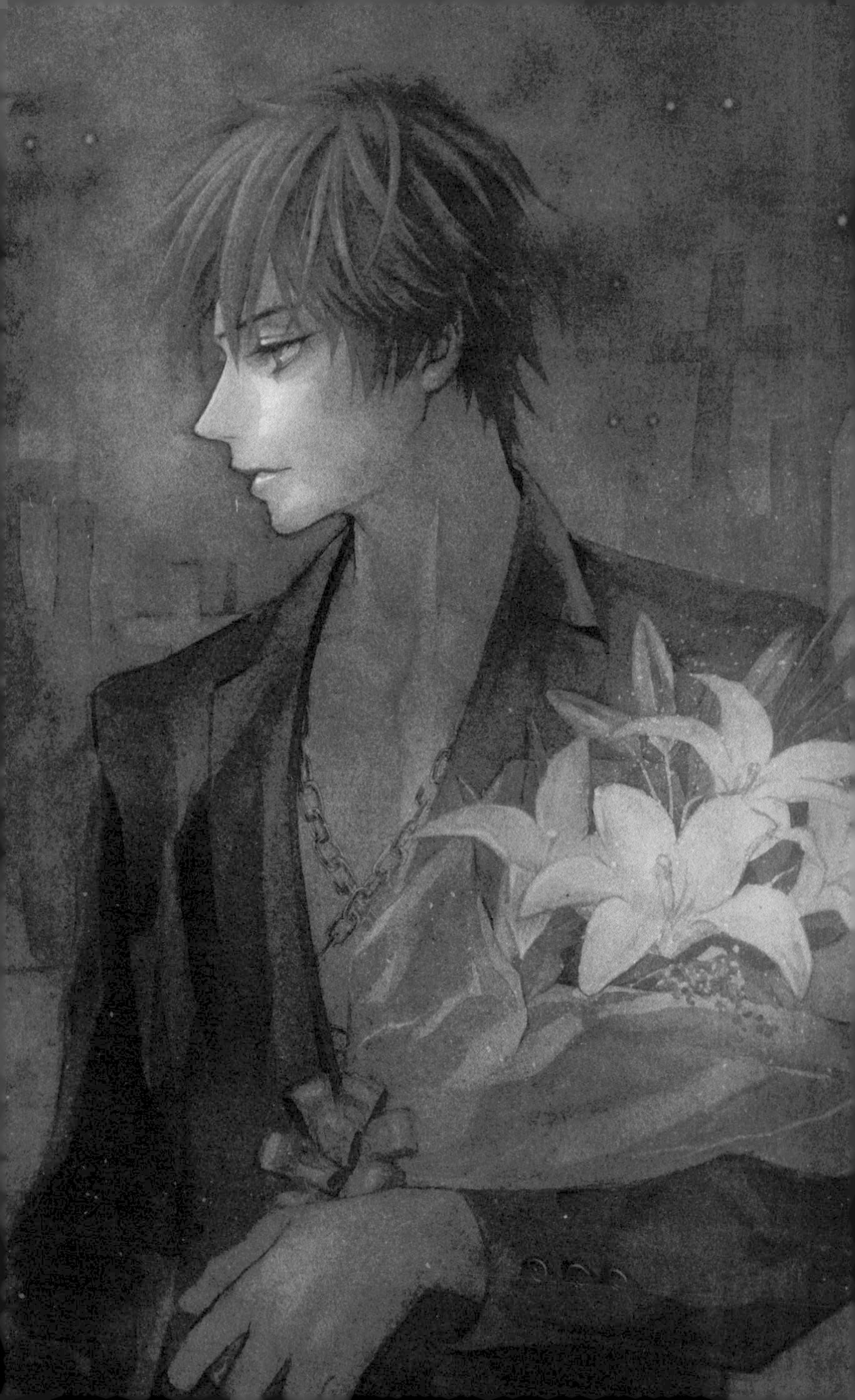

GHOST REAPER GIRL

1
CONTENTS

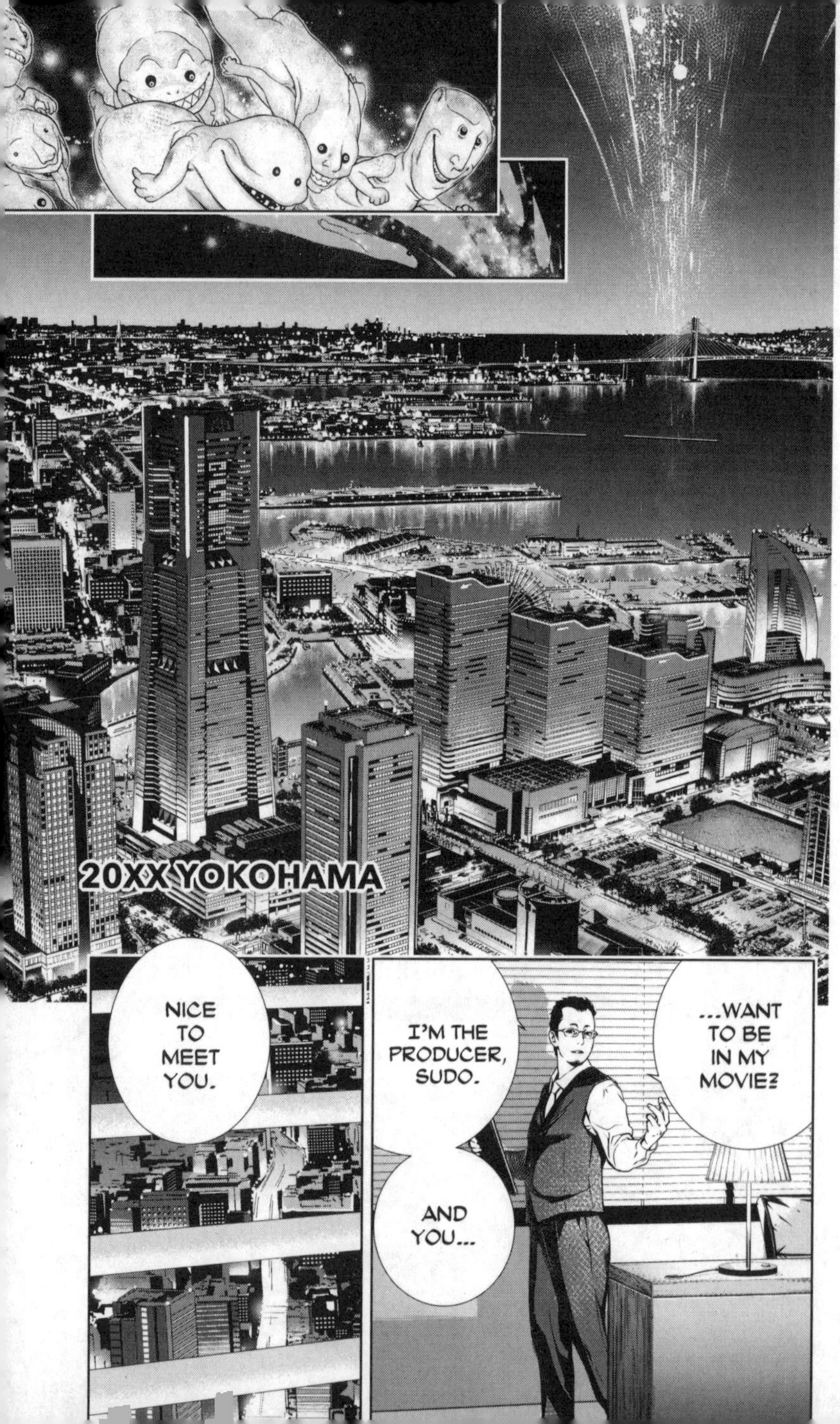
20XX YOKOHAMA
NICE TO MEET YOU.
I'M THE PRODUCER, SUDO.
AND YOU...
...WANT TO BE IN MY MOVIE?

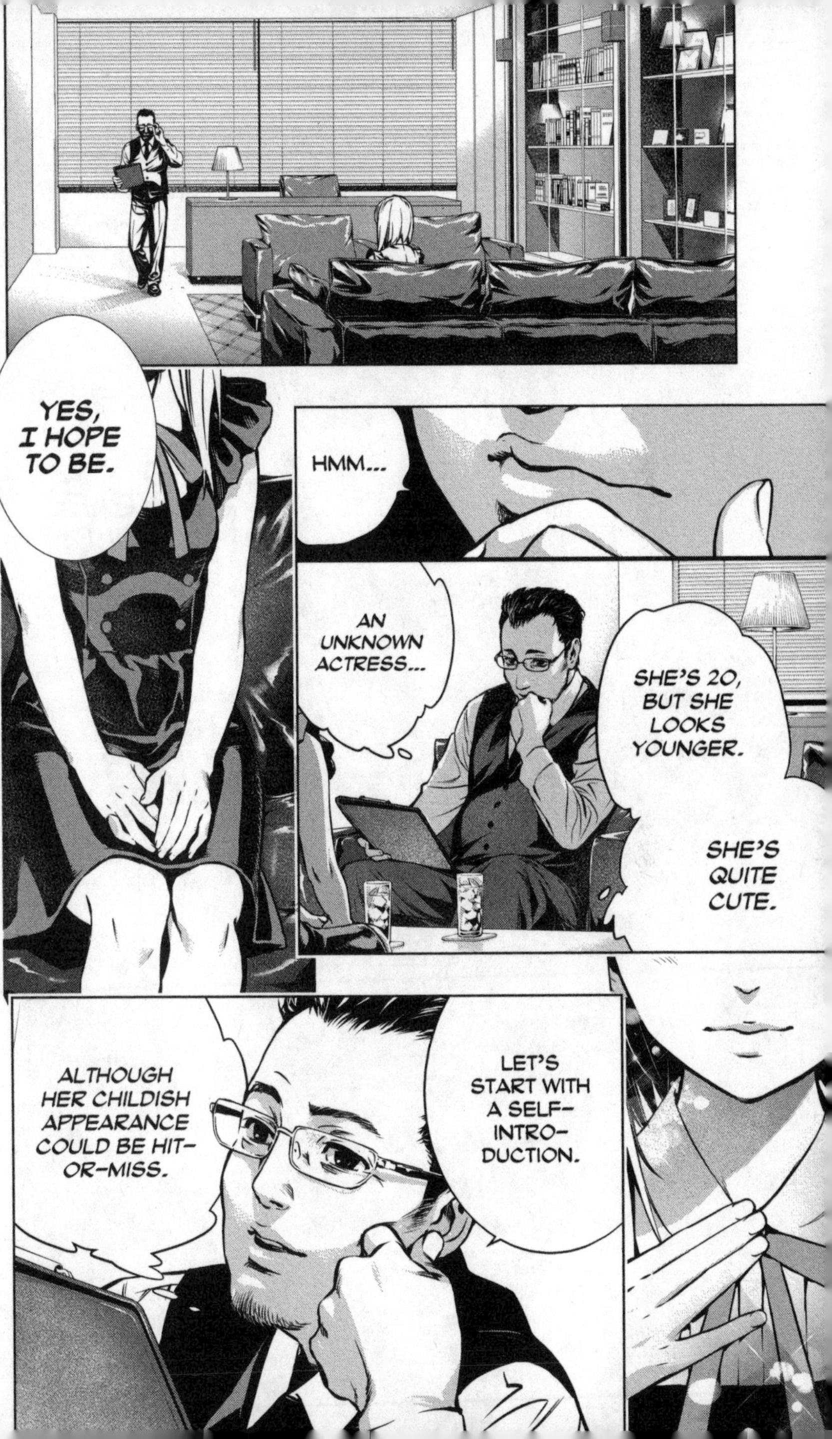
YES, I HOPE TO BE.
HMM...
SHE'S 20, BUT SHE LOOKS YOUNGER.
AN UNKNOWN ACTRESS...
SHE'S QUITE CUTE.
ALTHOUGH HER CHILDISH APPEARANCE COULD BE HIT-OR-MISS.
LET'S START WITH A SELF-INTRODUCTION.

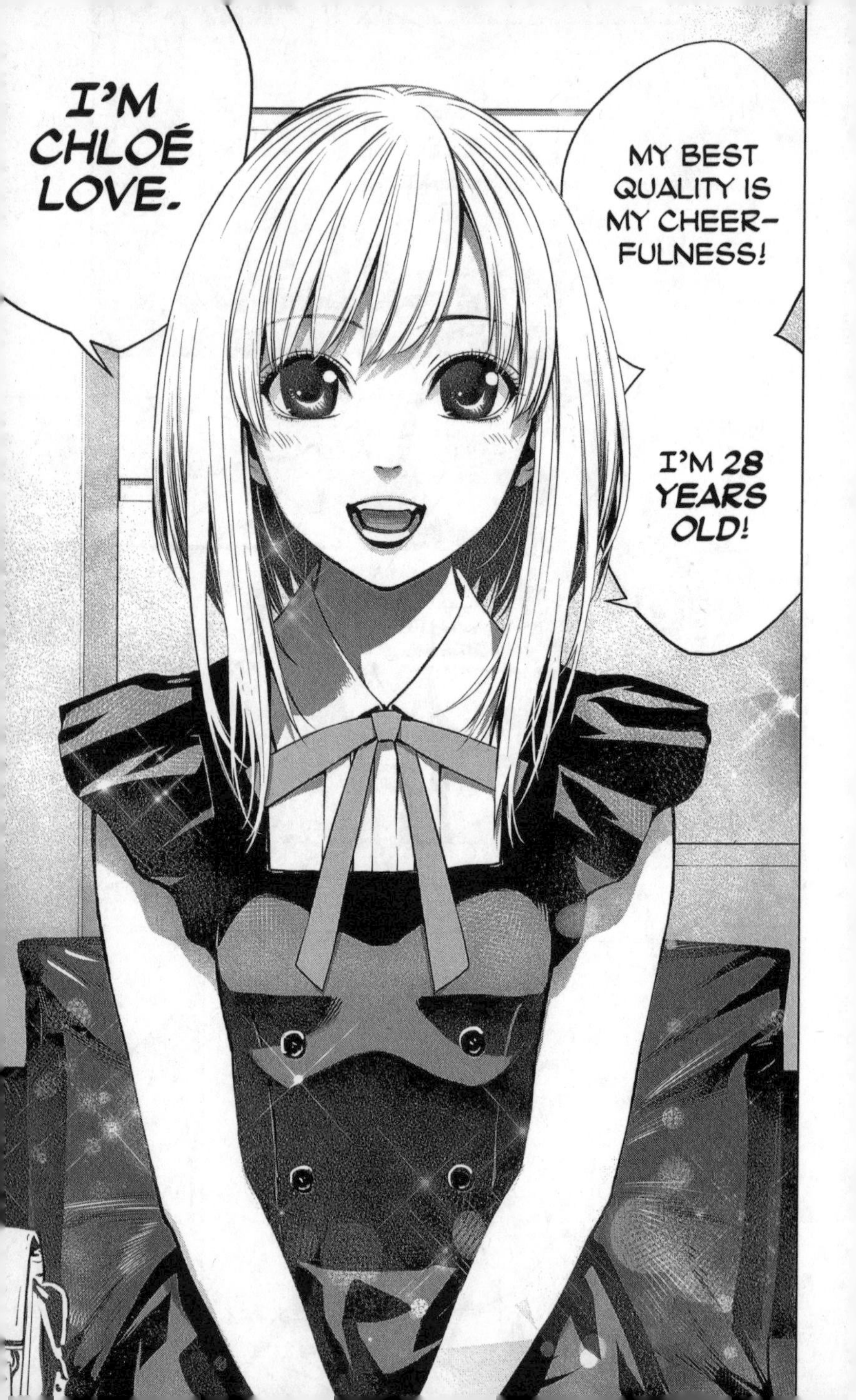
MY BEST QUALITY IS MY CHEER-FULNESS!
I'M 28 YEARS OLD!
I'M CHLOÉ LOVE.

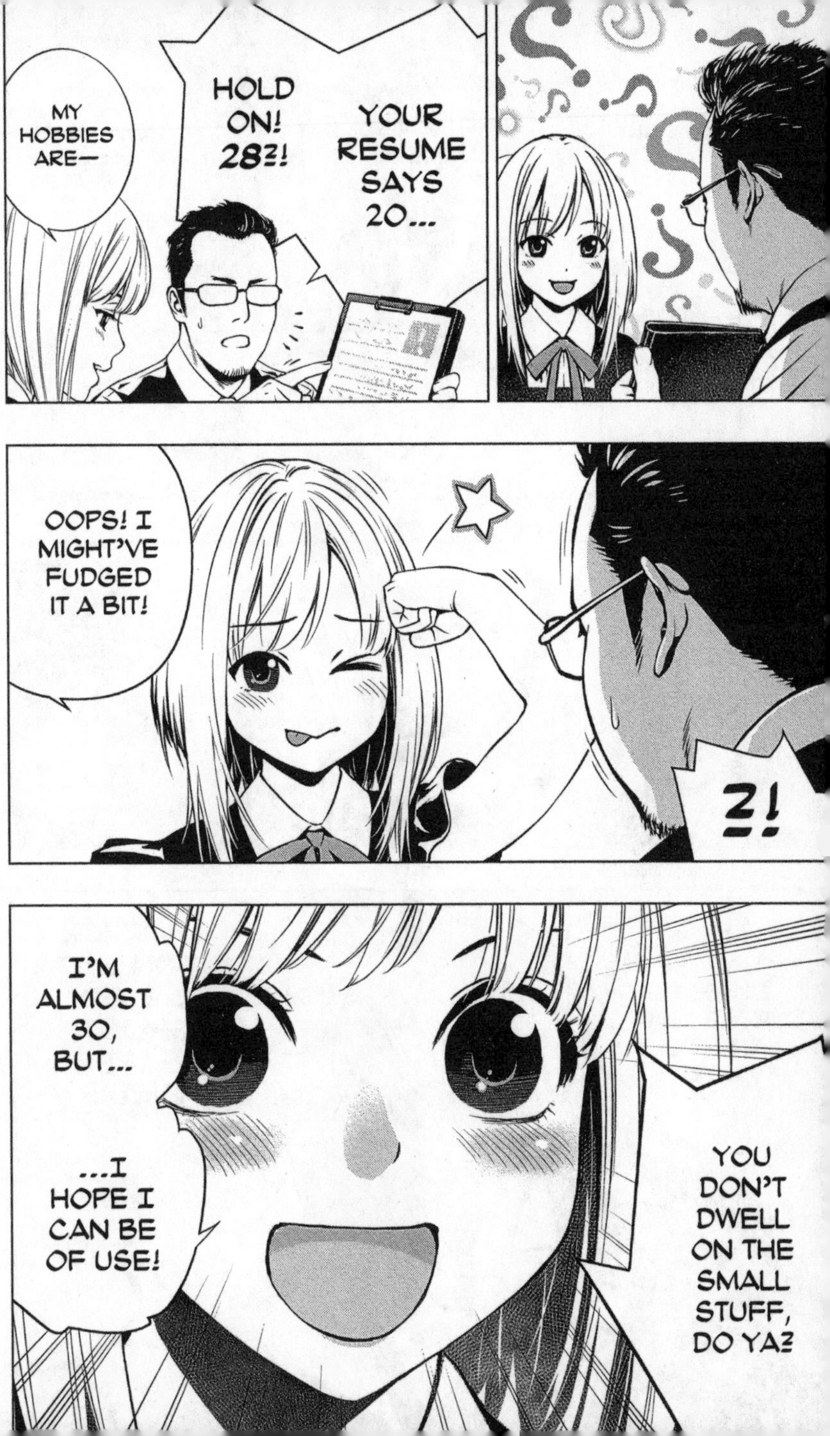
MY HOBBIES ARE—
HOLD ON! 28?!
YOUR RESUME SAYS 20...
OOPS! I MIGHT'VE FUDGED IT A BIT!
?!
I'M ALMOST 30, BUT...
...I HOPE I CAN BE OF USE!
YOU DON'T DWELL ON THE SMALL STUFF, DO YA?

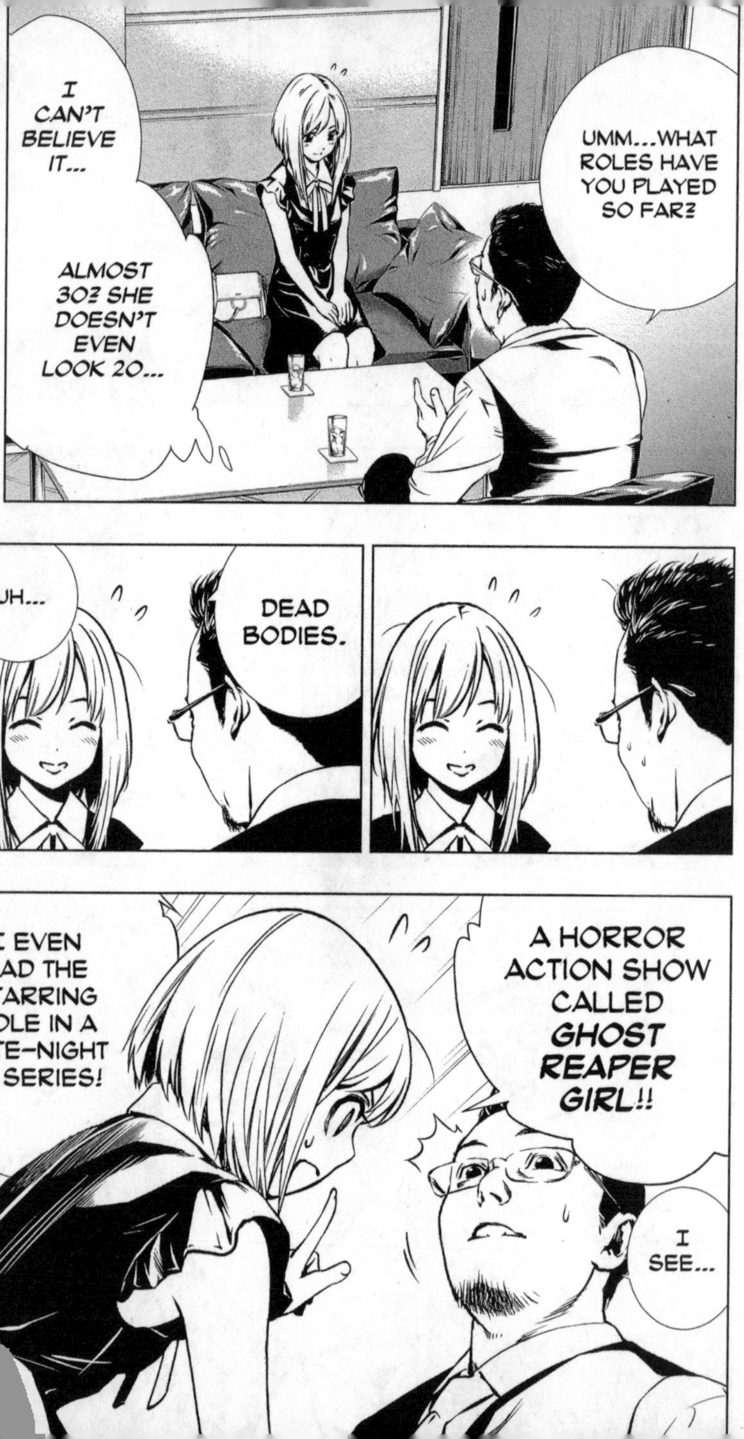
UMM...WHAT ROLES HAVE YOU PLAYED SO FAR?
I CAN'T BELIEVE IT...
ALMOST 30? SHE DOESN'T EVEN LOOK 20...
DEAD BODIES.
UH...
I EVEN HAD THE STARRING ROLE IN A LATE-NIGHT TV SERIES!
A HORROR ACTION SHOW CALLED GHOST REAPER GIRL!!
I SEE...

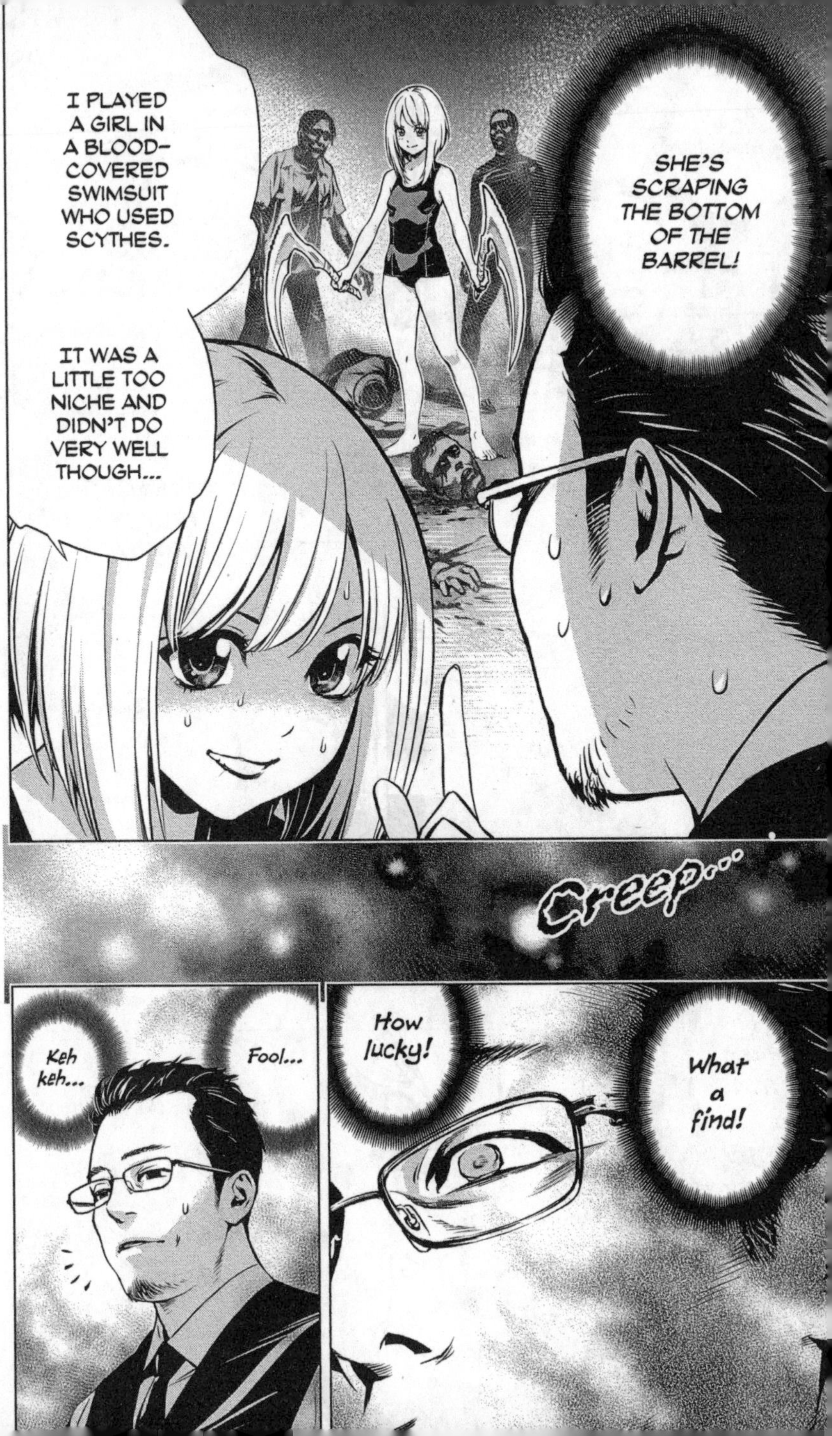
SHE'S SCRAPING THE BOTTOM OF THE BARREL!
I PLAYED A GIRL IN A BLOOD-COVERED SWIMSUIT WHO USED SCYTHES.
IT WAS A LITTLE TOO NICHE AND DIDN'T DO VERY WELL THOUGH...
Creep...
What a find!
How lucky!
Fool...
Keh keh...

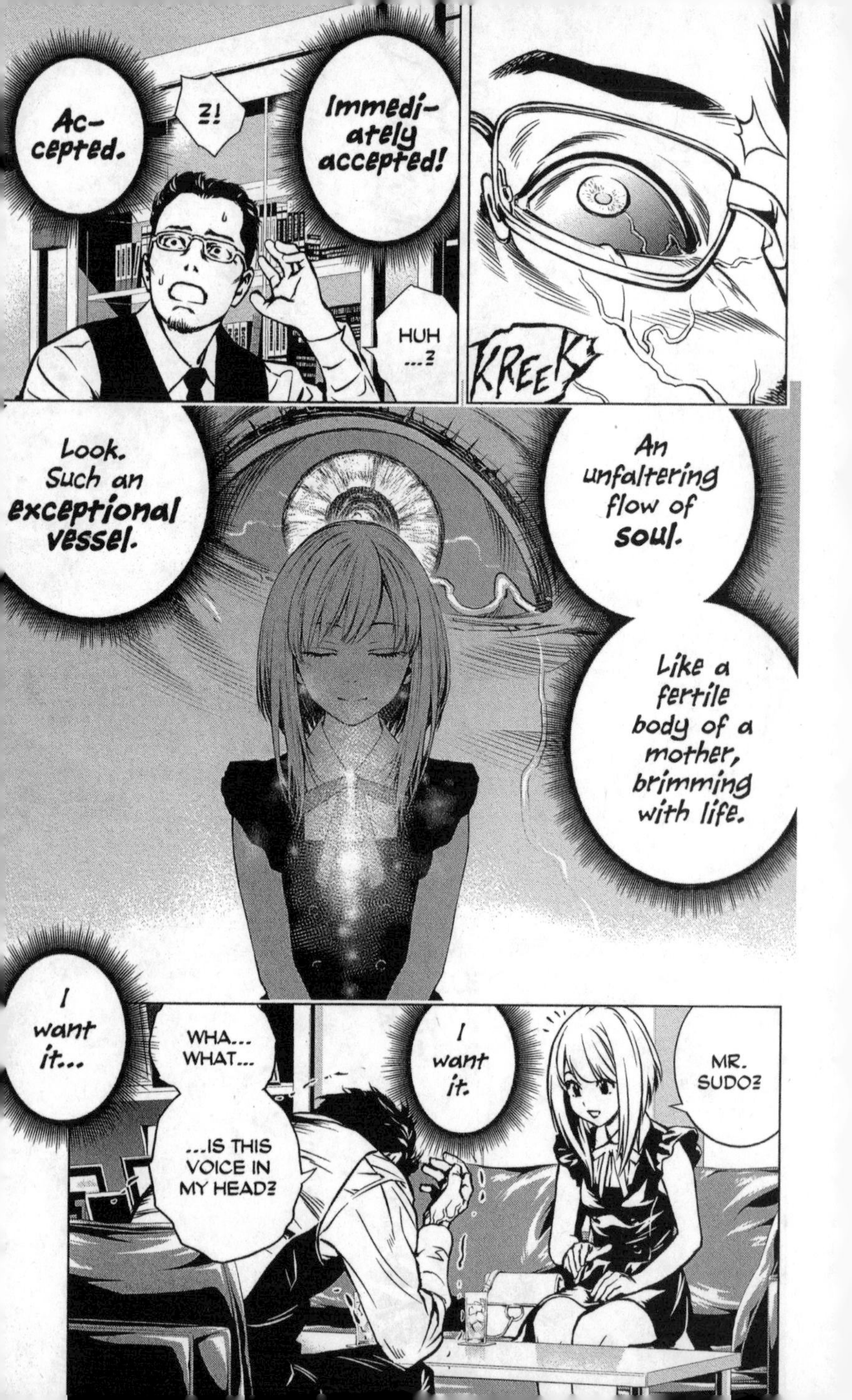
KREEK
Immedi-ately accepted!
?!
Ac-cepted.
HUH...?
An unfaltering flow of soul.
Like a fertile body of a mother, brimming with life.
Look. Such an exceptional vessel.
MR. SUDO?
I want it.
WHA... WHAT...
...IS THIS VOICE IN MY HEAD?
I want it...

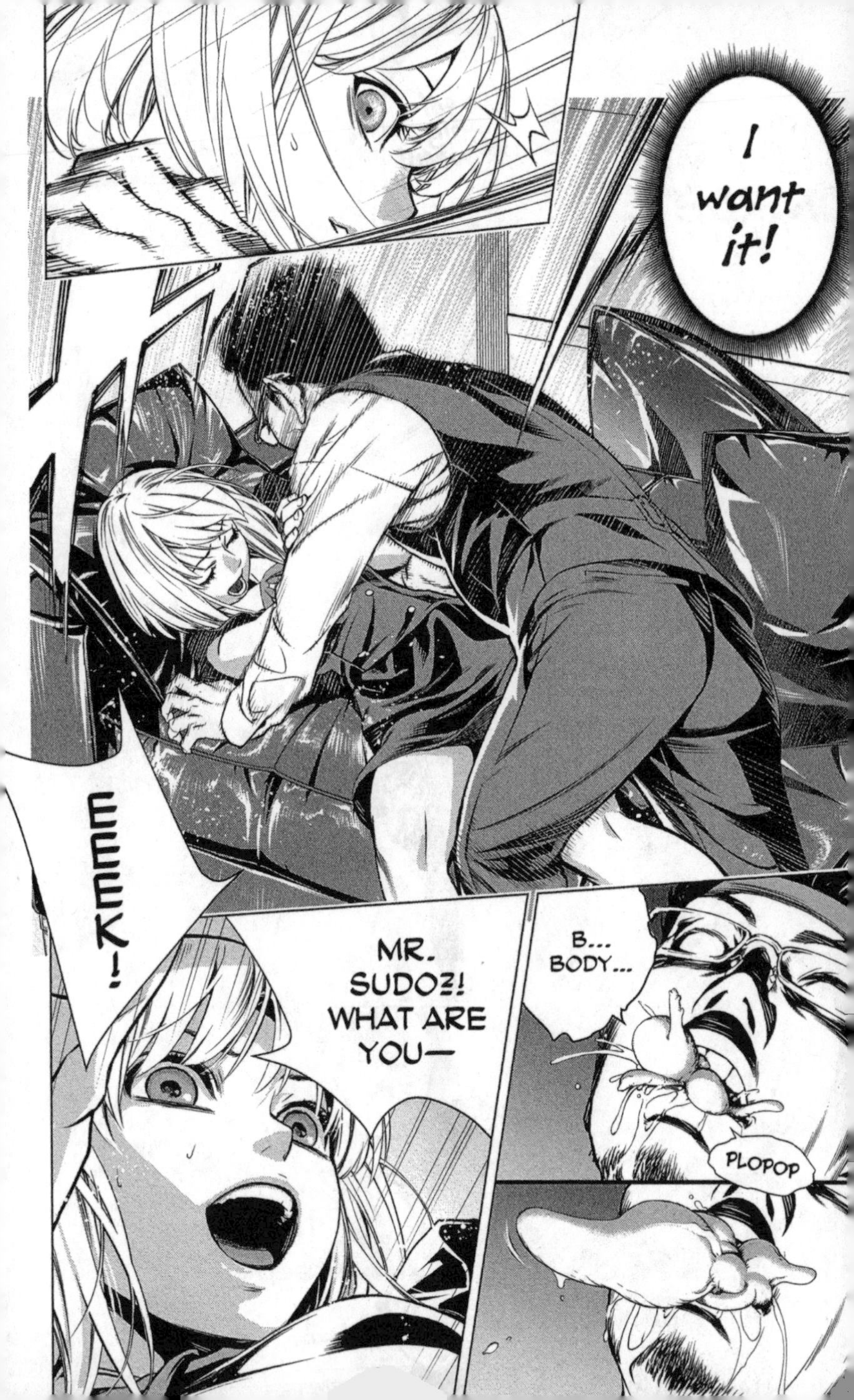
I want it!
EEEEK!
B... BODY...
PLOPOP
MR. SUDO?! WHAT ARE YOU—

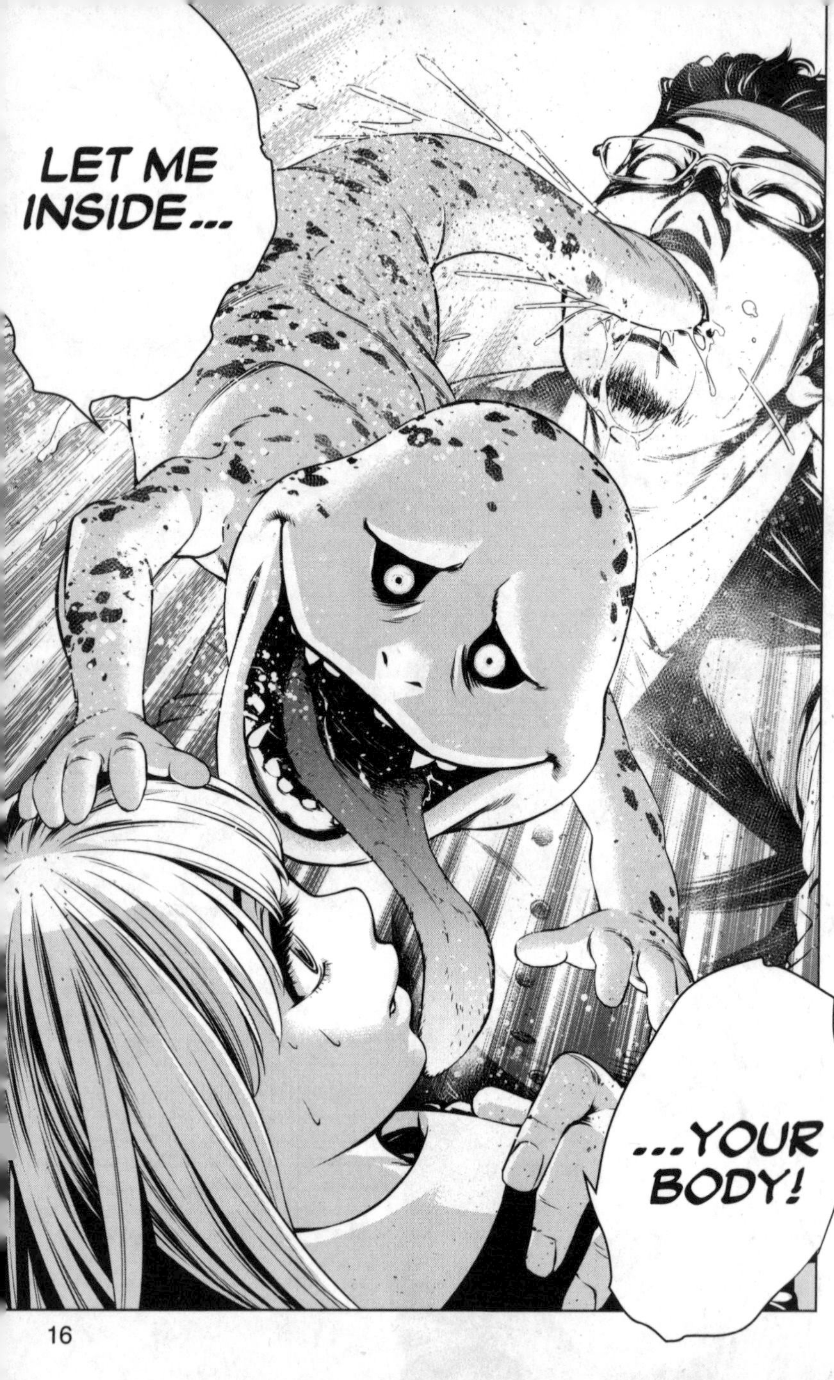
LET ME INSIDE...
...YOUR BODY!

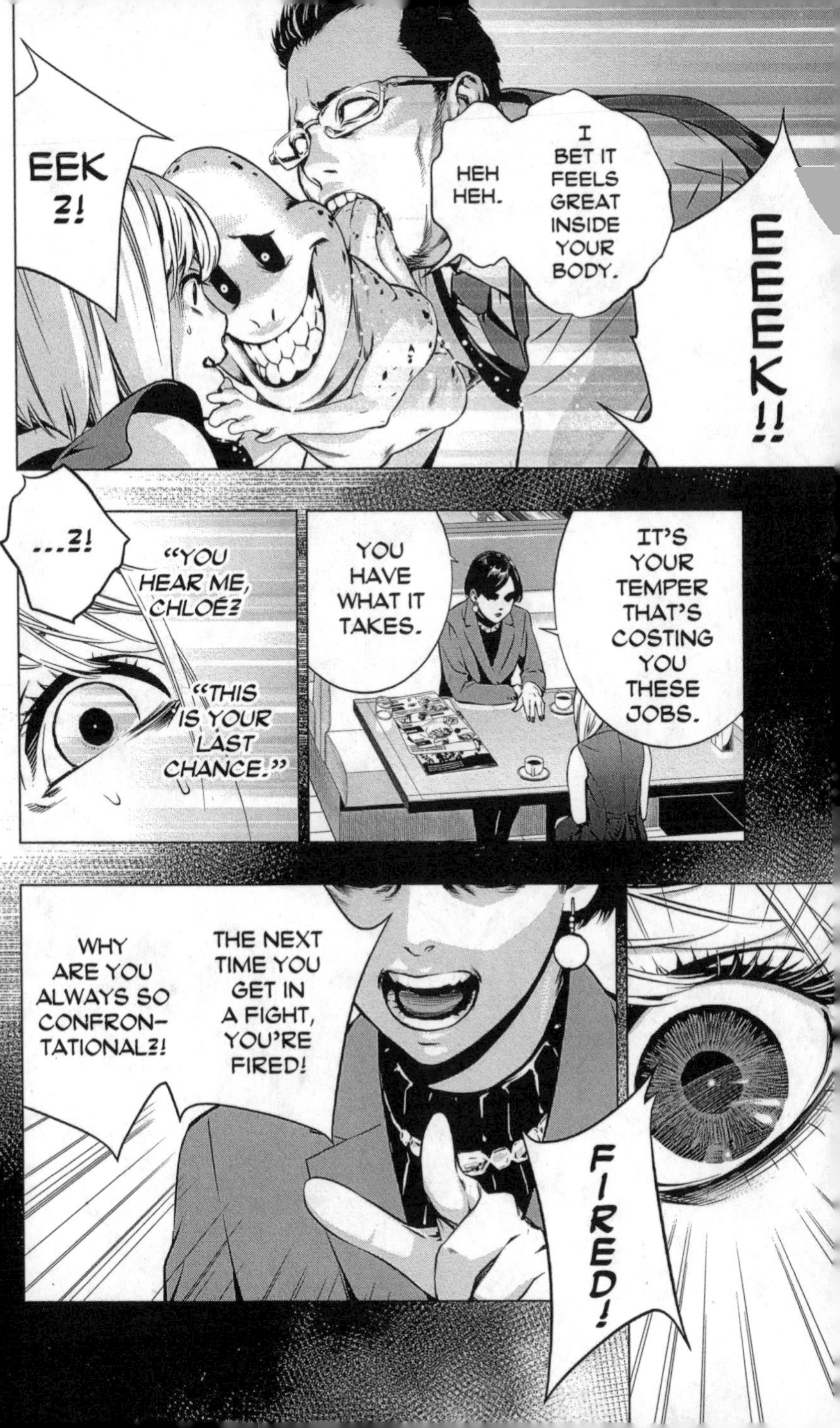
EEEEK!!
I BET IT FEELS GREAT INSIDE YOUR BODY.
HEH HEH.
EEK ?!
IT'S YOUR TEMPER THAT'S COSTING YOU THESE JOBS.
YOU HAVE WHAT IT TAKES.
"YOU HEAR ME, CHLOÉ?
"THIS IS YOUR LAST CHANCE."
...?!
FIRED!
THE NEXT TIME YOU GET IN A FIGHT, YOU'RE FIRED!
WHY ARE YOU ALWAYS SO CONFRON-TATIONAL?!

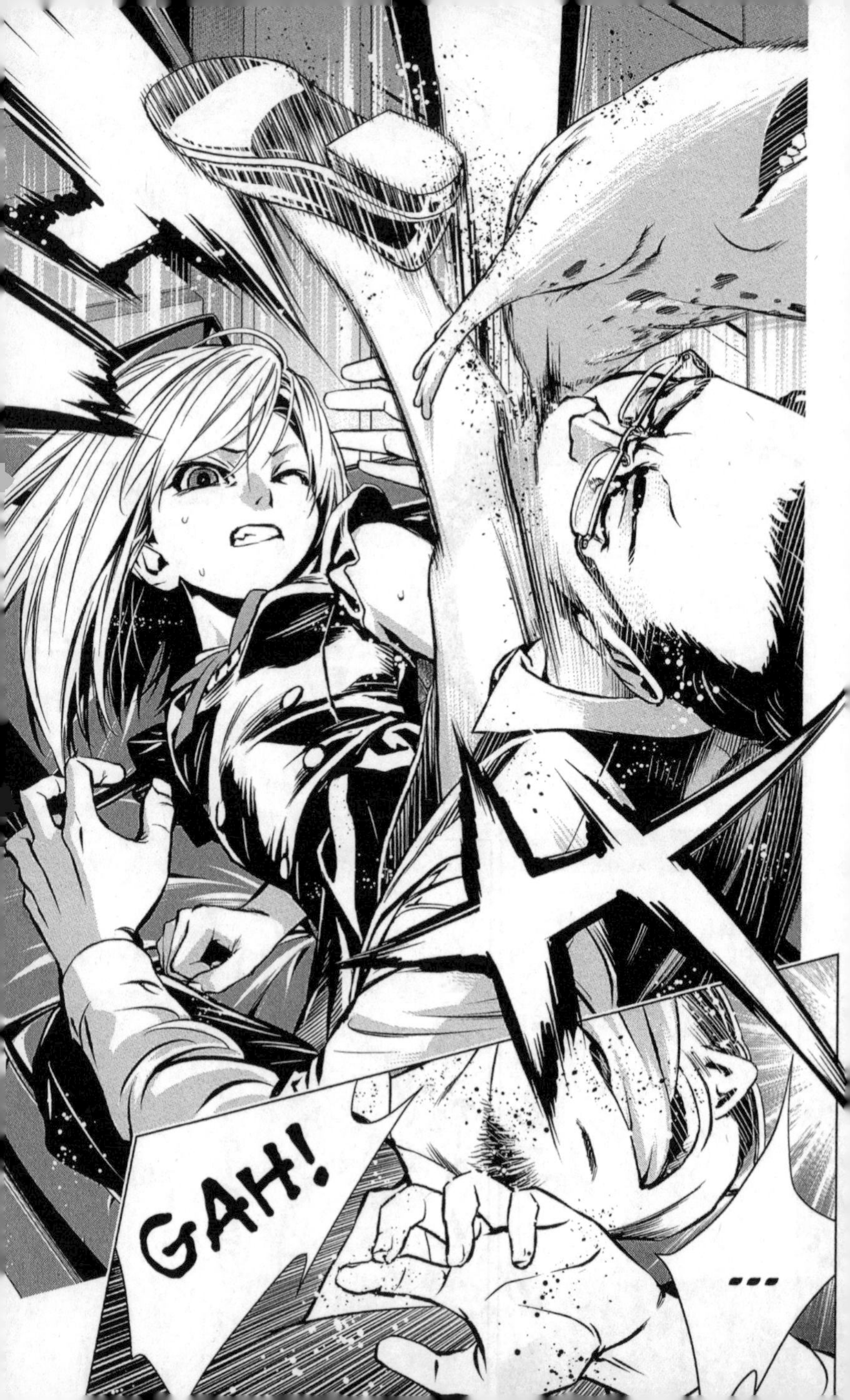
GAH!
...

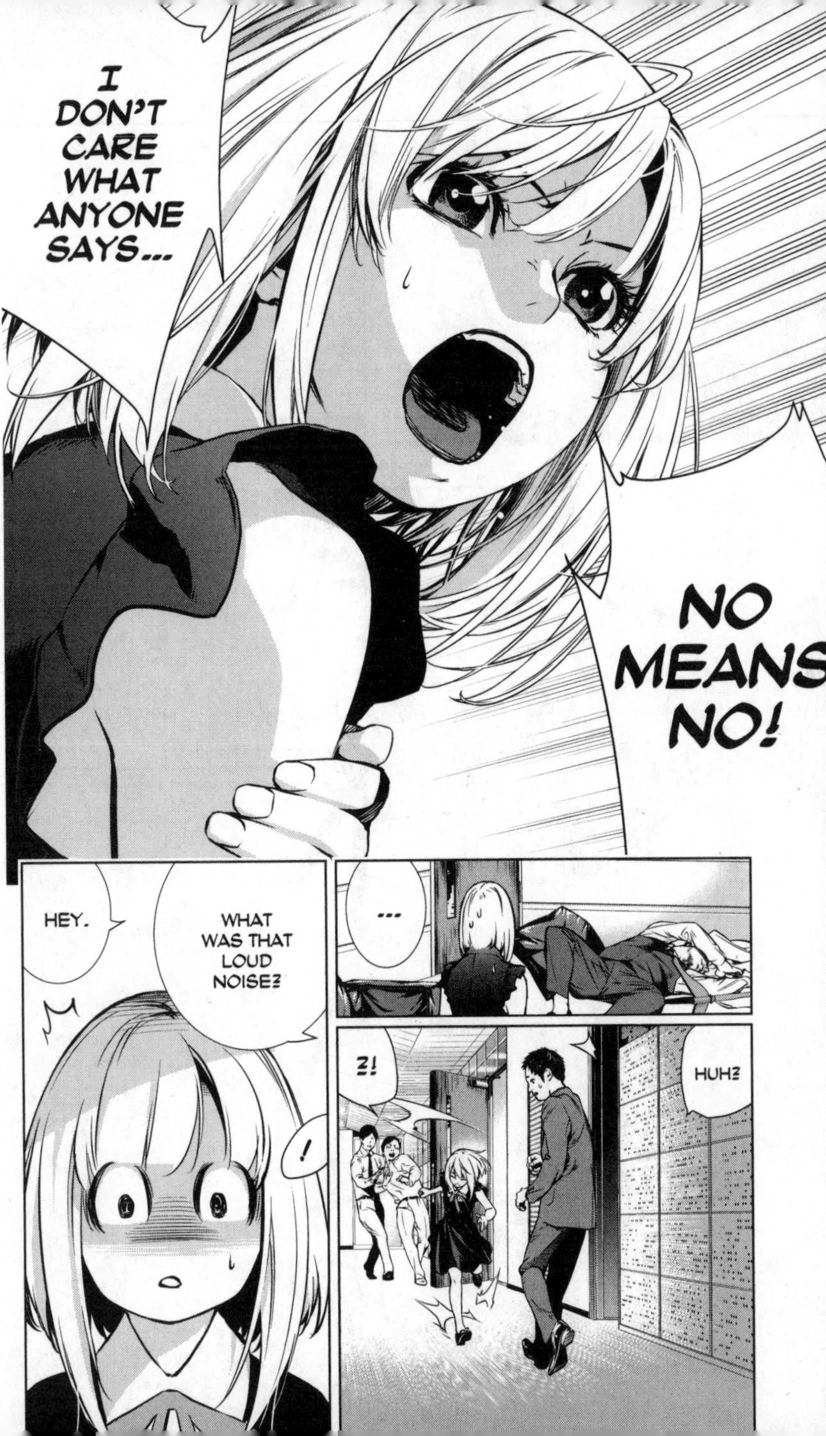
I DON'T CARE WHAT ANYONE SAYS...
NO MEANS NO!
...
HUH?
?!
HEY.
WHAT WAS THAT LOUD NOISE?
!

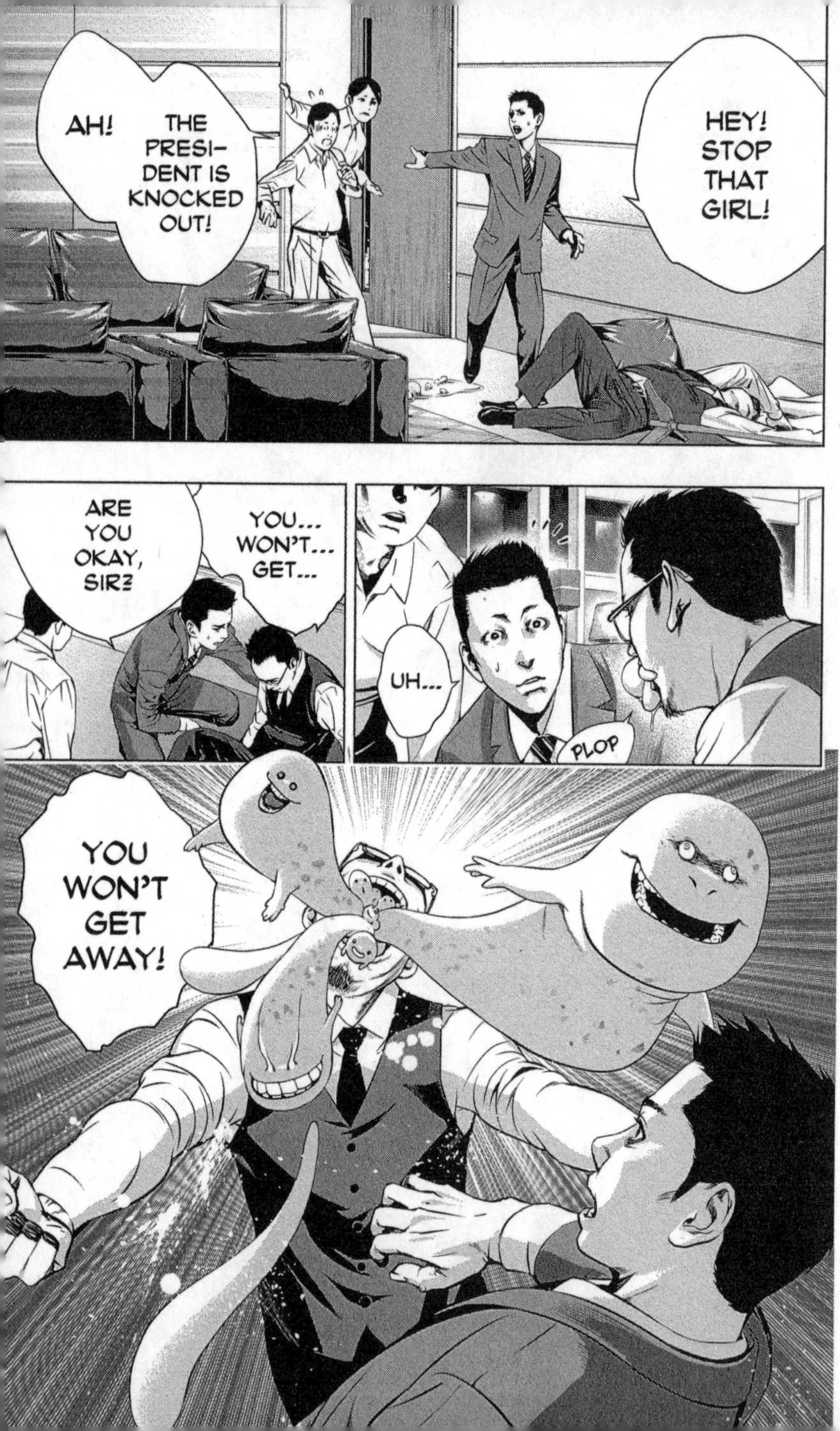
AH! THE PRESIDENT IS KNOCKED OUT!
HEY! STOP THAT GIRL!
ARE YOU OKAY, SIR?
YOU... WON'T... GET...
UH...
PLOP
YOU WON'T GET AWAY!

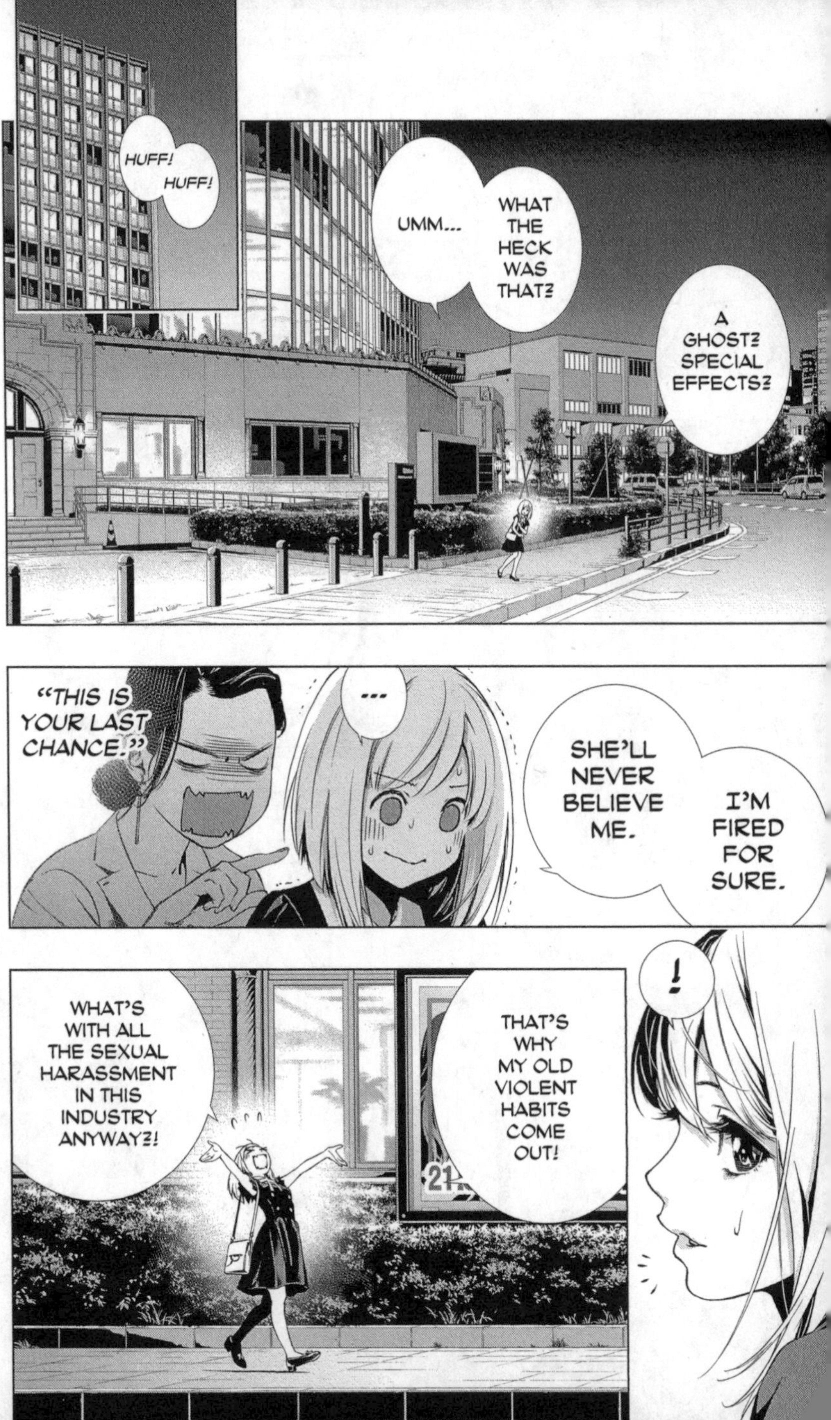
HUFF! HUFF!
A GHOST? SPECIAL EFFECTS?
WHAT THE HECK WAS THAT?
UMM...
I'M FIRED FOR SURE.
SHE'LL NEVER BELIEVE ME.
...
"THIS IS YOUR LAST CHANCE."
!
THAT'S WHY MY OLD VIOLENT HABITS COME OUT!
WHAT'S WITH ALL THE SEXUAL HARASSMENT IN THIS INDUSTRY ANYWAY?!

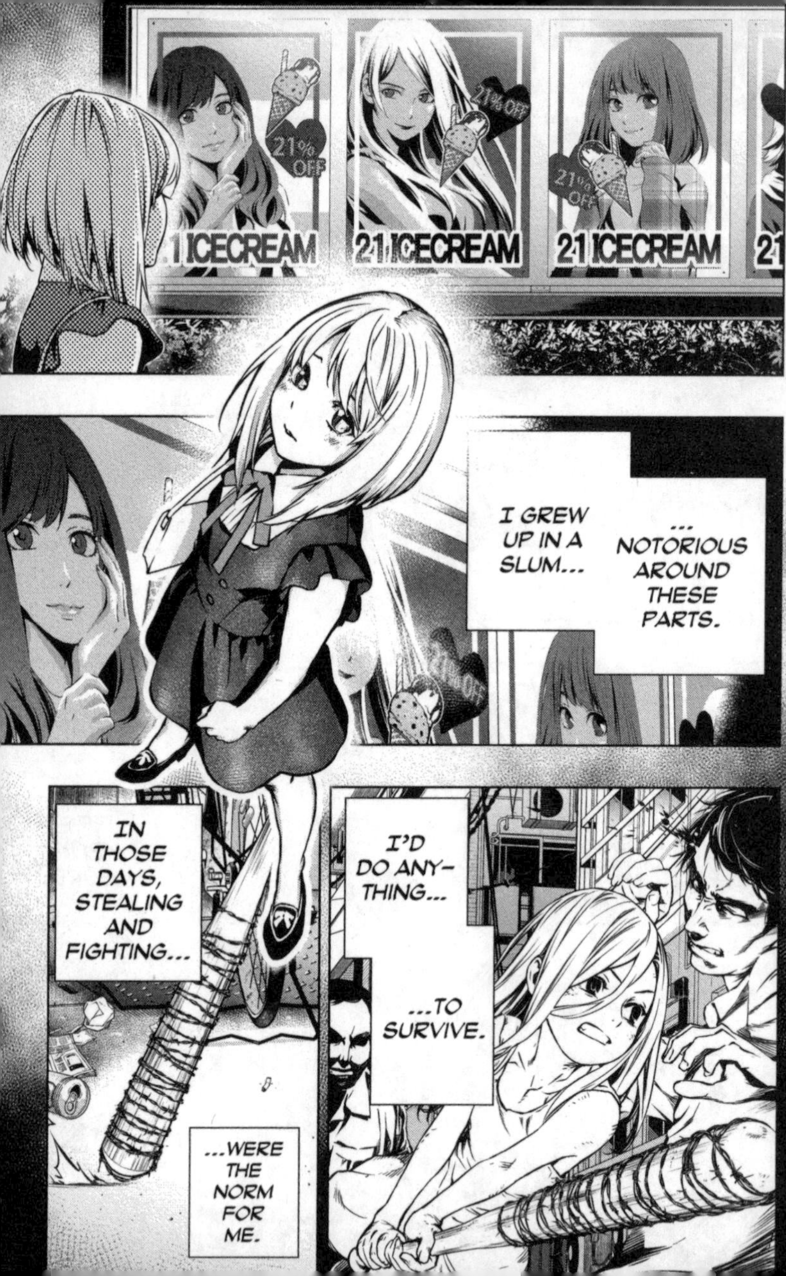
21% OFF
21 ICECREAM
21% OFF
21 ICECREAM
21% OFF
21 ICECREAM
I GREW UP IN A SLUM...
...NOTORIOUS AROUND THESE PARTS.
I'D DO ANYTHING...
...TO SURVIVE.
IN THOSE DAYS, STEALING AND FIGHTING...
...WERE THE NORM FOR ME.

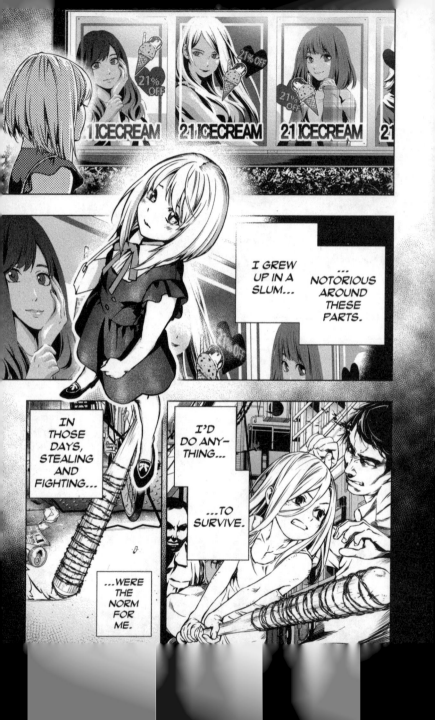

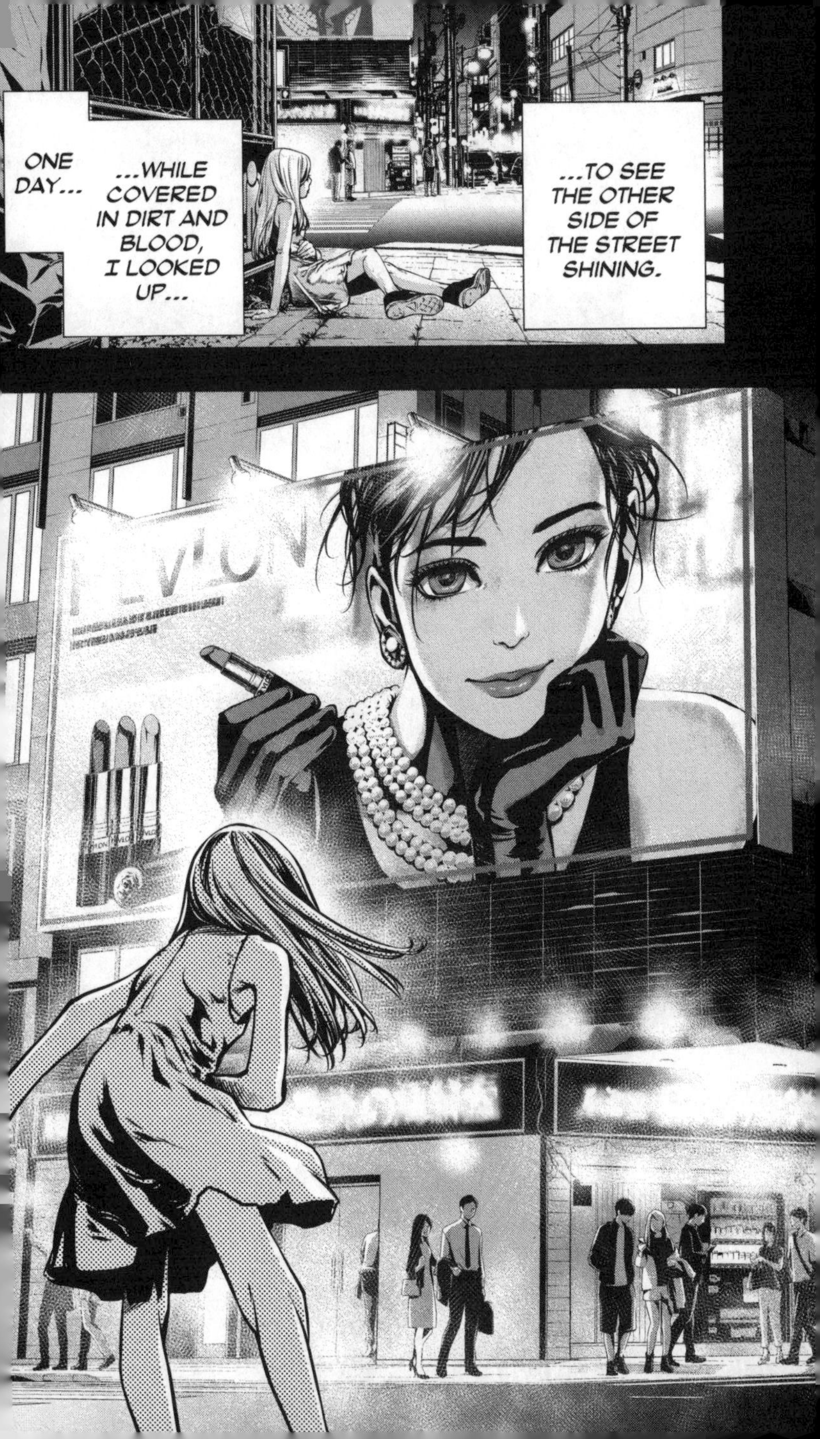
ONE DAY...
...WHILE COVERED IN DIRT AND BLOOD, I LOOKED UP...
...TO SEE THE OTHER SIDE OF THE STREET SHINING.

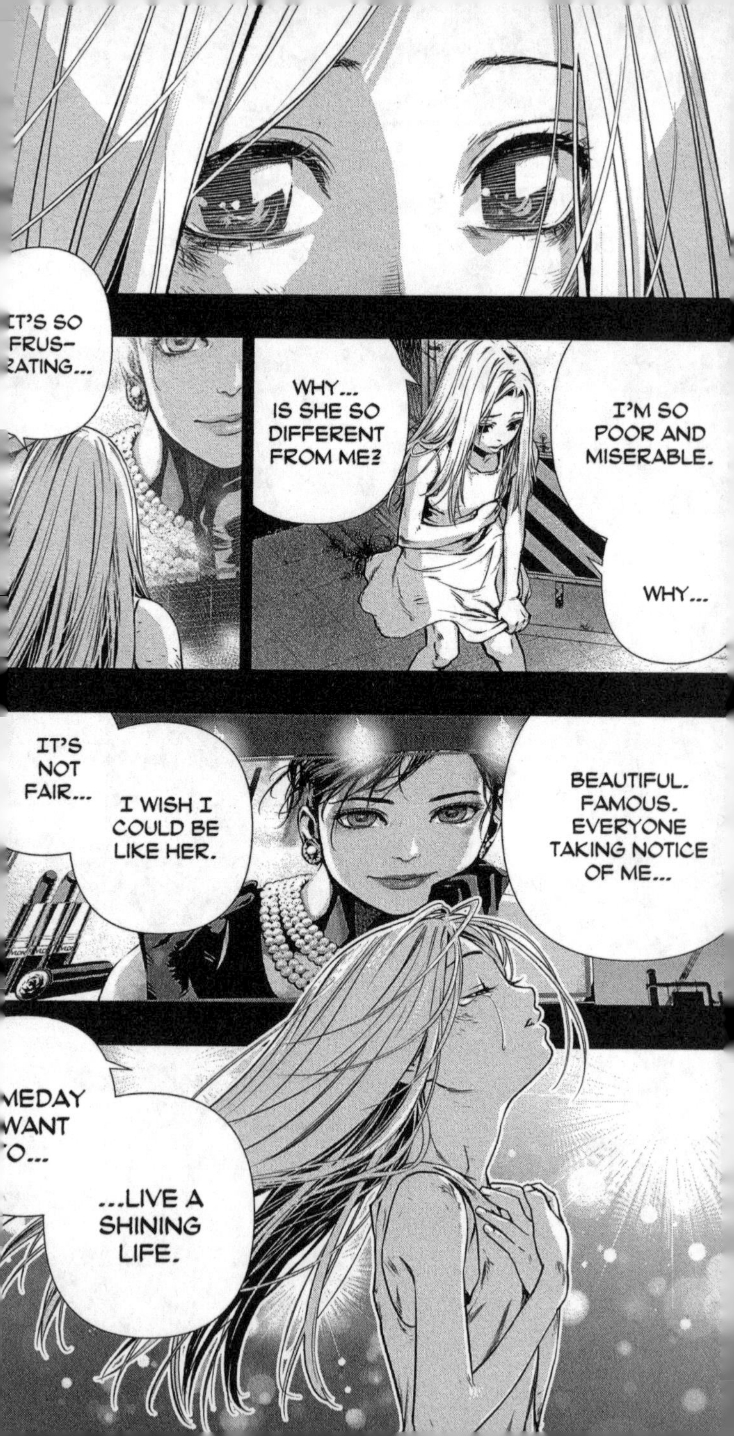
I'M SO POOR AND MISERABLE.
WHY...
WHY... IS SHE SO DIFFERENT FROM ME?
IT'S SO FRUS-RATING...
BEAUTIFUL. FAMOUS. EVERYONE TAKING NOTICE OF ME...
I WISH I COULD BE LIKE HER.
IT'S NOT FAIR...
MEDAY WANT TO...
...LIVE A SHINING LIFE.

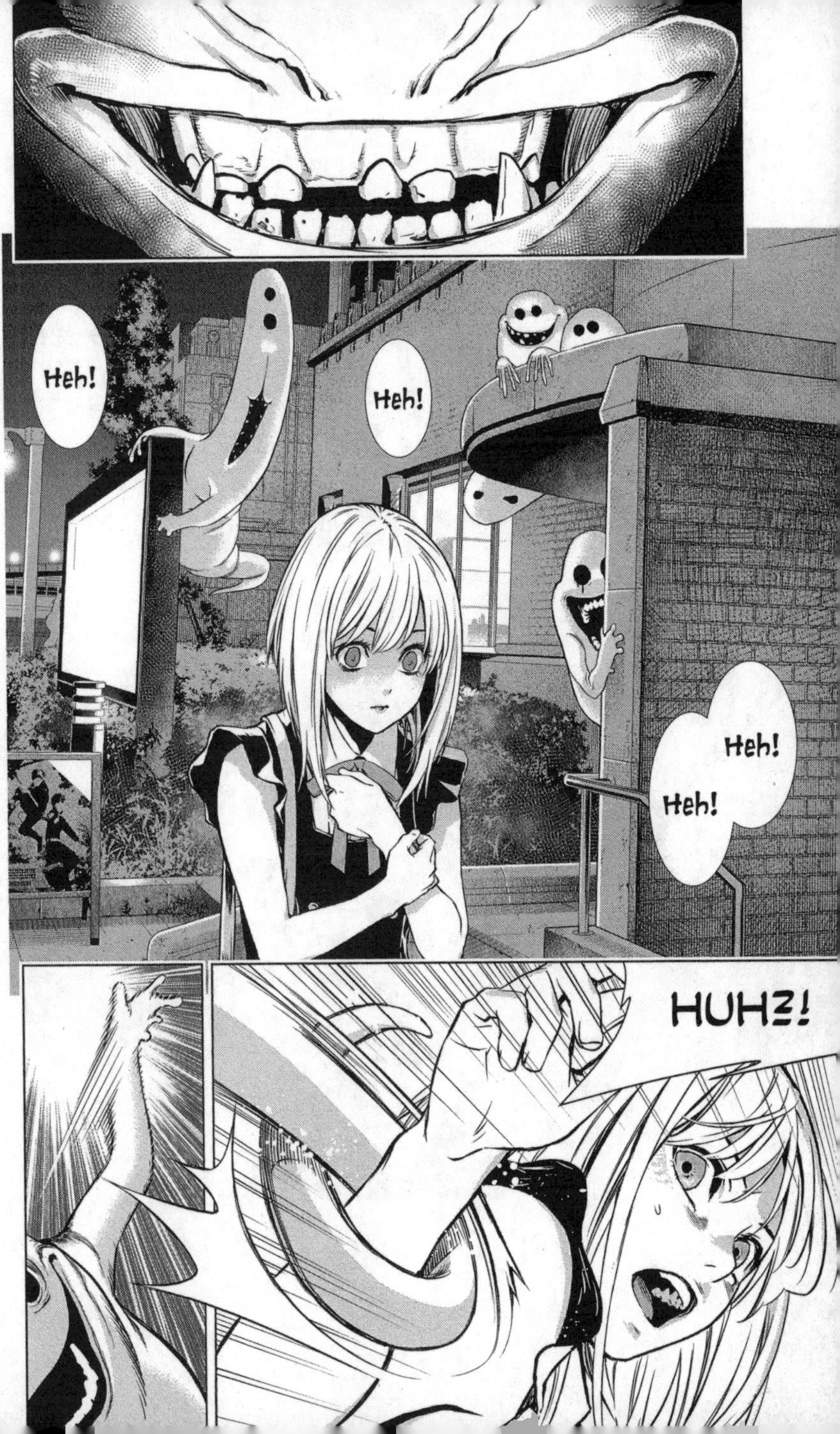
Heh! Heh!
Heh!
Heh!
HUH?!

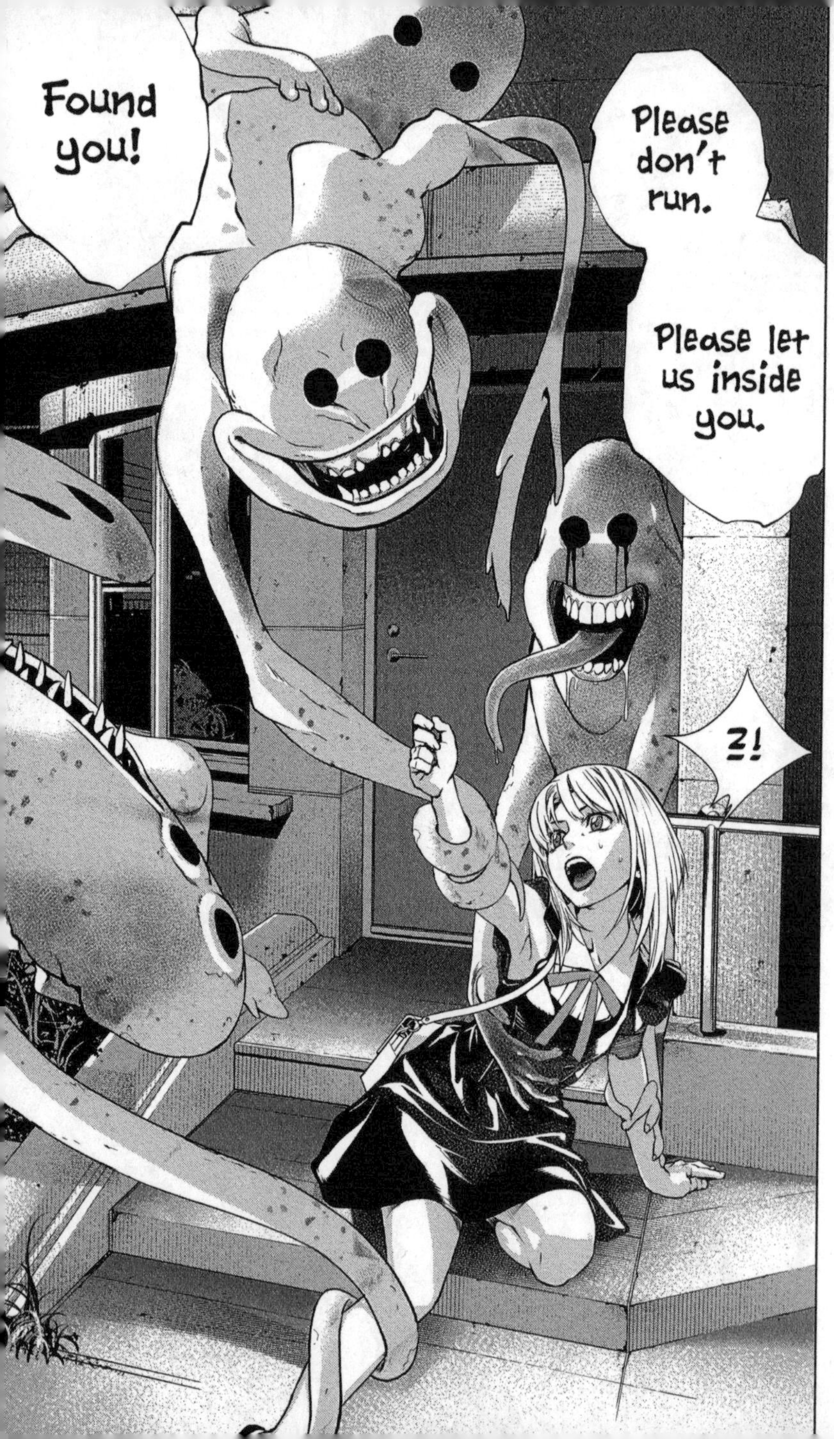
Please don't run.
Please let us inside you.
Found you!
?!

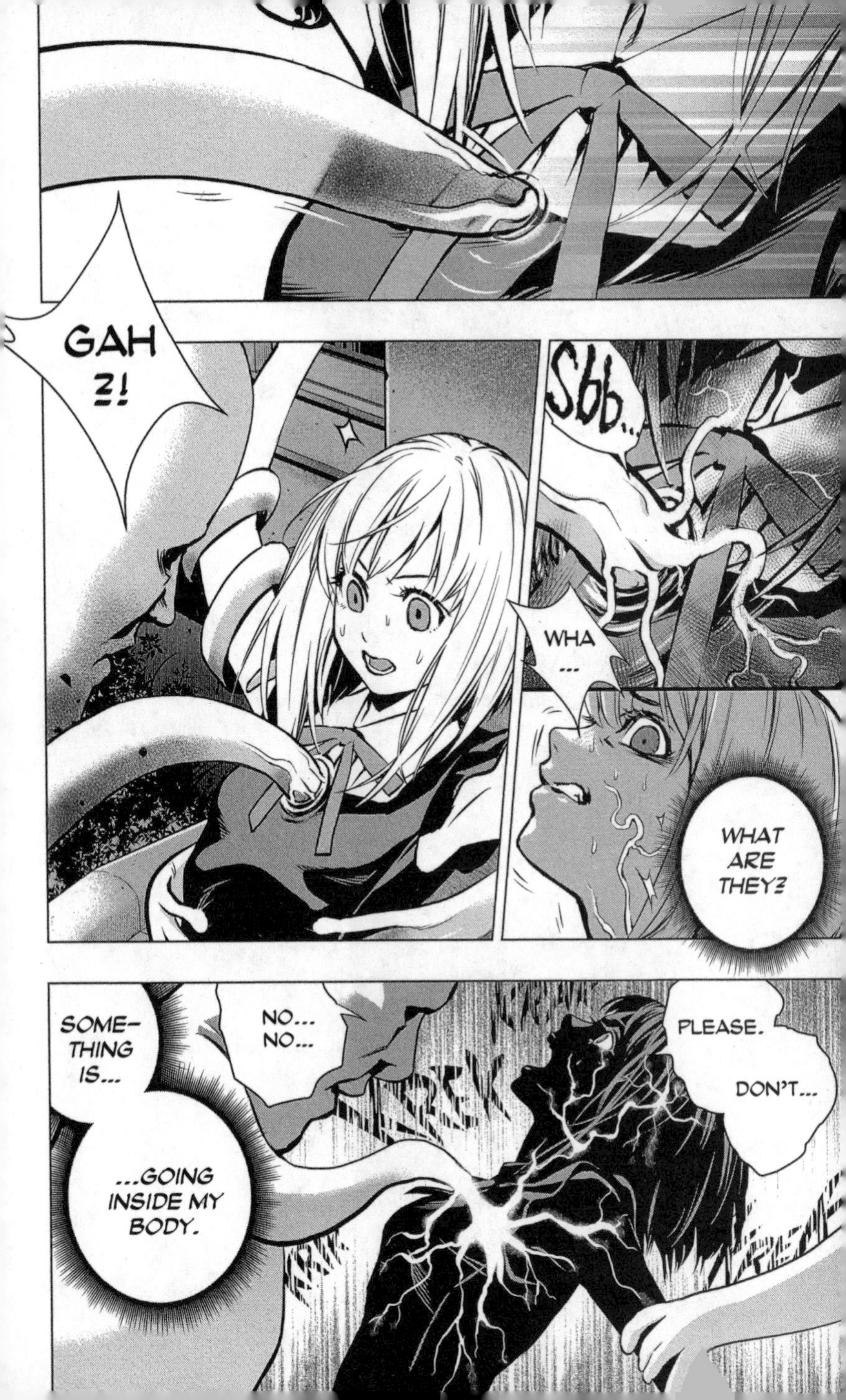
Sbb...
WHA...
WHAT ARE THEY?
GAH ?!
PLEASE.
DON'T...
NO... NO...
SOME-THING IS...
...GOING INSIDE MY BODY.

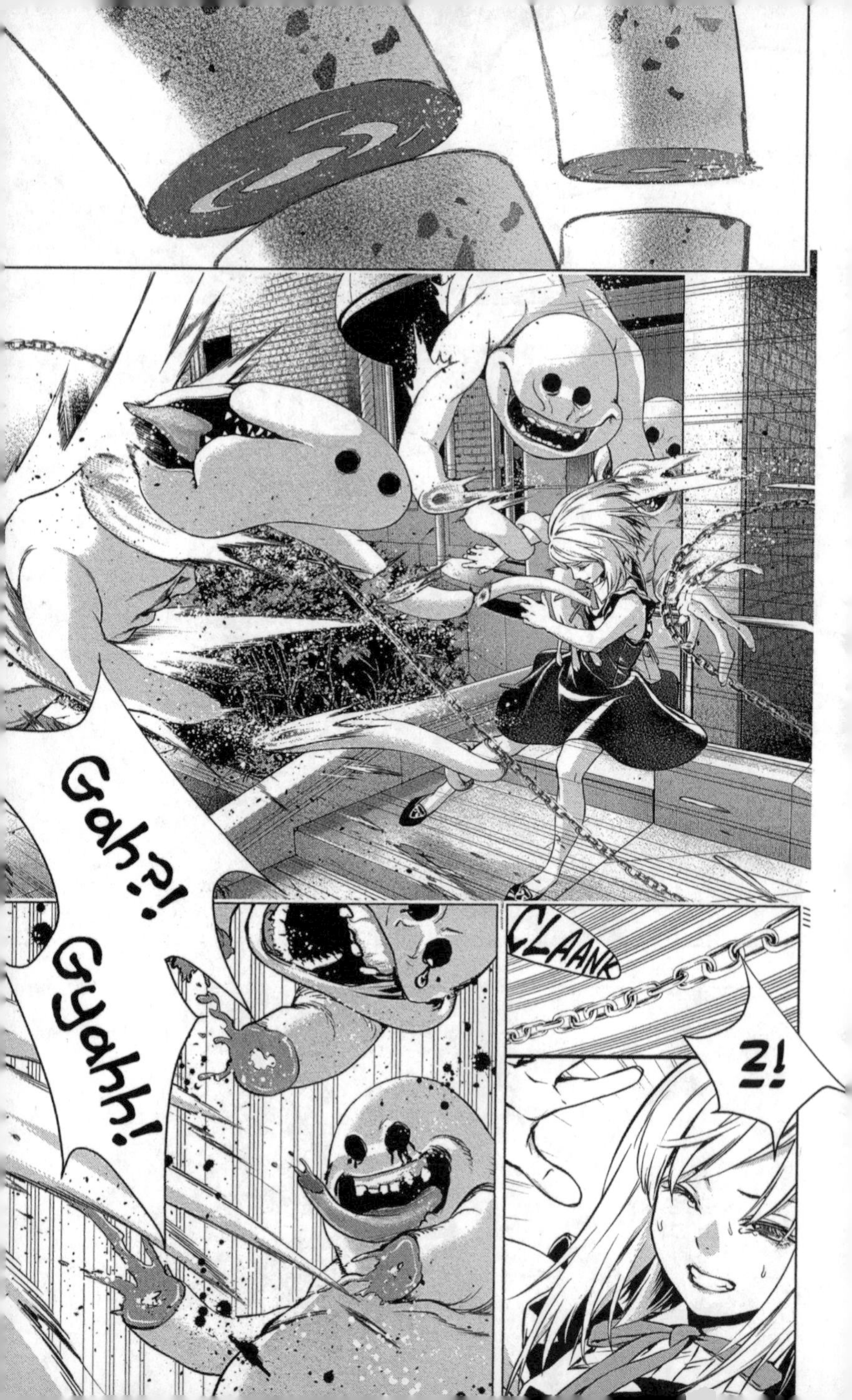
CLAANK
!?
Gah?! Gyahh!

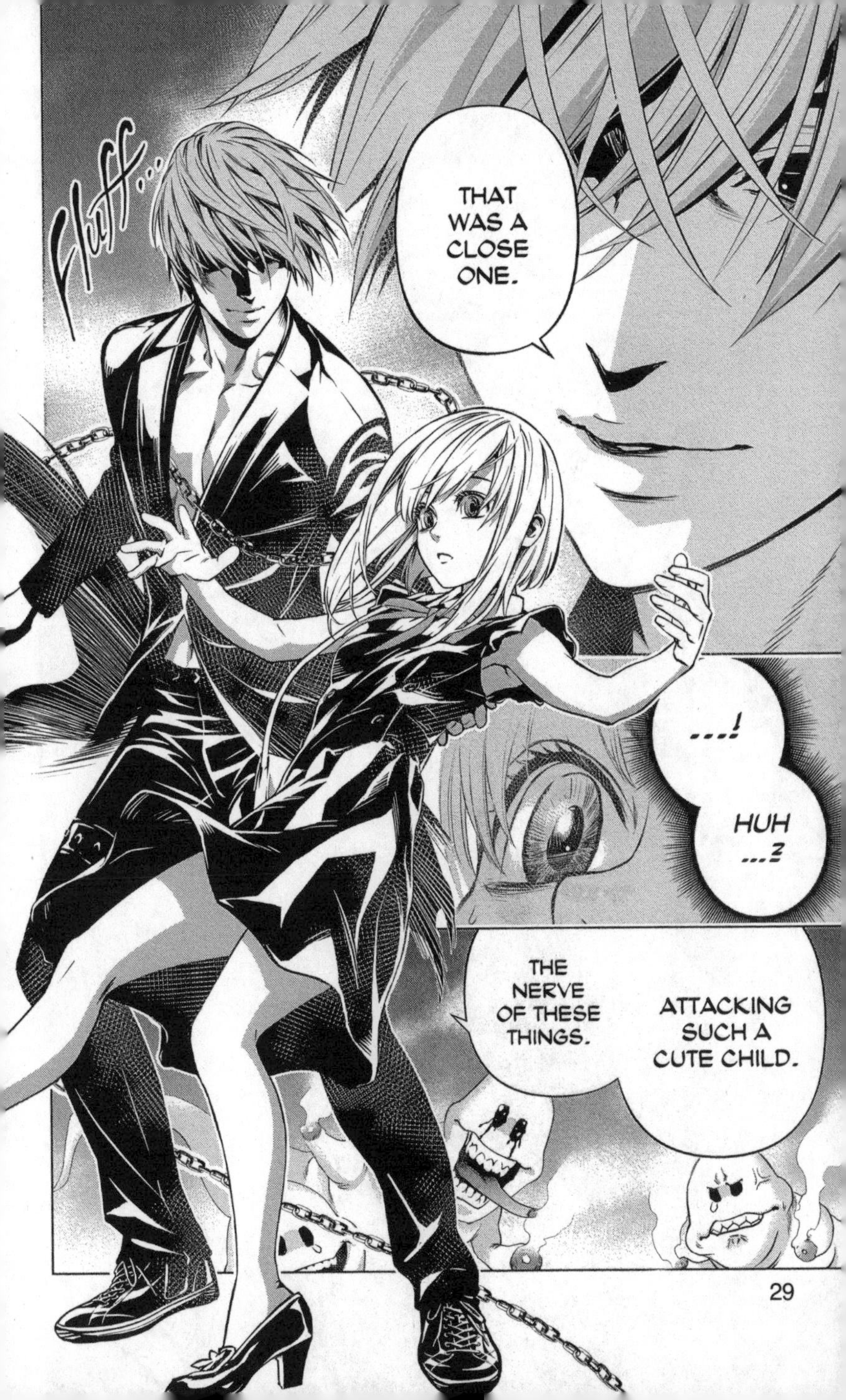
THAT WAS A CLOSE ONE.
...!
HUH ...?
ATTACKING SUCH A CUTE CHILD.
THE NERVE OF THESE THINGS.
Fluff...

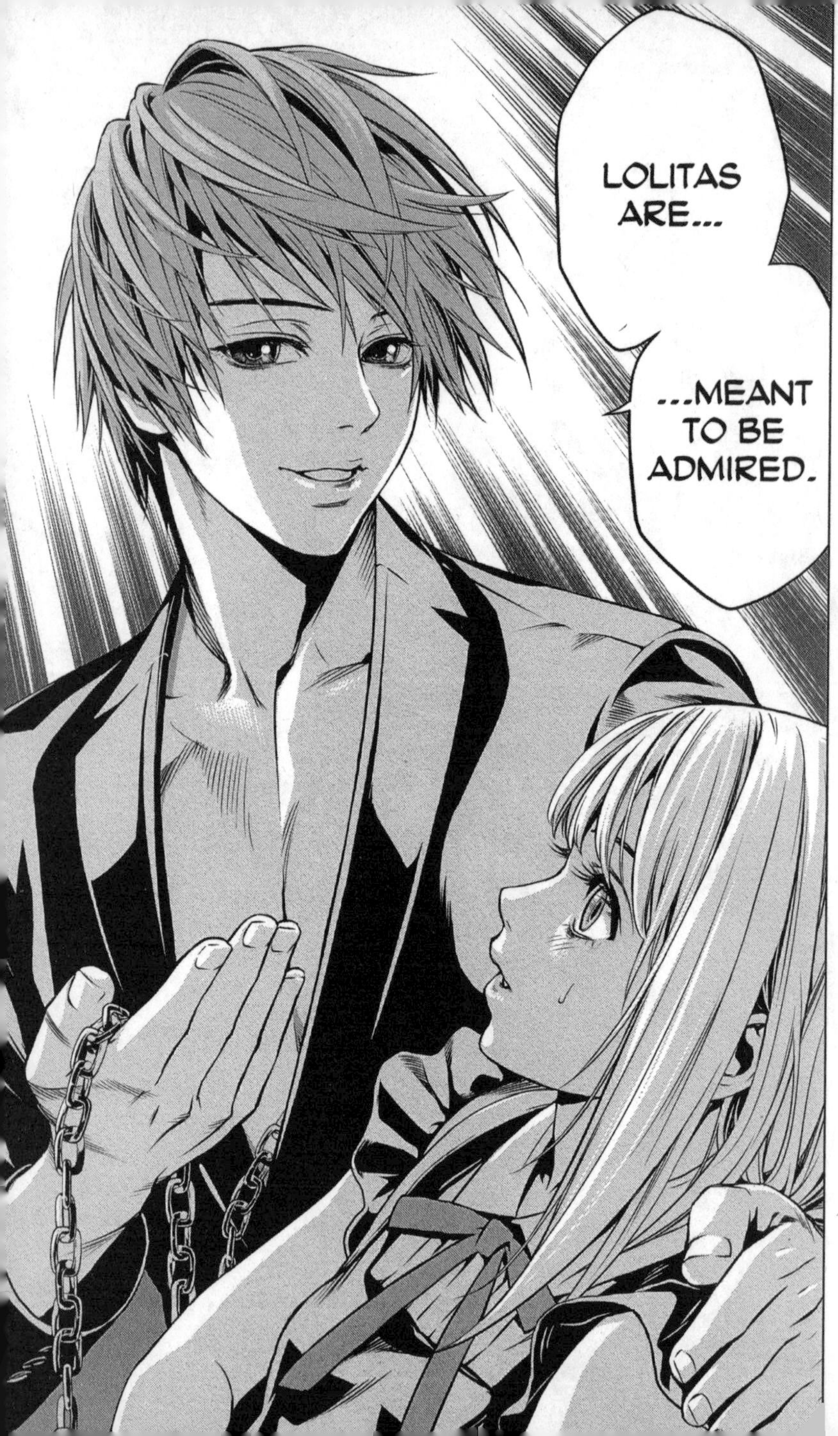
LOLITAS ARE...
...MEANT TO BE ADMIRED.

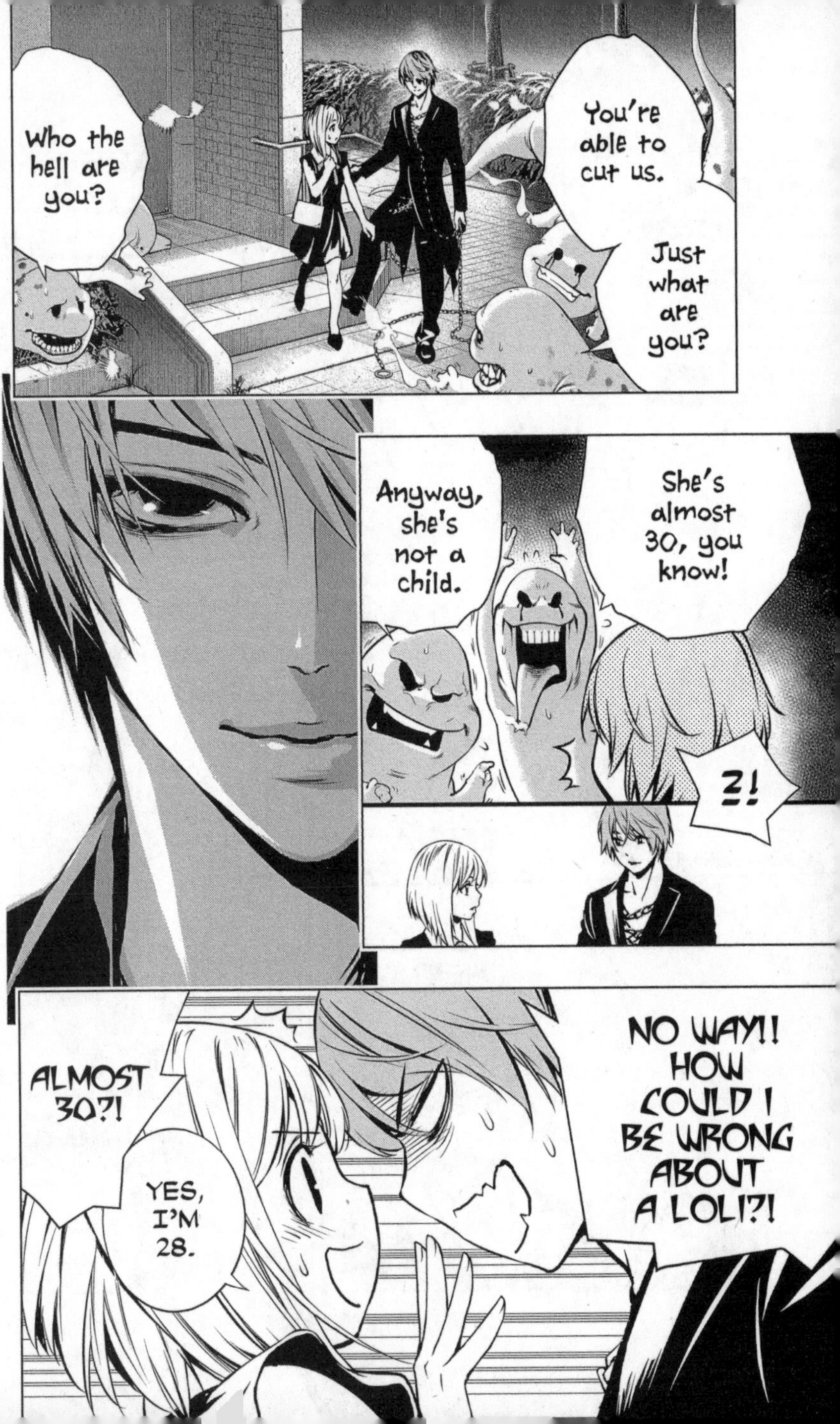
You're able to cut us.
Just what are you?
Who the hell are you?
She's almost 30, you know!
Anyway, she's not a child.
?!
NO WAY!! HOW COULD I BE WRONG ABOUT A LOLI?!
ALMOST 30?!
YES, I'M 28.

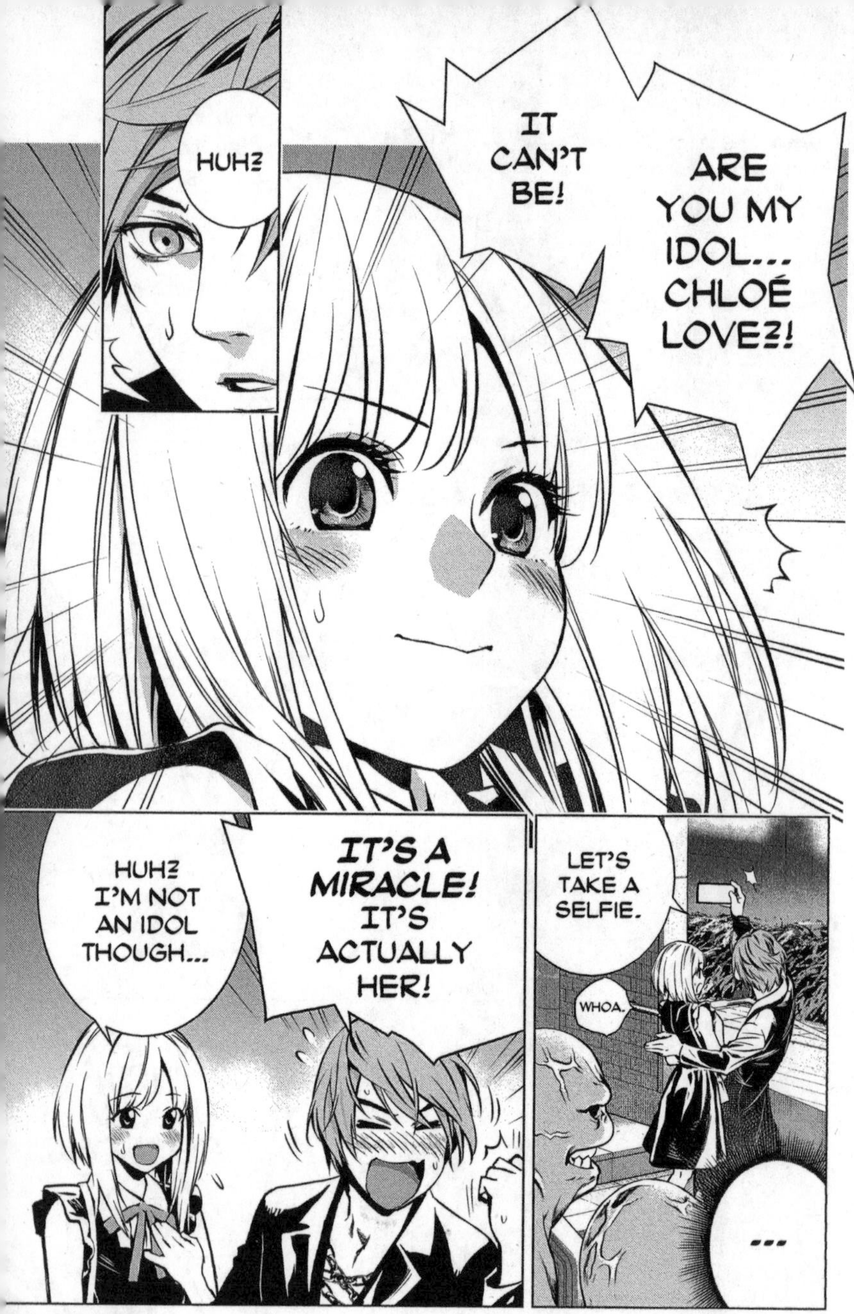
IT CAN'T BE!
ARE YOU MY IDOL... CHLOÉ LOVE?!
HUH?
LET'S TAKE A SELFIE.
WHOA.
...
IT'S A MIRACLE! IT'S ACTUALLY HER!
HUH? I'M NOT AN IDOL THOUGH...

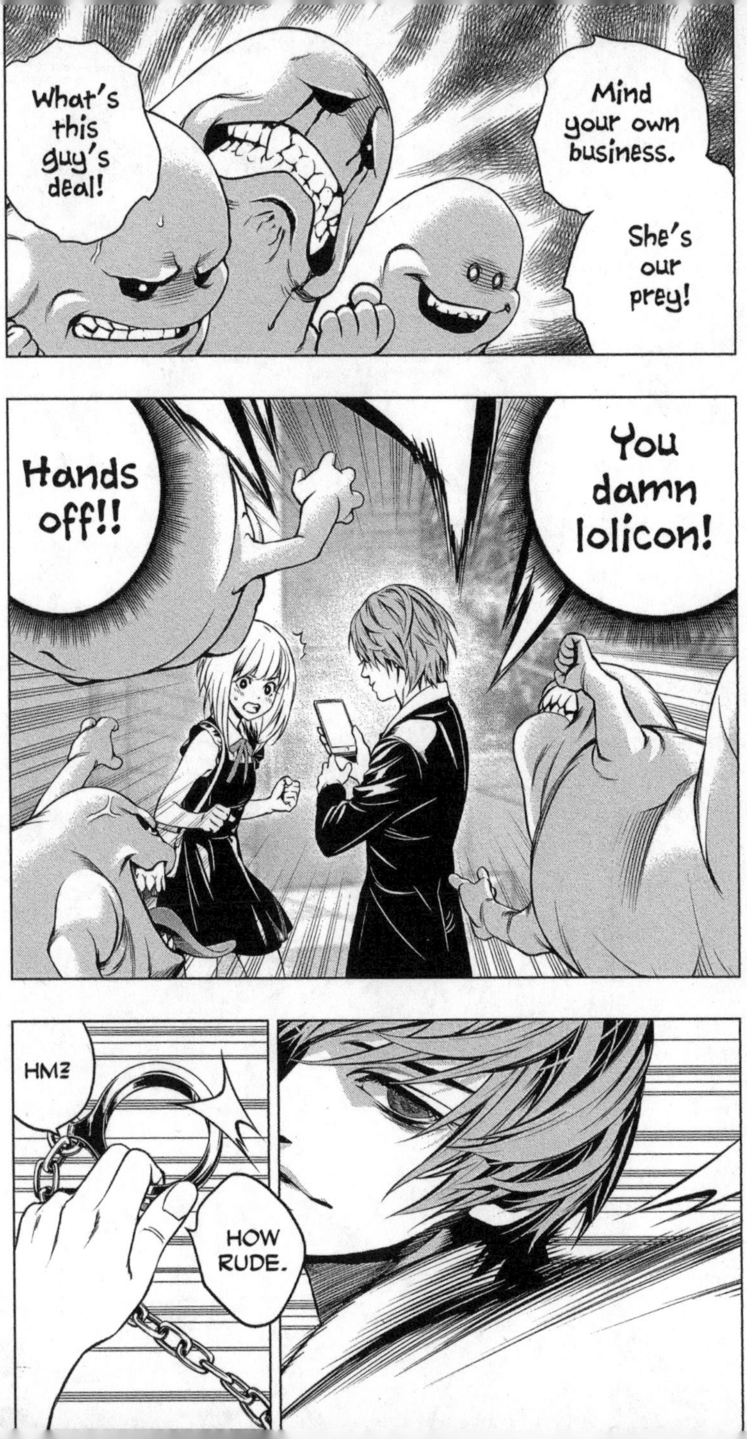
Mind your own business.
She's our prey!
What's this guy's deal!
You damn lolicon!
Hands off!!
HM?
HOW RUDE.

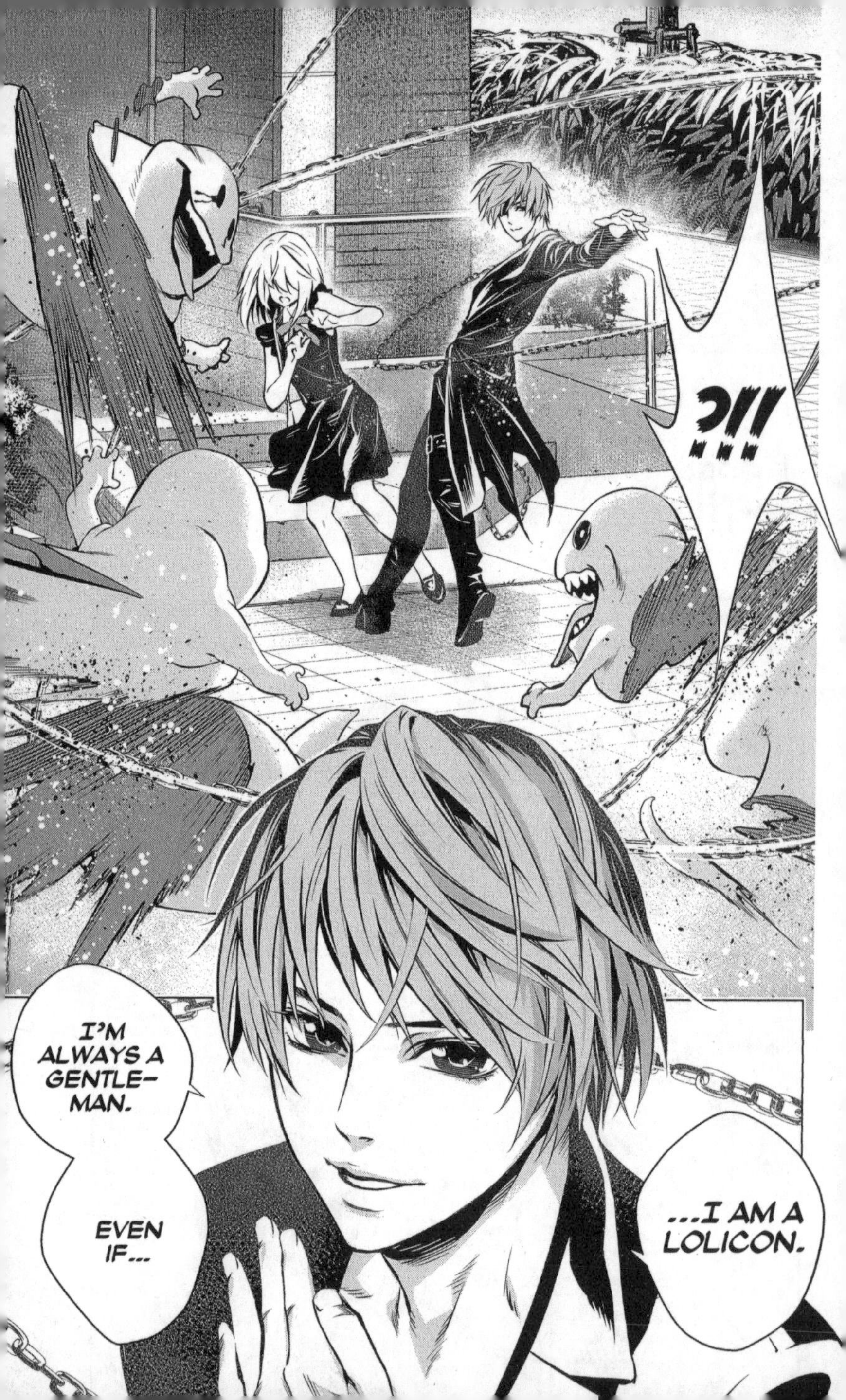
?!!
I'M ALWAYS A GENTLE-MAN.
...I AM A LOLICON.
EVEN IF...

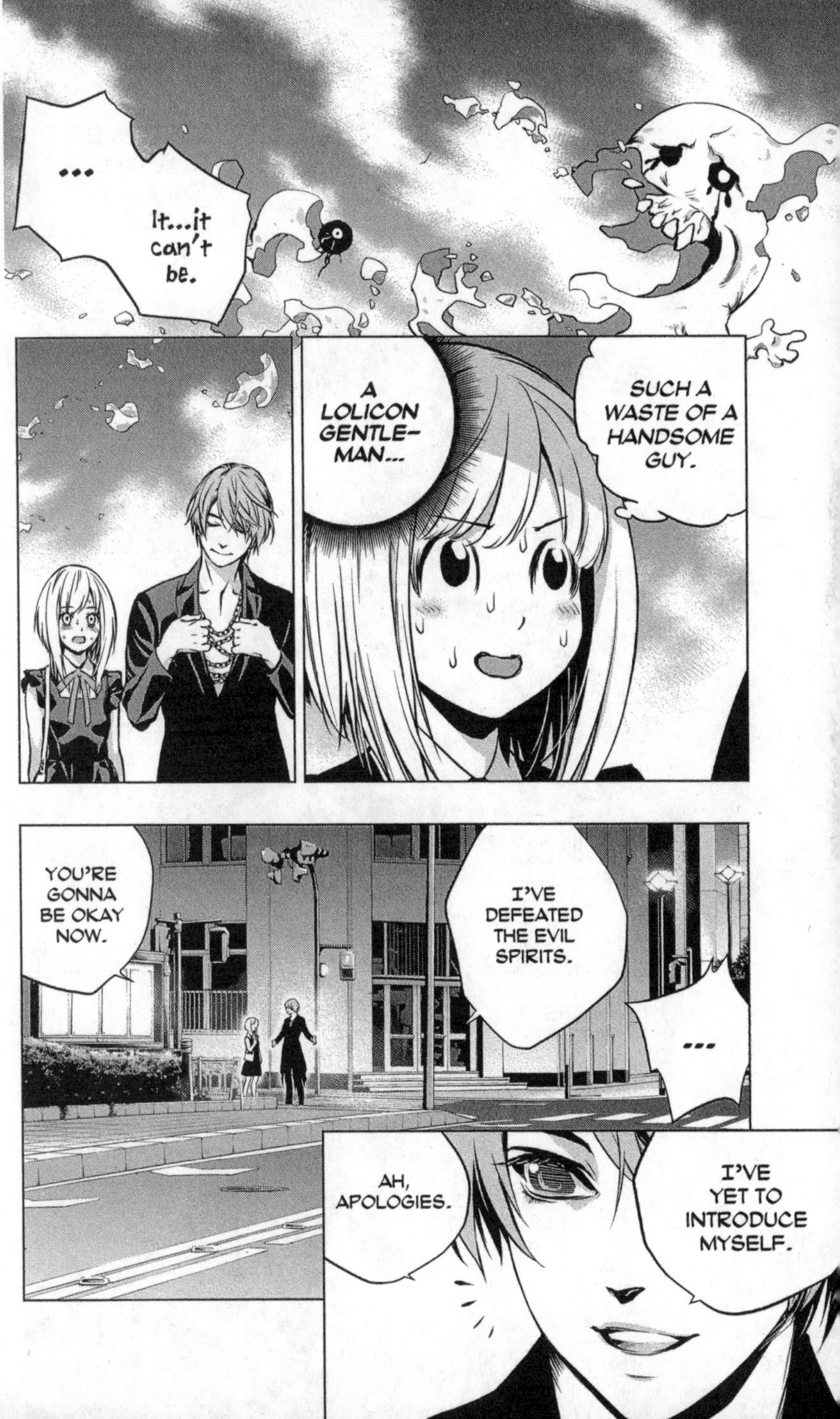
...
It...it can't be.
SUCH A WASTE OF A HANDSOME GUY.
A LOLICON GENTLE-MAN...
I'VE DEFEATED THE EVIL SPIRITS.
YOU'RE GONNA BE OKAY NOW.
...
I'VE YET TO INTRODUCE MYSELF.
AH, APOLOGIES.

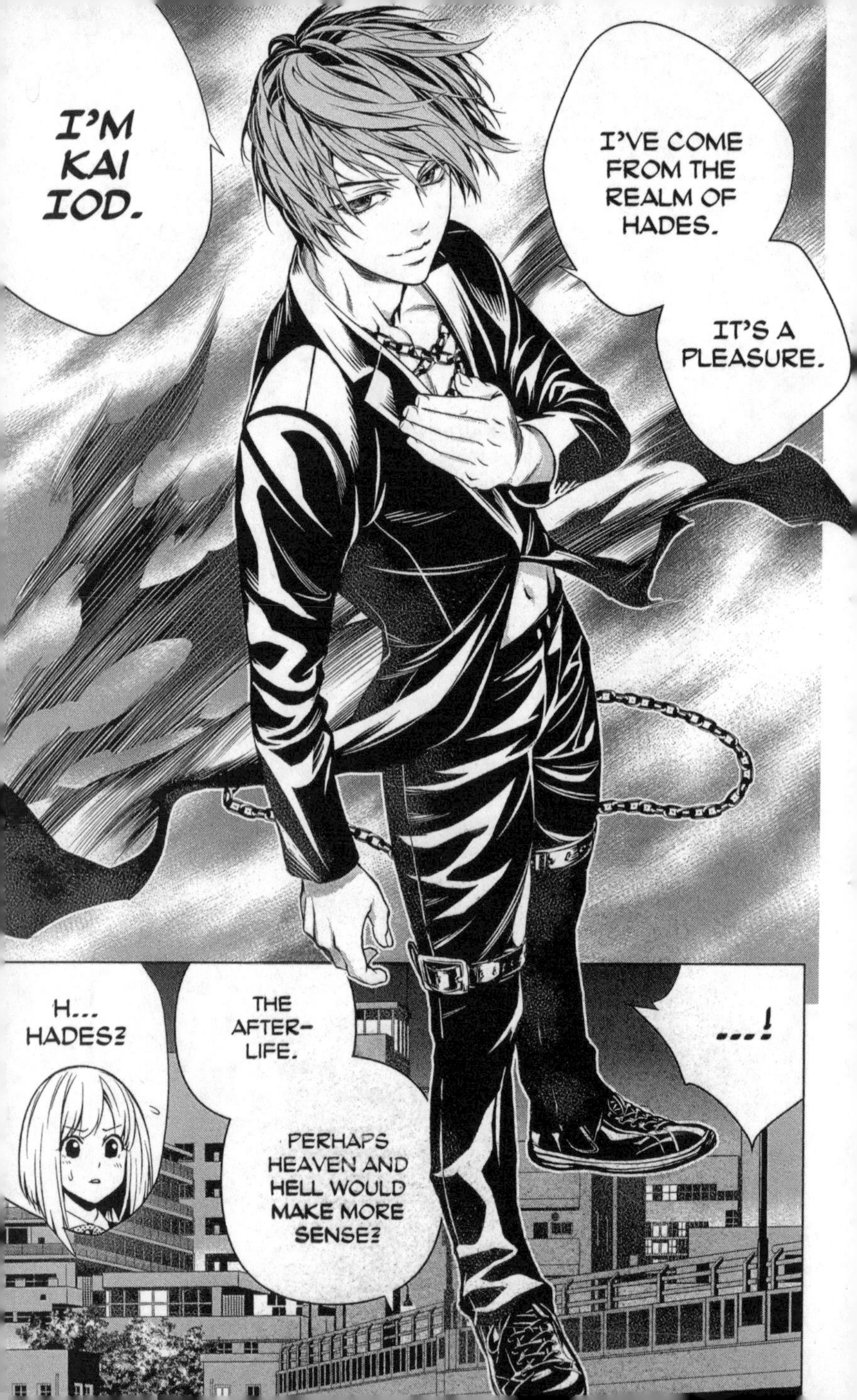
I'M KAI IOD.
I'VE COME FROM THE REALM OF HADES.
IT'S A PLEASURE.
...!
H... HADES?
THE AFTER-LIFE.
PERHAPS HEAVEN AND HELL WOULD MAKE MORE SENSE?

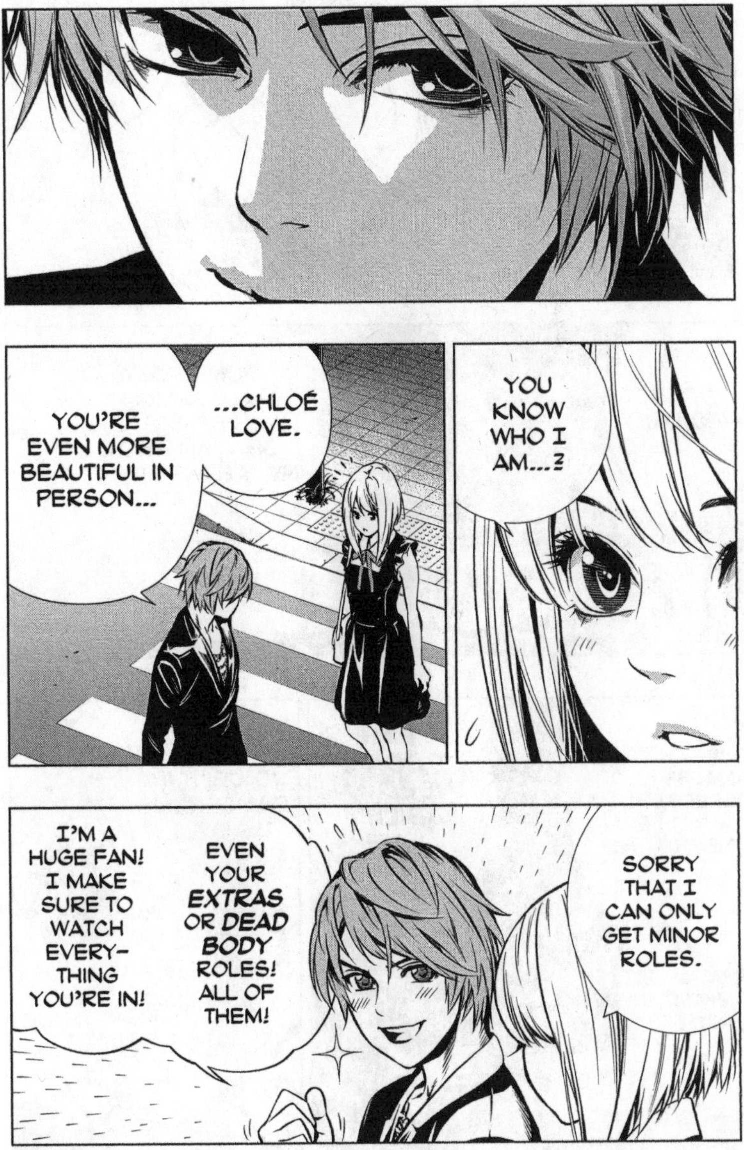
YOU KNOW WHO I AM...?
...CHLOÉ LOVE.
YOU'RE EVEN MORE BEAUTIFUL IN PERSON...
SORRY THAT I CAN ONLY GET MINOR ROLES.
EVEN YOUR *EXTRAS* OR *DEAD BODY* ROLES! ALL OF THEM!
I'M A HUGE FAN! I MAKE SURE TO WATCH EVERY-THING YOU'RE IN!

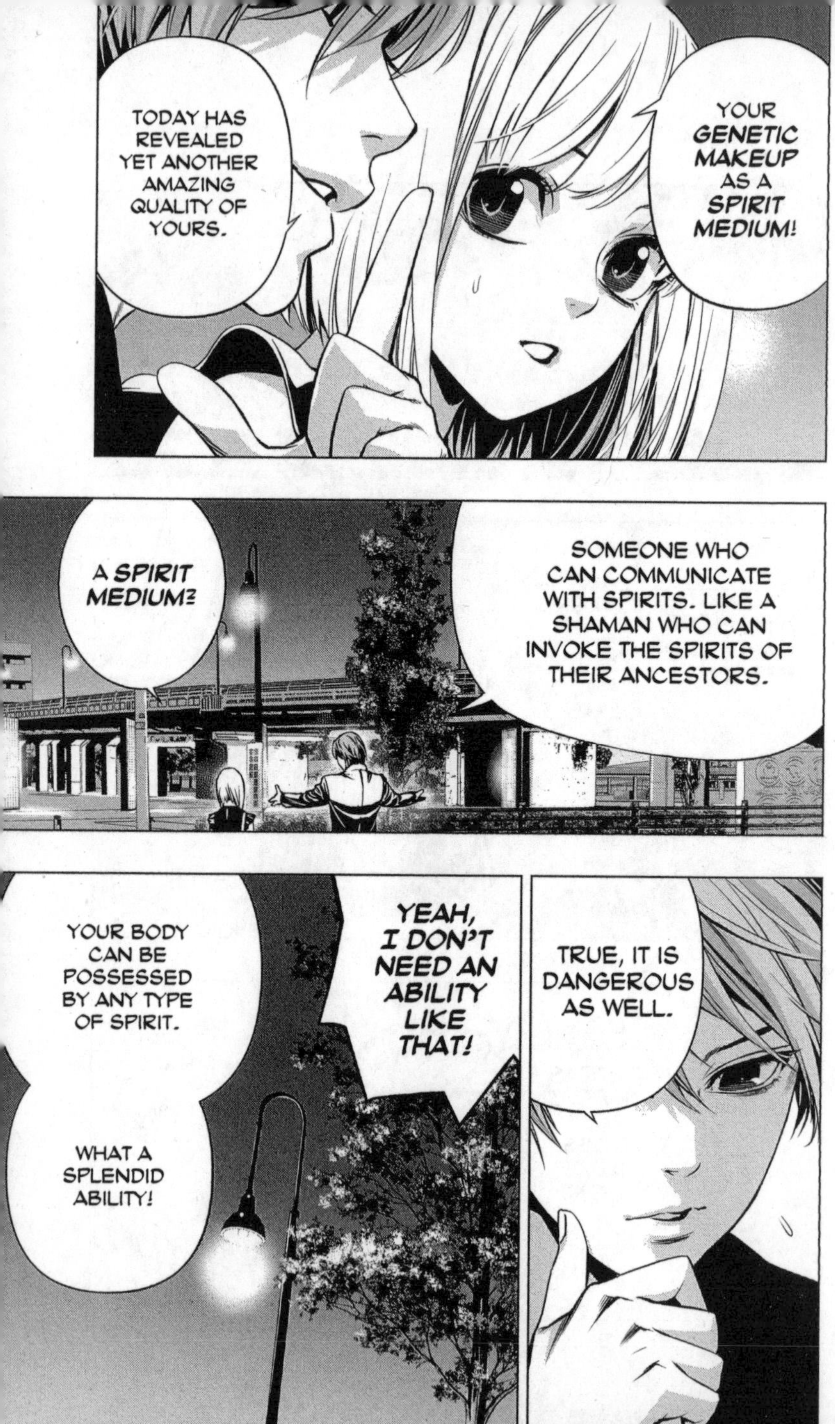
TODAY HAS REVEALED YET ANOTHER AMAZING QUALITY OF YOURS.
YOUR GENETIC MAKEUP AS A SPIRIT MEDIUM!
A SPIRIT MEDIUM?
SOMEONE WHO CAN COMMUNICATE WITH SPIRITS. LIKE A SHAMAN WHO CAN INVOKE THE SPIRITS OF THEIR ANCESTORS.
YOUR BODY CAN BE POSSESSED BY ANY TYPE OF SPIRIT.
WHAT A SPLENDID ABILITY!
YEAH, I DON'T NEED AN ABILITY LIKE THAT!
TRUE, IT IS DANGEROUS AS WELL.

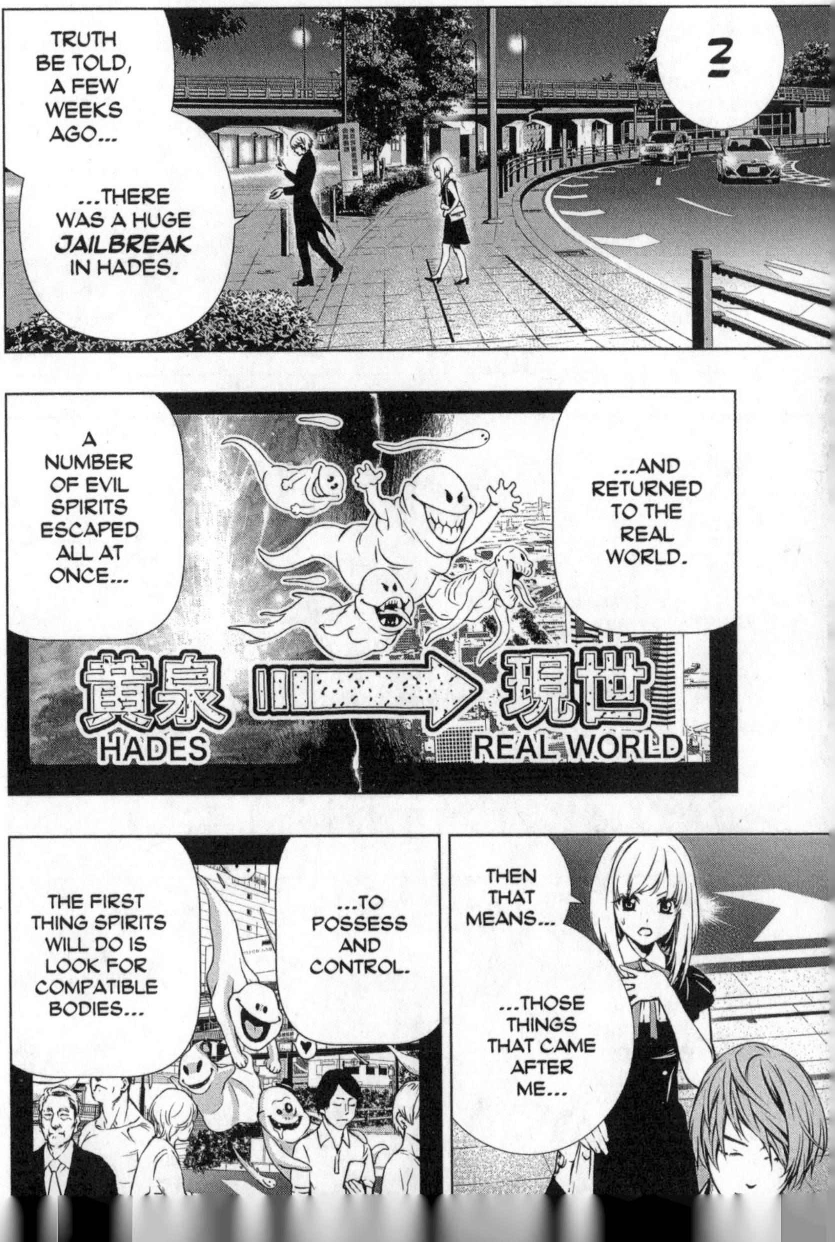
TRUTH BE TOLD, A FEW WEEKS AGO...
...THERE WAS A HUGE JAILBREAK IN HADES.
?
A NUMBER OF EVIL SPIRITS ESCAPED ALL AT ONCE...
...AND RETURNED TO THE REAL WORLD.
黄泉
HADES
現世
REAL WORLD
THE FIRST THING SPIRITS WILL DO IS LOOK FOR COMPATIBLE BODIES...
...TO POSSESS AND CONTROL.
THEN THAT MEANS...
...THOSE THINGS THAT CAME AFTER ME...

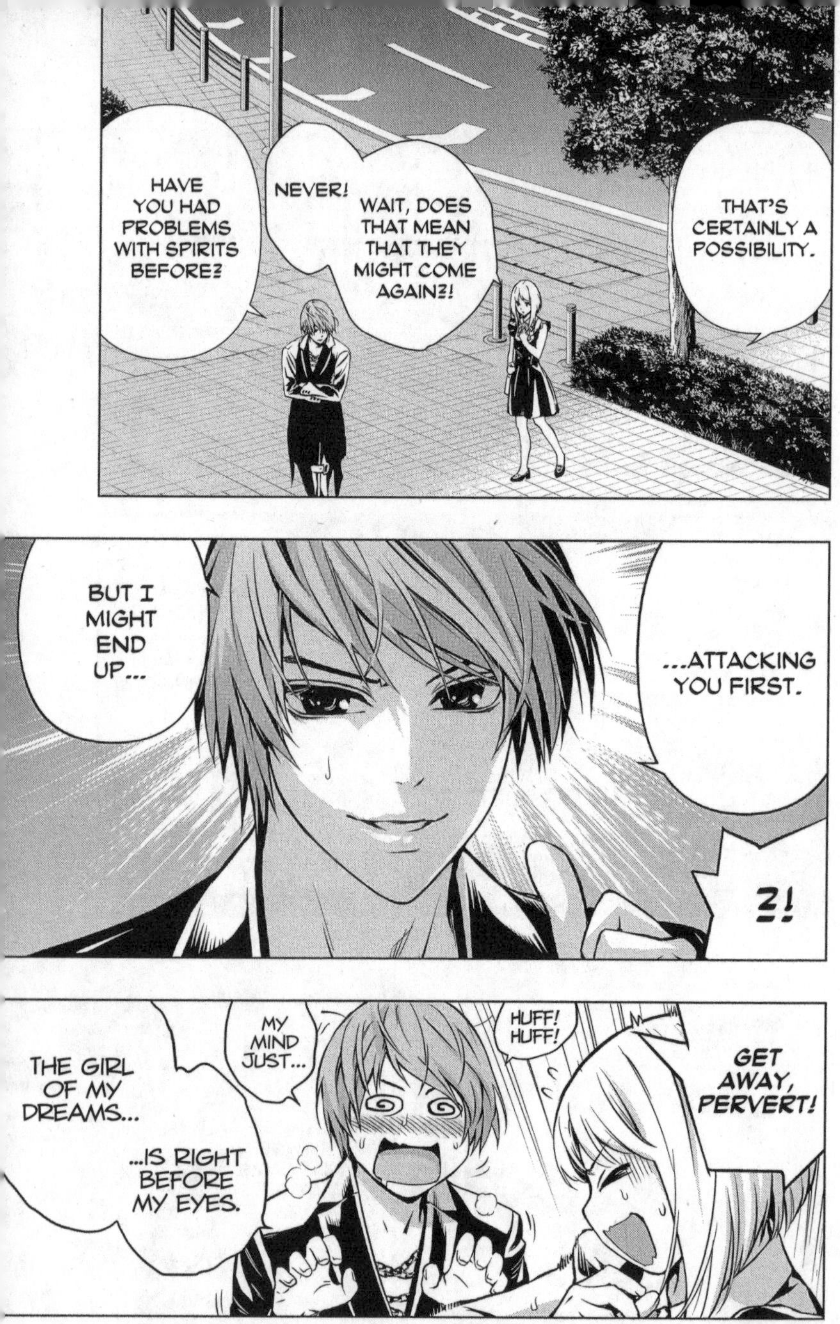
HAVE YOU HAD PROBLEMS WITH SPIRITS BEFORE?
NEVER!
WAIT, DOES THAT MEAN THAT THEY MIGHT COME AGAIN?!
THAT'S CERTAINLY A POSSIBILITY.
BUT I MIGHT END UP...
...ATTACKING YOU FIRST.
?!
THE GIRL OF MY DREAMS...
...IS RIGHT BEFORE MY EYES.
MY MIND JUST...
HUFF! HUFF!
GET AWAY, PERVERT!

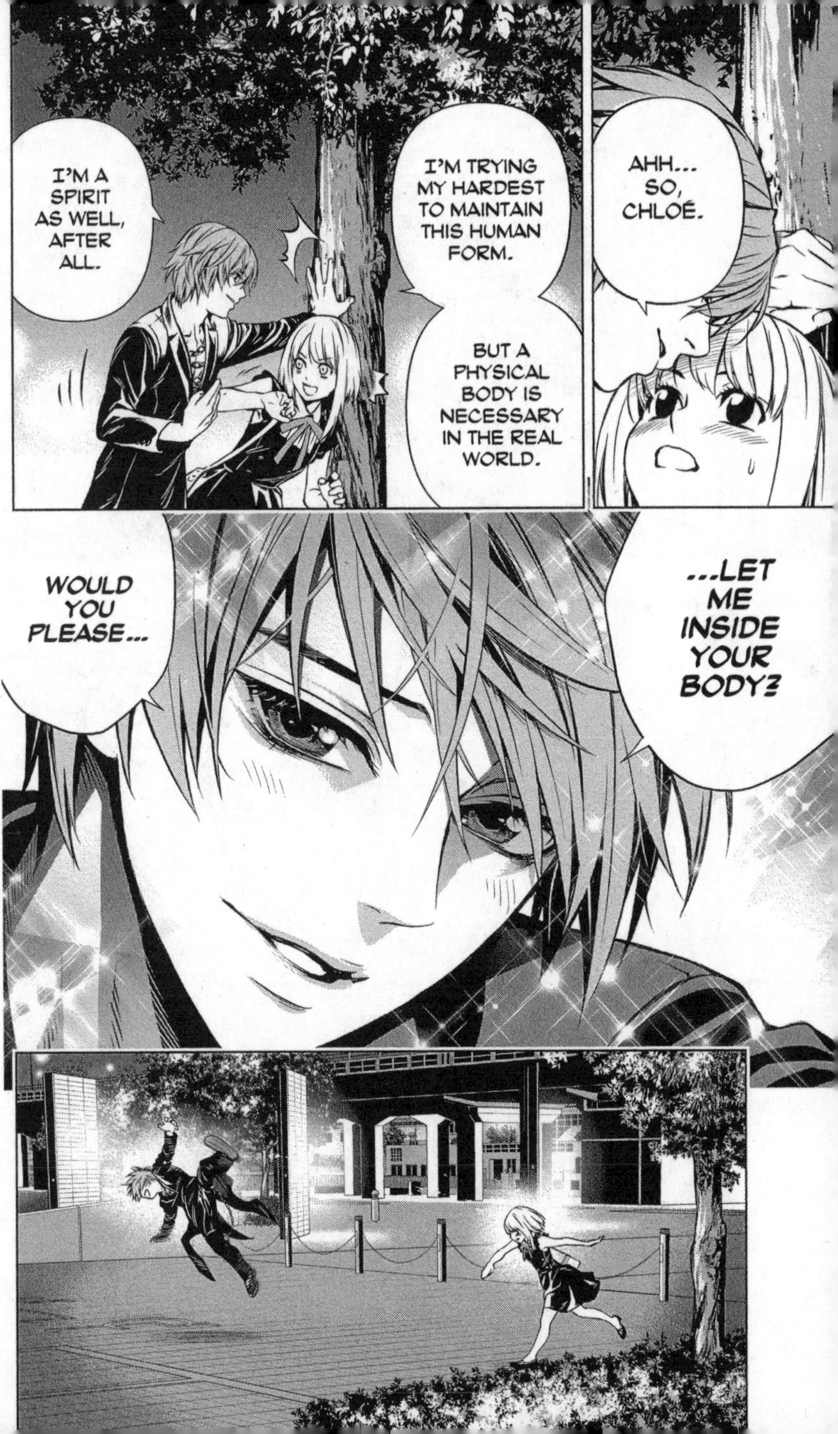
AHH... SO, CHLOÉ.
I'M TRYING MY HARDEST TO MAINTAIN THIS HUMAN FORM.
BUT A PHYSICAL BODY IS NECESSARY IN THE REAL WORLD.
I'M A SPIRIT AS WELL, AFTER ALL.
WOULD YOU PLEASE...
...LET ME INSIDE YOUR BODY?

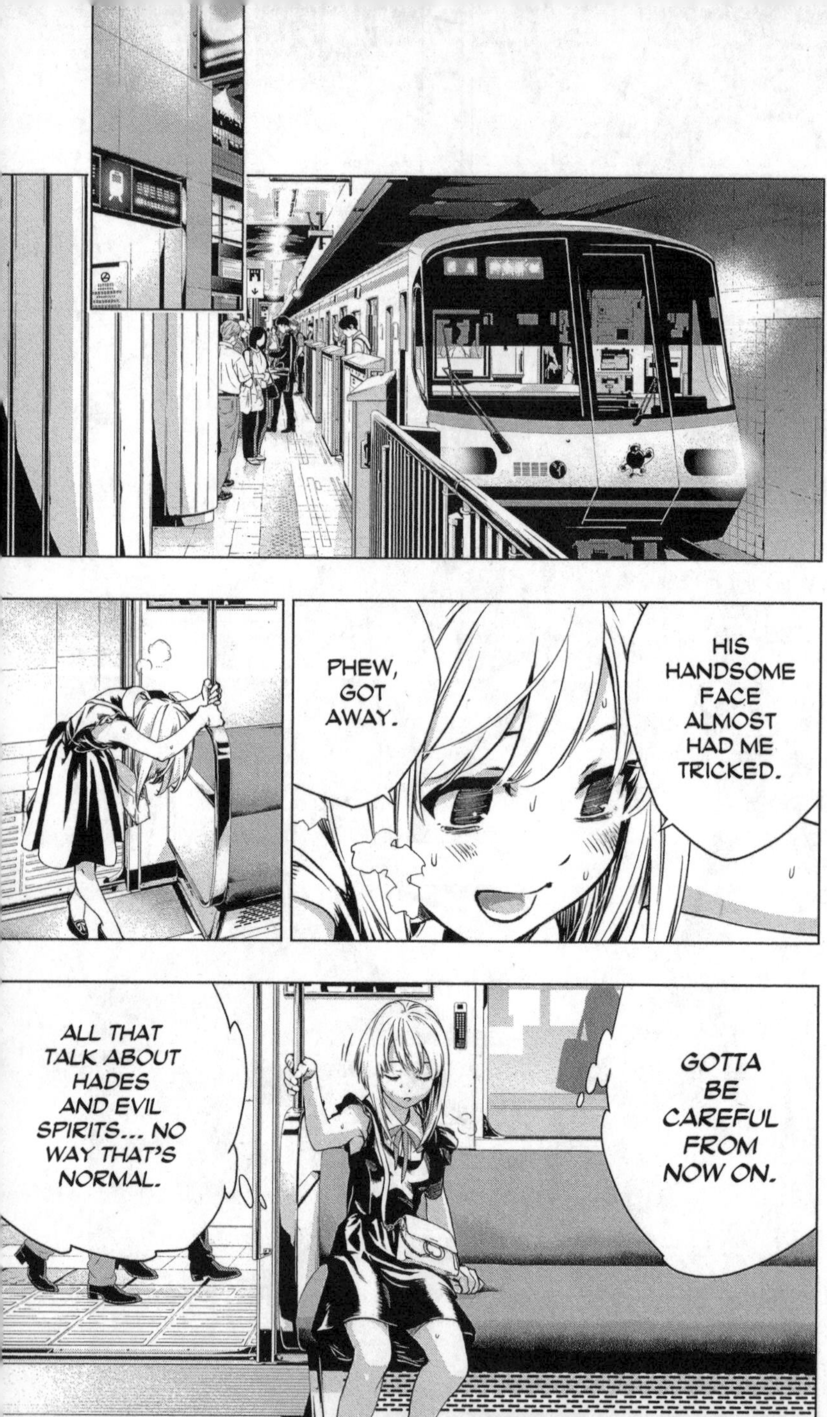
PHEW, GOT AWAY.
HIS HANDSOME FACE ALMOST HAD ME TRICKED.
ALL THAT TALK ABOUT HADES AND EVIL SPIRITS... NO WAY THAT'S NORMAL.
GOTTA BE CAREFUL FROM NOW ON.

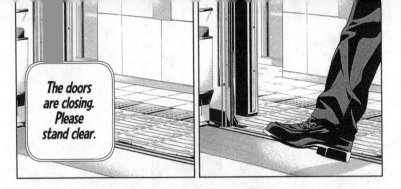

The doors are closing. Please stand clear.

BUT THAT WAS THE FIRST TIME...

...SOMEONE SAID THEY'RE A FAN OF MINE.

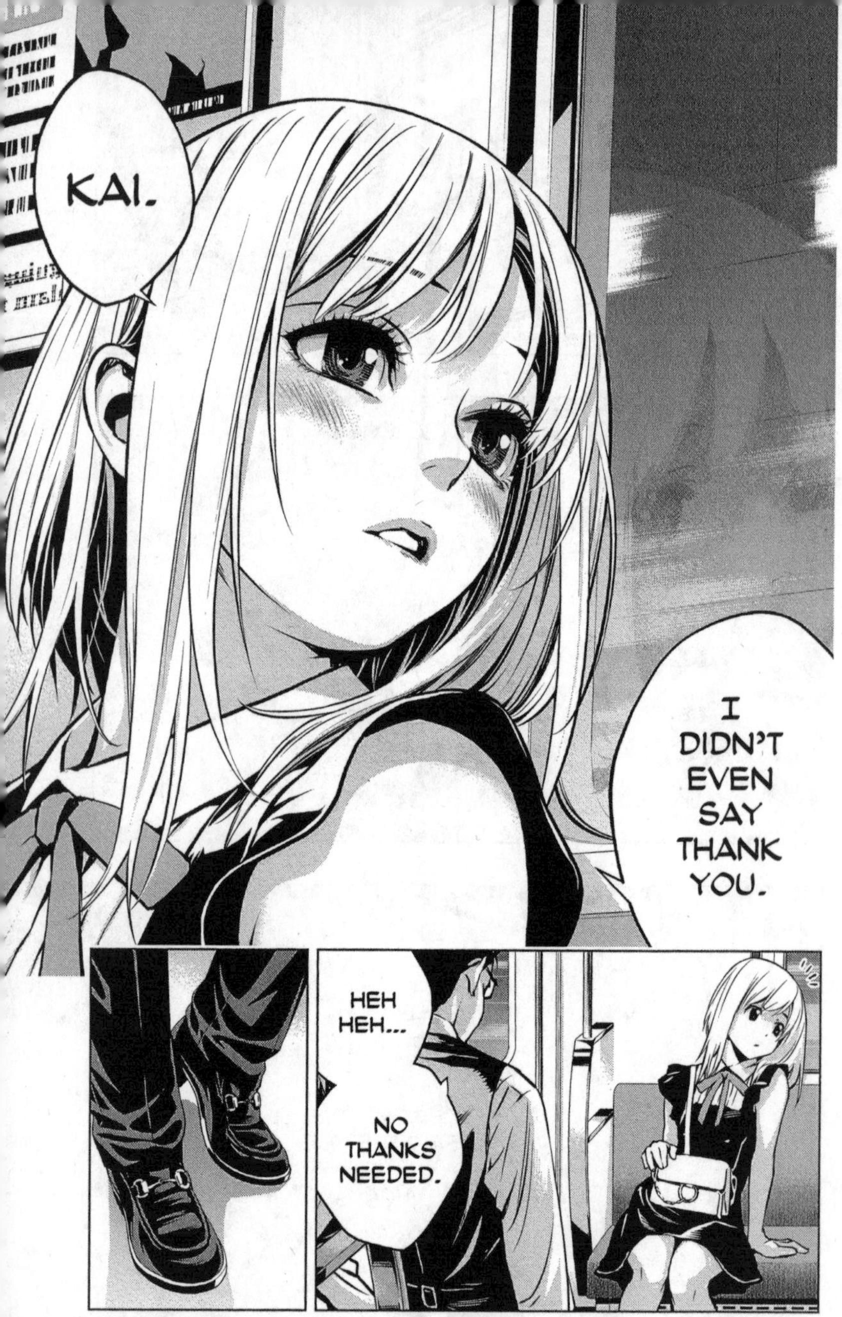
KAI.
I DIDN'T EVEN SAY THANK YOU.
HEH HEH...
NO THANKS NEEDED.

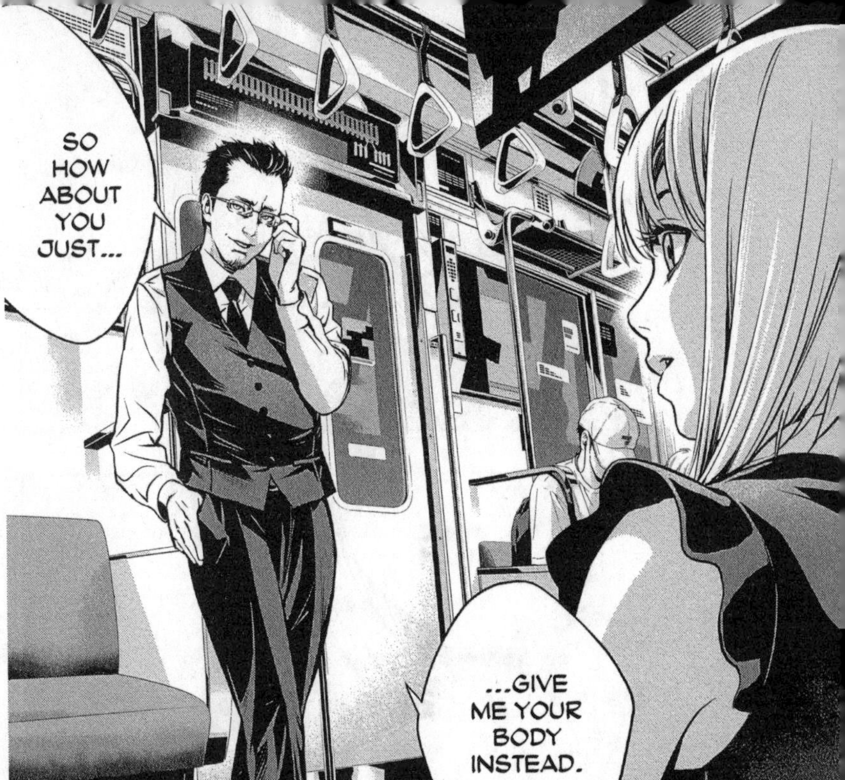
SO HOW ABOUT YOU JUST...
...GIVE ME YOUR BODY INSTEAD.

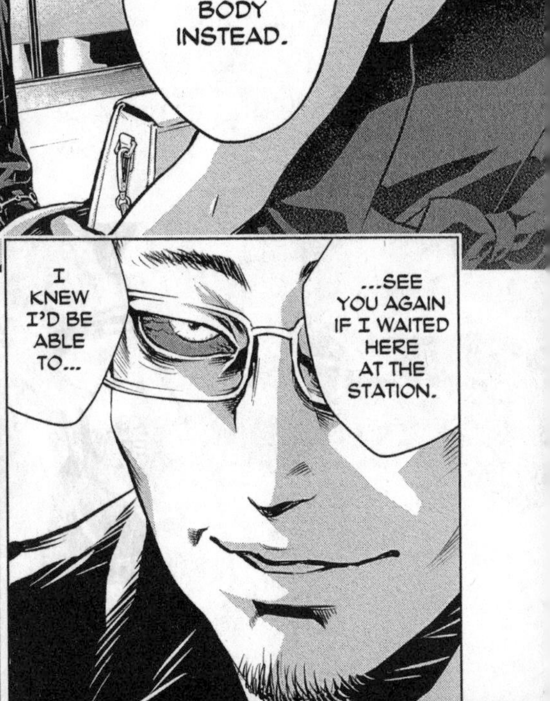
I KNEW I'D BE ABLE TO...
...SEE YOU AGAIN IF I WAITED HERE AT THE STATION.

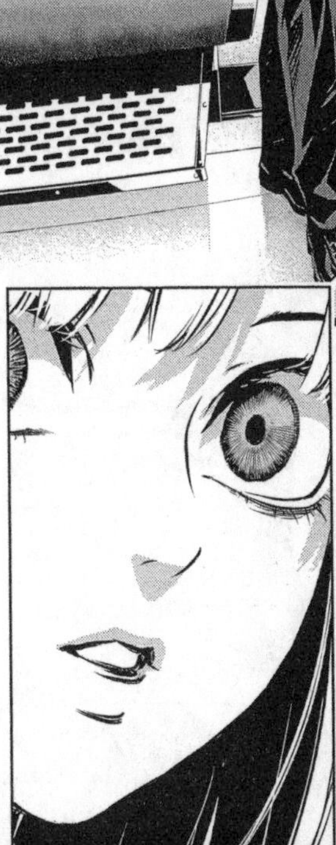

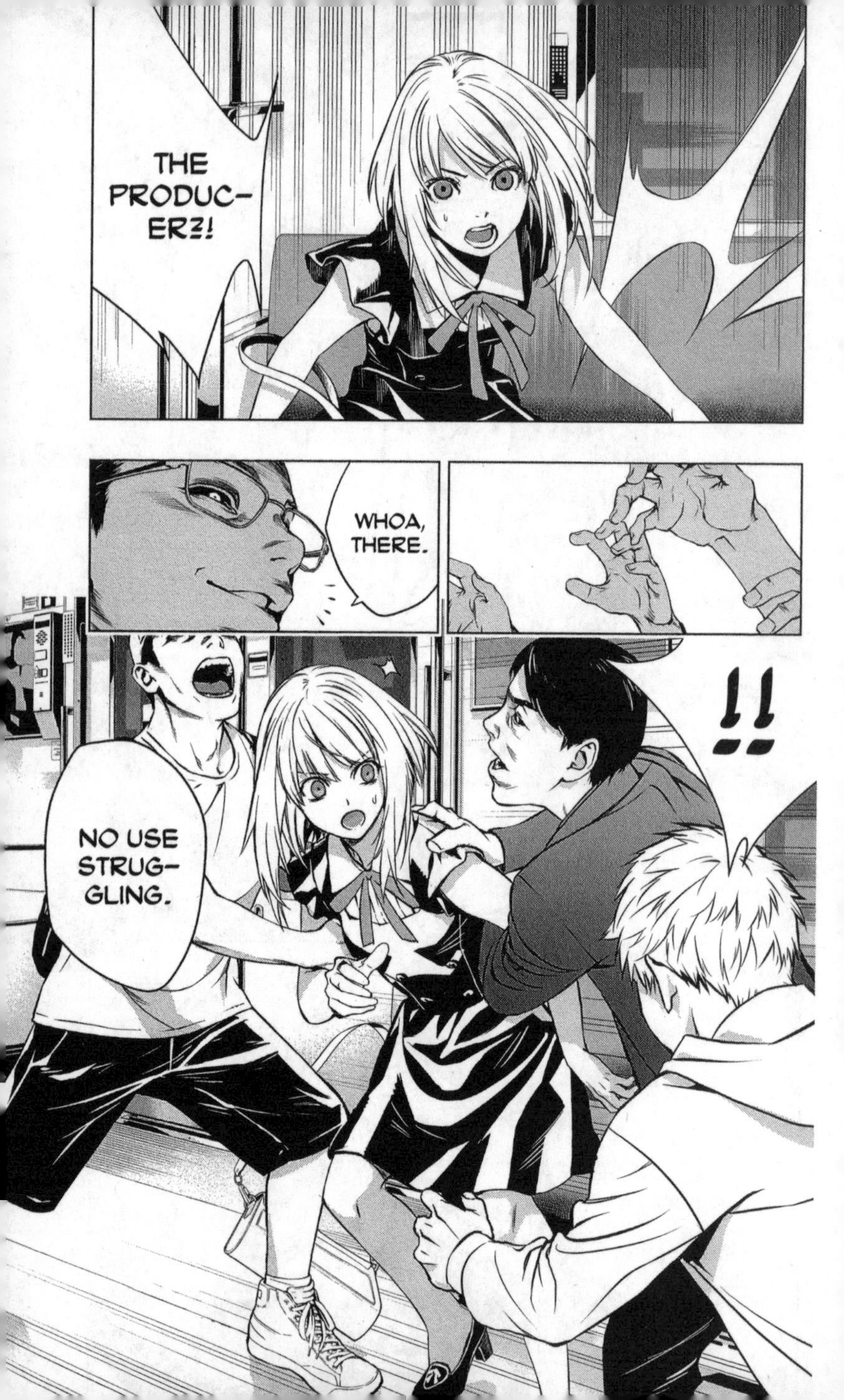
THE PRODUC-ER?!
WHOA, THERE.
!!
NO USE STRUG-GLING.

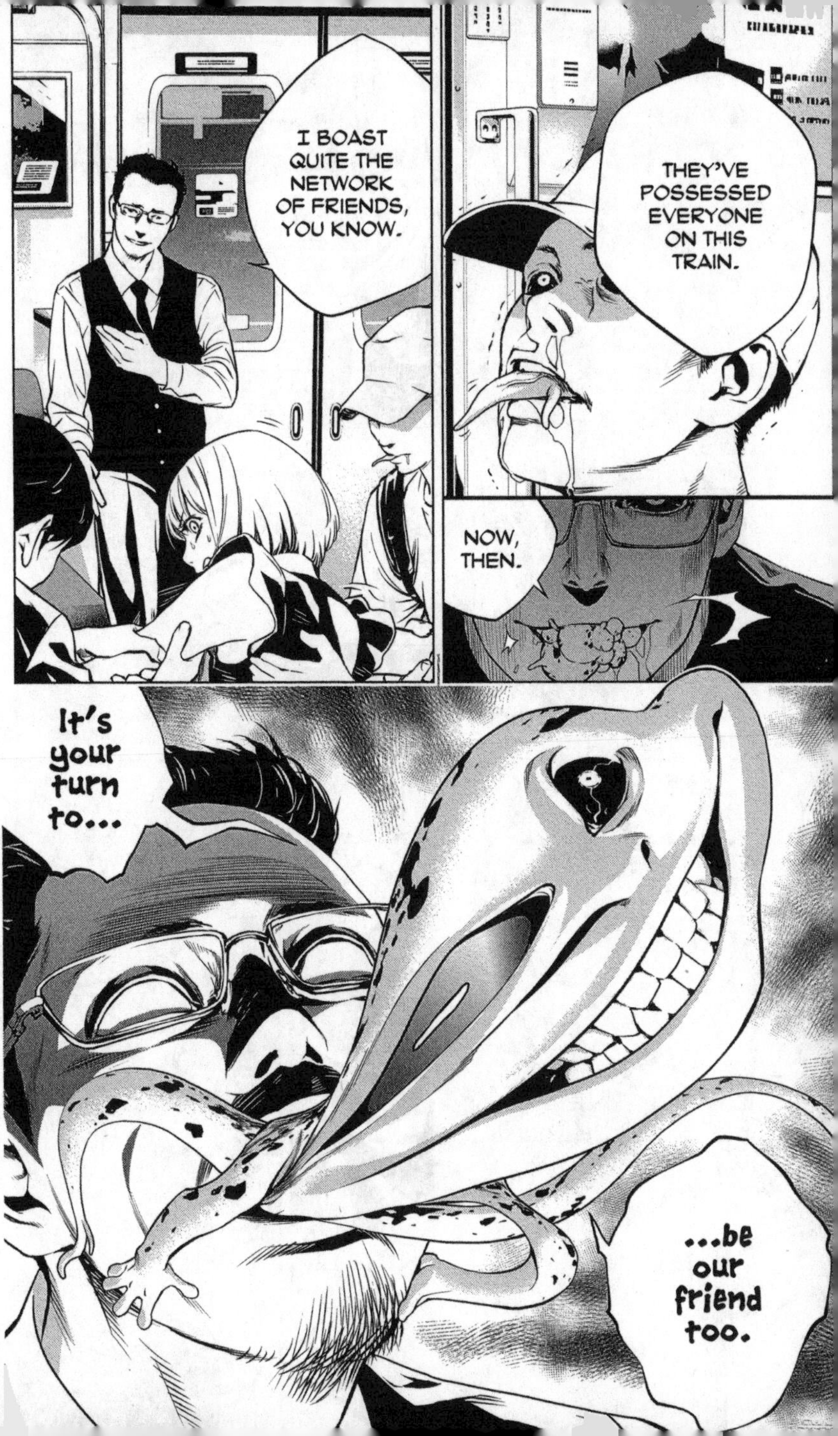
I BOAST QUITE THE NETWORK OF FRIENDS, YOU KNOW.
THEY'VE POSSESSED EVERYONE ON THIS TRAIN.
NOW, THEN.
It's your turn to...
...be our friend too.

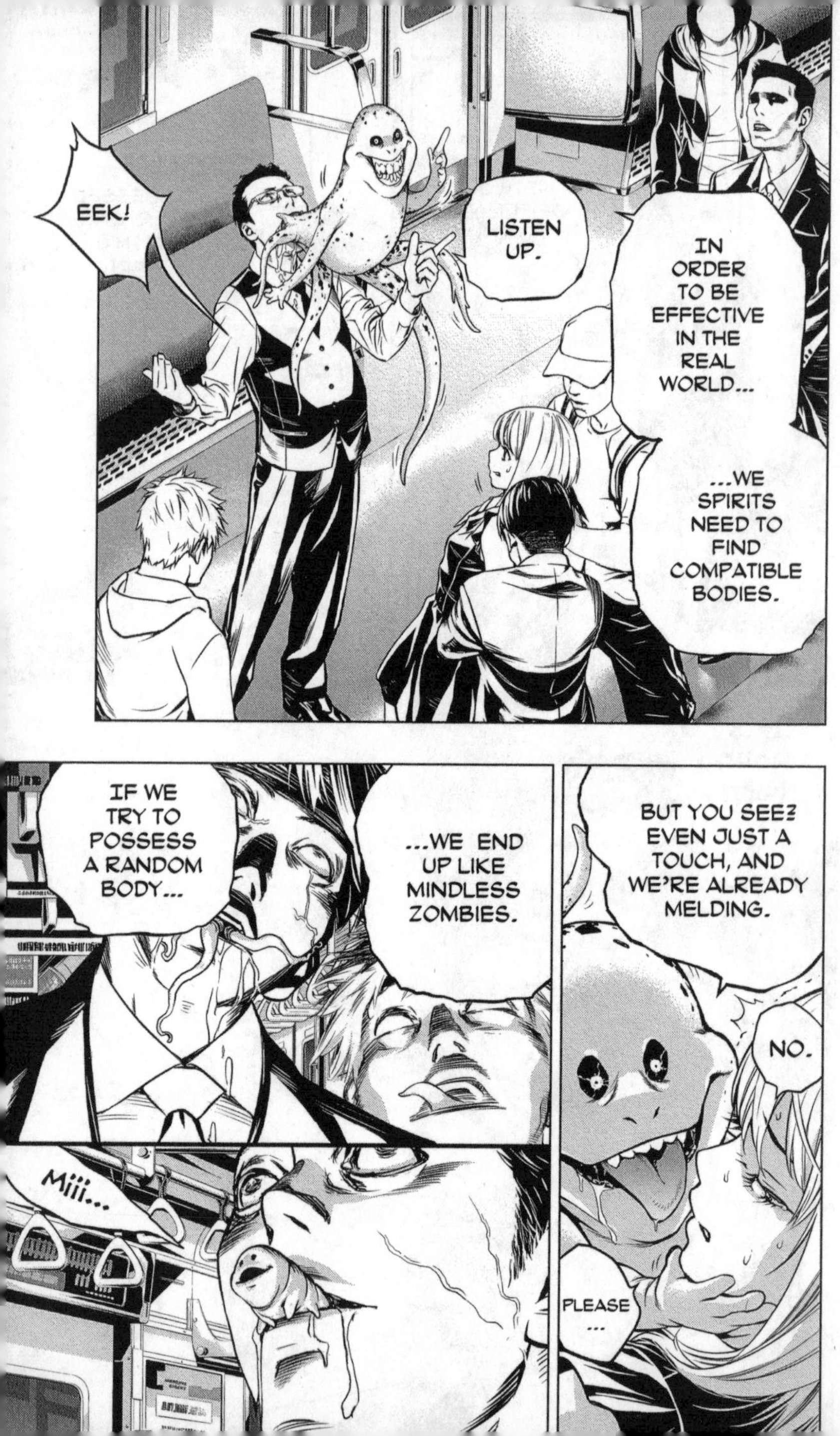
EEK!
LISTEN UP.
IN ORDER TO BE EFFECTIVE IN THE REAL WORLD...
...WE SPIRITS NEED TO FIND COMPATIBLE BODIES.
IF WE TRY TO POSSESS A RANDOM BODY...
...WE END UP LIKE MINDLESS ZOMBIES.
Miii...
BUT YOU SEE? EVEN JUST A TOUCH, AND WE'RE ALREADY MELDING.
NO.
PLEASE ...

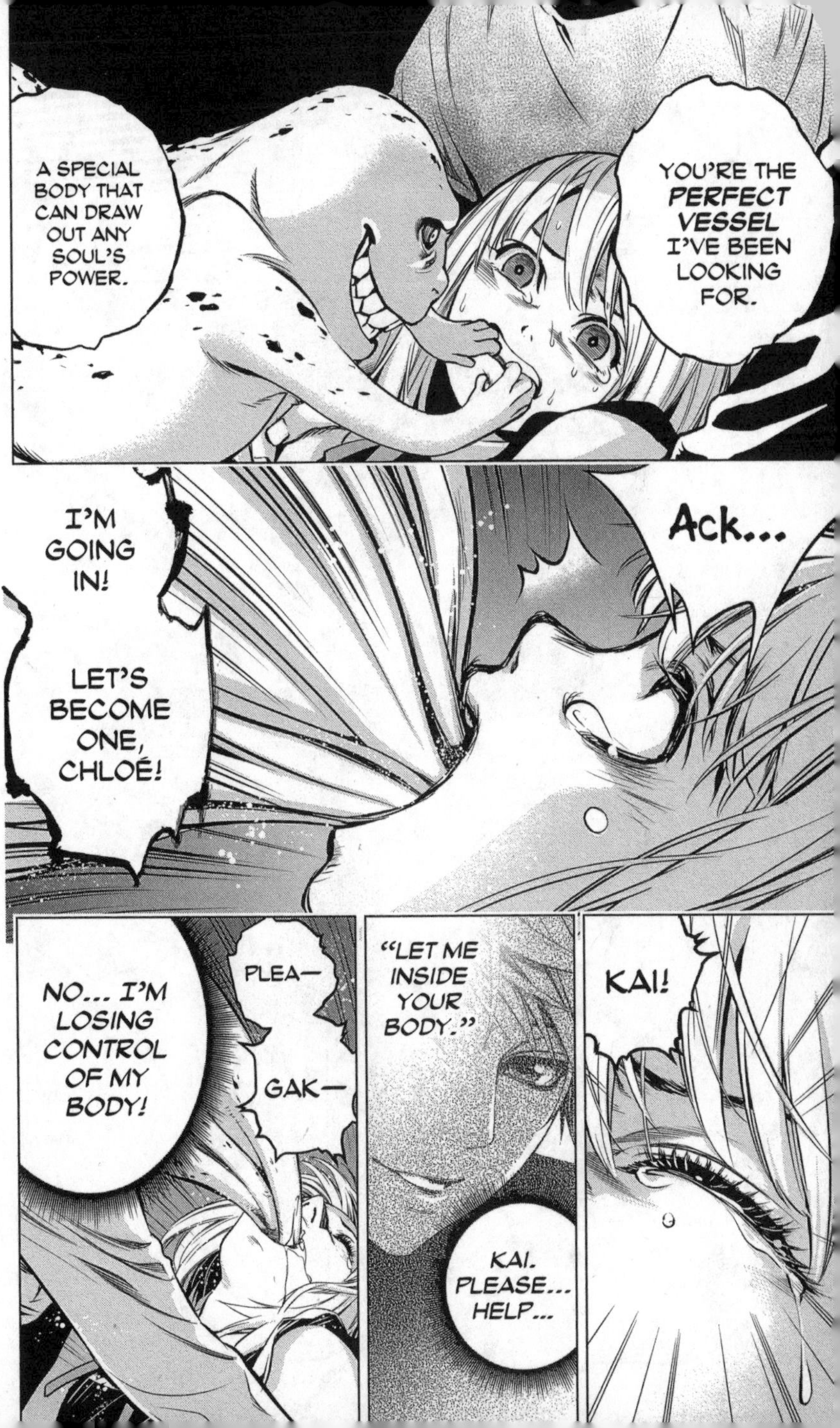
YOU'RE THE PERFECT VESSEL I'VE BEEN LOOKING FOR.
A SPECIAL BODY THAT CAN DRAW OUT ANY SOUL'S POWER.
Ack...
I'M GOING IN!
LET'S BECOME ONE, CHLOÉ!
KAI!
"LET ME INSIDE YOUR BODY."
KAI. PLEASE... HELP...
NO... I'M LOSING CONTROL OF MY BODY!
PLEA—
GAK—

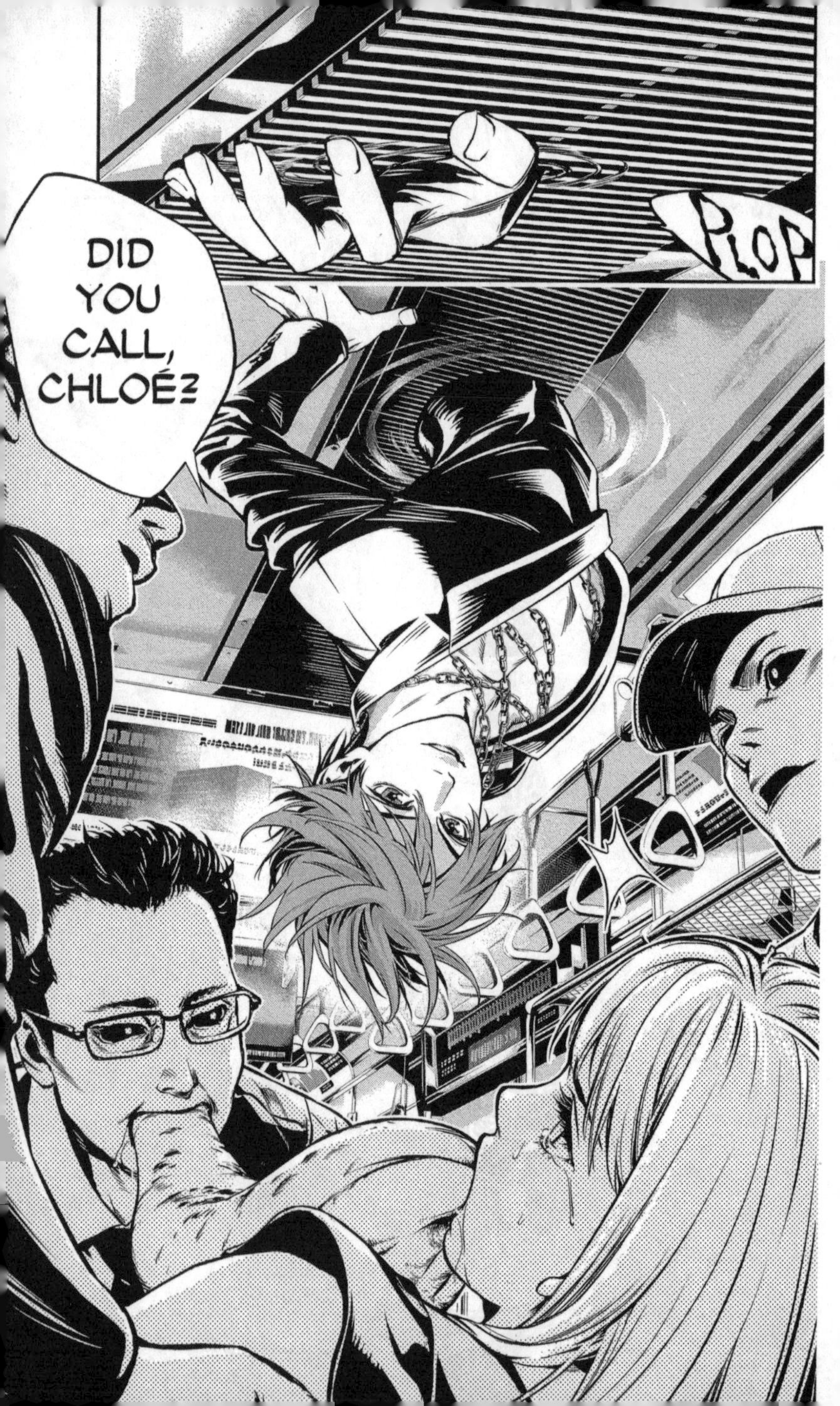
PLOP
DID YOU CALL, CHLOÉ?

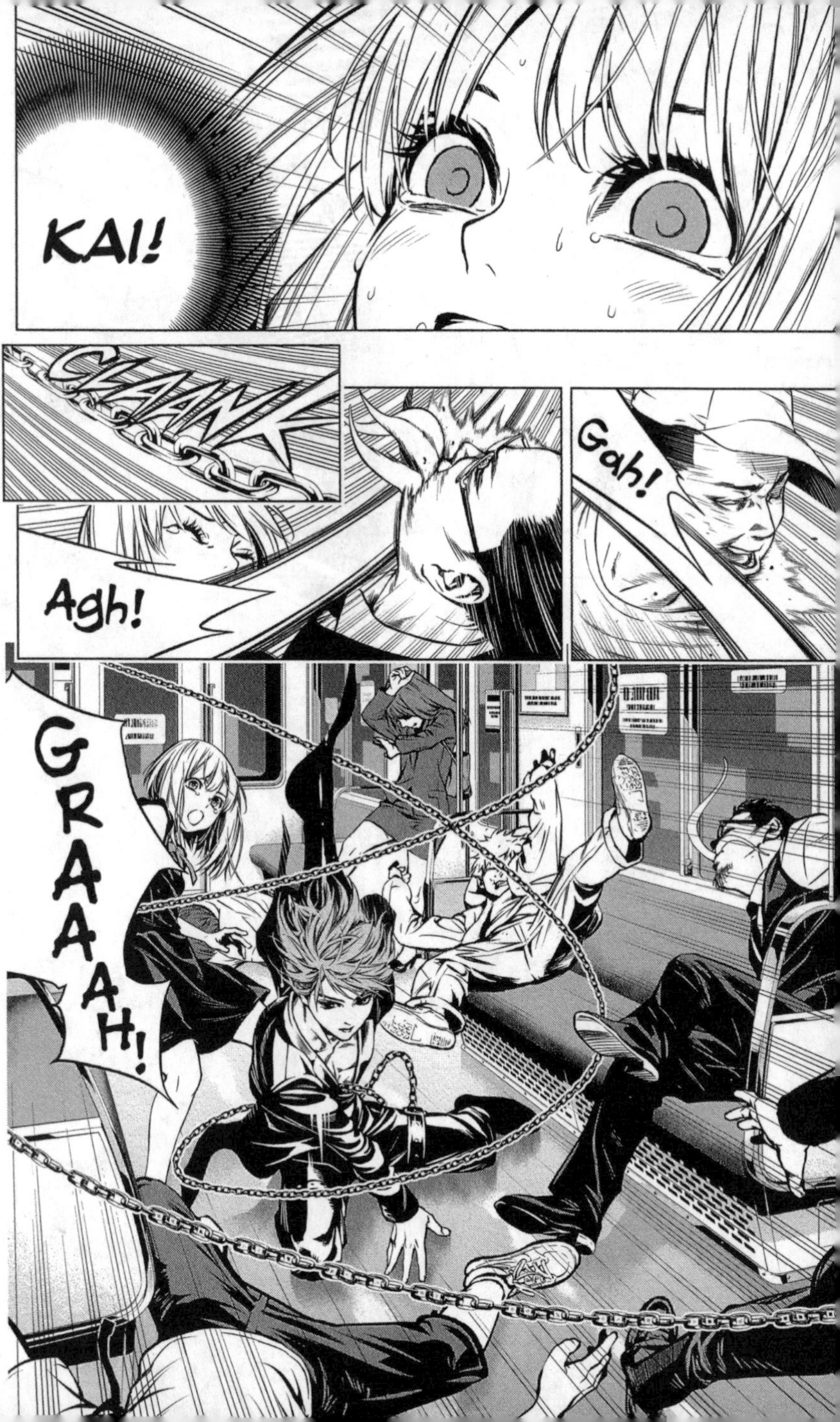
KAI!
Gah!
CLANK
Agh!
GRAAAAH!

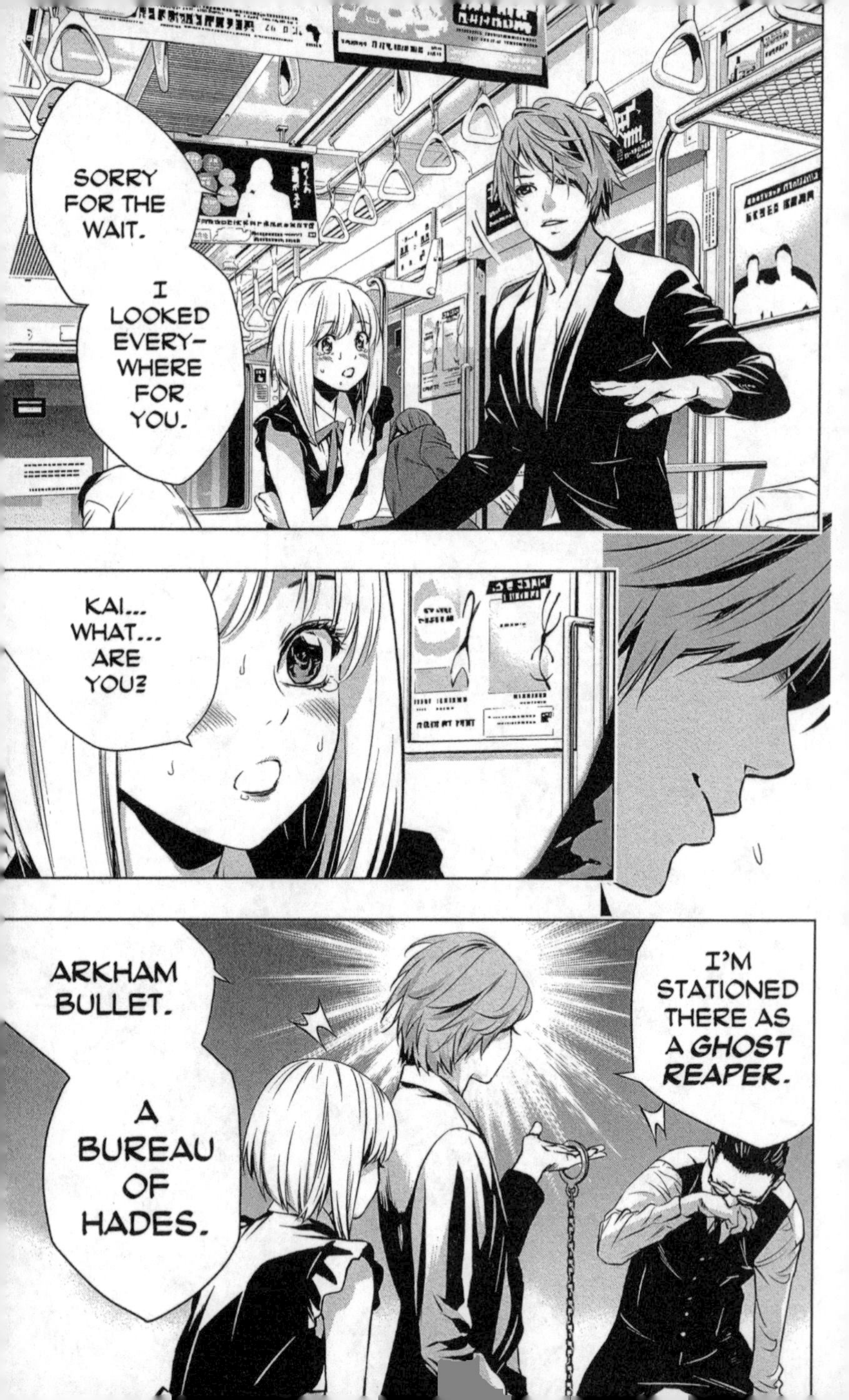
SORRY FOR THE WAIT.
I LOOKED EVERY-WHERE FOR YOU.
KAI... WHAT... ARE YOU?
ARKHAM BULLET.
A BUREAU OF HADES.
I'M STATIONED THERE AS A *GHOST REAPER*.

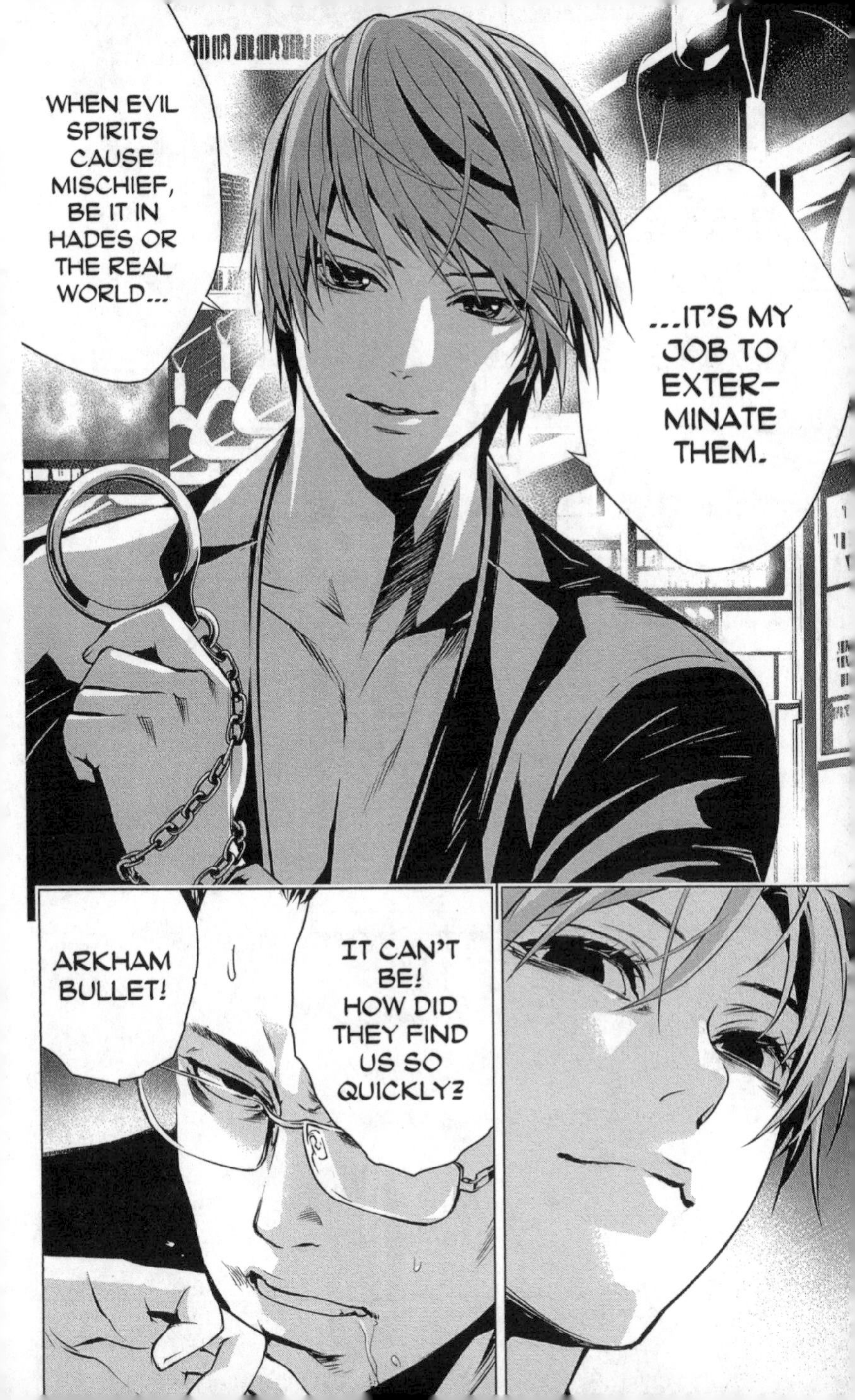
WHEN EVIL SPIRITS CAUSE MISCHIEF, BE IT IN HADES OR THE REAL WORLD...
...IT'S MY JOB TO EXTER-MINATE THEM.
IT CAN'T BE! HOW DID THEY FIND US SO QUICKLY?
ARKHAM BULLET!

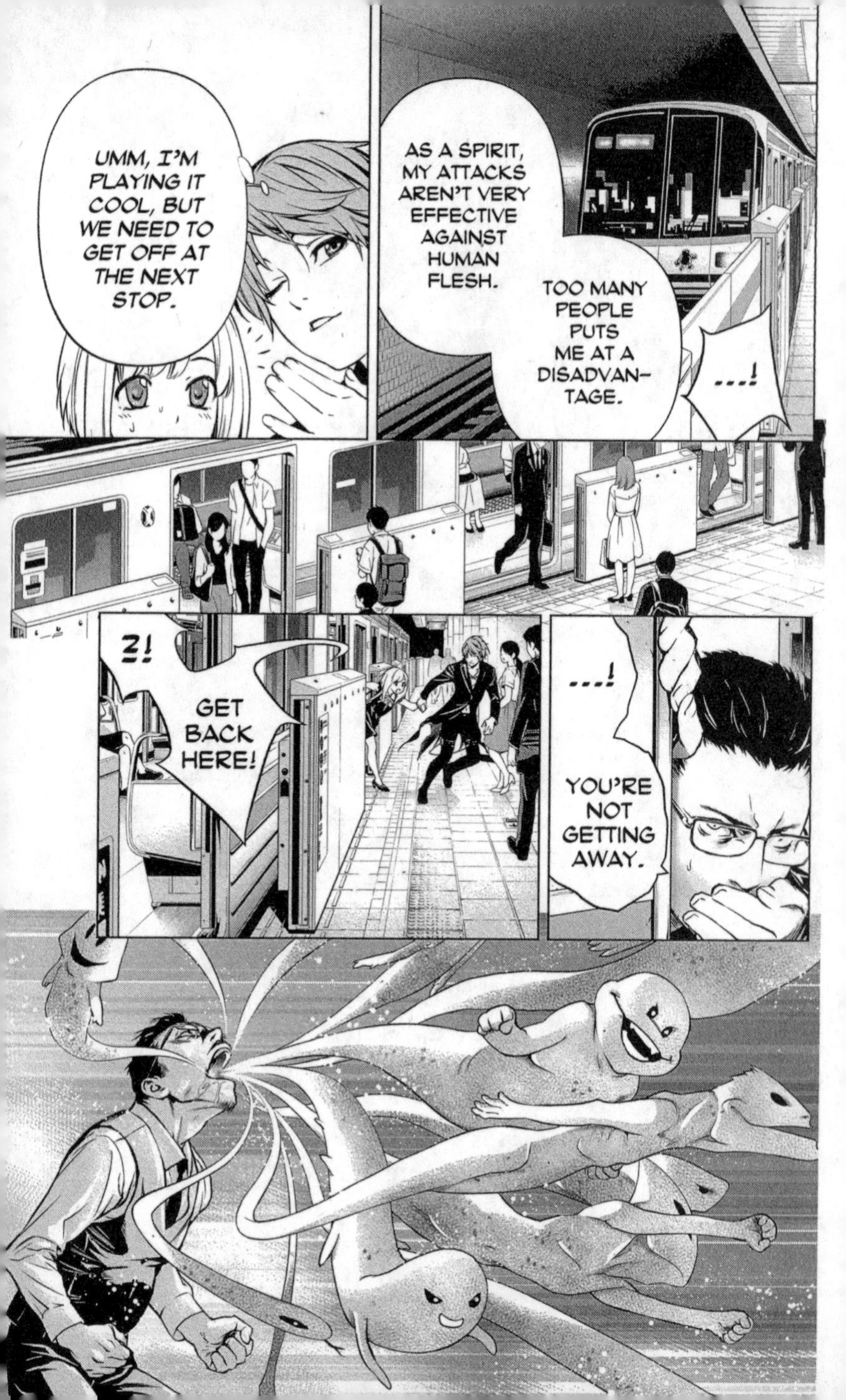
AS A SPIRIT, MY ATTACKS AREN'T VERY EFFECTIVE AGAINST HUMAN FLESH.
TOO MANY PEOPLE PUTS ME AT A DISADVANTAGE.
...!
UMM, I'M PLAYING IT COOL, BUT WE NEED TO GET OFF AT THE NEXT STOP.
...!
YOU'RE NOT GETTING AWAY.
Z!
GET BACK HERE!

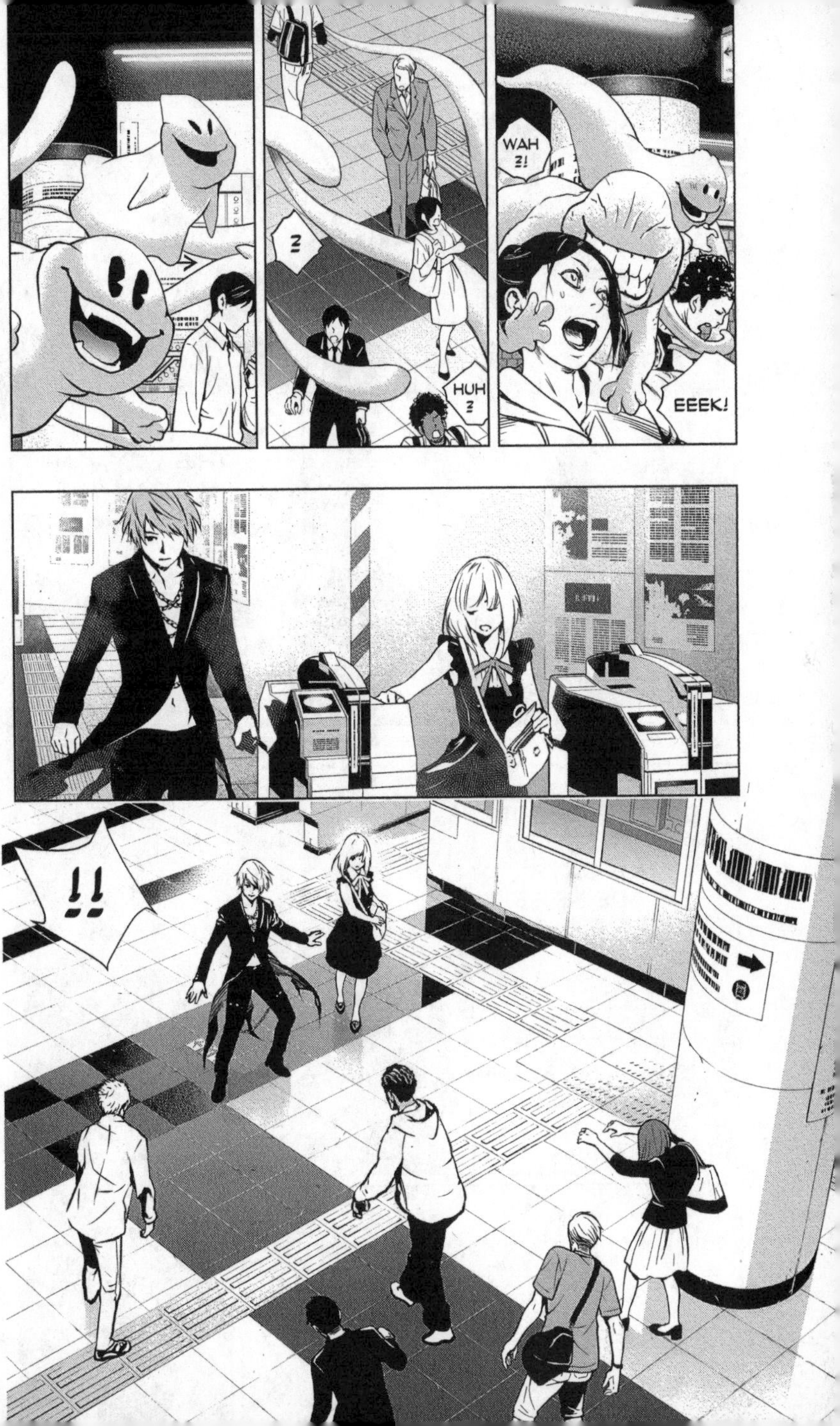
WAH?!
EEEK!
?
HUH?
!!

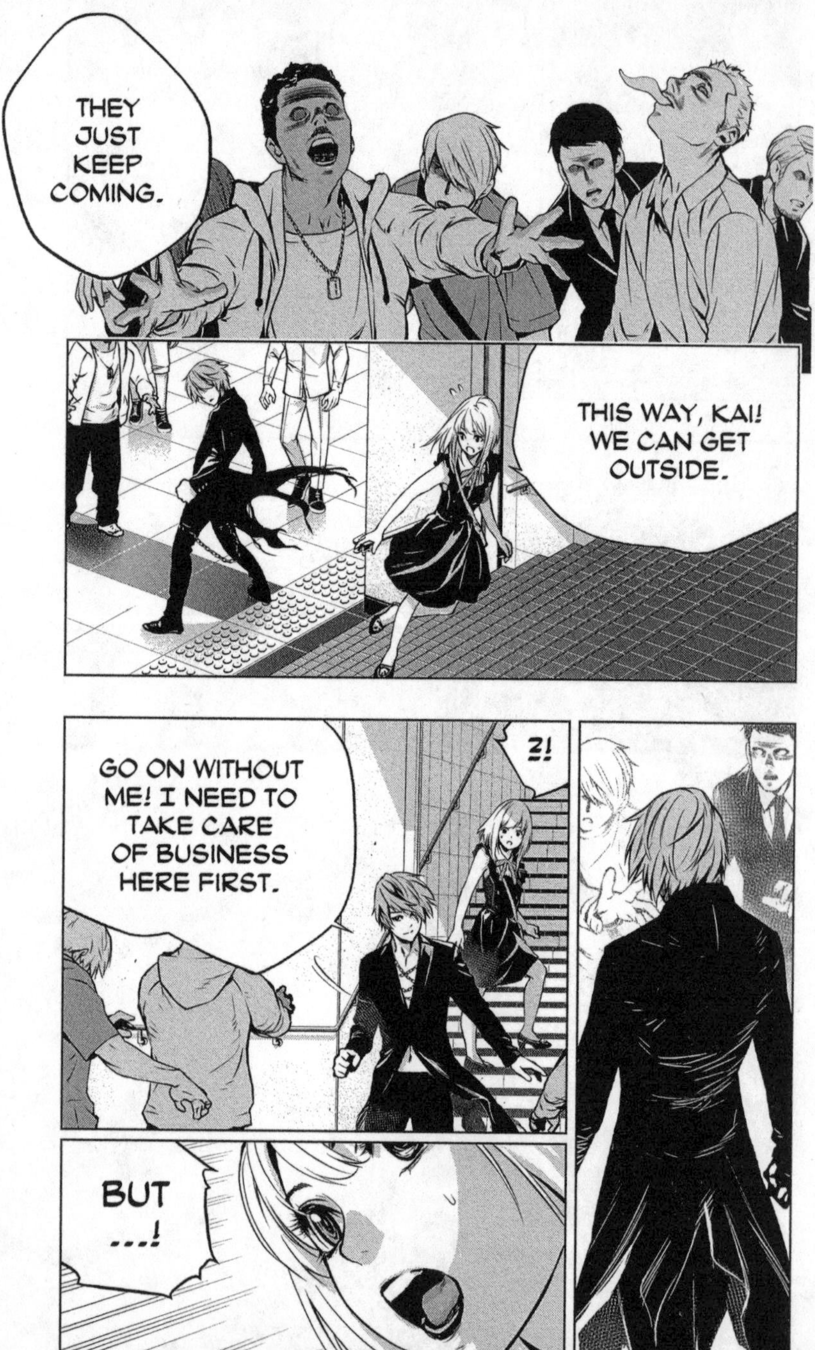
THEY JUST KEEP COMING.
THIS WAY, KAI! WE CAN GET OUTSIDE.
GO ON WITHOUT ME! I NEED TO TAKE CARE OF BUSINESS HERE FIRST.
?!
BUT ...!

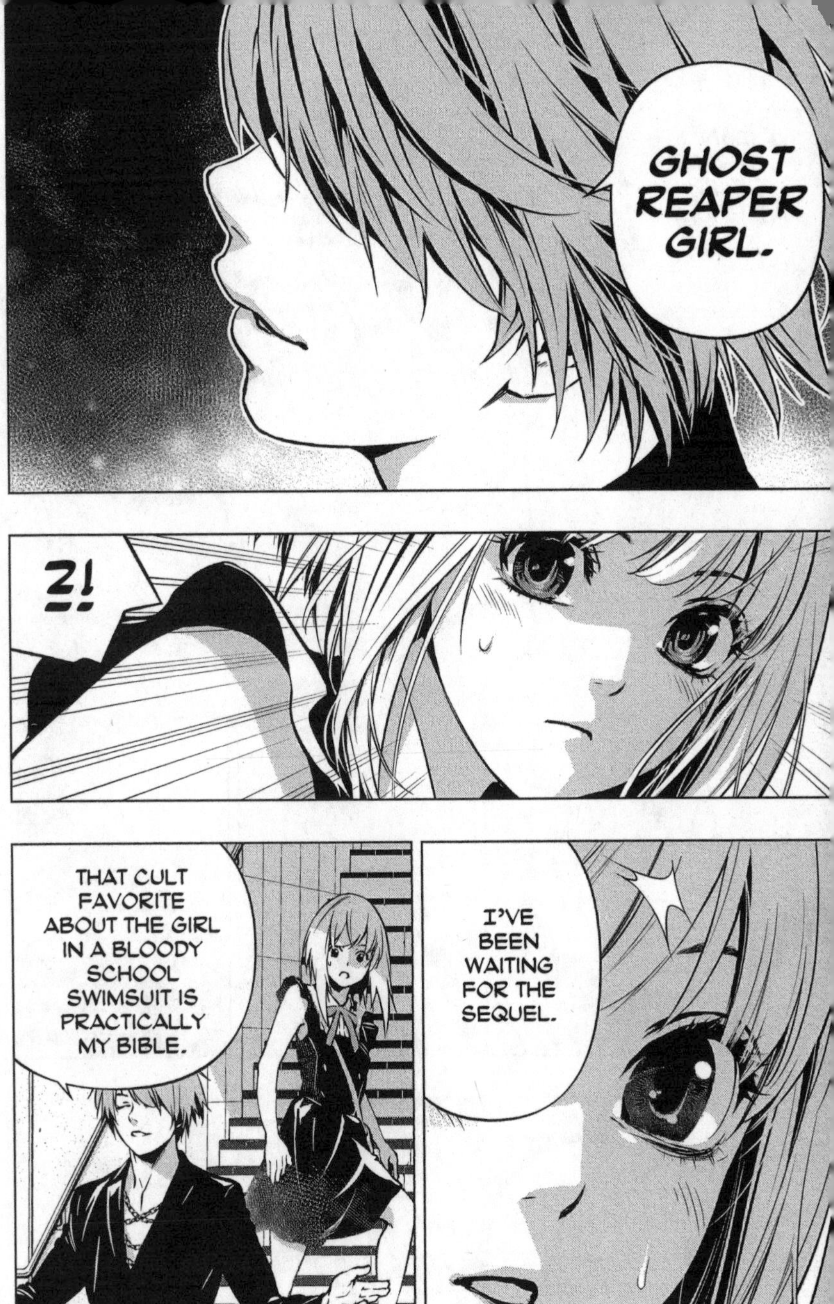
GHOST REAPER GIRL.
?!
I'VE BEEN WAITING FOR THE SEQUEL.
THAT CULT FAVORITE ABOUT THE GIRL IN A BLOODY SCHOOL SWIMSUIT IS PRACTICALLY MY BIBLE.

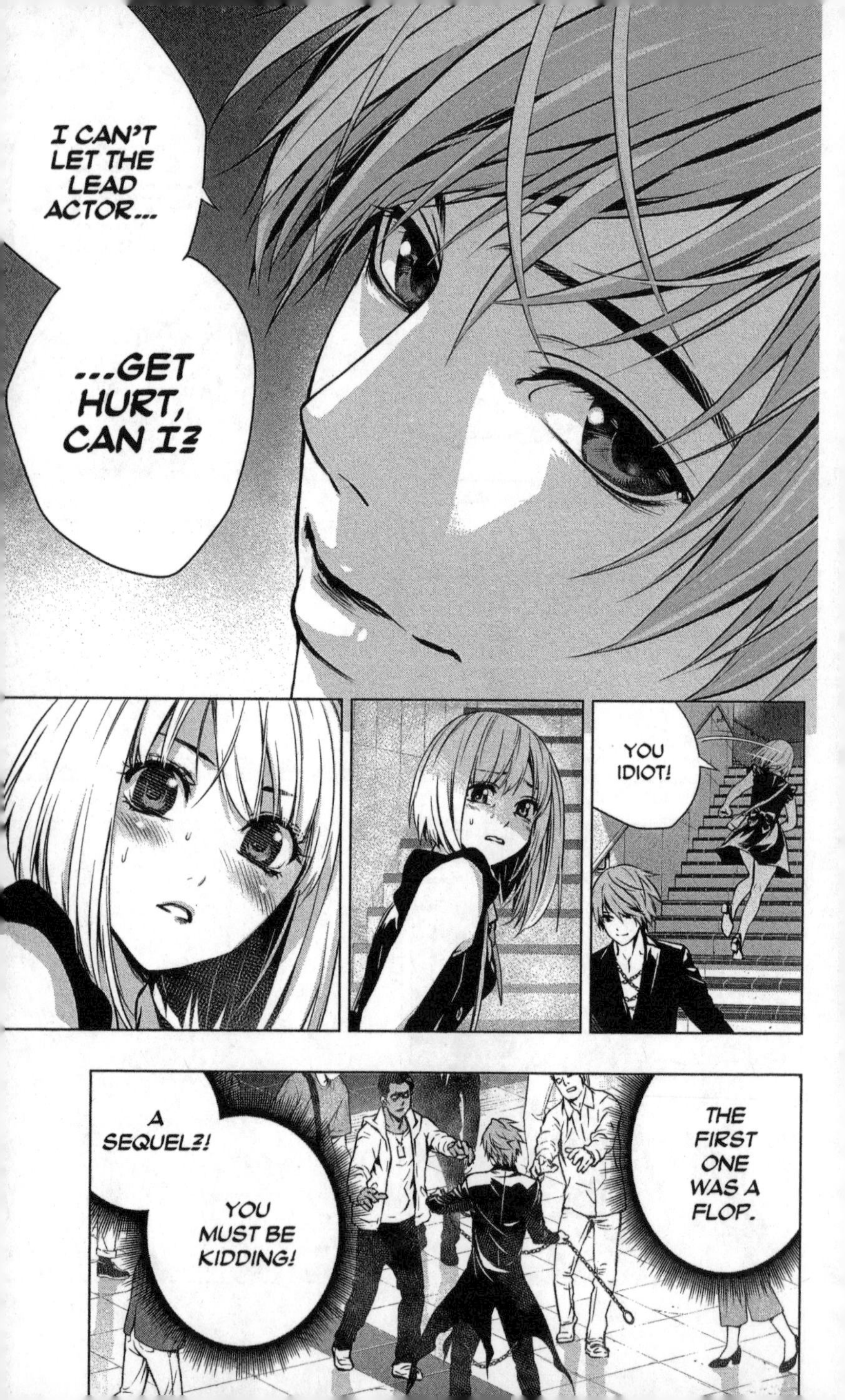
I CAN'T LET THE LEAD ACTOR...
...GET HURT, CAN I?
YOU IDIOT!
THE FIRST ONE WAS A FLOP.
A SEQUEL?!
YOU MUST BE KIDDING!

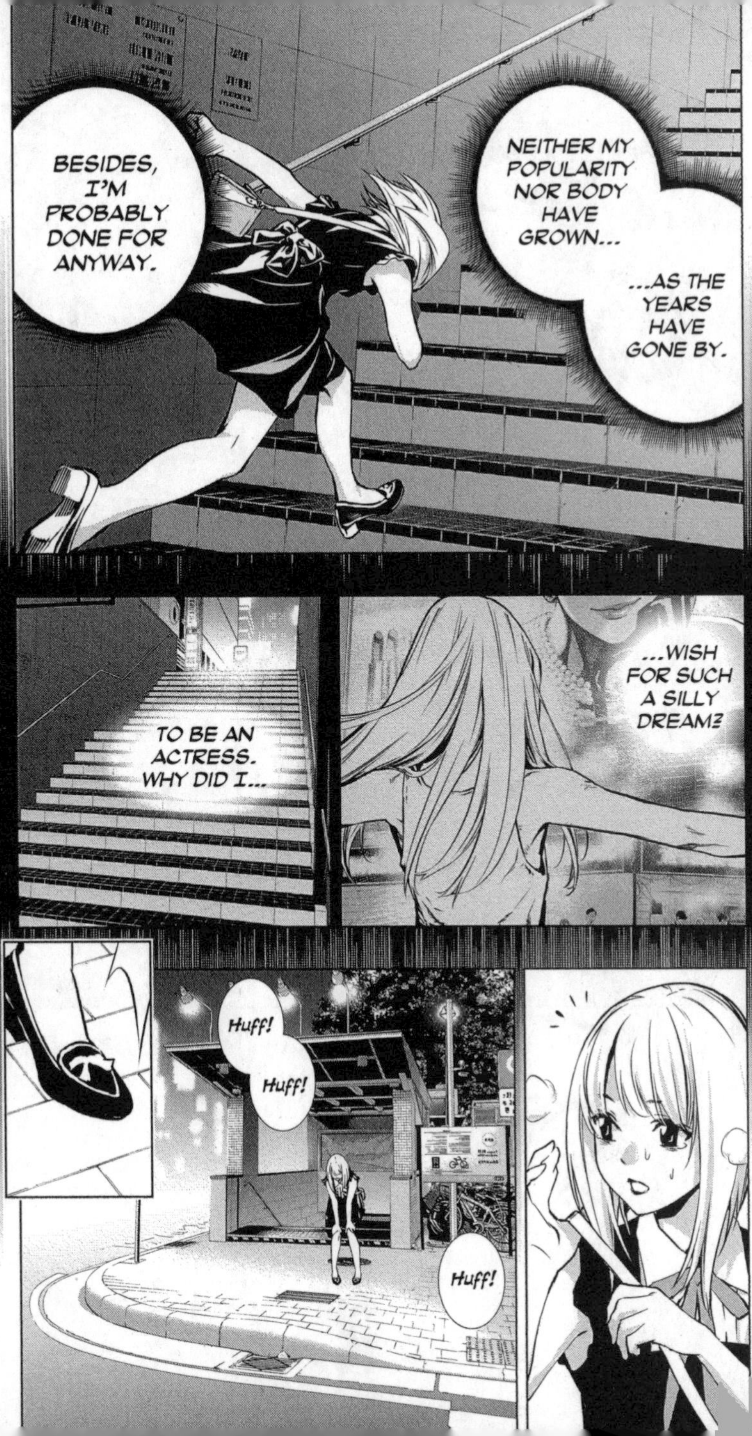
NEITHER MY POPULARITY NOR BODY HAVE GROWN...
...AS THE YEARS HAVE GONE BY.
BESIDES, I'M PROBABLY DONE FOR ANYWAY.
...WISH FOR SUCH A SILLY DREAM?
TO BE AN ACTRESS. WHY DID I...
Huff!
Huff!
Huff!

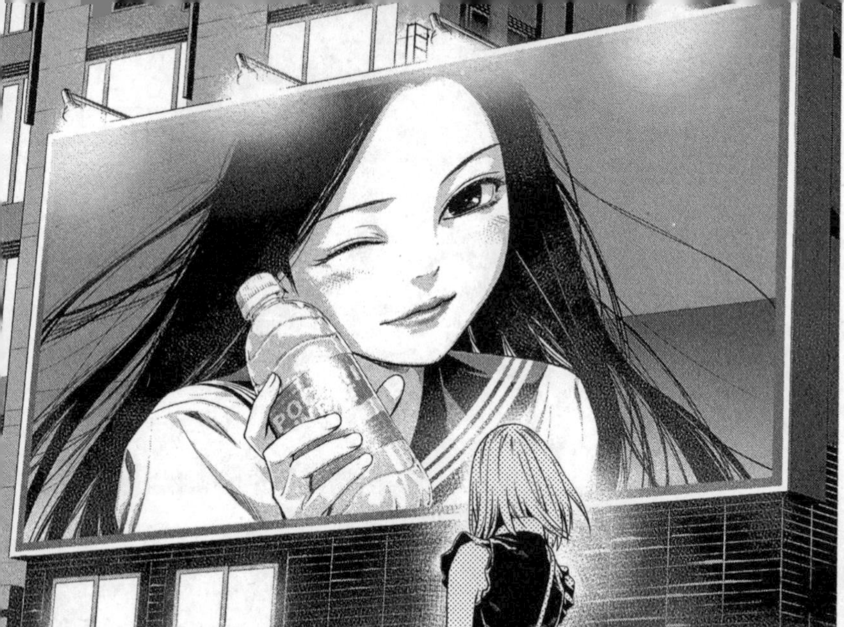
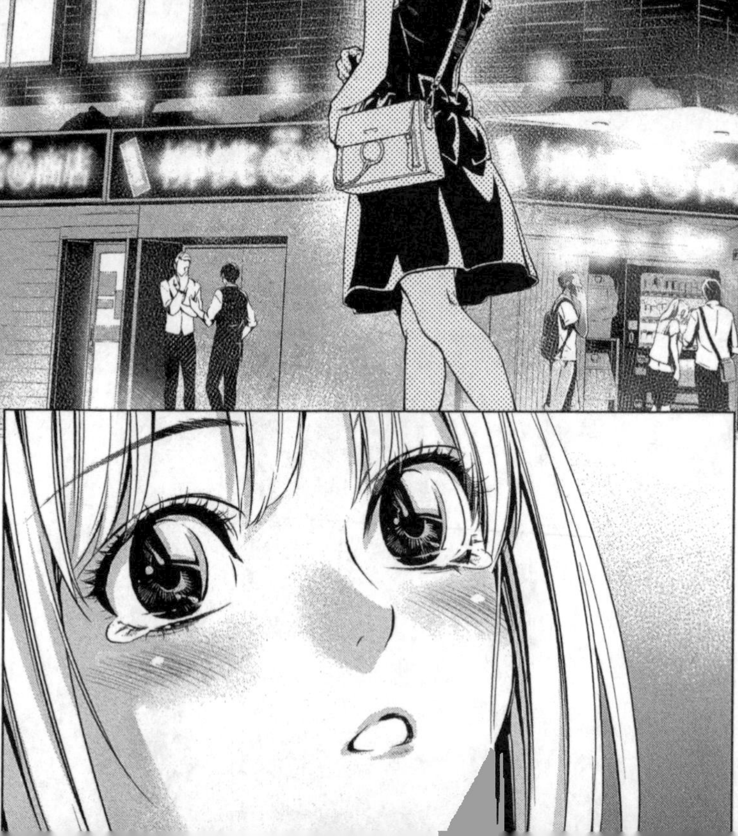

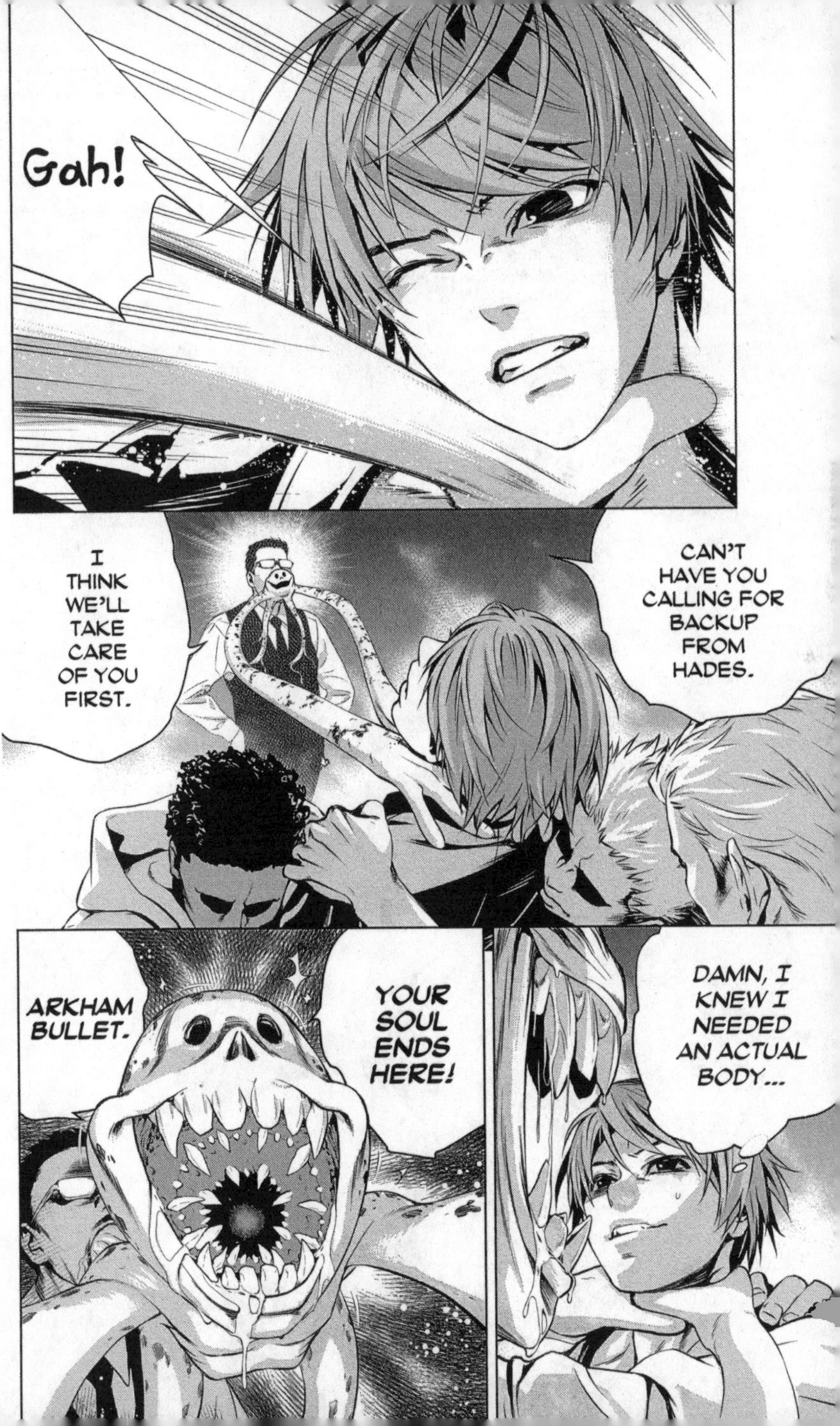
Gah!
CAN'T HAVE YOU CALLING FOR BACKUP FROM HADES.
I THINK WE'LL TAKE CARE OF YOU FIRST.
DAMN, I KNEW I NEEDED AN ACTUAL BODY...
YOUR SOUL ENDS HERE!
ARKHAM BULLET.

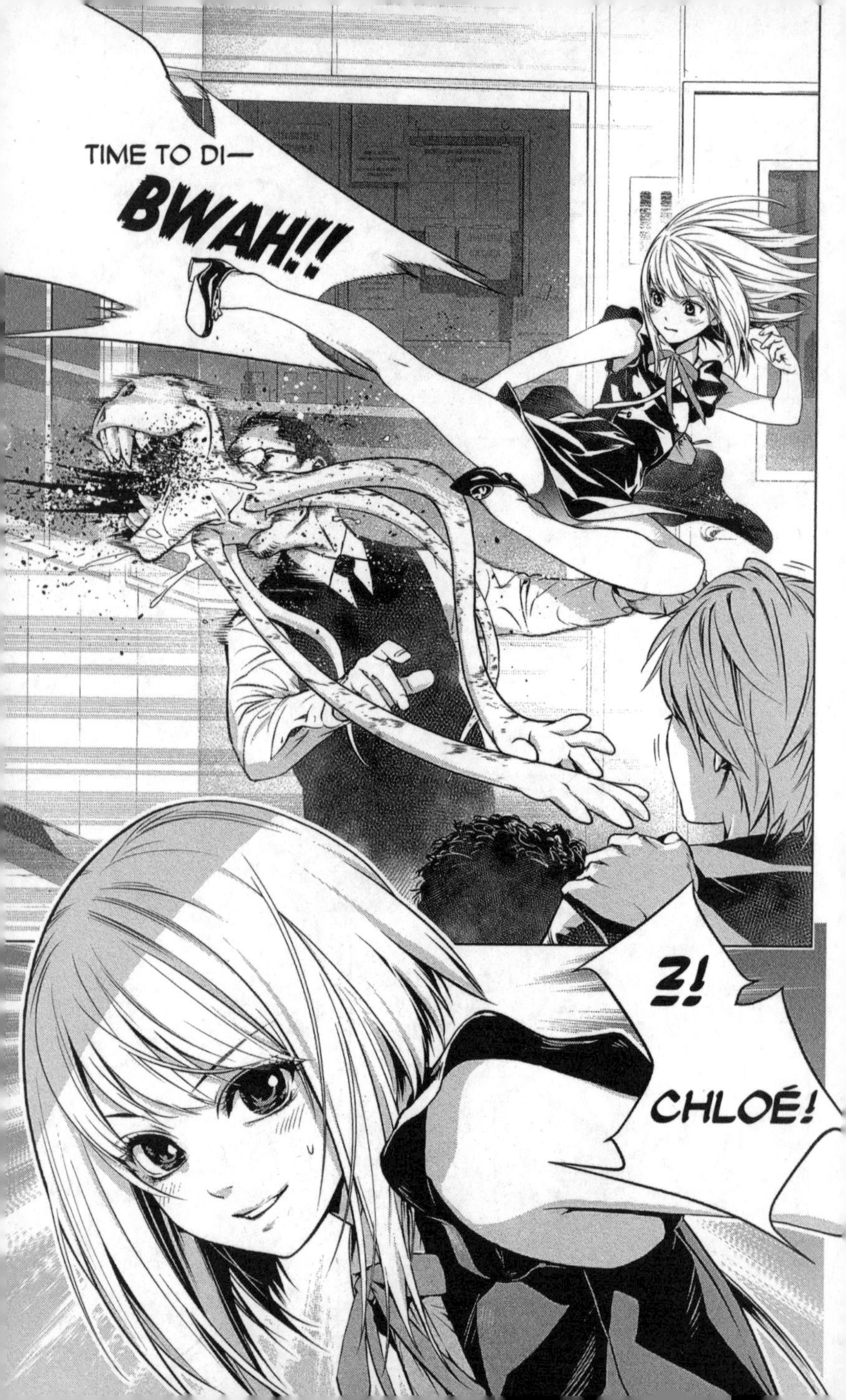
TIME TO DI—
BWAH!!
Z!
CHLOÉ!

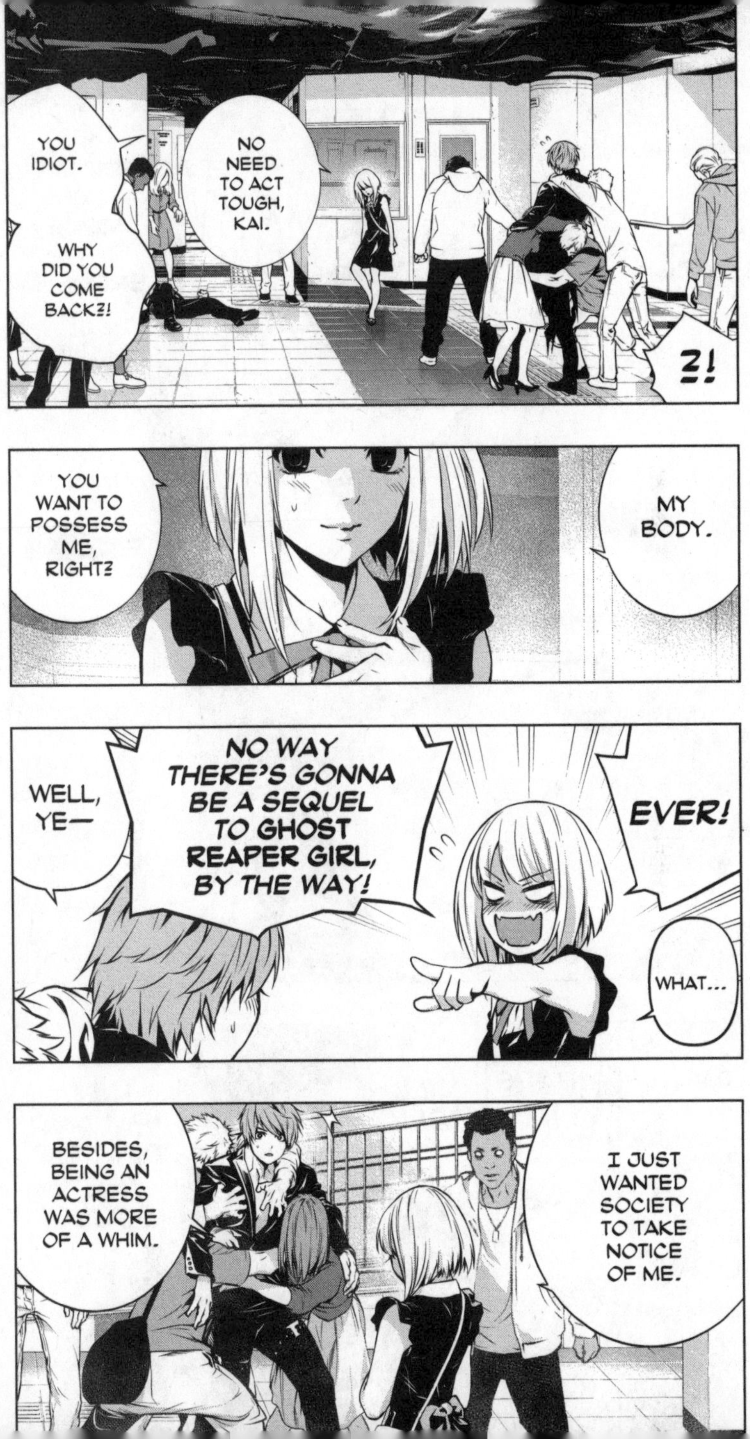
YOU IDIOT.
WHY DID YOU COME BACK?!
NO NEED TO ACT TOUGH, KAI.
?!
YOU WANT TO POSSESS ME, RIGHT?
MY BODY.
WELL, YE—
NO WAY THERE'S GONNA BE A SEQUEL TO GHOST REAPER GIRL, BY THE WAY!
EVER!
WHAT...
BESIDES, BEING AN ACTRESS WAS MORE OF A WHIM.
I JUST WANTED SOCIETY TO TAKE NOTICE OF ME.

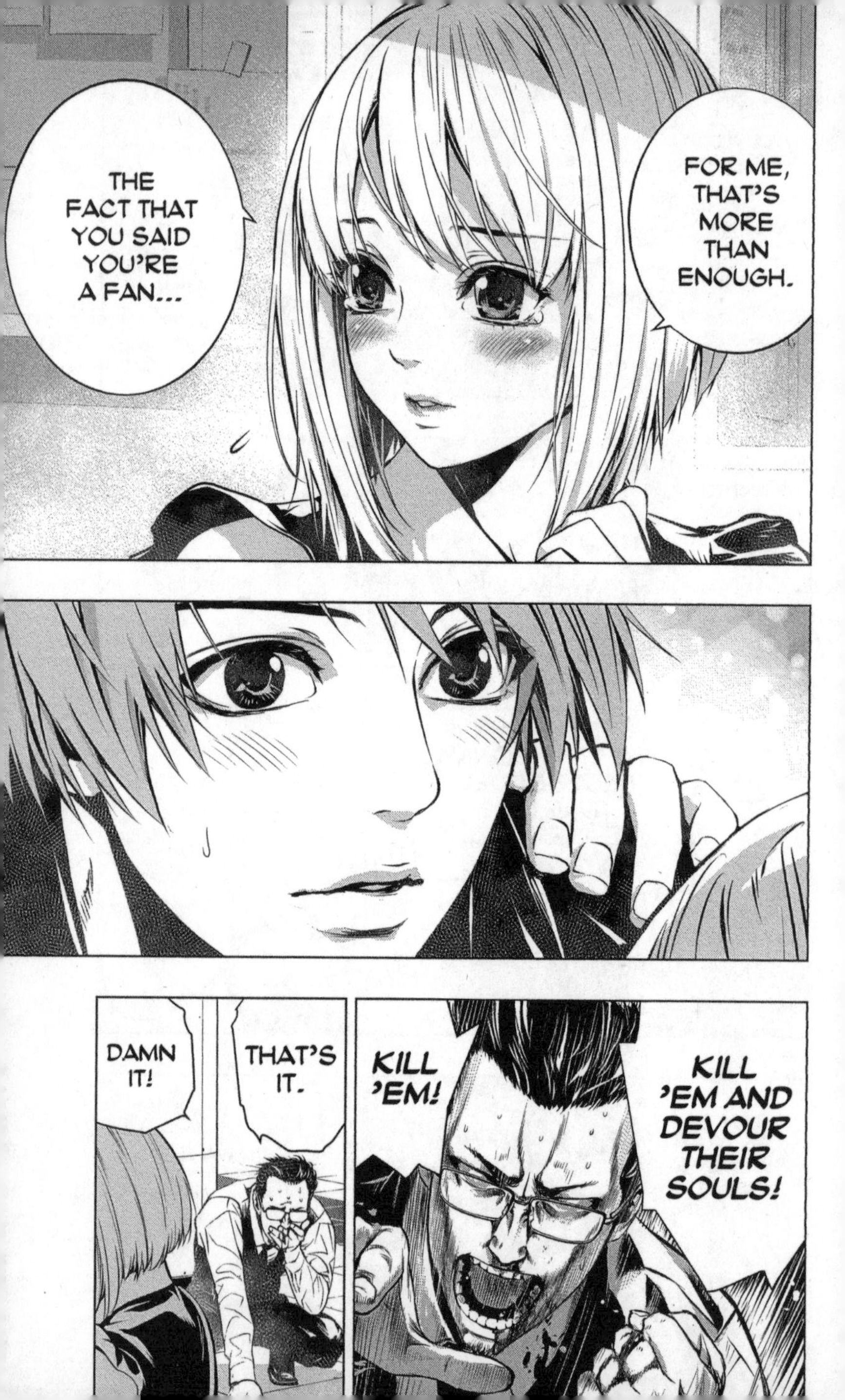
THE FACT THAT YOU SAID YOU'RE A FAN...
FOR ME, THAT'S MORE THAN ENOUGH.
DAMN IT!
THAT'S IT.
KILL 'EM!
KILL 'EM AND DEVOUR THEIR SOULS!

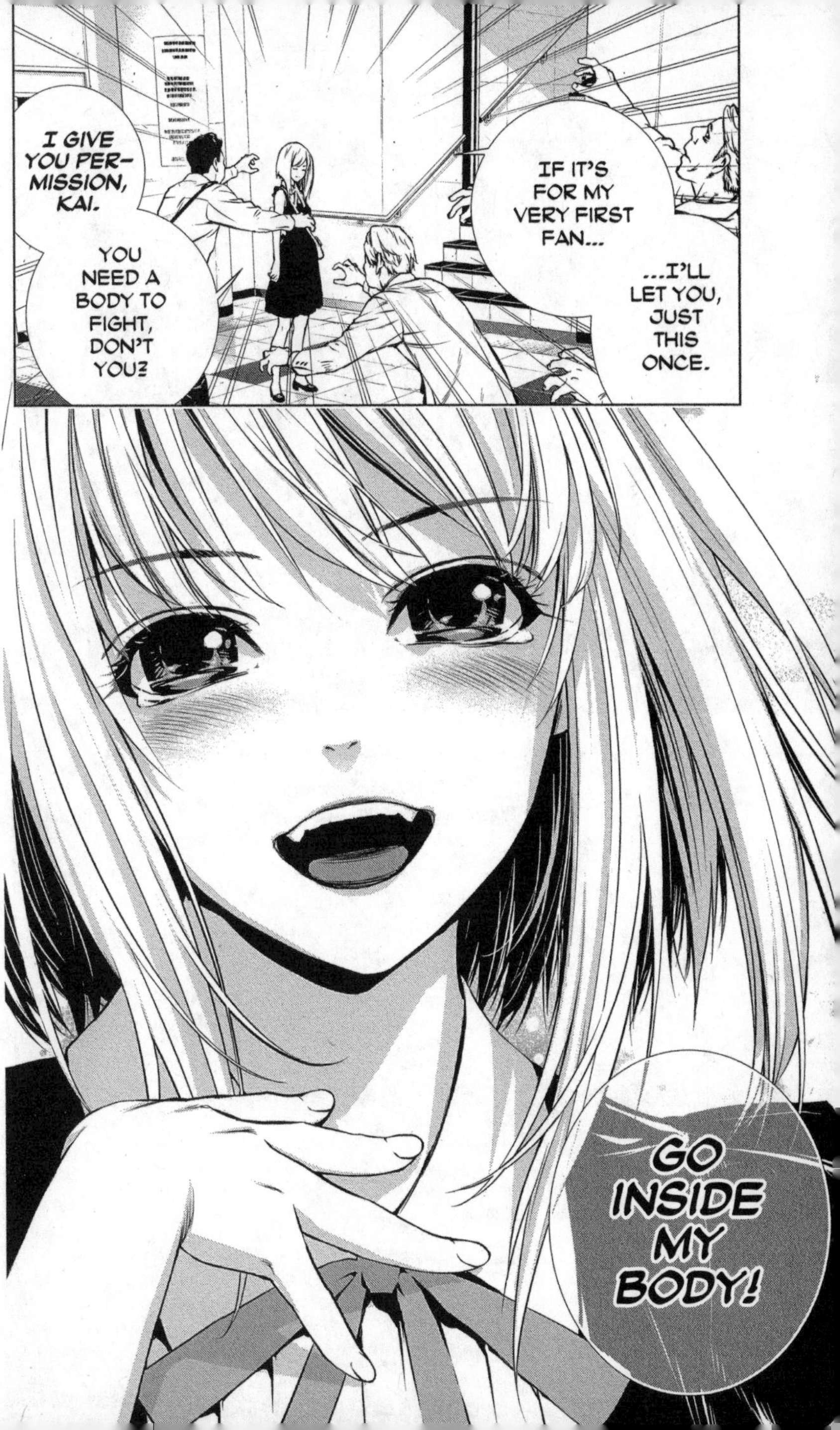
IF IT'S FOR MY VERY FIRST FAN...
...I'LL LET YOU, JUST THIS ONCE.
I GIVE YOU PER-MISSION, KAI.
YOU NEED A BODY TO FIGHT, DON'T YOU?
GO INSIDE MY BODY!

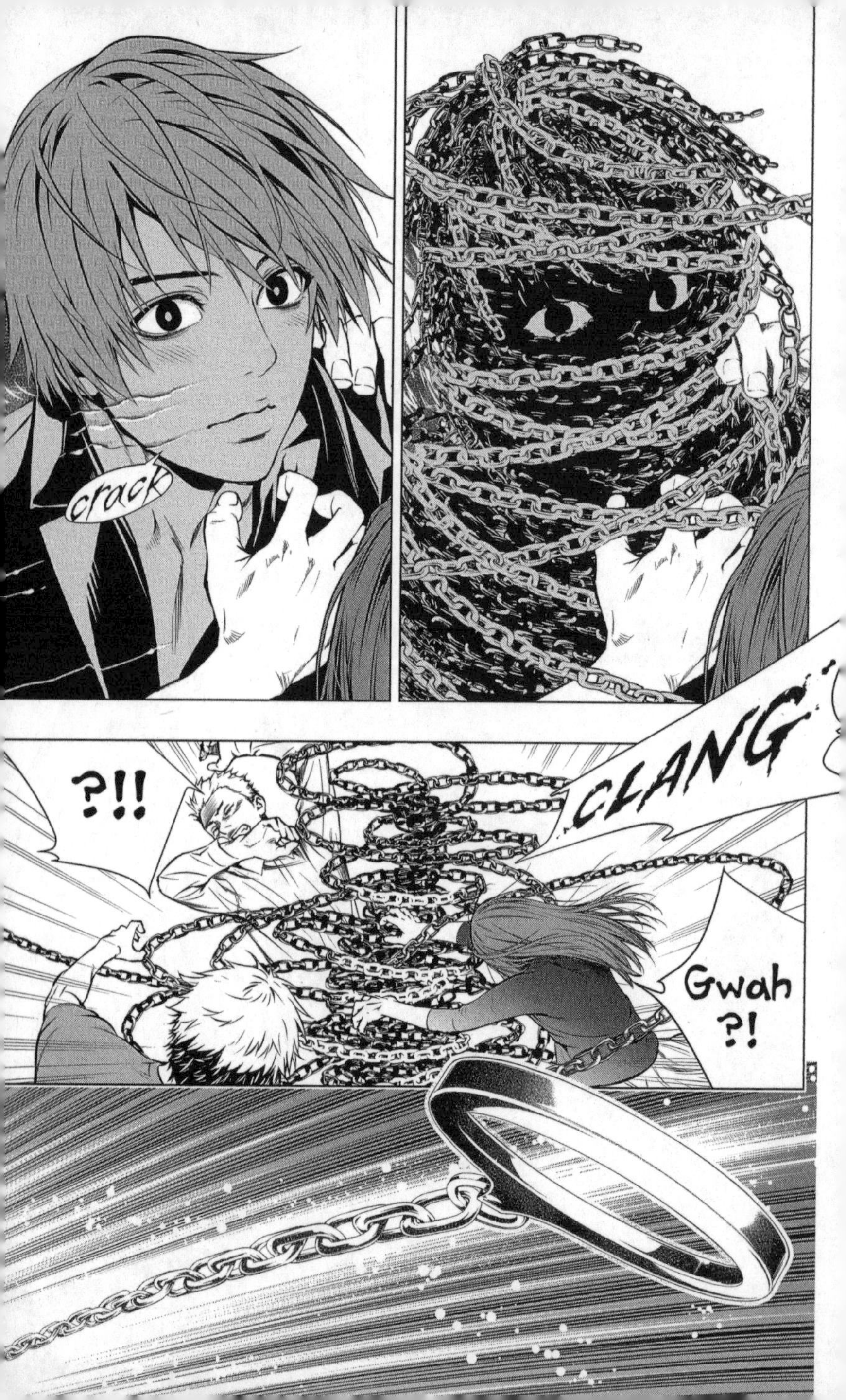
crack
CLANG
Gwah ?!
?!!

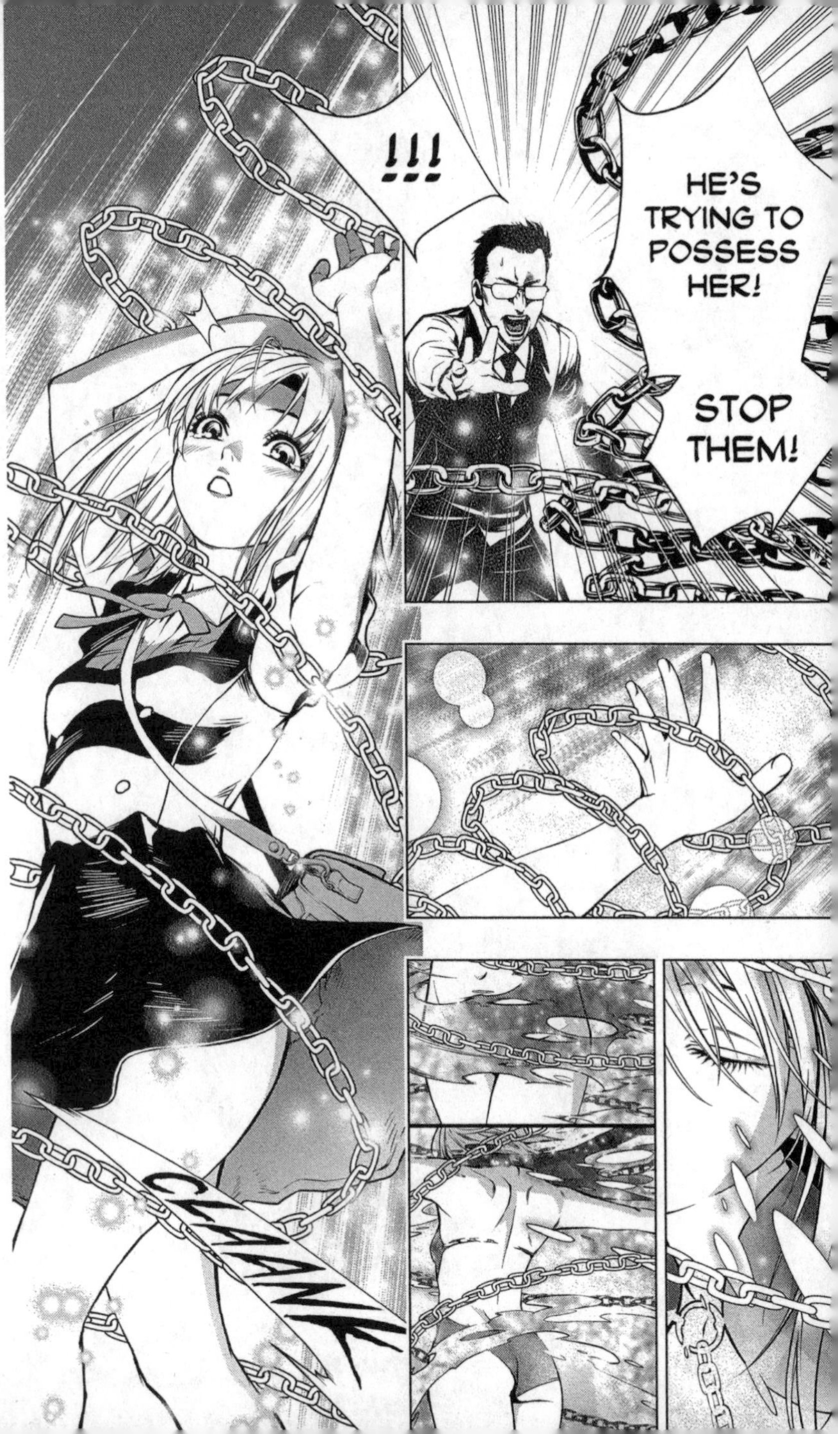
HE'S TRYING TO POSSESS HER!
STOP THEM!
!!!
CLAANK

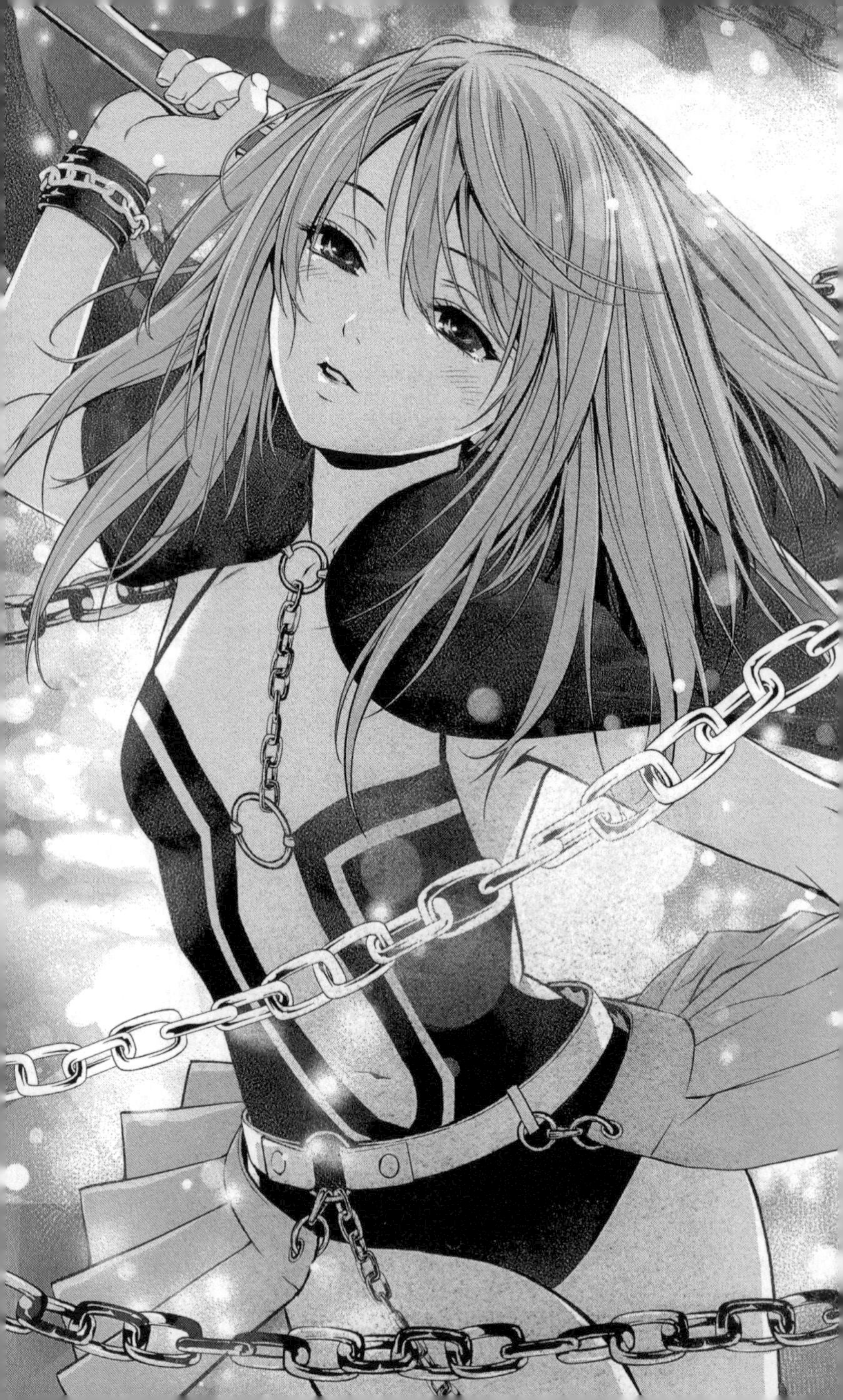

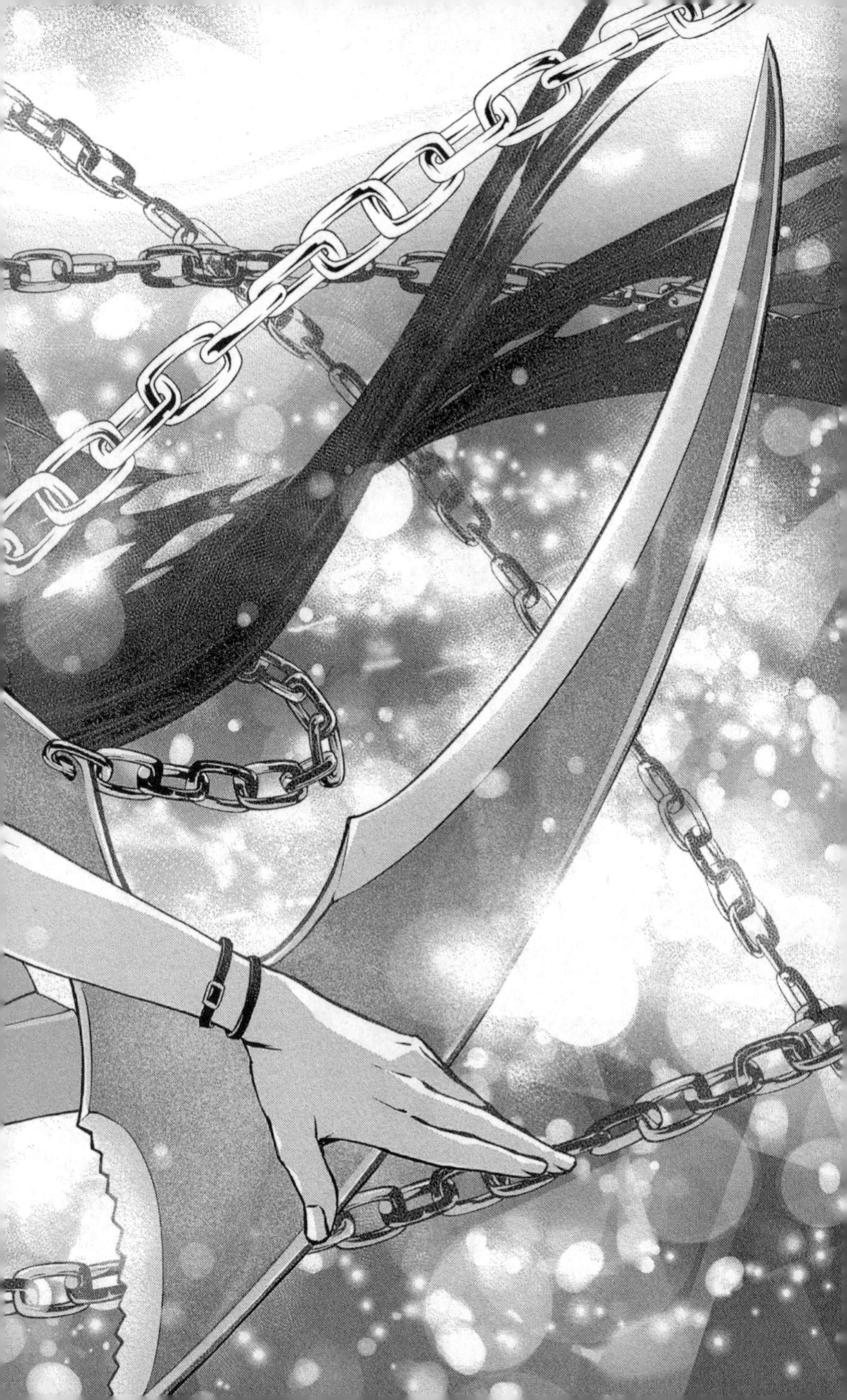

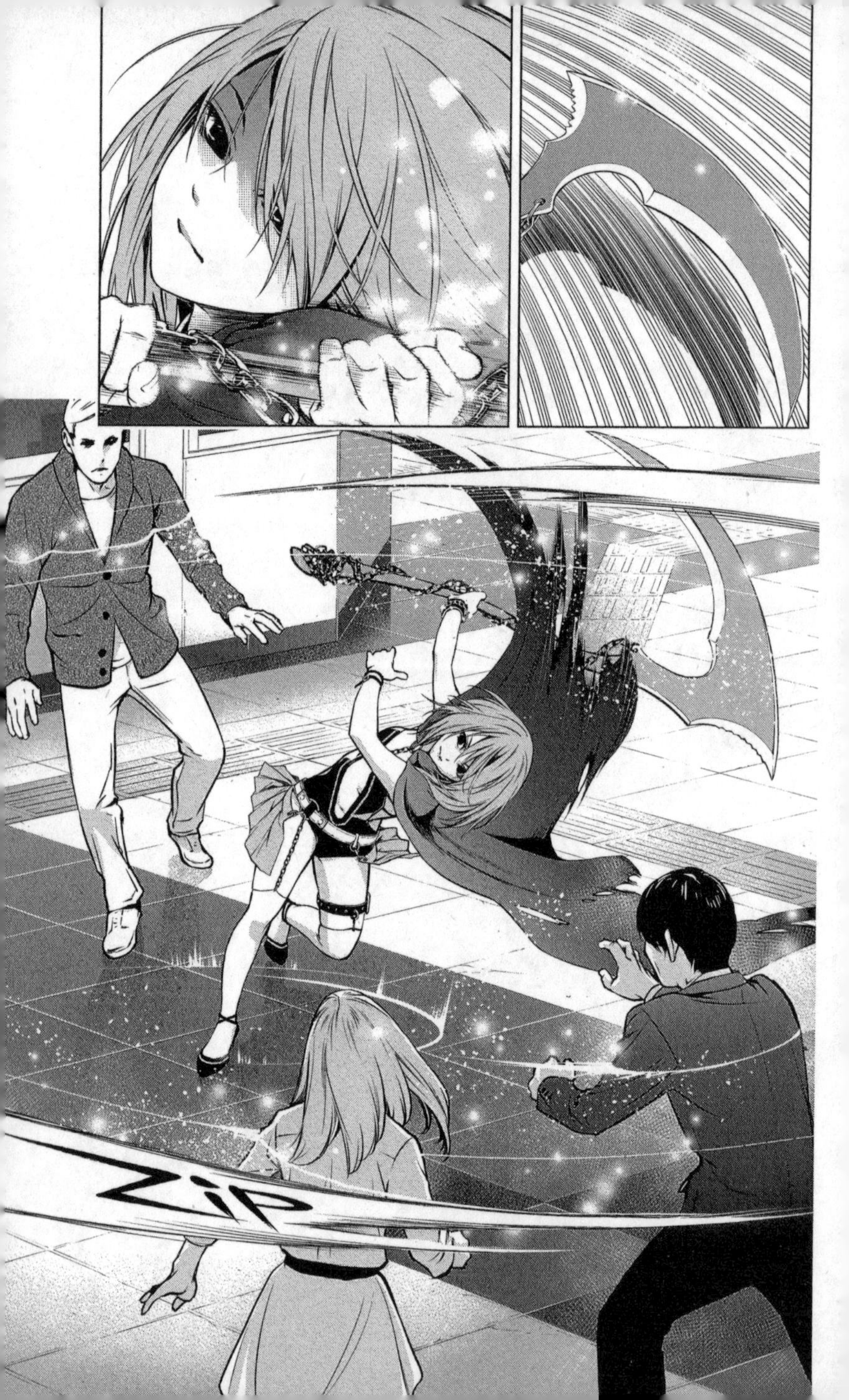
ZiP

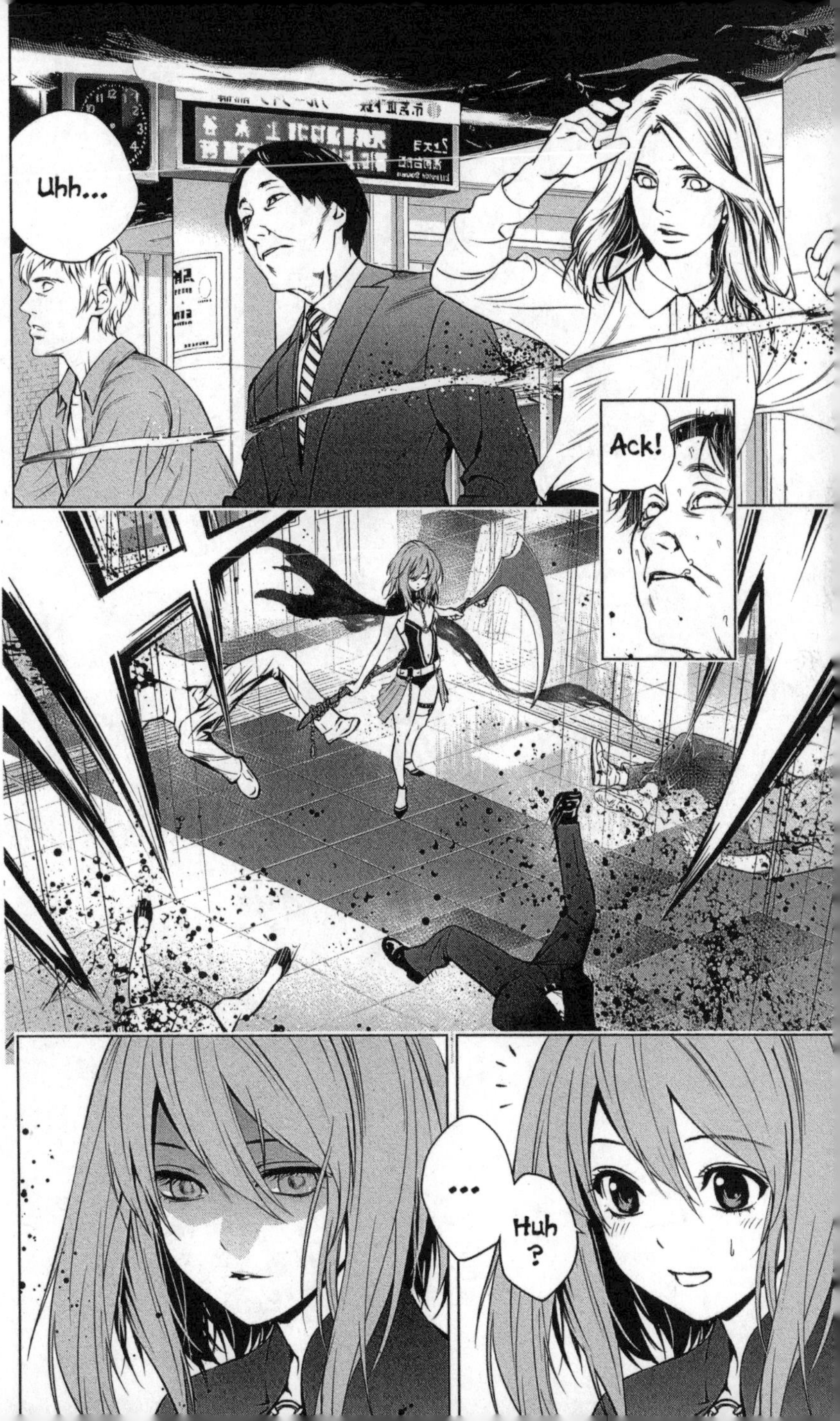
Uhh...
Ack!
...
Huh?

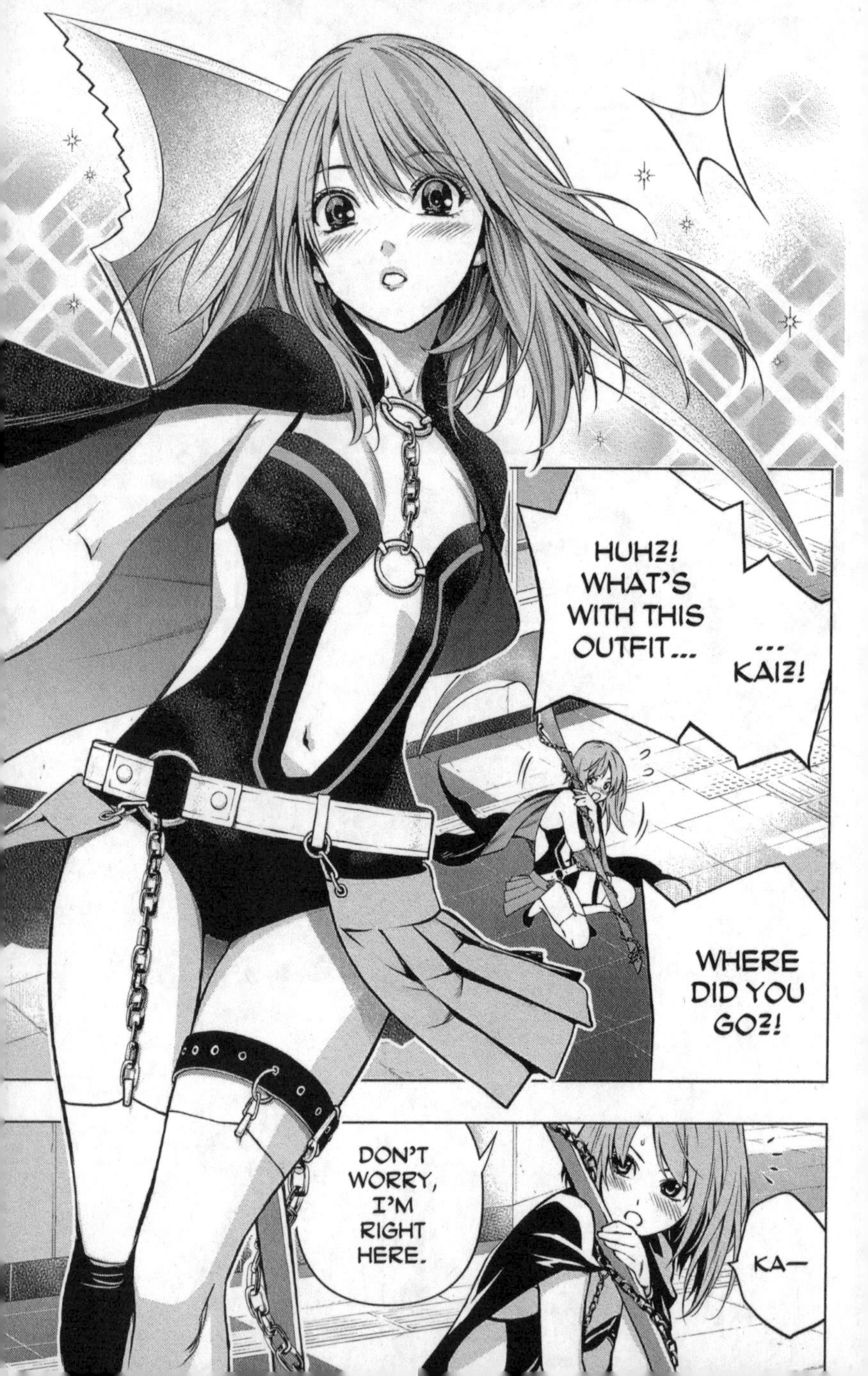
HUH?! WHAT'S WITH THIS OUTFIT... ...KAI?!
WHERE DID YOU GO?!
KA—
DON'T WORRY, I'M RIGHT HERE.

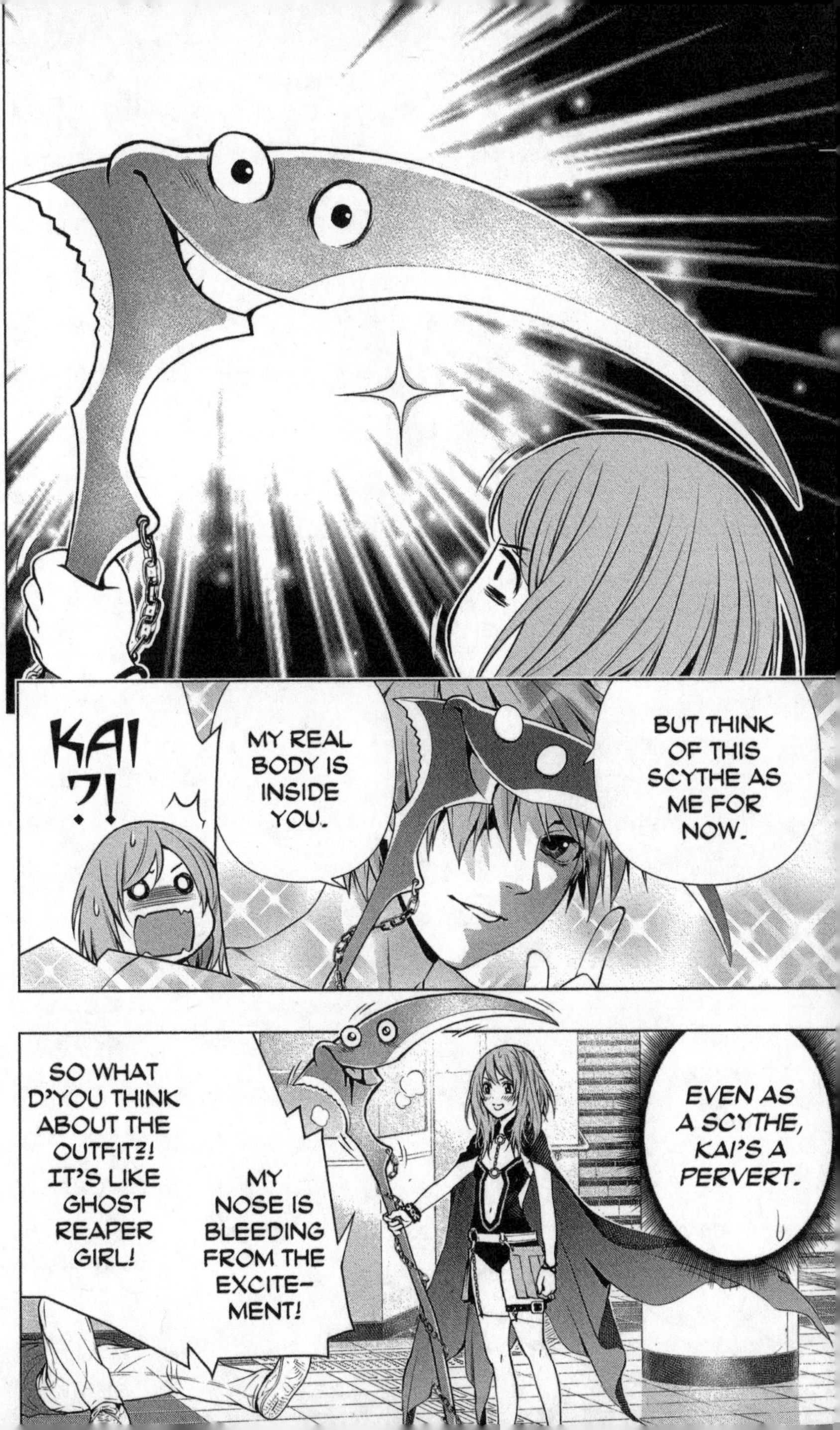
BUT THINK OF THIS SCYTHE AS ME FOR NOW.
MY REAL BODY IS INSIDE YOU.
KAI ?!
EVEN AS A SCYTHE, KAI'S A PERVERT.
MY NOSE IS BLEEDING FROM THE EXCITE-MENT!
SO WHAT D'YOU THINK ABOUT THE OUTFIT?! IT'S LIKE GHOST REAPER GIRL!

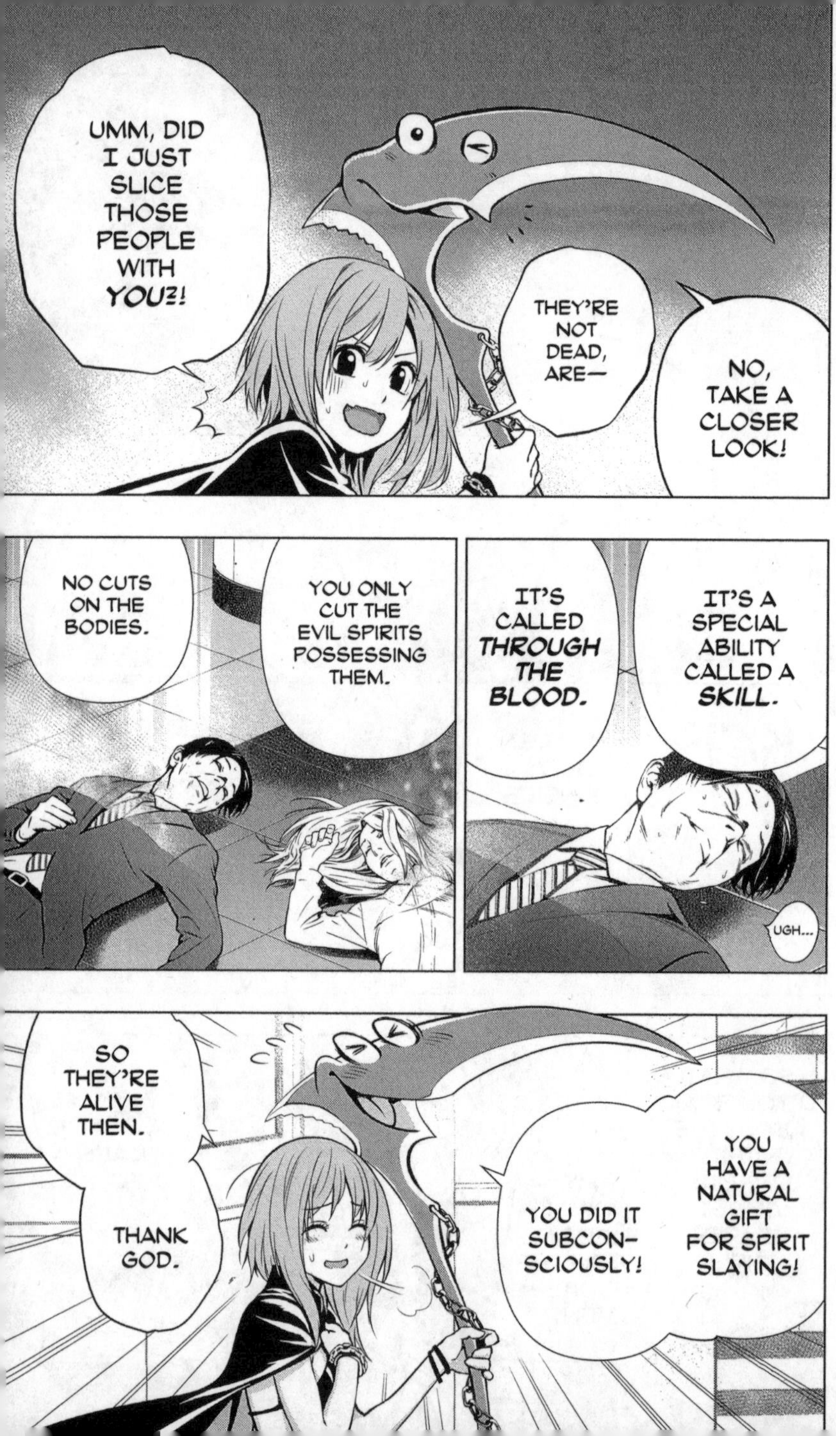
UMM, DID I JUST SLICE THOSE PEOPLE WITH *YOU*?!
THEY'RE NOT DEAD, ARE—
NO, TAKE A CLOSER LOOK!
NO CUTS ON THE BODIES.
YOU ONLY CUT THE EVIL SPIRITS POSSESSING THEM.
IT'S CALLED ***THROUGH THE BLOOD.***
IT'S A SPECIAL ABILITY CALLED A ***SKILL.***
UGH...
SO THEY'RE ALIVE THEN.
THANK GOD.
YOU DID IT SUBCON-SCIOUSLY!
YOU HAVE A NATURAL GIFT FOR SPIRIT SLAYING!

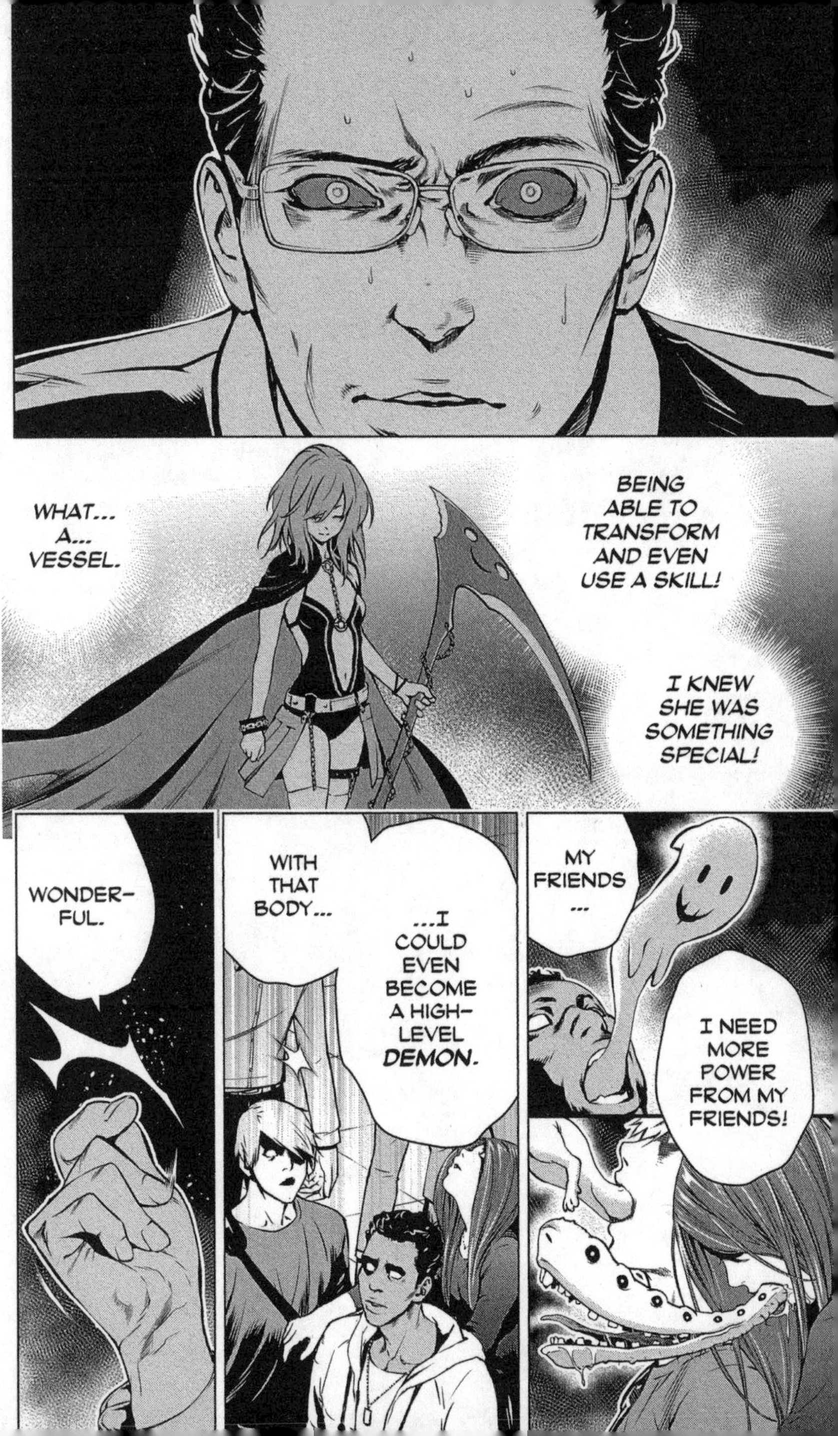
BEING ABLE TO TRANSFORM AND EVEN USE A SKILL!
WHAT... A... VESSEL.
I KNEW SHE WAS SOMETHING SPECIAL!
MY FRIENDS ...
I NEED MORE POWER FROM MY FRIENDS!
WITH THAT BODY...
...I COULD EVEN BECOME A HIGH-LEVEL DEMON.
WONDER-FUL.

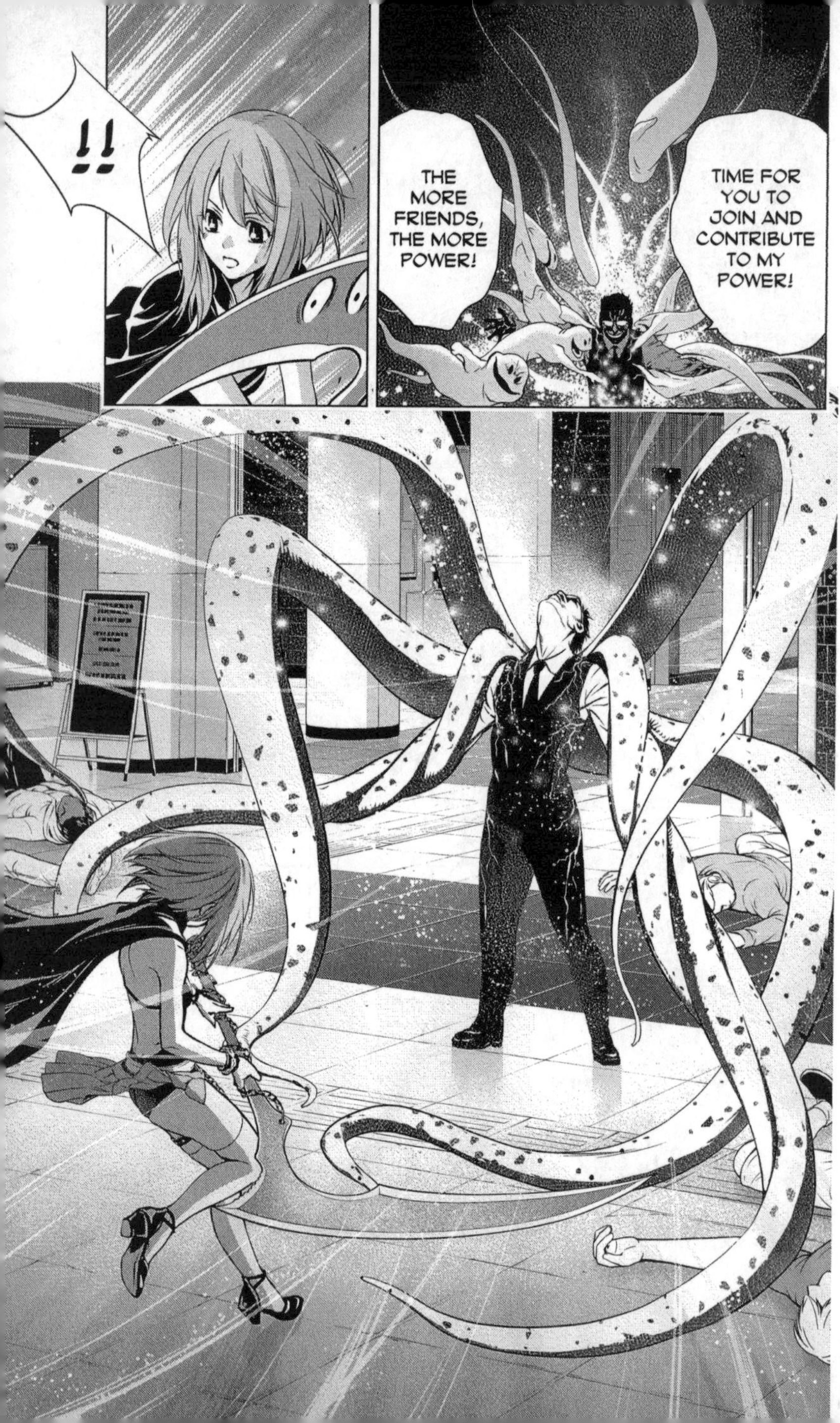
TIME FOR YOU TO JOIN AND CONTRIBUTE TO MY POWER!
THE MORE FRIENDS, THE MORE POWER!
!!

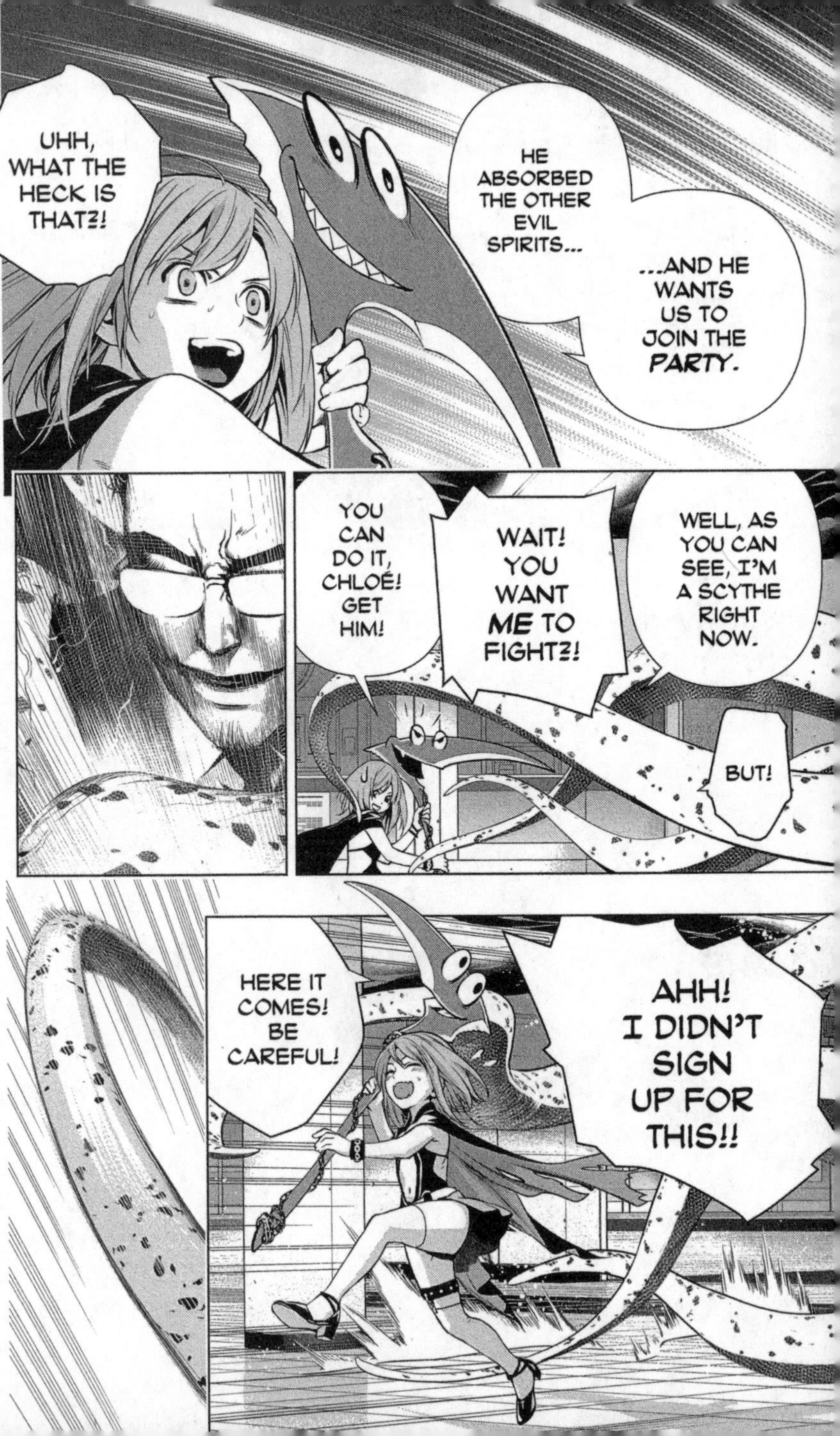
UHH, WHAT THE HECK IS THAT?!
HE ABSORBED THE OTHER EVIL SPIRITS...
...AND HE WANTS US TO JOIN THE *PARTY*.
YOU CAN DO IT, CHLOÉ! GET HIM!
WAIT! YOU WANT *ME* TO FIGHT?!
WELL, AS YOU CAN SEE, I'M A SCYTHE RIGHT NOW.
BUT!
HERE IT COMES! BE CAREFUL!
AHH! I DIDN'T SIGN UP FOR THIS!!

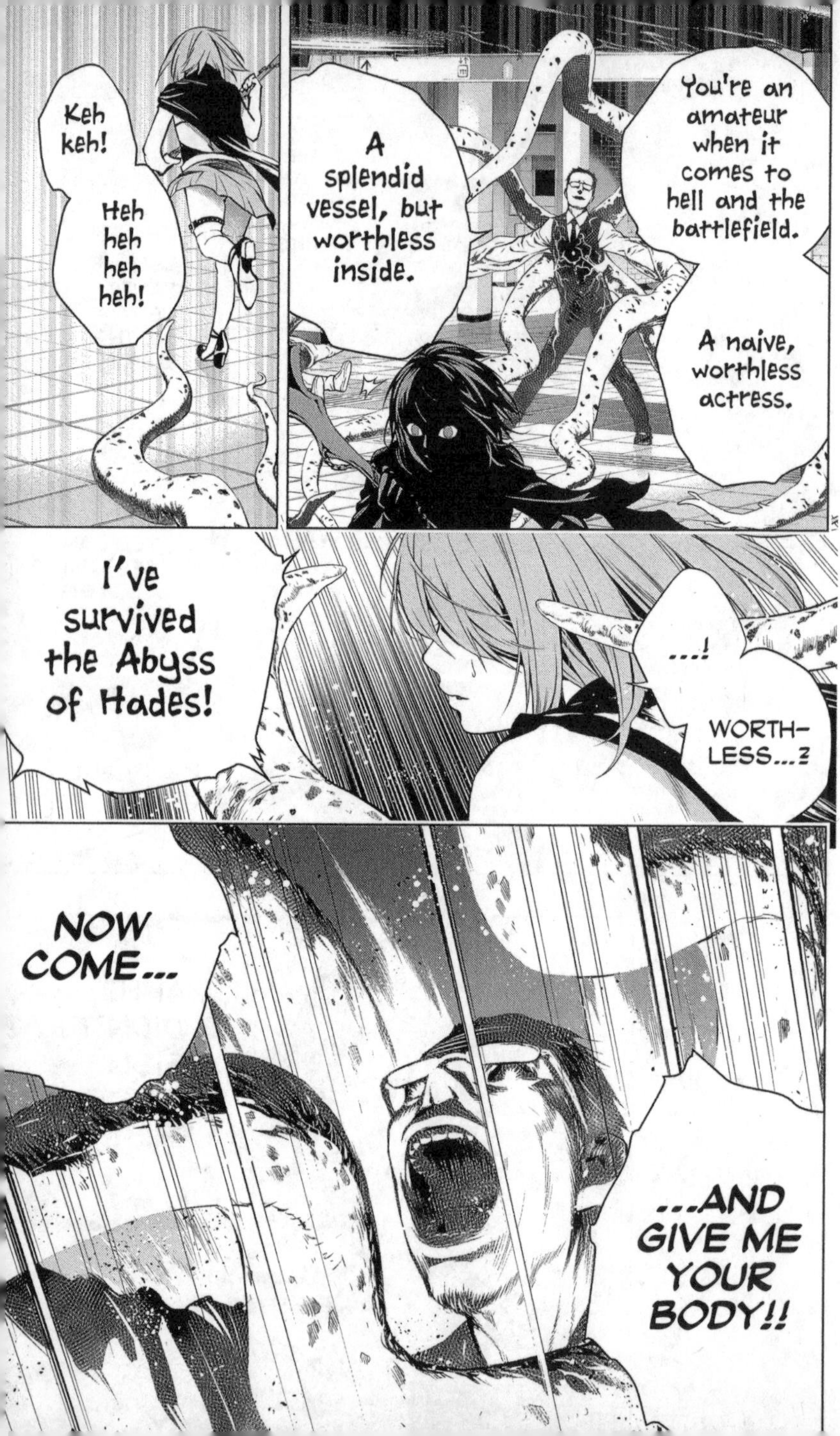
You're an amateur when it comes to hell and the battlefield.
A splendid vessel, but worthless inside.
A naive, worthless actress.
Keh keh!
Heh heh heh heh!
...!
WORTH-LESS...?
I've survived the Abyss of Hades!
NOW COME...
...AND GIVE ME YOUR BODY!!

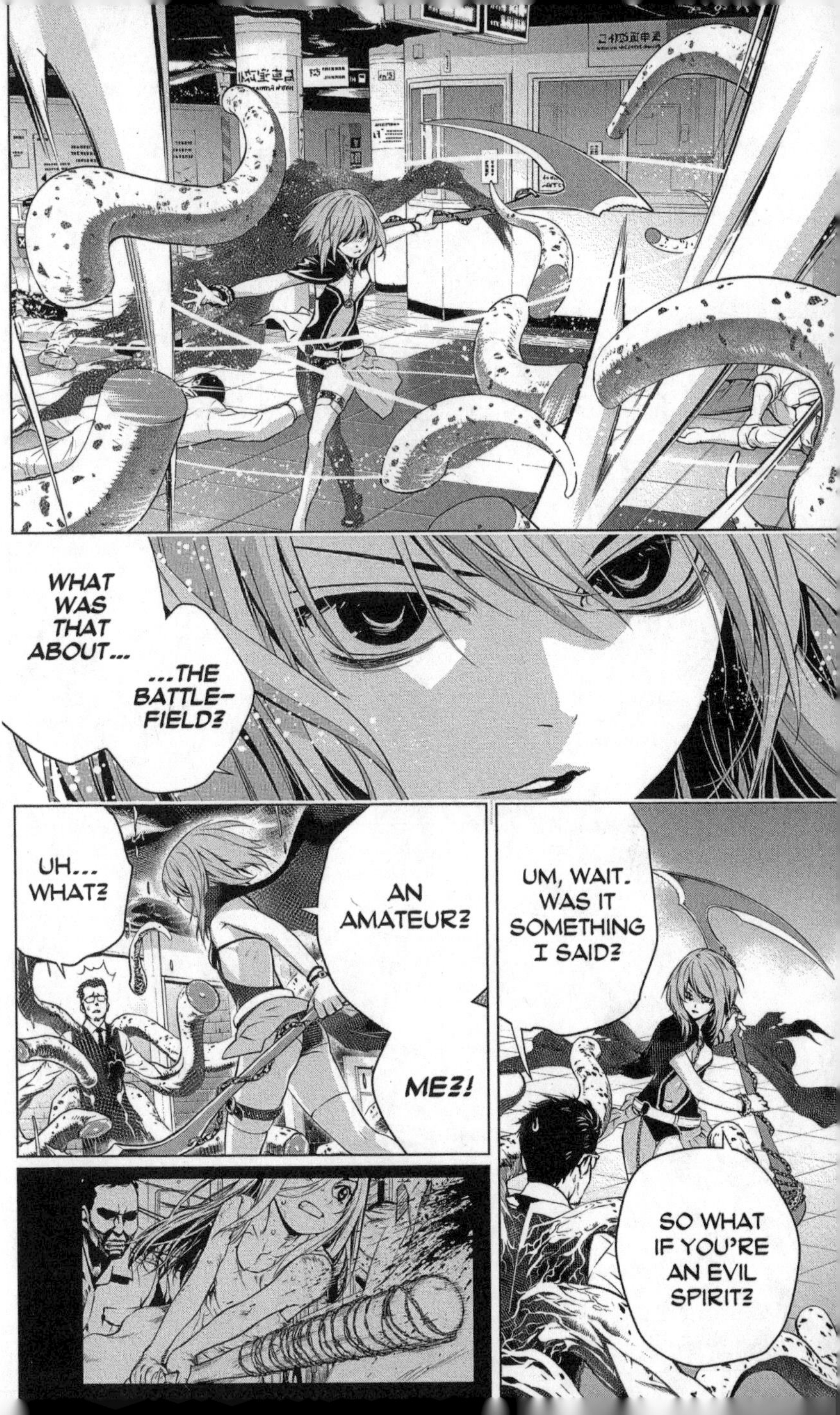
WHAT WAS THAT ABOUT...
...THE BATTLE-FIELD?
UM, WAIT. WAS IT SOMETHING I SAID?
SO WHAT IF YOU'RE AN EVIL SPIRIT?
AN AMATEUR?
ME?!
UH... WHAT?

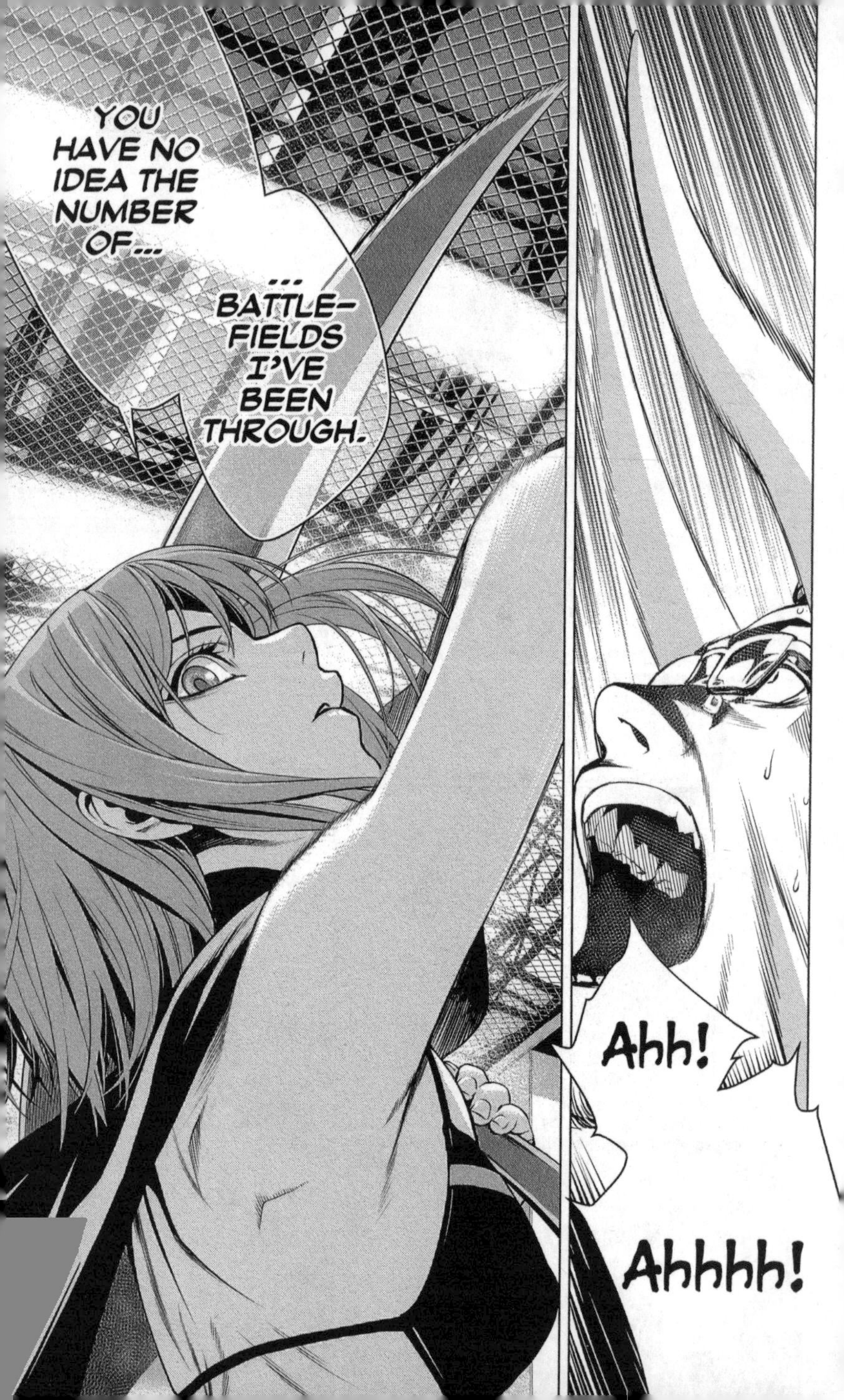
Ahh!
Ahhhh!
YOU HAVE NO IDEA THE NUMBER OF...
...BATTLE-FIELDS I'VE BEEN THROUGH.

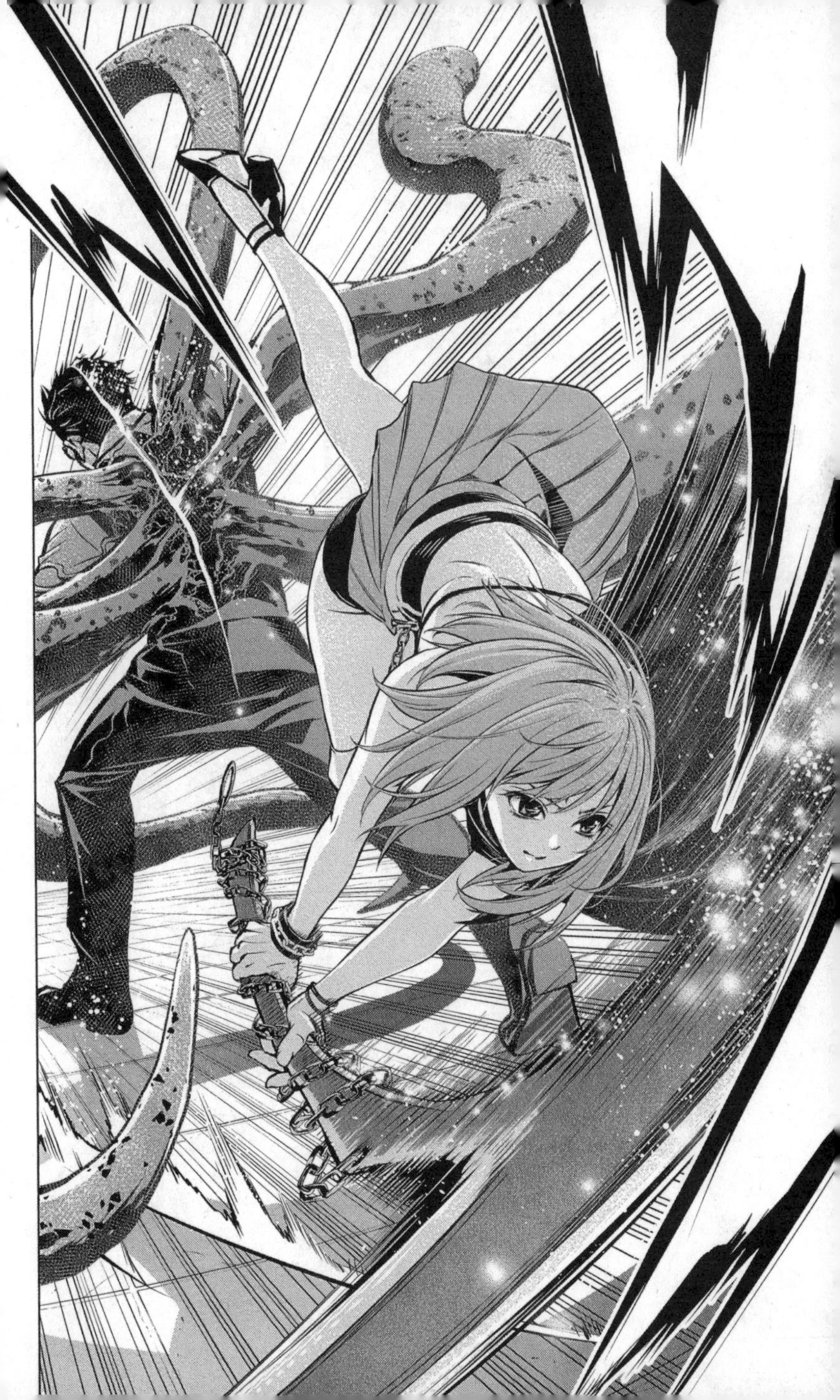

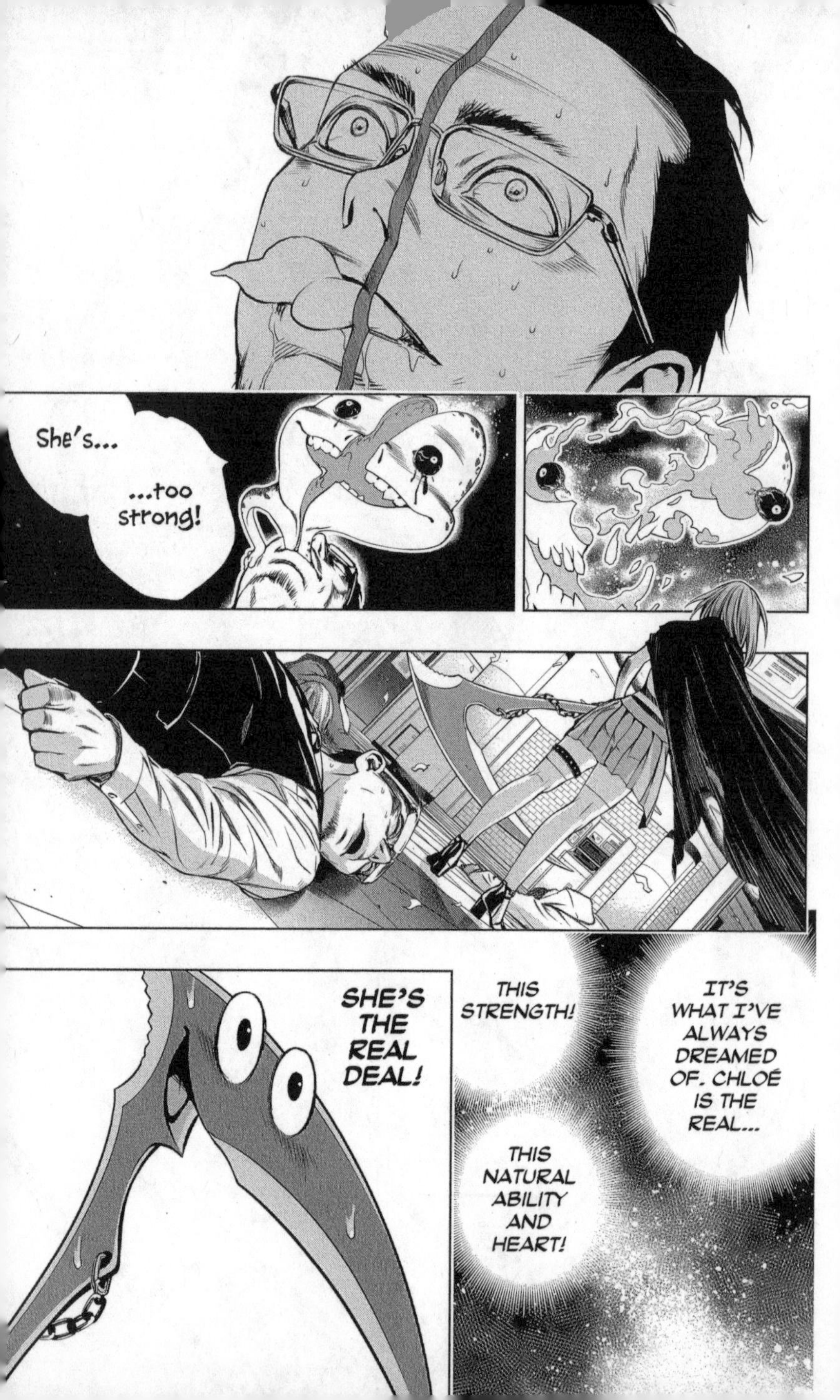
She's...
...too strong!
IT'S WHAT I'VE ALWAYS DREAMED OF. CHLOÉ IS THE REAL...
THIS STRENGTH!
THIS NATURAL ABILITY AND HEART!
SHE'S THE REAL DEAL!

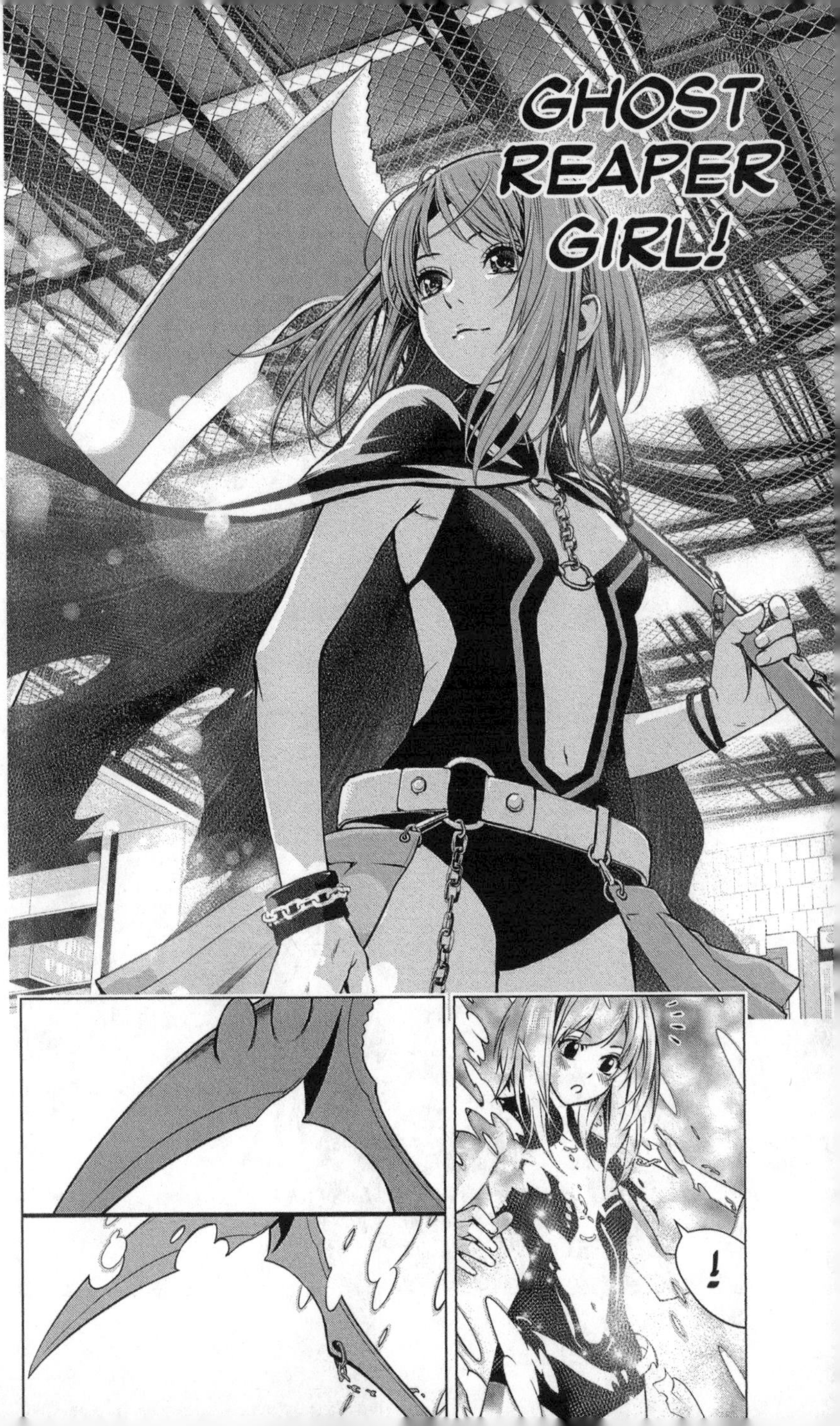
GHOST REAPER GIRL!
!

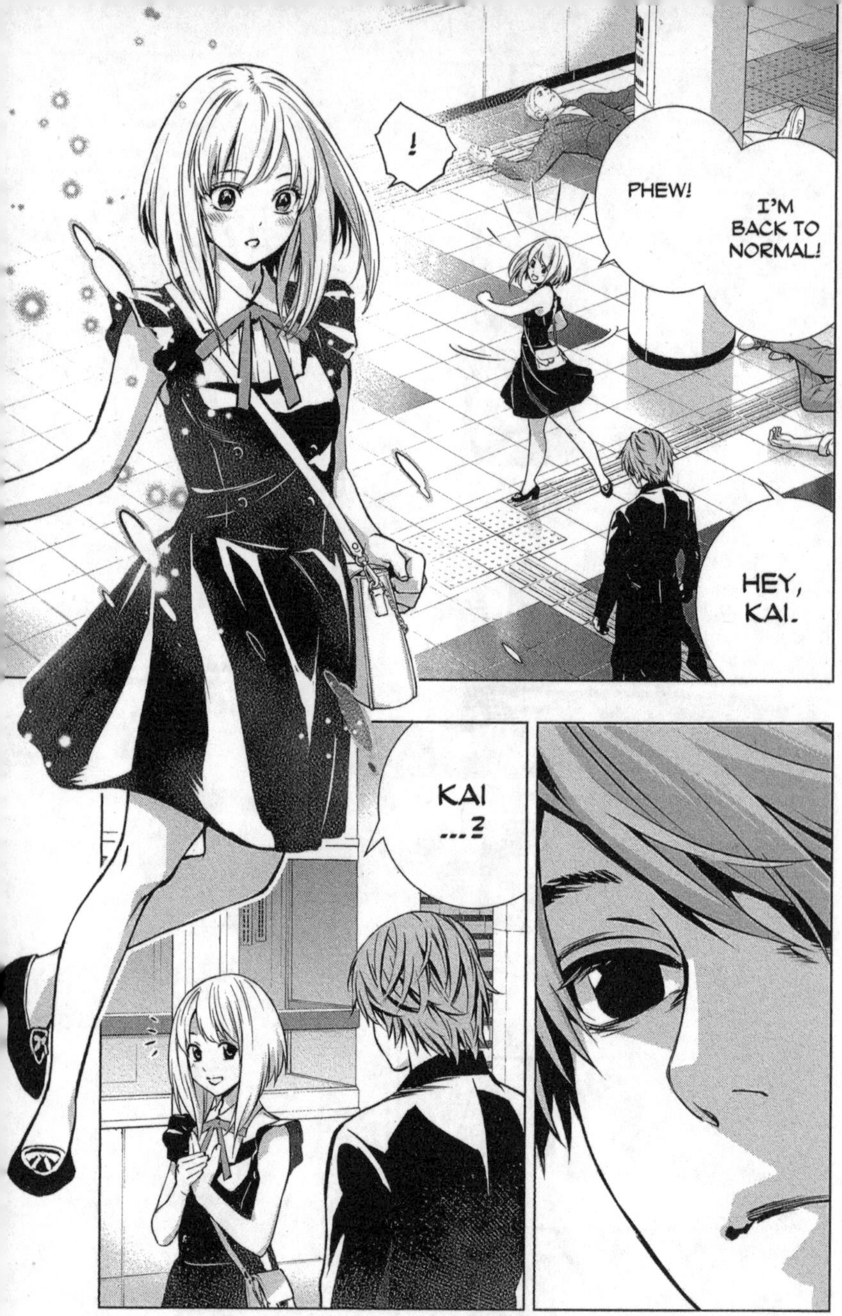
PHEW!
I'M BACK TO NORMAL!
HEY, KAI.
!
KAI ...?

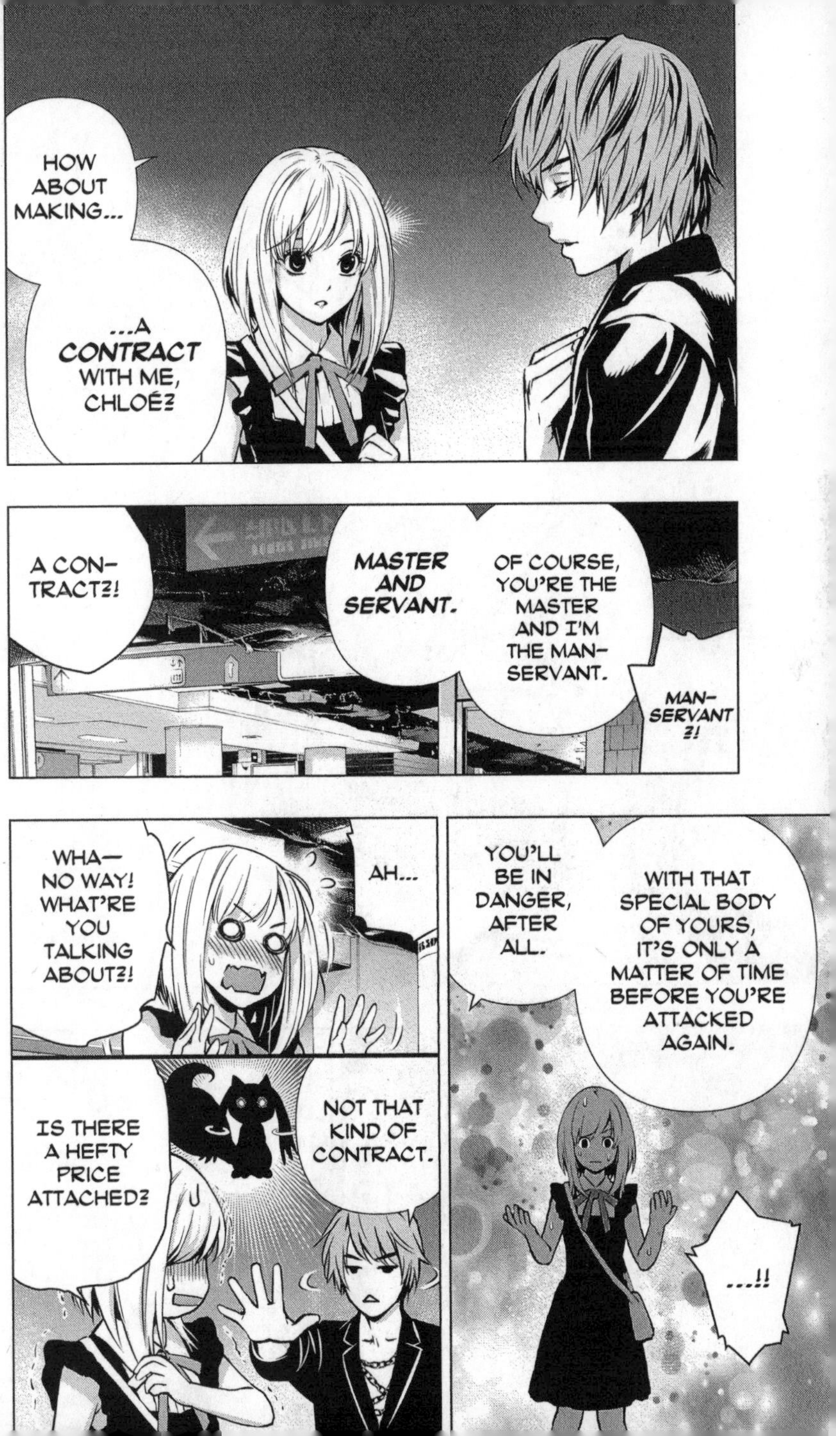
HOW ABOUT MAKING...
...A CONTRACT WITH ME, CHLOÉ?
A CON-TRACT?!
MASTER AND SERVANT.
OF COURSE, YOU'RE THE MASTER AND I'M THE MAN-SERVANT.
MAN-SERVANT?!
WITH THAT SPECIAL BODY OF YOURS, IT'S ONLY A MATTER OF TIME BEFORE YOU'RE ATTACKED AGAIN.
YOU'LL BE IN DANGER, AFTER ALL.
...!!
AH...
WHA— NO WAY! WHAT'RE YOU TALKING ABOUT?!
IS THERE A HEFTY PRICE ATTACHED?
NOT THAT KIND OF CONTRACT.

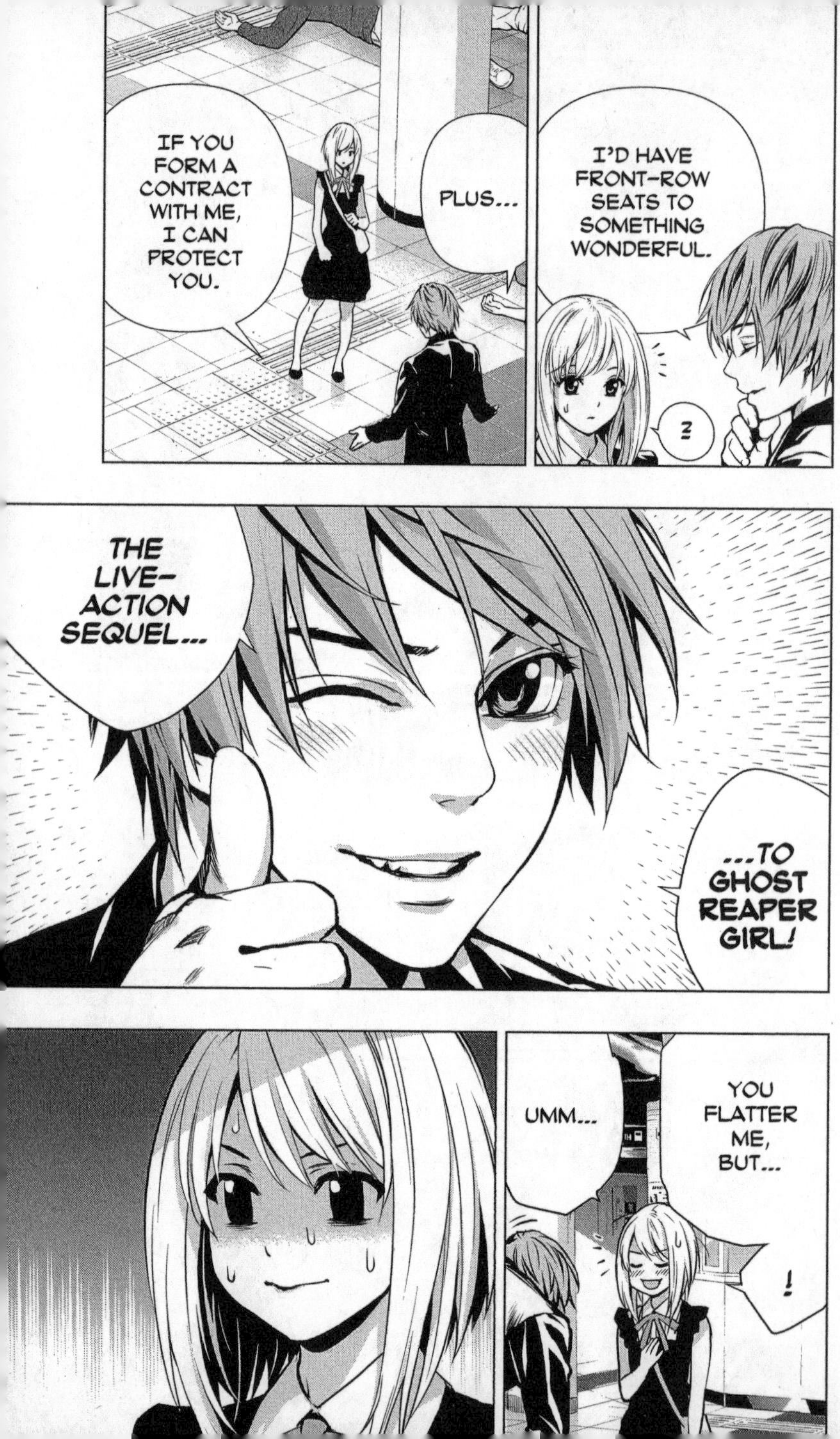
IF YOU FORM A CONTRACT WITH ME, I CAN PROTECT YOU.
PLUS...
I'D HAVE FRONT-ROW SEATS TO SOMETHING WONDERFUL.
?
THE LIVE-ACTION SEQUEL...
...TO GHOST REAPER GIRL!
UMM...
YOU FLATTER ME, BUT...
!

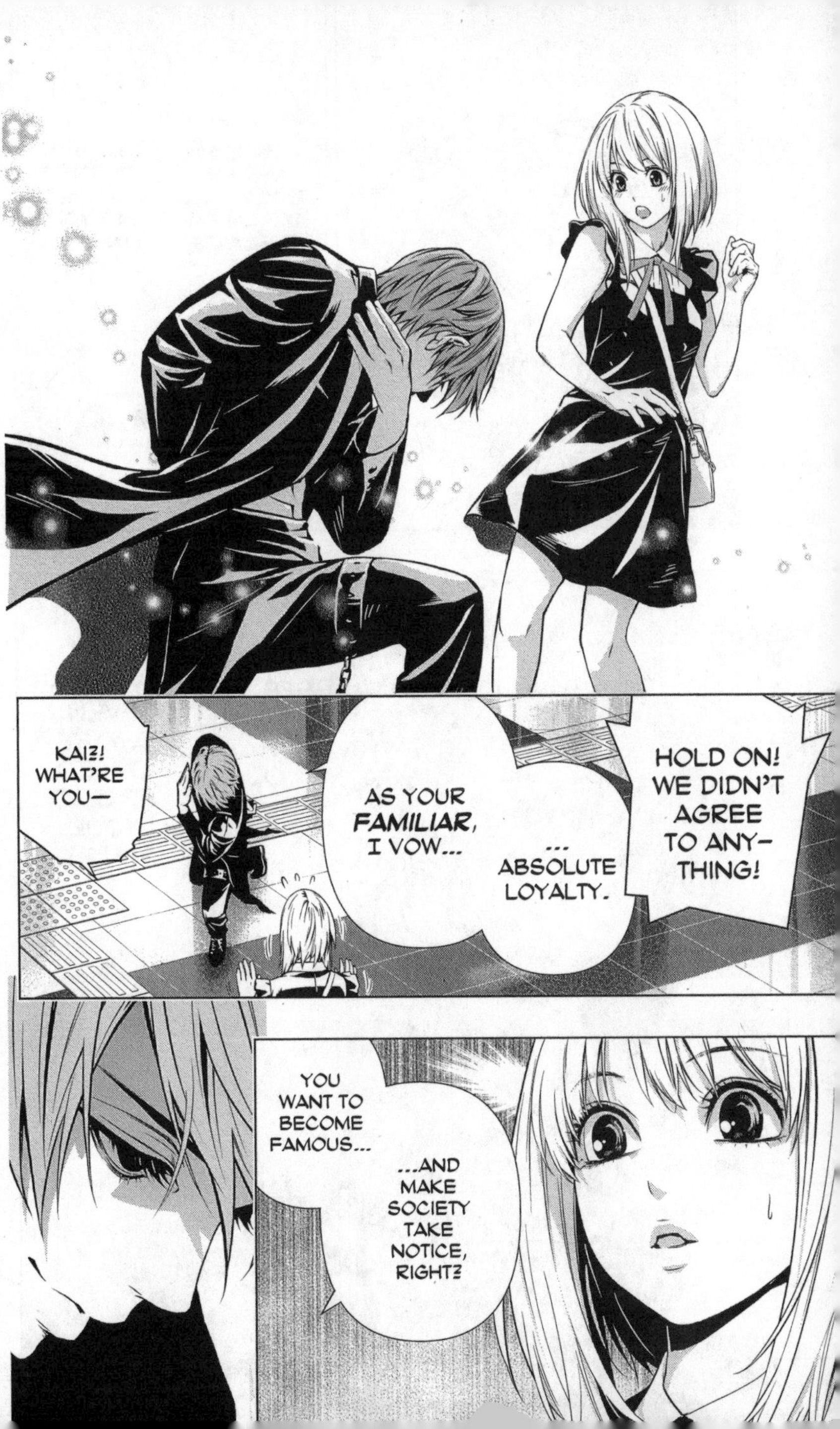
KAI?! WHAT'RE YOU—
AS YOUR *FAMILIAR*, I VOW...
...ABSOLUTE LOYALTY.
HOLD ON! WE DIDN'T AGREE TO ANYTHING!
YOU WANT TO BECOME FAMOUS...
...AND MAKE SOCIETY TAKE NOTICE, RIGHT?

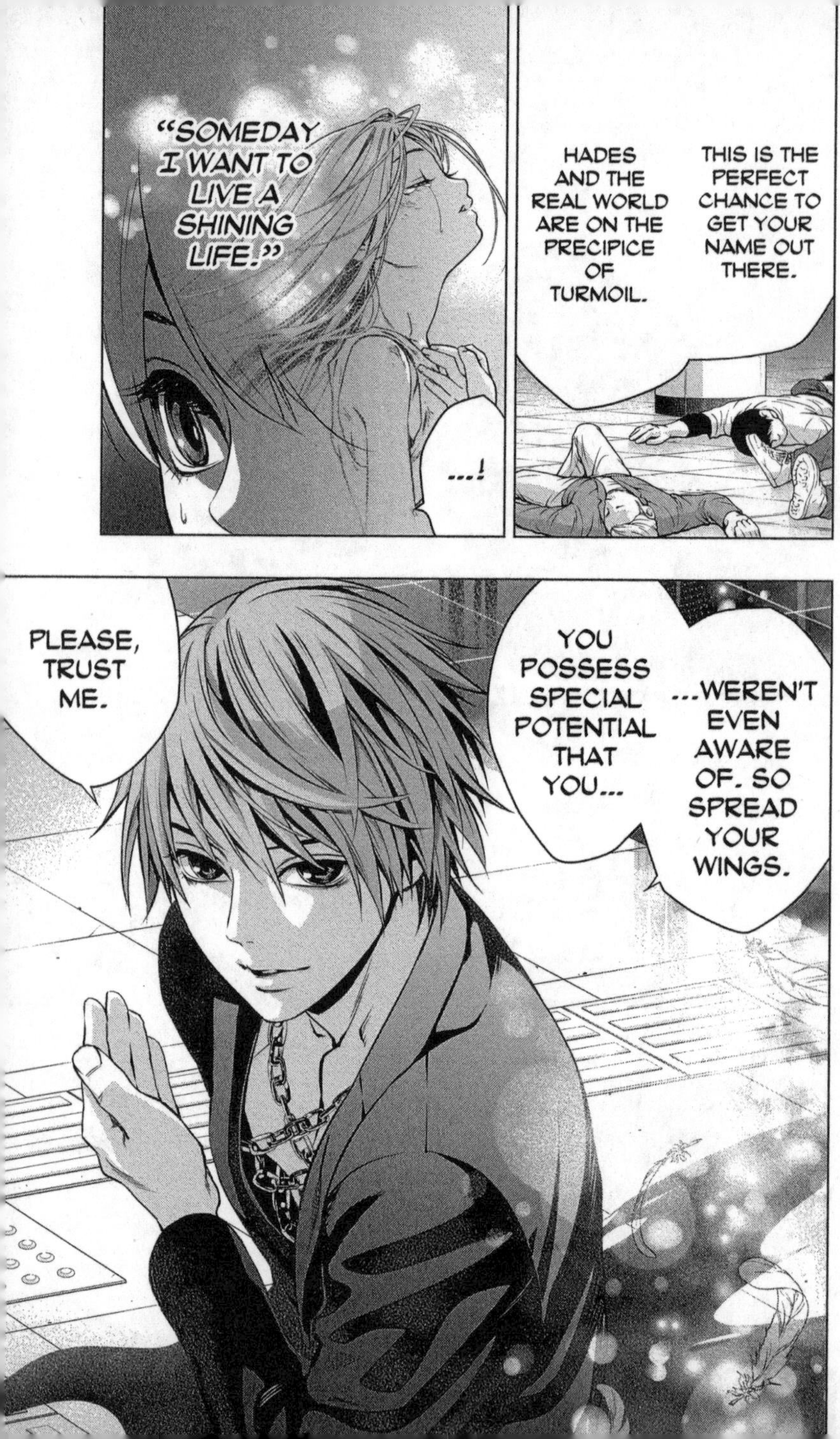
HADES AND THE REAL WORLD ARE ON THE PRECIPICE OF TURMOIL.
THIS IS THE PERFECT CHANCE TO GET YOUR NAME OUT THERE.
"SOMEDAY I WANT TO LIVE A SHINING LIFE."
...!
YOU POSSESS SPECIAL POTENTIAL THAT YOU...
...WEREN'T EVEN AWARE OF. SO SPREAD YOUR WINGS.
PLEASE, TRUST ME.

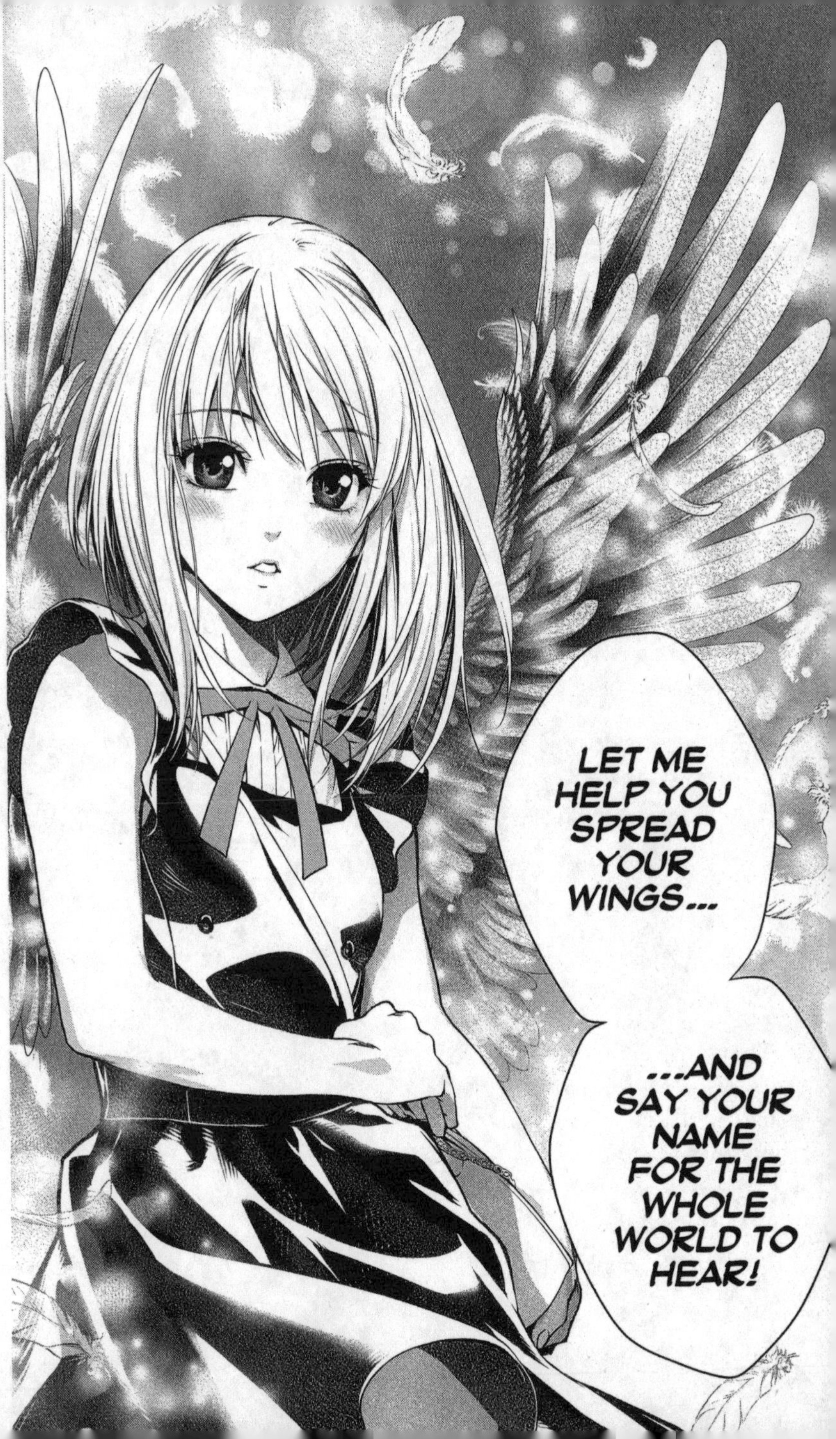
LET ME HELP YOU SPREAD YOUR WINGS...
...AND SAY YOUR NAME FOR THE WHOLE WORLD TO HEAR!

GHOST REAPER GIRL

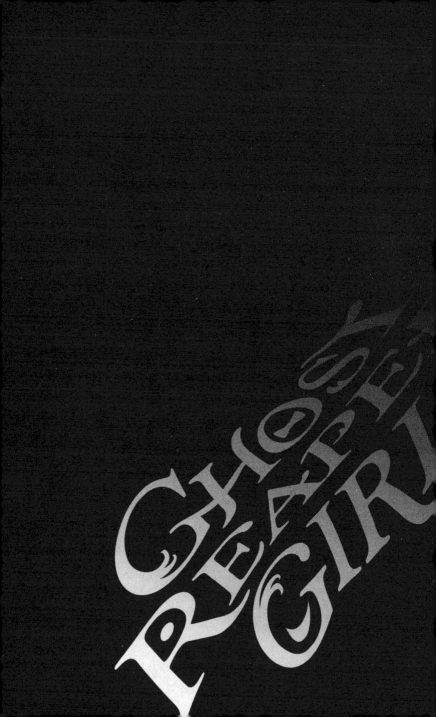

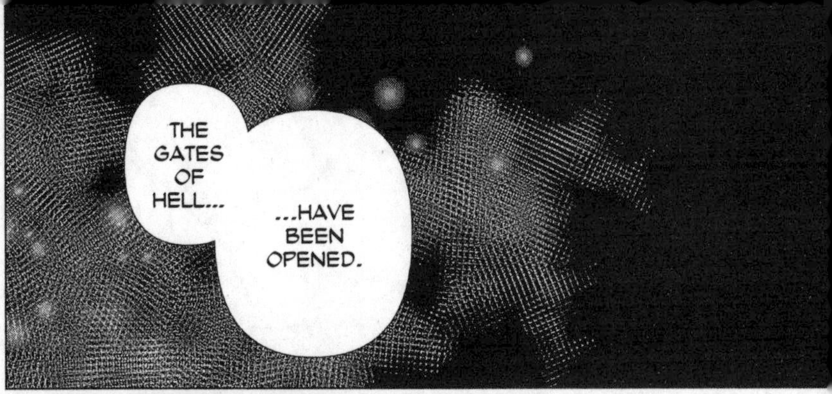
THE GATES OF HELL...
...HAVE BEEN OPENED.

#2: Soul Predator Noel

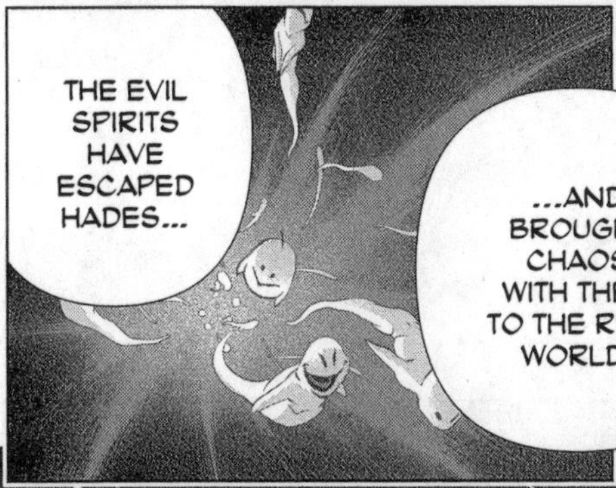
THE EVIL SPIRITS HAVE ESCAPED HADES...

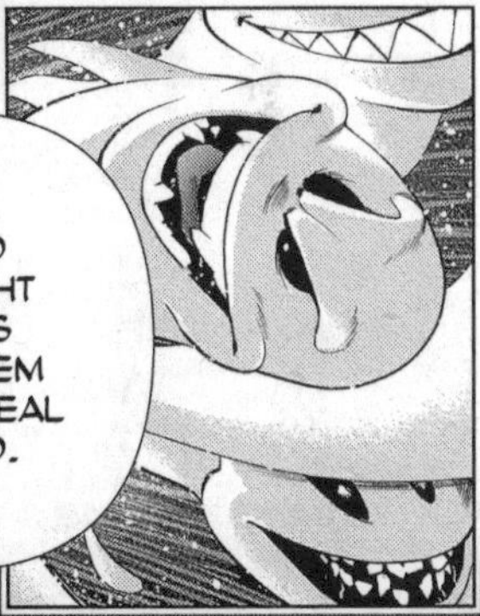
...AND BROUGHT CHAOS WITH THEM TO THE REAL WORLD.

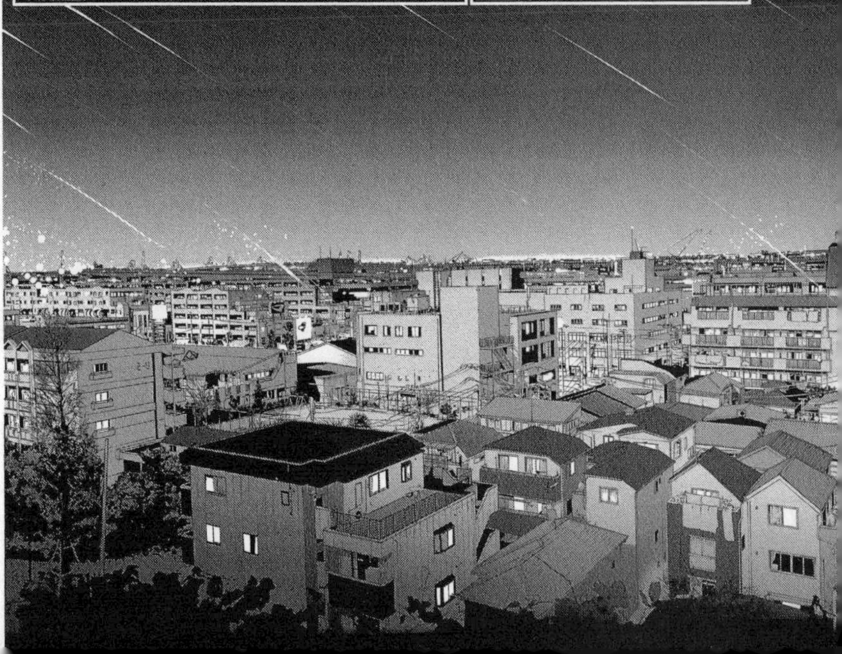

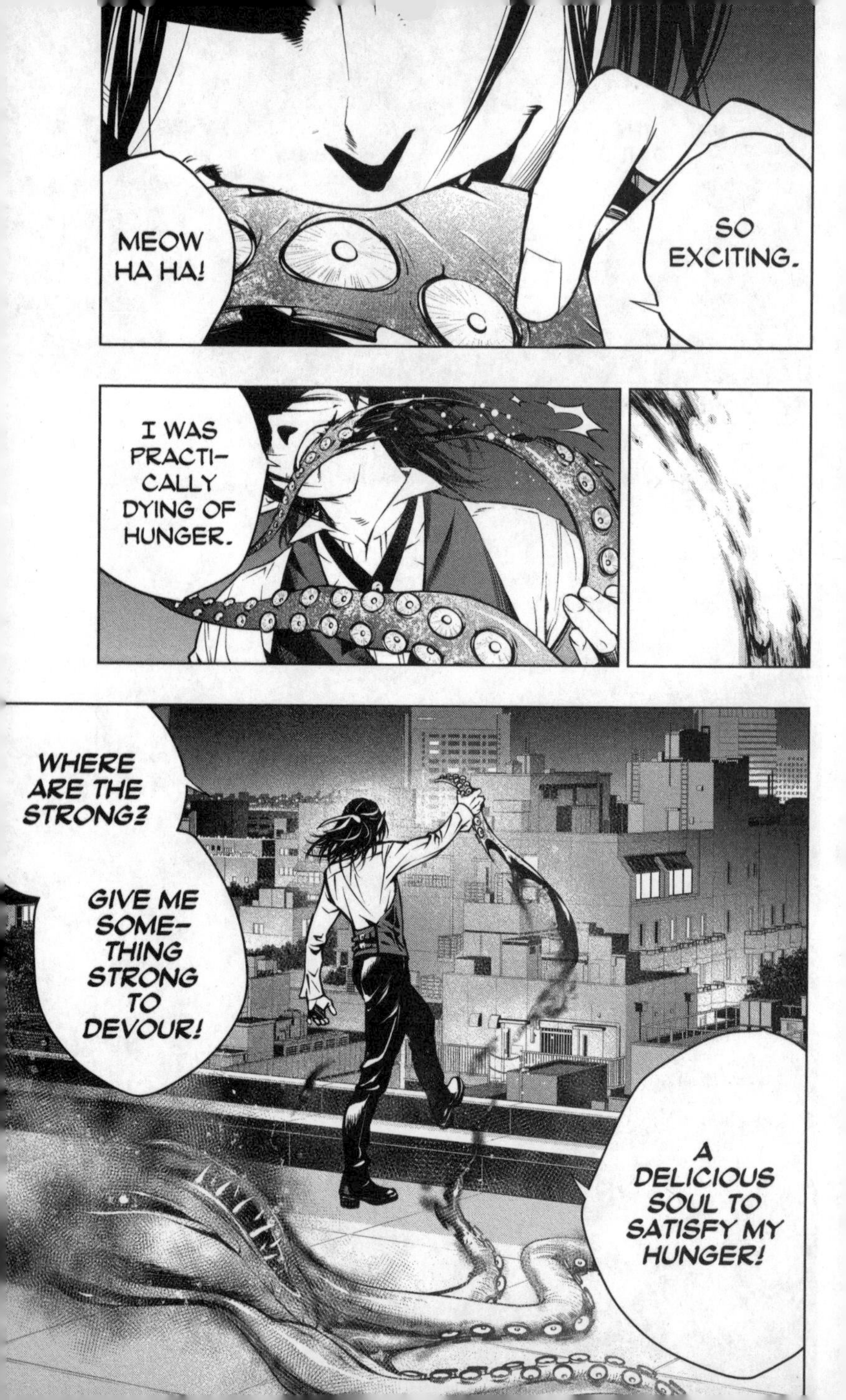
SO EXCITING.
MEOW HA HA!
I WAS PRACTI-CALLY DYING OF HUNGER.
A DELICIOUS SOUL TO SATISFY MY HUNGER!
WHERE ARE THE STRONG?
GIVE ME SOME-THING STRONG TO DEVOUR!

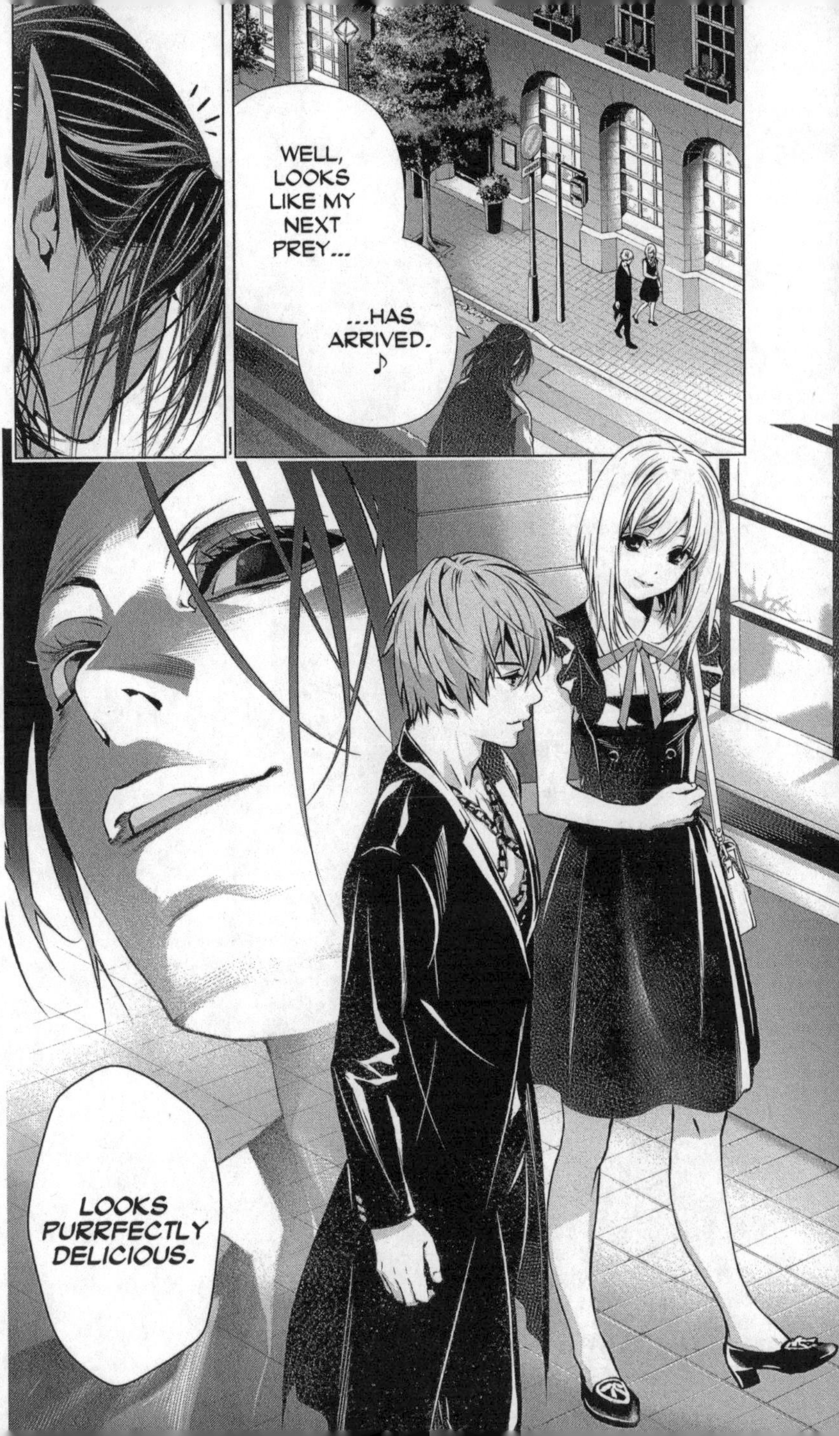
WELL, LOOKS LIKE MY NEXT PREY...
...HAS ARRIVED. ♪
LOOKS PURRFECTLY DELICIOUS.

#2: Soul Predator Noel

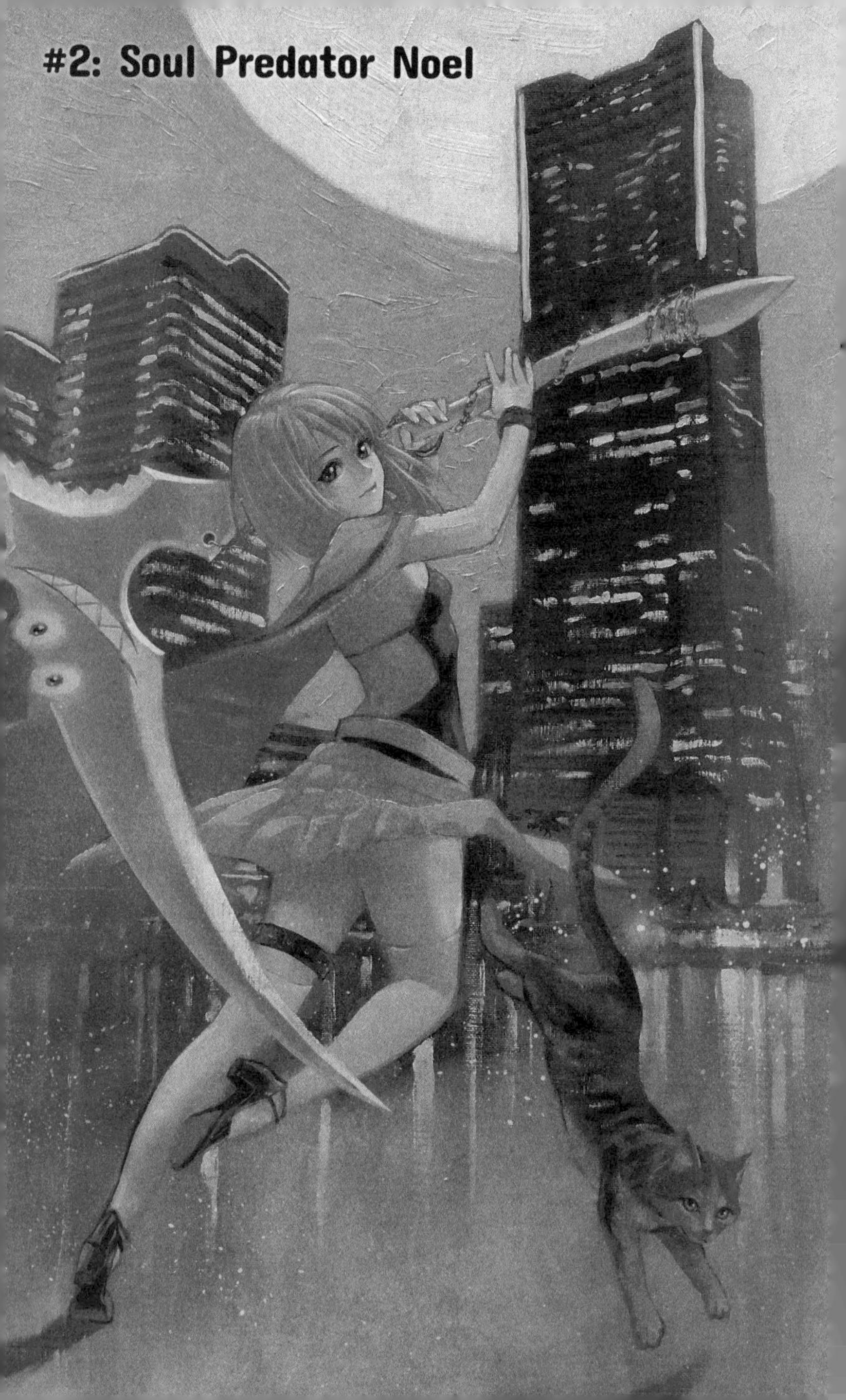

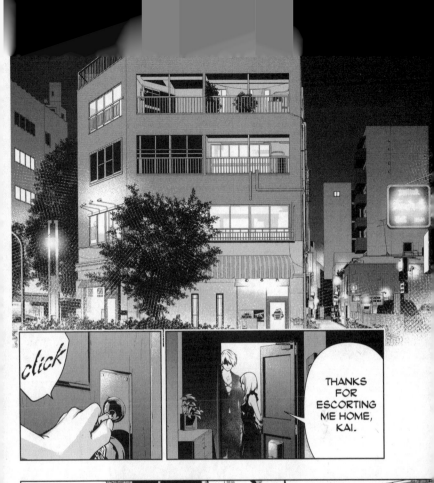

click

THANKS FOR ESCORTING ME HOME, KAI.

IT WAS A CRAZY DAY BEING ATTACKED BY GHOSTS AND ALL...

...BUT I MADE IT HOME SAFELY THANKS TO YOU.

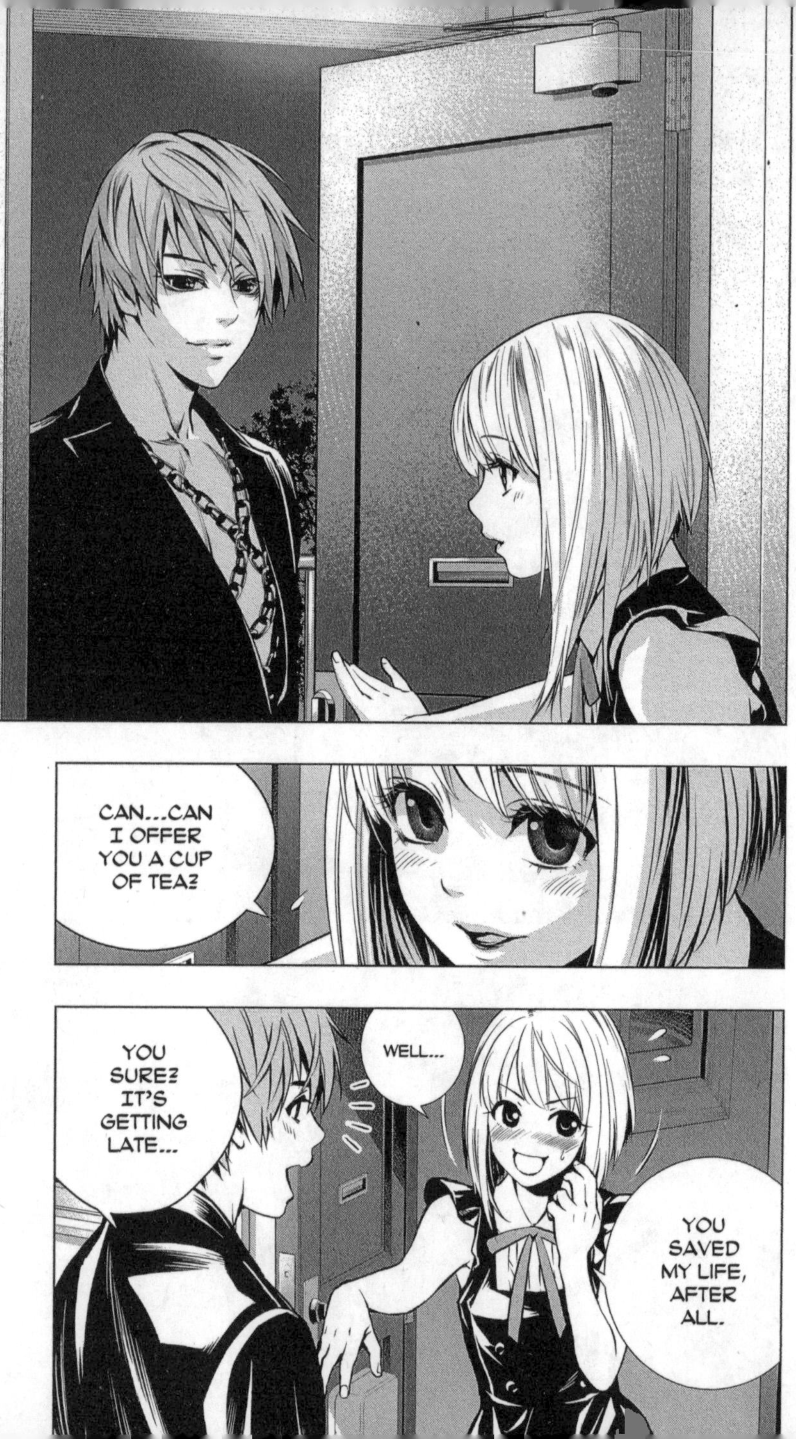
CAN...CAN I OFFER YOU A CUP OF TEA?
YOU SURE? IT'S GETTING LATE...
WELL...
YOU SAVED MY LIFE, AFTER ALL.

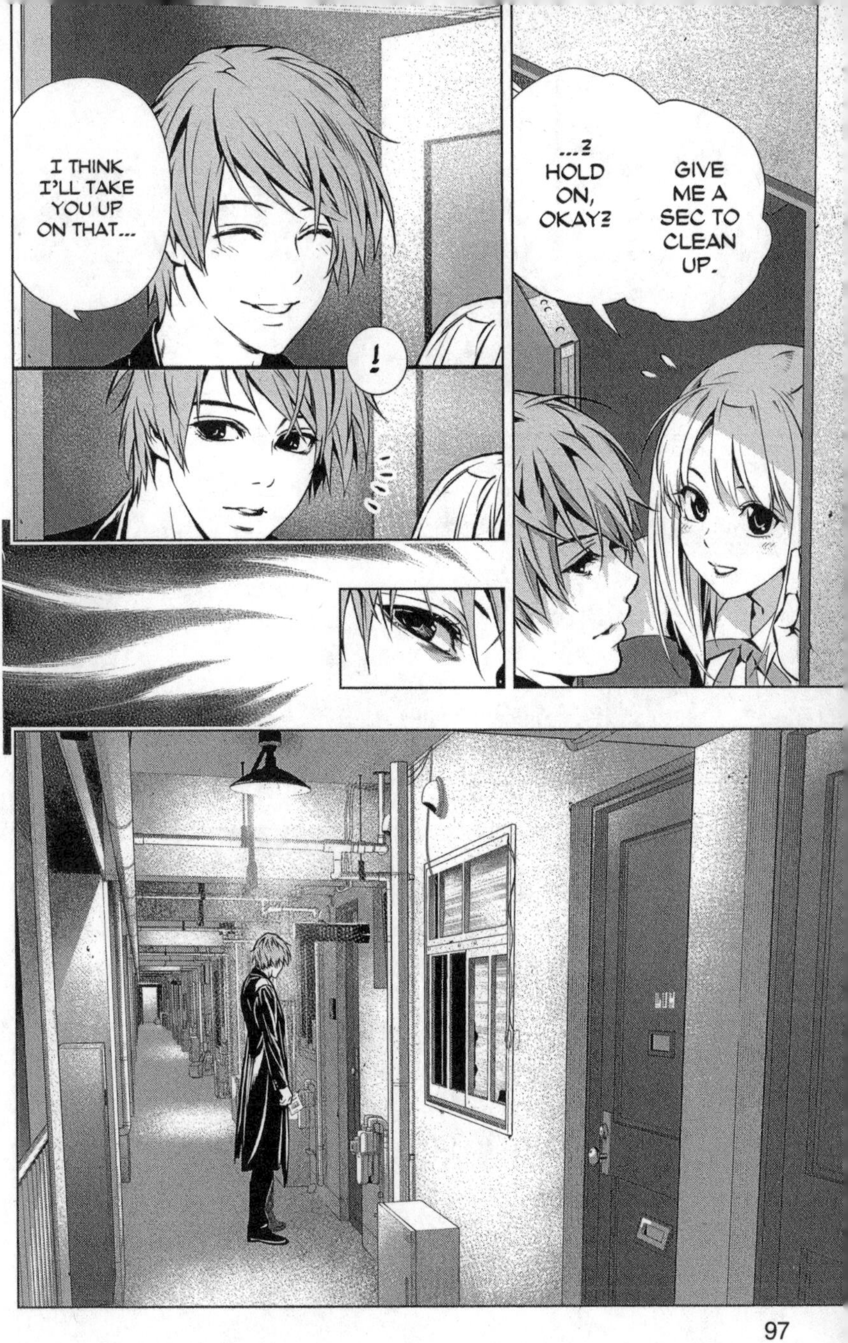
I THINK I'LL TAKE YOU UP ON THAT...
!
GIVE ME A SEC TO CLEAN UP.
...? HOLD ON, OKAY?

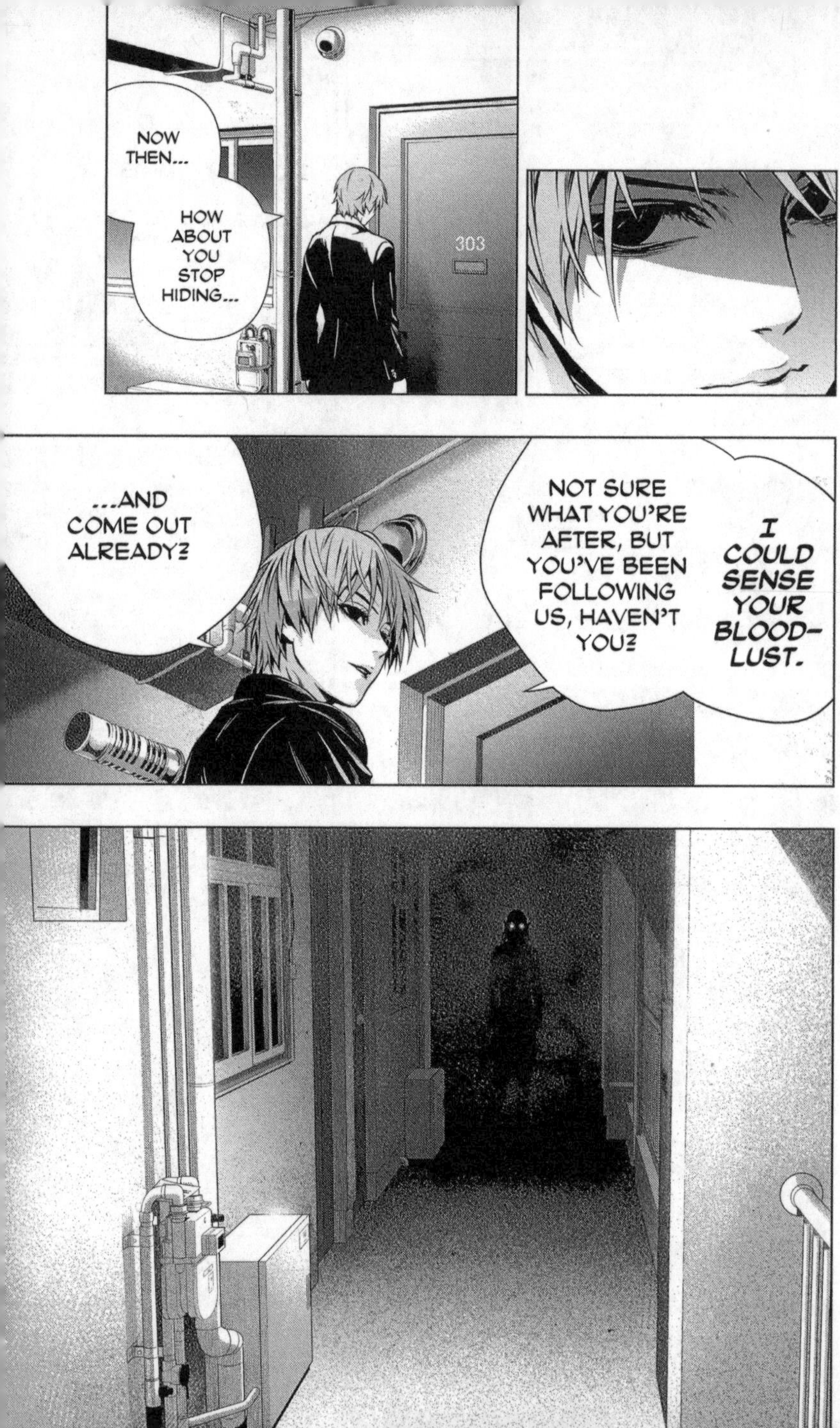
NOW THEN...
HOW ABOUT YOU STOP HIDING...
303
...AND COME OUT ALREADY?
NOT SURE WHAT YOU'RE AFTER, BUT YOU'VE BEEN FOLLOWING US, HAVEN'T YOU?
I COULD SENSE YOUR BLOOD-LUST.

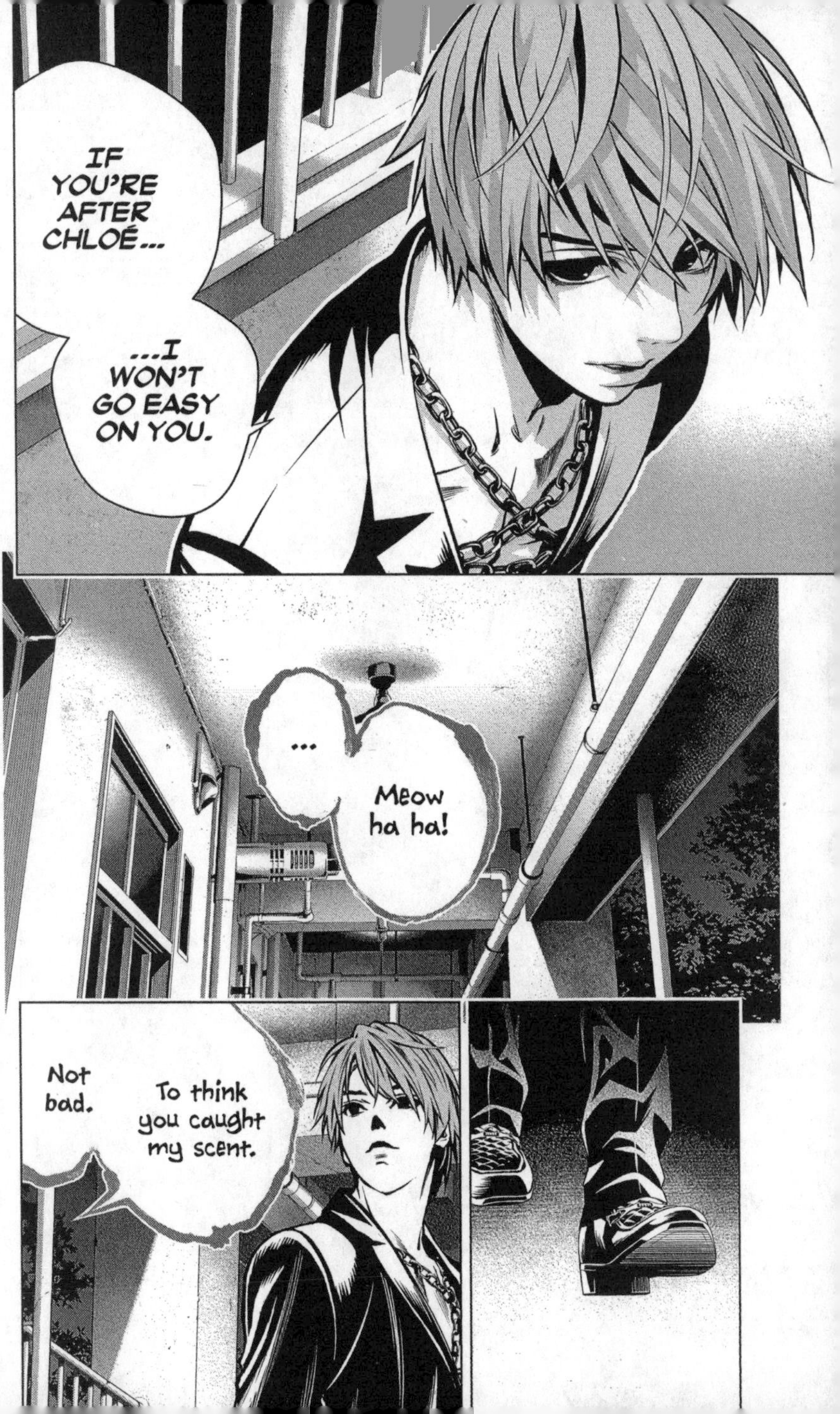
IF YOU'RE AFTER CHLOÉ...
...I WON'T GO EASY ON YOU.
...
Meow ha ha!
Not bad.
To think you caught my scent.

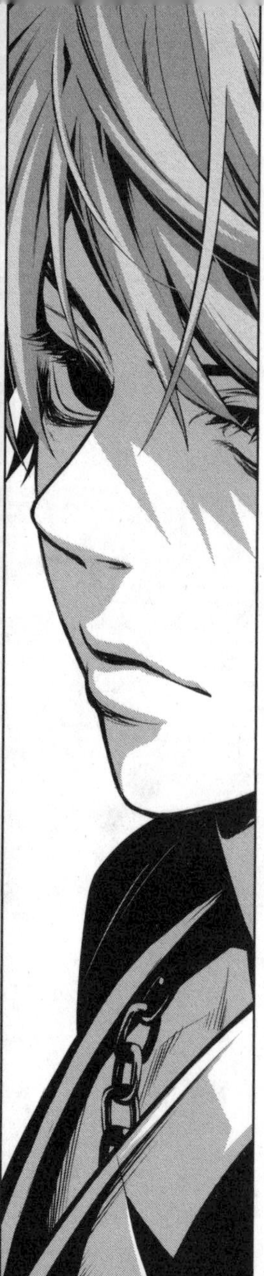
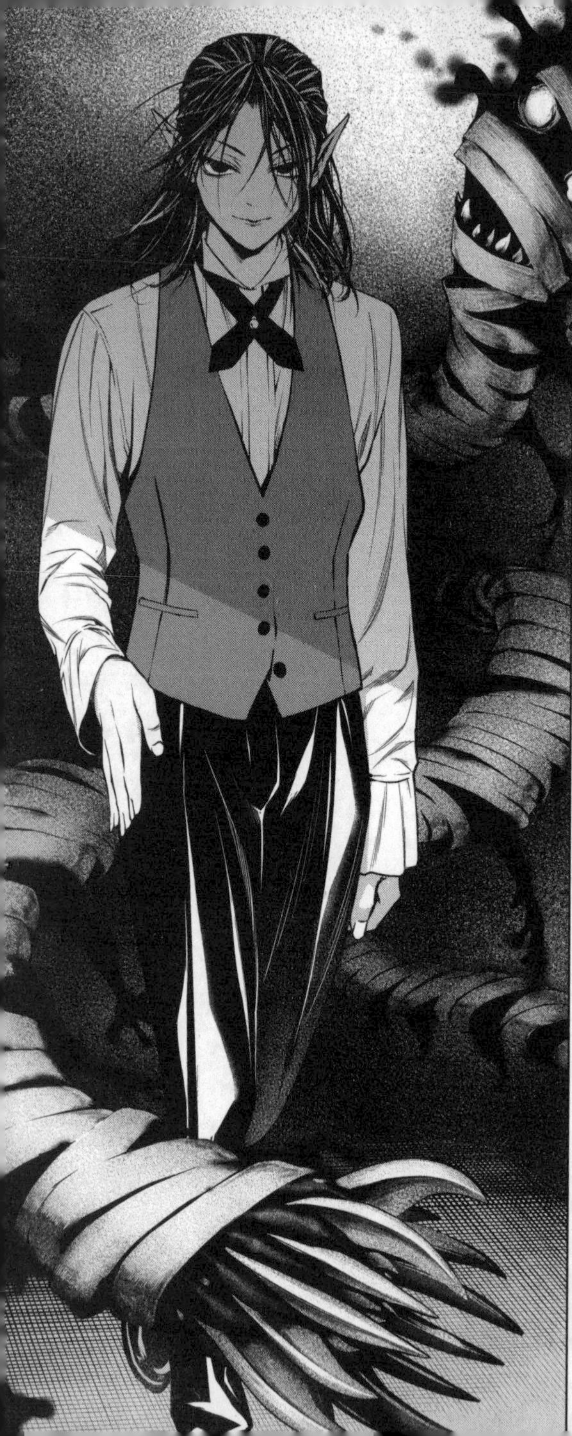

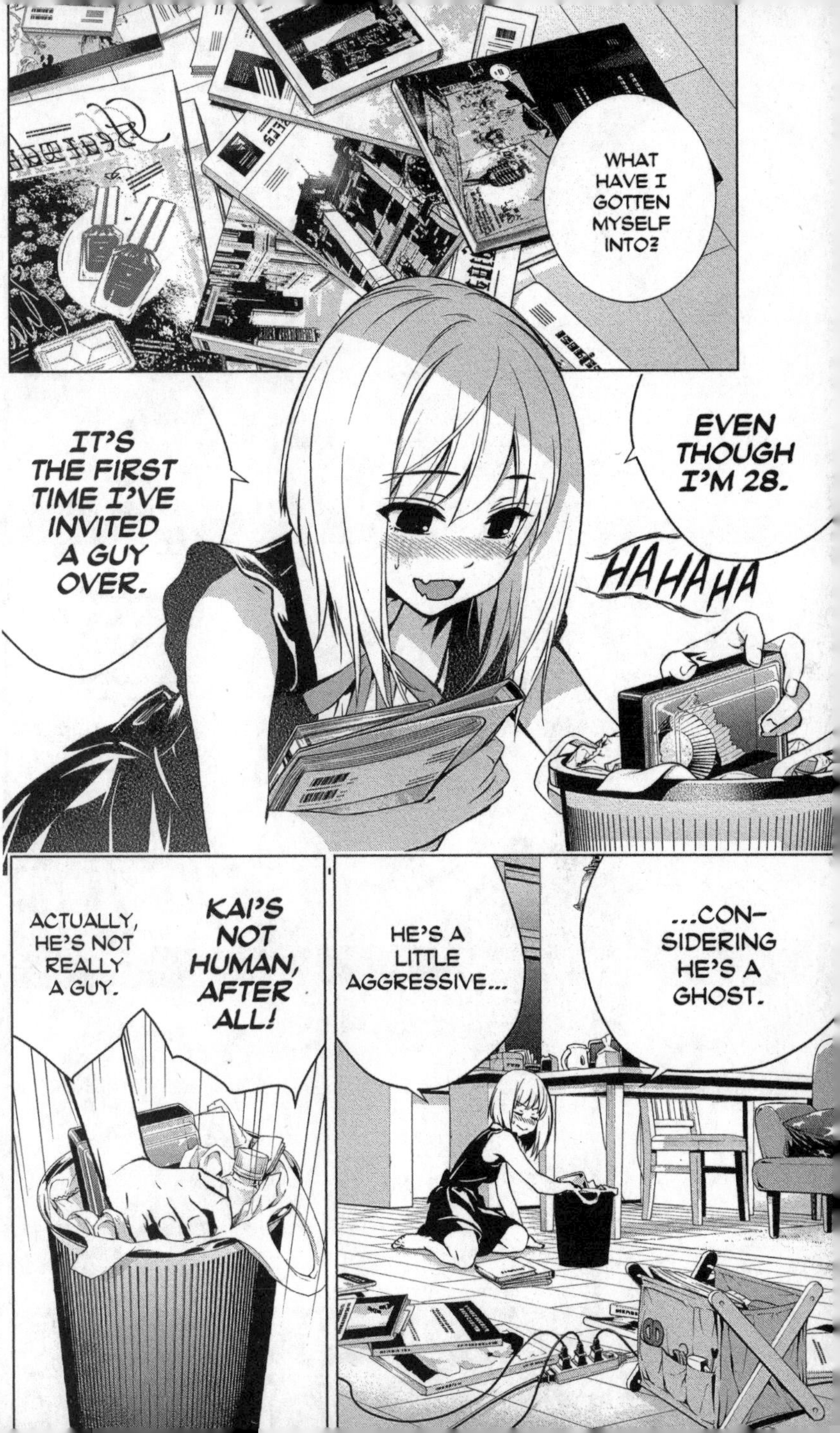
WHAT HAVE I GOTTEN MYSELF INTO?
IT'S THE FIRST TIME I'VE INVITED A GUY OVER.
EVEN THOUGH I'M 28.
HAHAHA
ACTUALLY, HE'S NOT REALLY A GUY.
KAI'S NOT HUMAN, AFTER ALL!
HE'S A LITTLE AGGRESSIVE...
...CON-SIDERING HE'S A GHOST.

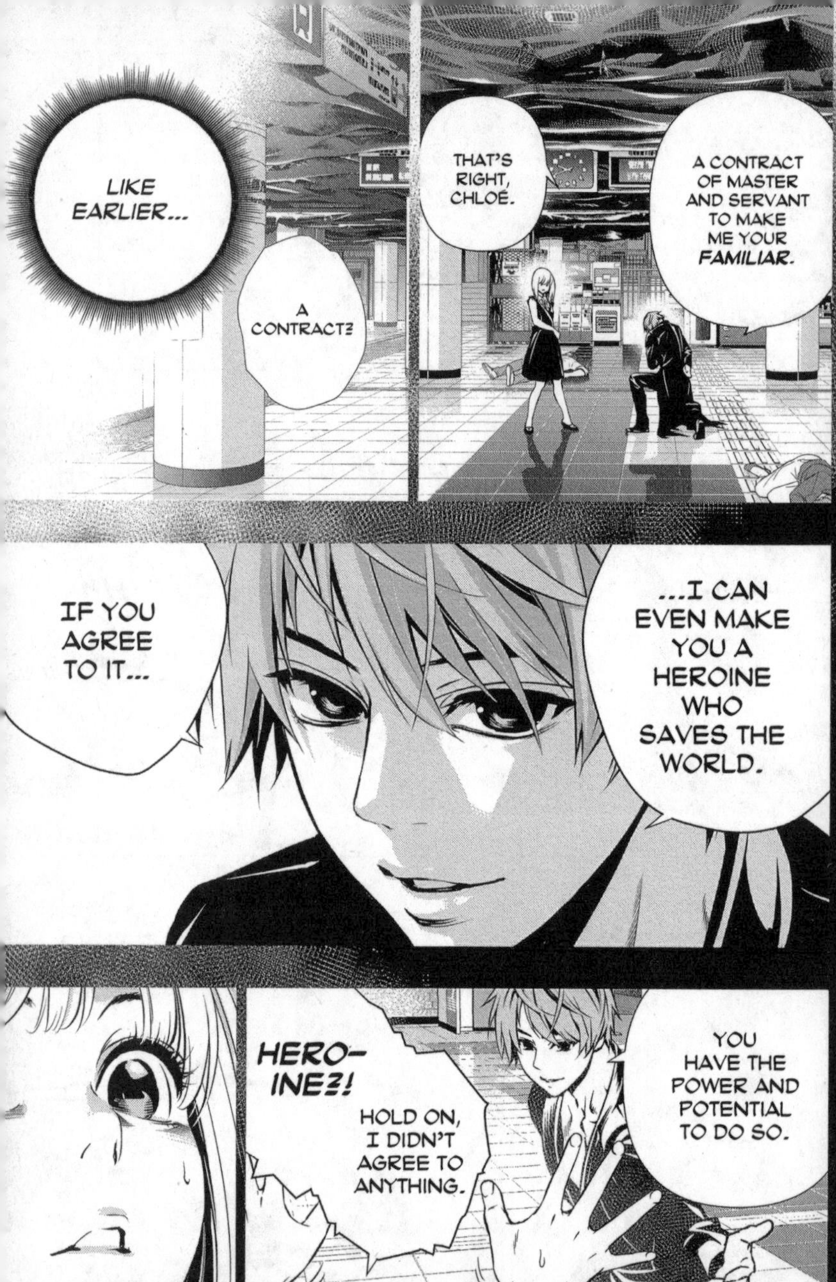
LIKE EARLIER...
A CONTRACT?
THAT'S RIGHT, CHLOÉ.
A CONTRACT OF MASTER AND SERVANT TO MAKE ME YOUR *FAMILIAR*.
IF YOU AGREE TO IT...
...I CAN EVEN MAKE YOU A HEROINE WHO SAVES THE WORLD.
HERO-INE?!
HOLD ON, I DIDN'T AGREE TO ANYTHING.
YOU HAVE THE POWER AND POTENTIAL TO DO SO.

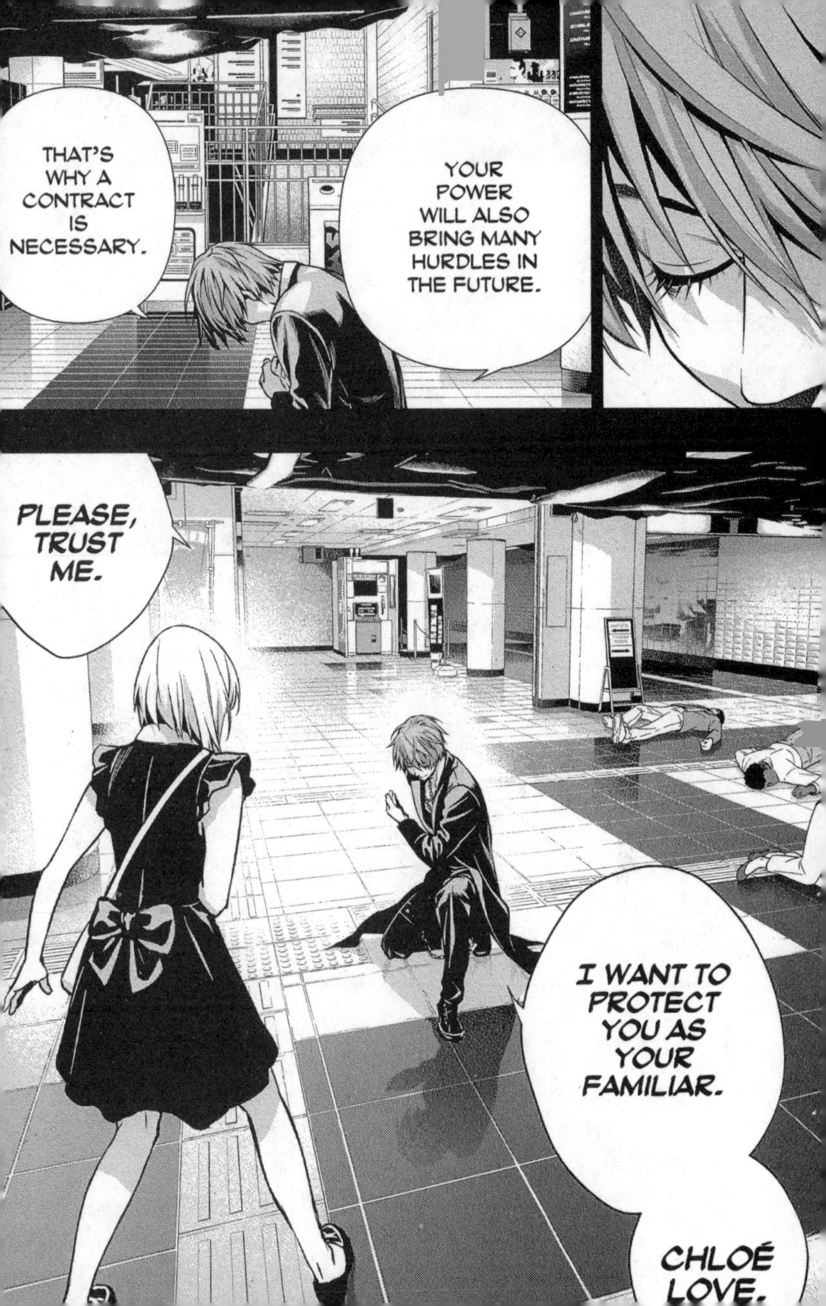
YOUR POWER WILL ALSO BRING MANY HURDLES IN THE FUTURE.
THAT'S WHY A CONTRACT IS NECESSARY.
PLEASE, TRUST ME.
I WANT TO PROTECT YOU AS YOUR FAMILIAR.
CHLOÉ LOVE.

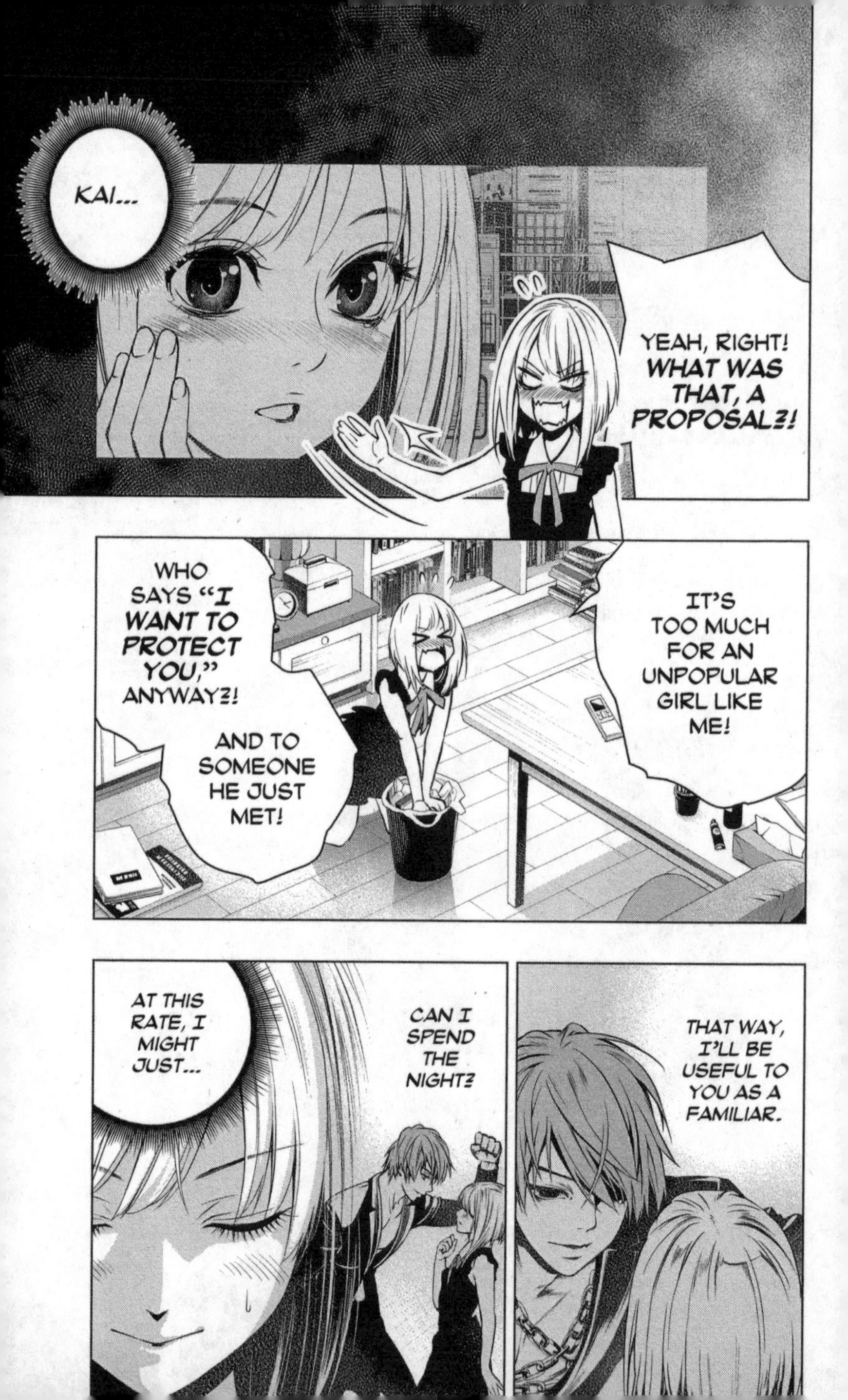
KAI...
YEAH, RIGHT! WHAT WAS THAT, A PROPOSAL?!
IT'S TOO MUCH FOR AN UNPOPULAR GIRL LIKE ME!
WHO SAYS "I WANT TO PROTECT YOU," ANYWAY?!
AND TO SOMEONE HE JUST MET!
THAT WAY, I'LL BE USEFUL TO YOU AS A FAMILIAR.
CAN I SPEND THE NIGHT?
AT THIS RATE, I MIGHT JUST...

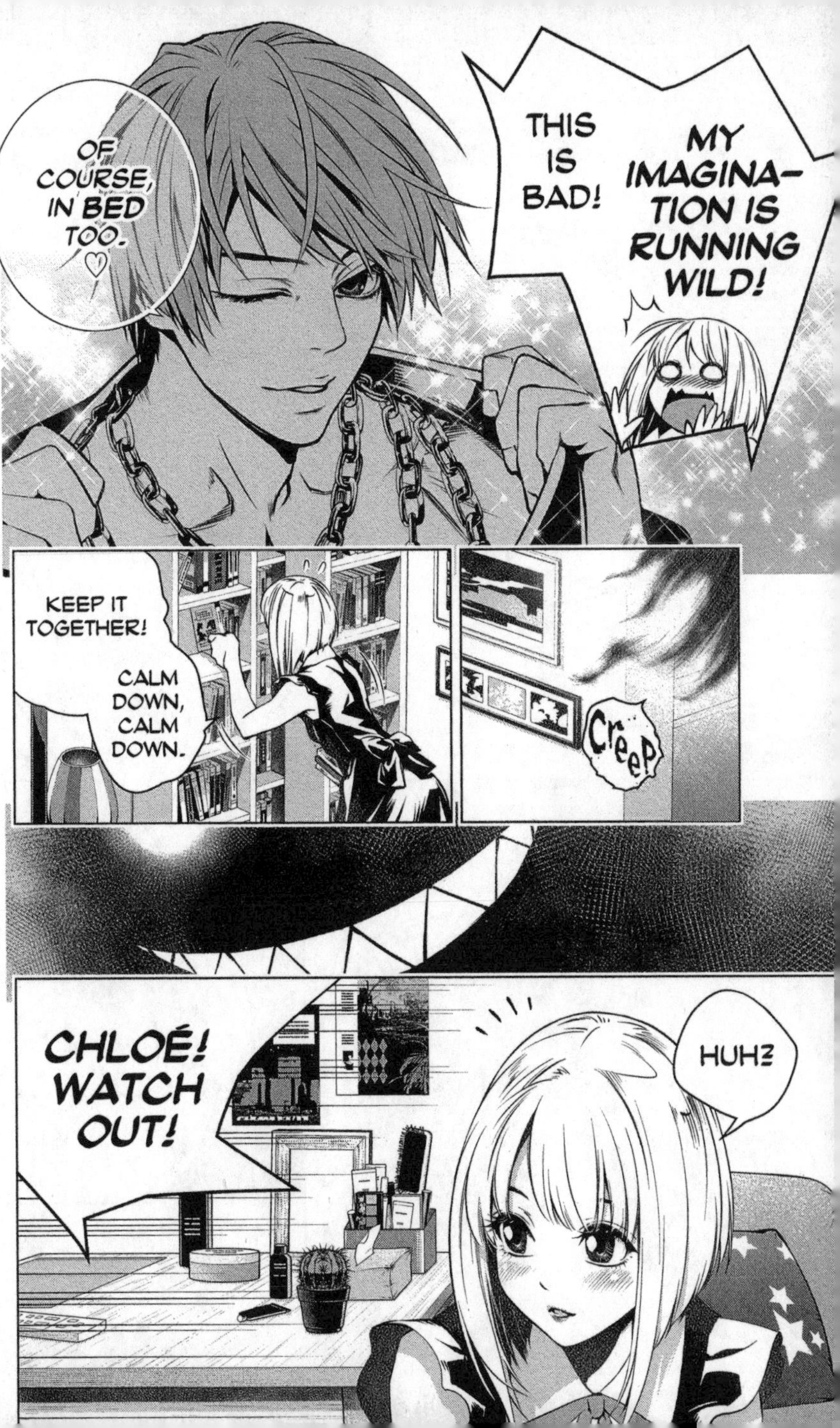
OF COURSE, IN BED TOO. ♡
THIS IS BAD!
MY IMAGINATION IS RUNNING WILD!
KEEP IT TOGETHER!
CALM DOWN, CALM DOWN.
CREEP
CHLOÉ! WATCH OUT!
HUH?

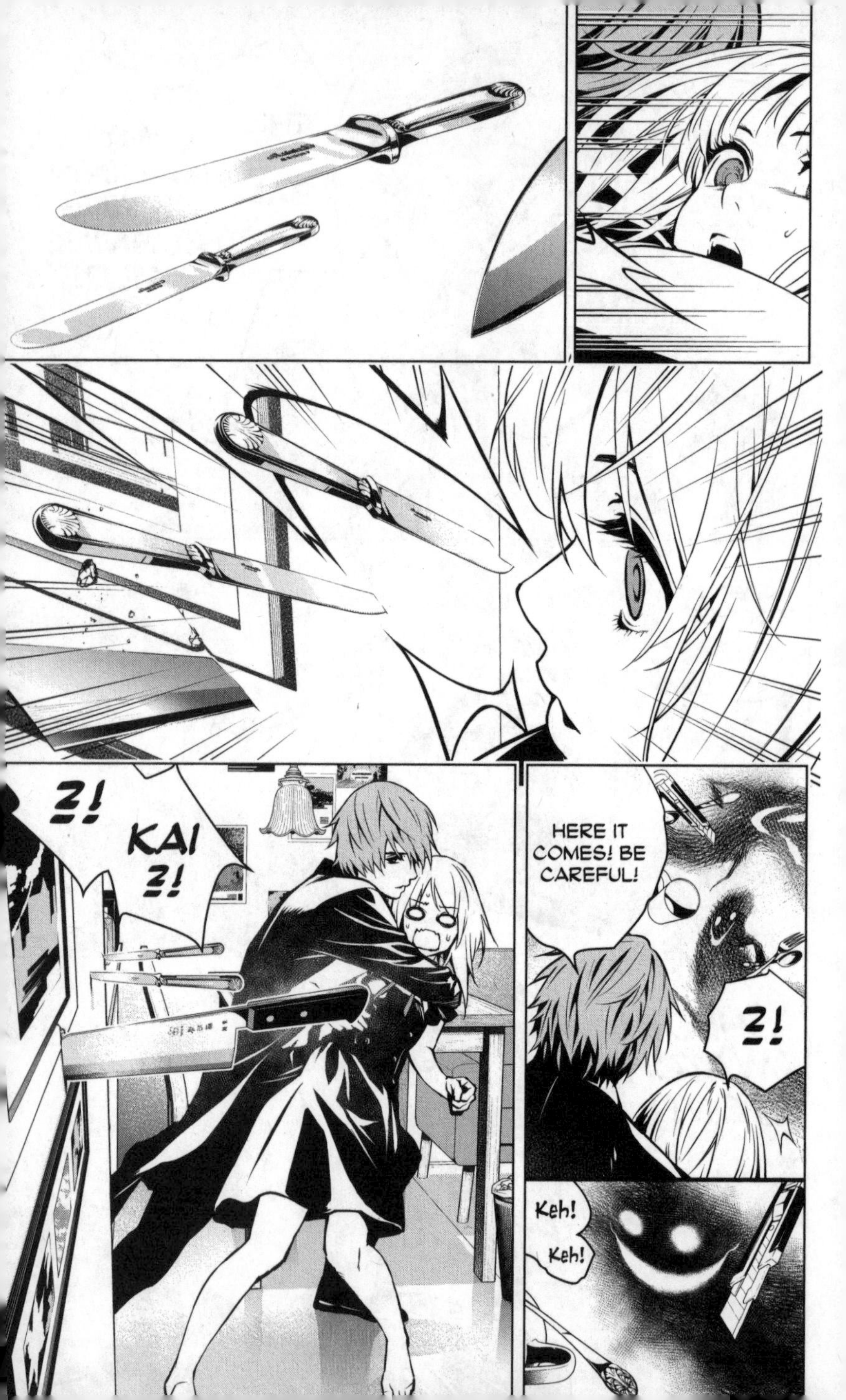
HERE IT COMES! BE CAREFUL!
?!
Keh!
Keh!
?!
KAI
?!

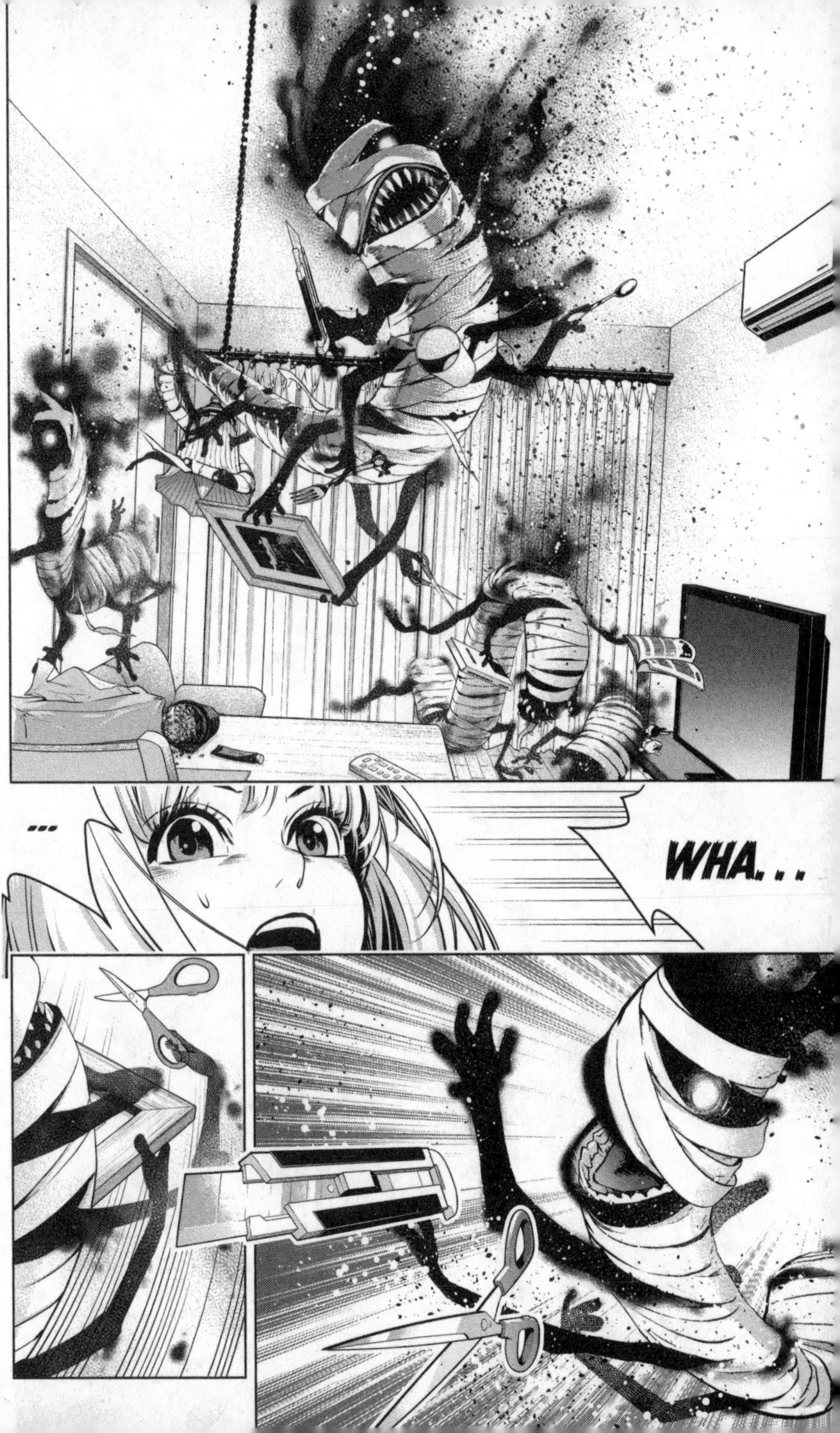

...
WHA...

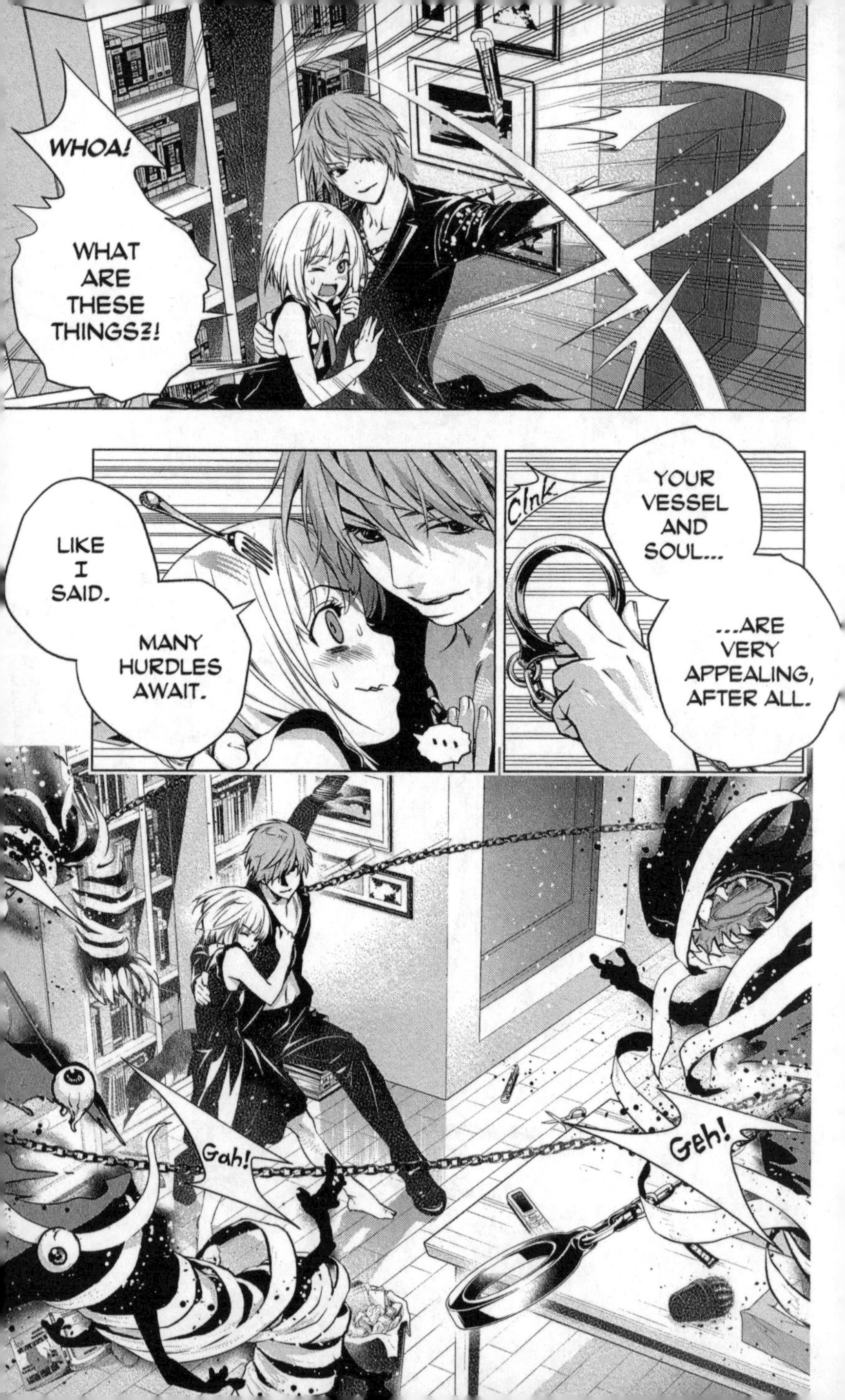
WHOA!
WHAT ARE THESE THINGS?!
Clnk
YOUR VESSEL AND SOUL...
...ARE VERY APPEALING, AFTER ALL.
LIKE I SAID.
MANY HURDLES AWAIT.
...
Geh!
Gah!

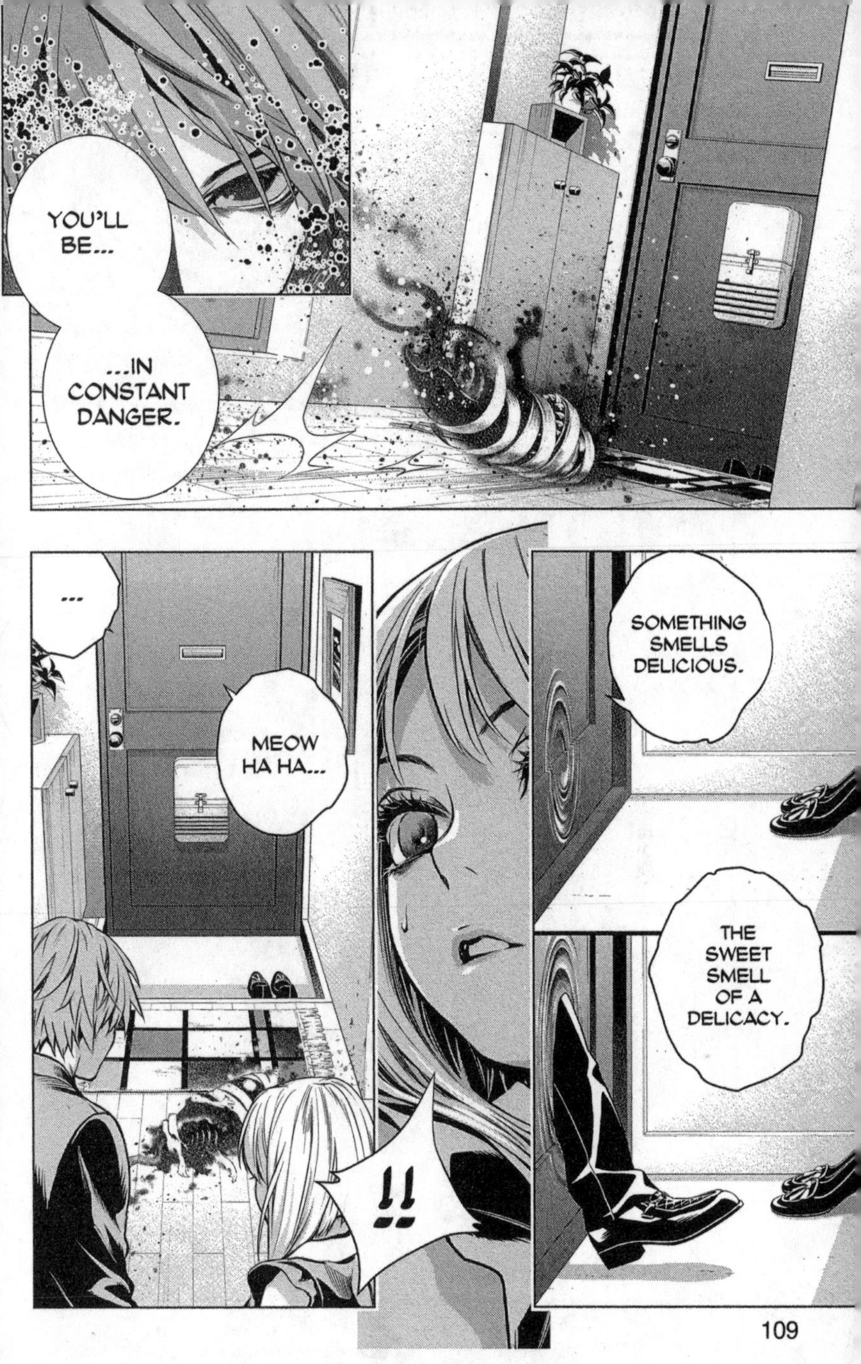
YOU'LL BE...
...IN CONSTANT DANGER.
SOMETHING SMELLS DELICIOUS.
THE SWEET SMELL OF A DELICACY.
!!
...
MEOW HA HA...

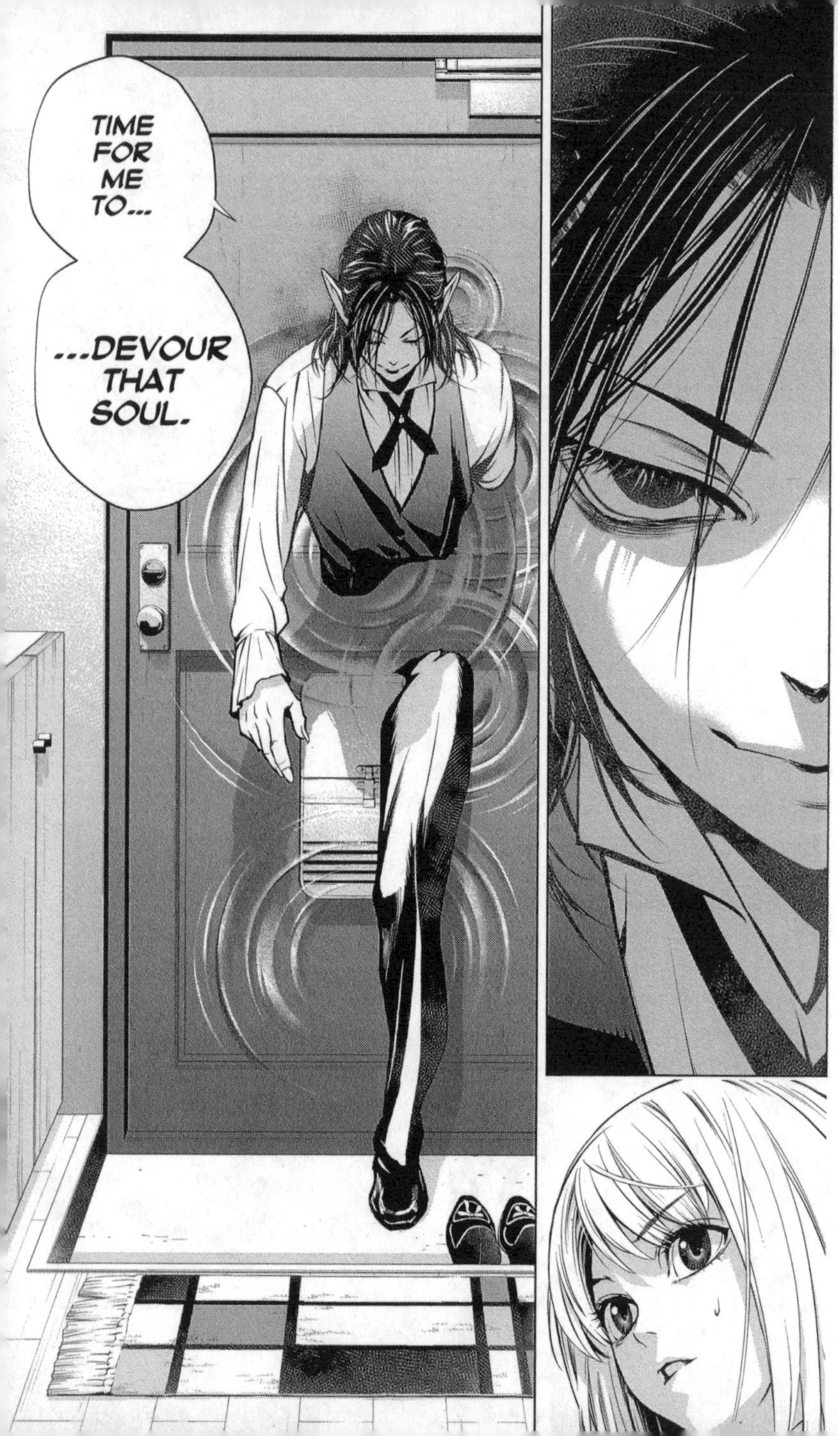
TIME FOR ME TO...
...DEVOUR THAT SOUL.

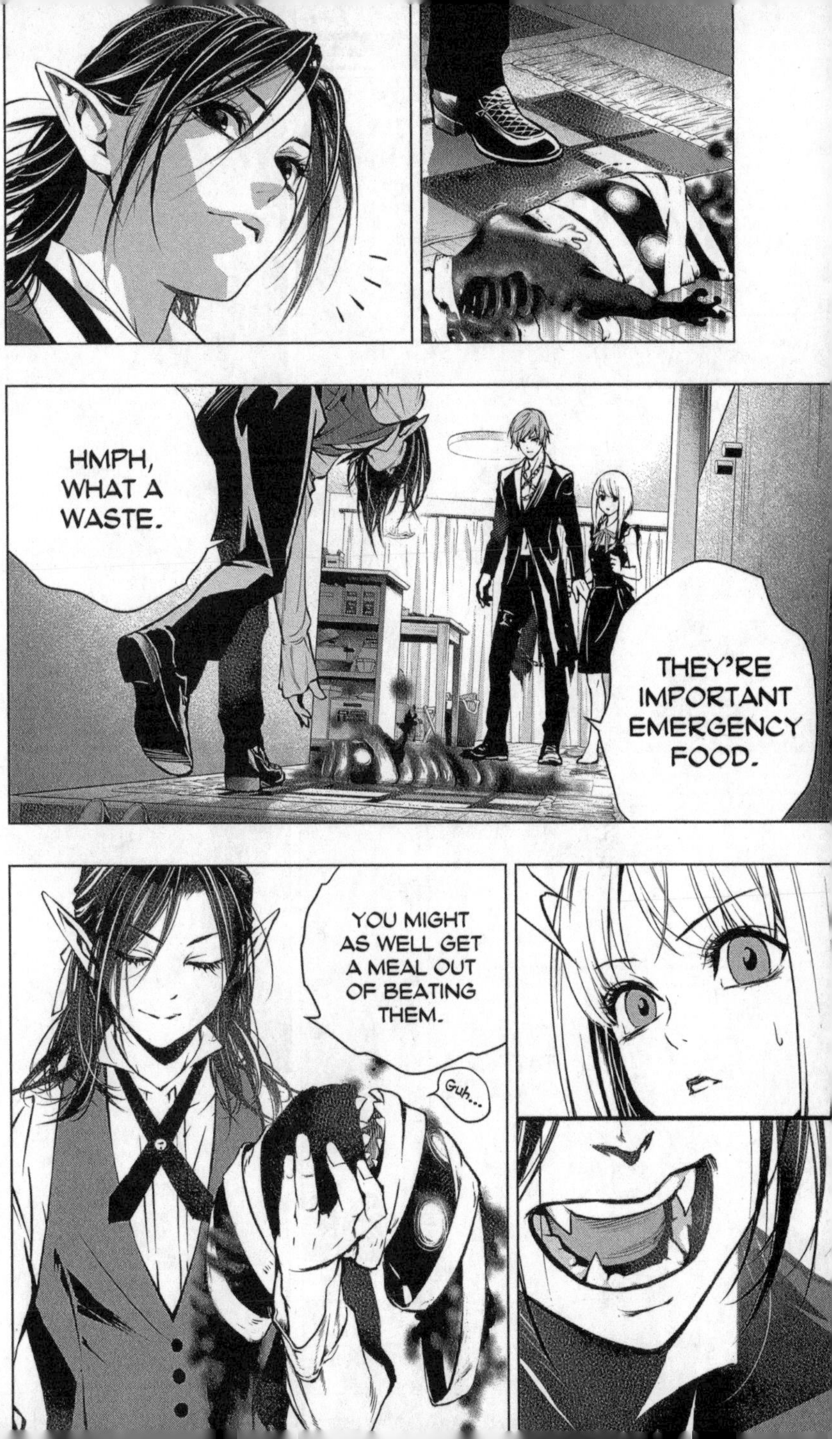
THEY'RE IMPORTANT EMERGENCY FOOD.
HMPH, WHAT A WASTE.
YOU MIGHT AS WELL GET A MEAL OUT OF BEATING THEM.
Guh...

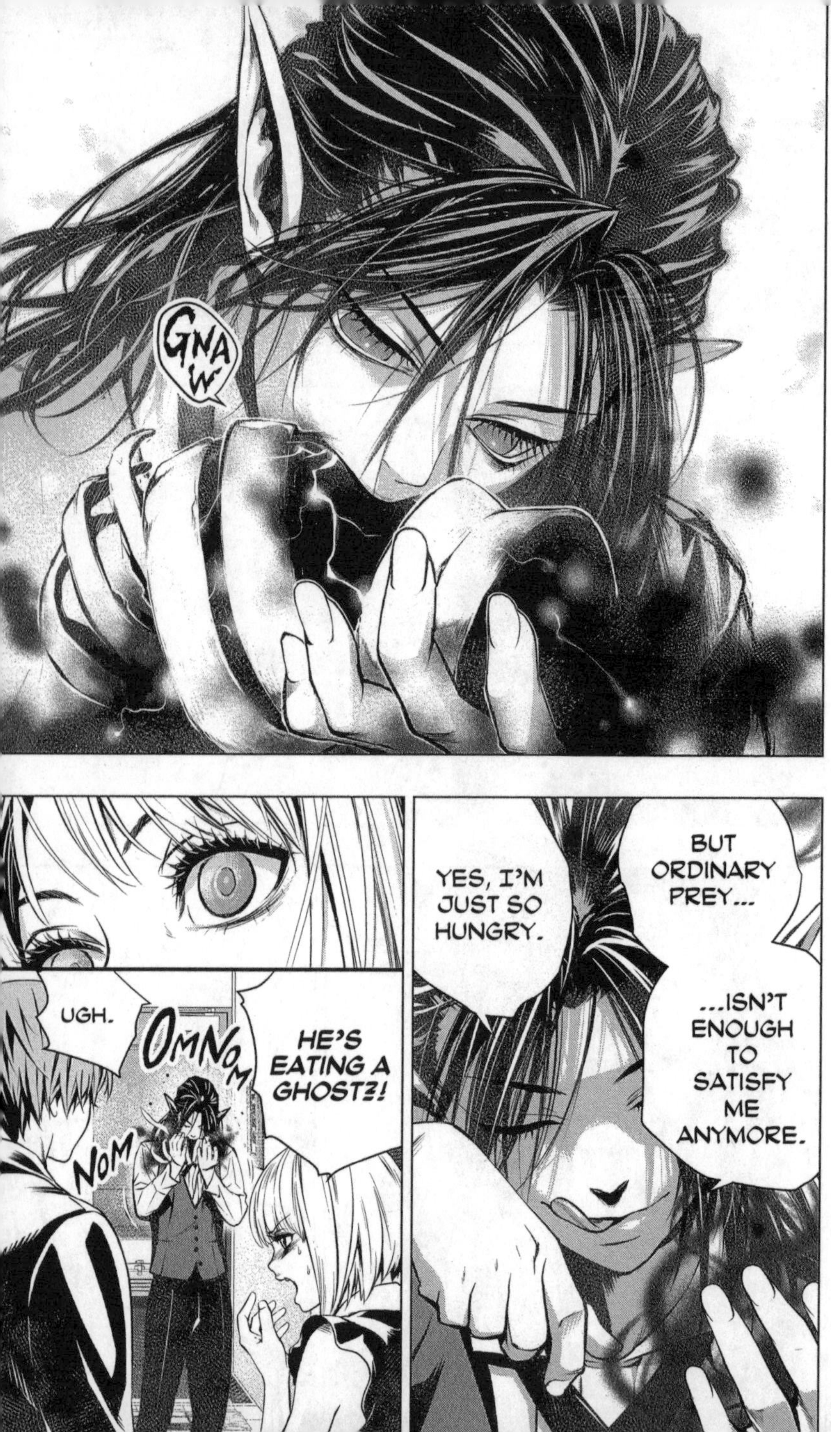
GNAW
UGH.
OMNOM
NOM
HE'S EATING A GHOST?!
YES, I'M JUST SO HUNGRY.
BUT ORDINARY PREY...
...ISN'T ENOUGH TO SATISFY ME ANYMORE.

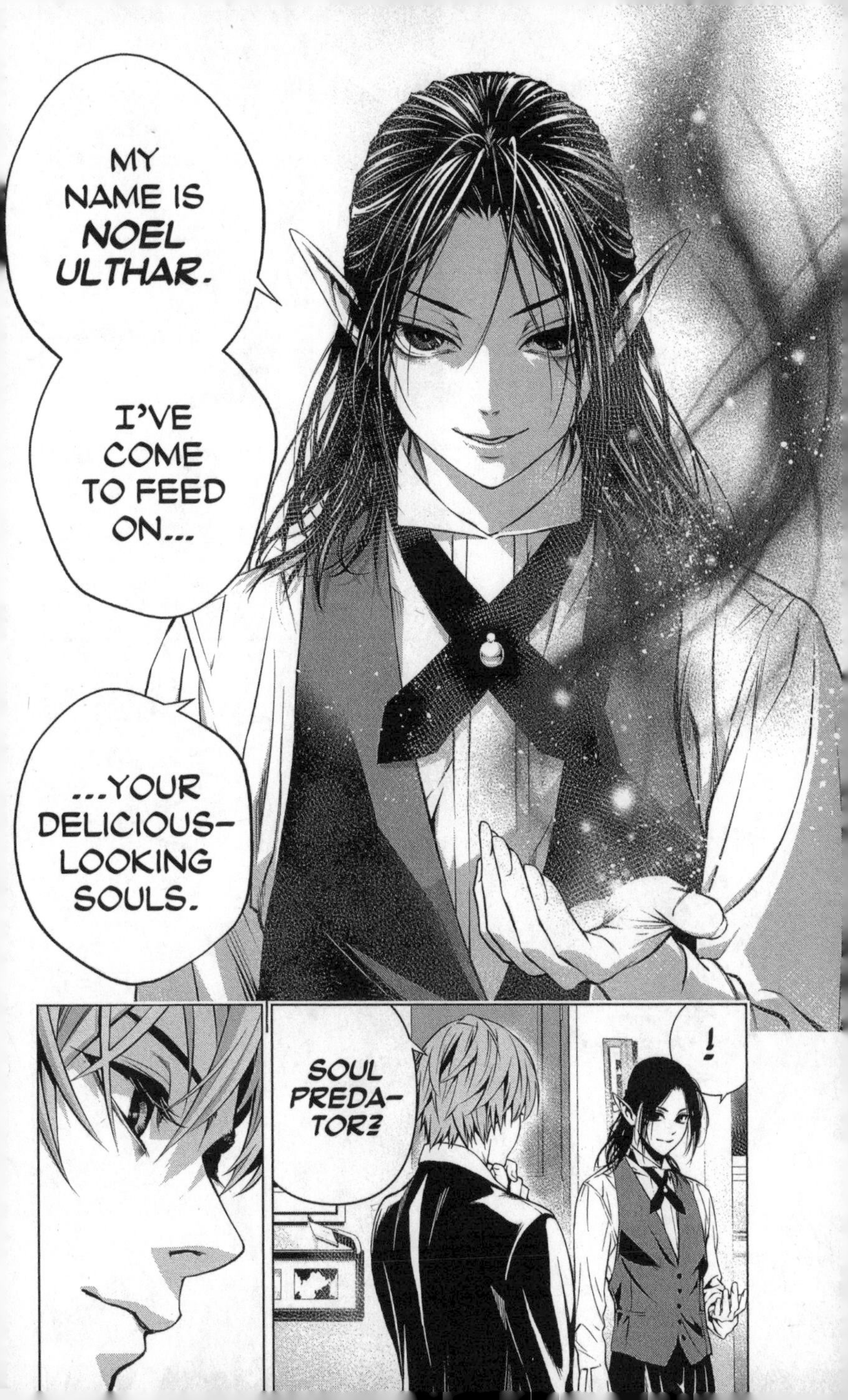
MY NAME IS NOEL ULTHAR.
I'VE COME TO FEED ON...
...YOUR DELICIOUS-LOOKING SOULS.
!
SOUL PREDA-TOR?

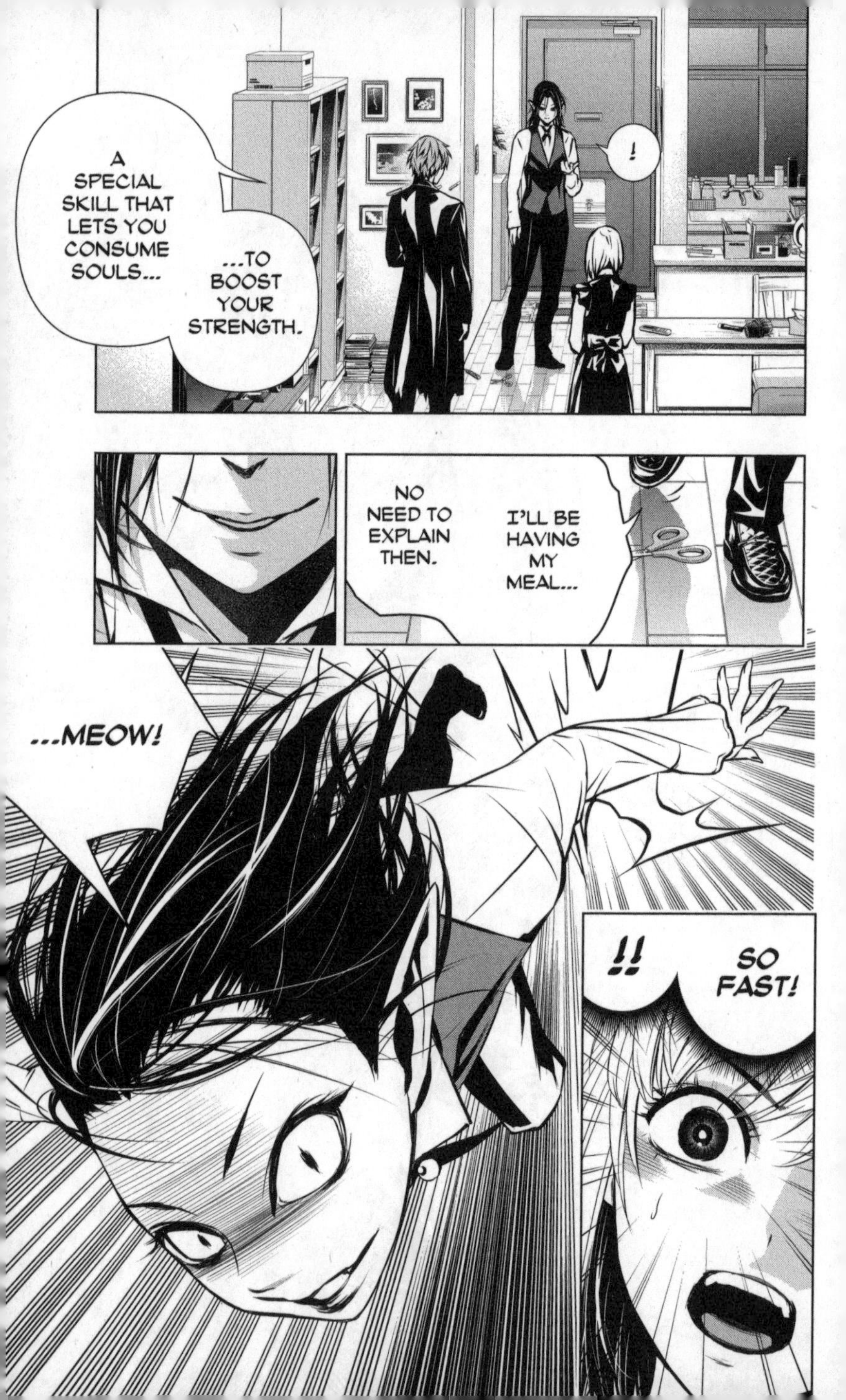
!
A SPECIAL SKILL THAT LETS YOU CONSUME SOULS...
...TO BOOST YOUR STRENGTH.
NO NEED TO EXPLAIN THEN.
I'LL BE HAVING MY MEAL...
...MEOW!
!!
SO FAST!

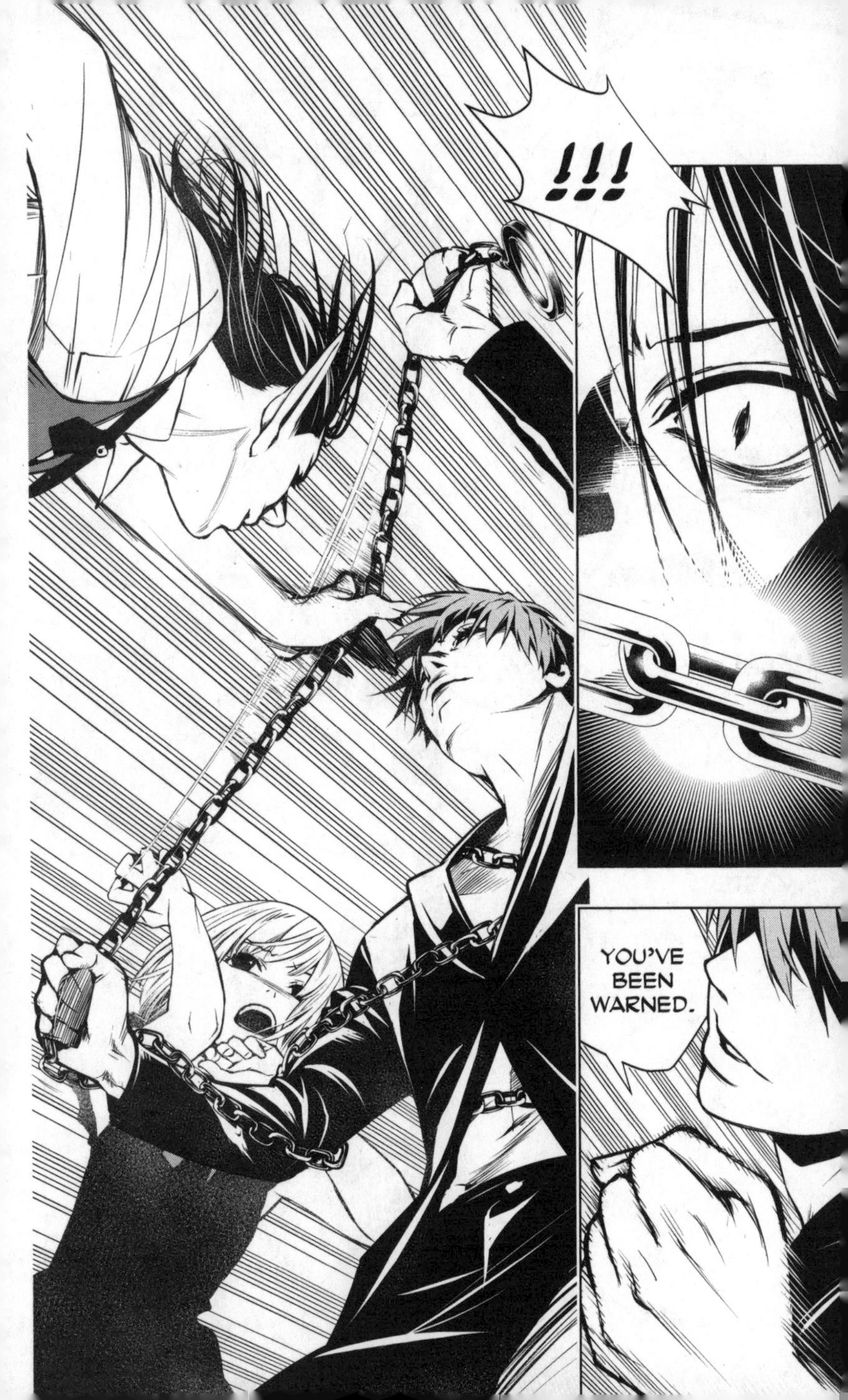
!!!
YOU'VE BEEN WARNED.

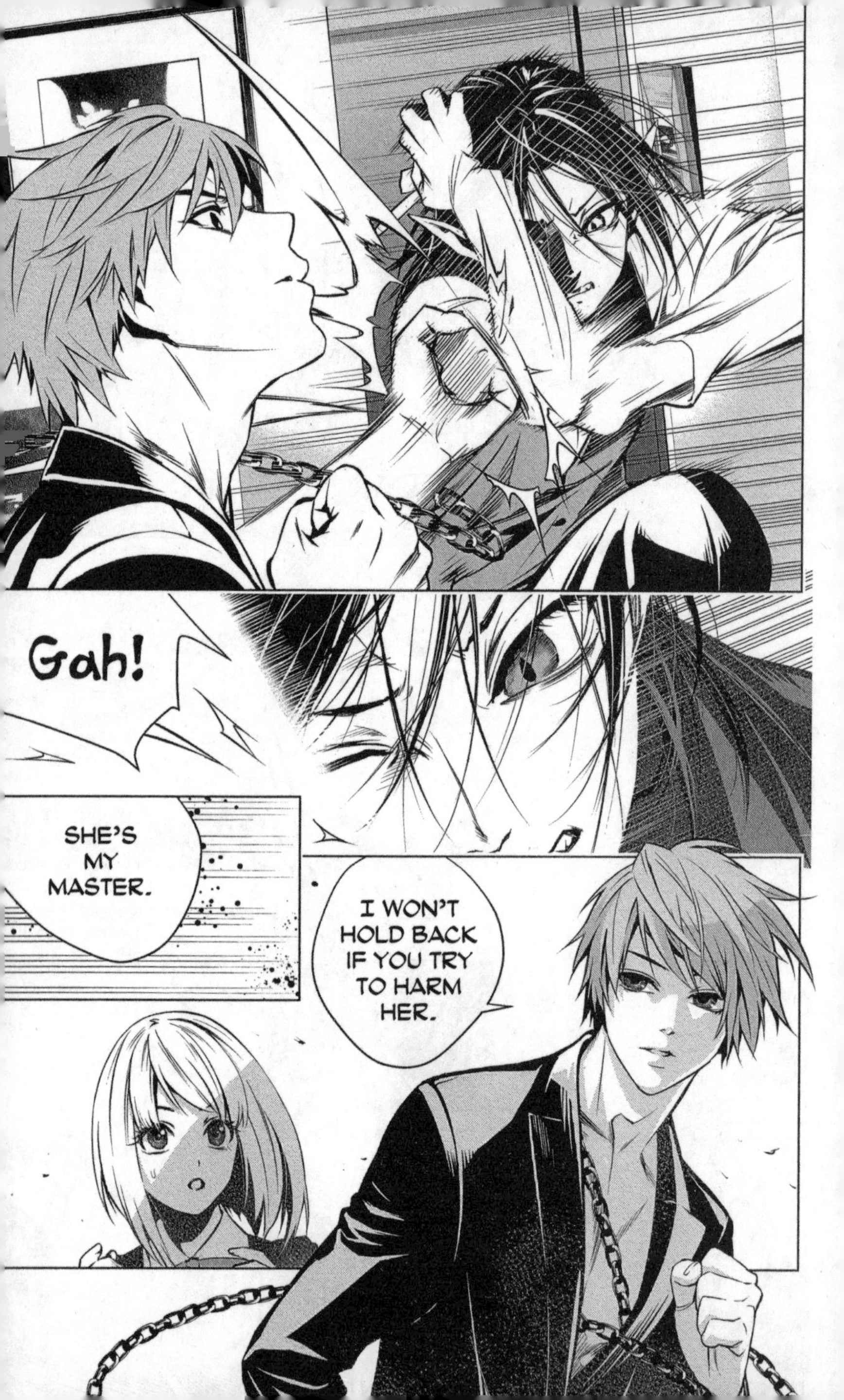
Gah!
SHE'S MY MASTER.
I WON'T HOLD BACK IF YOU TRY TO HARM HER.

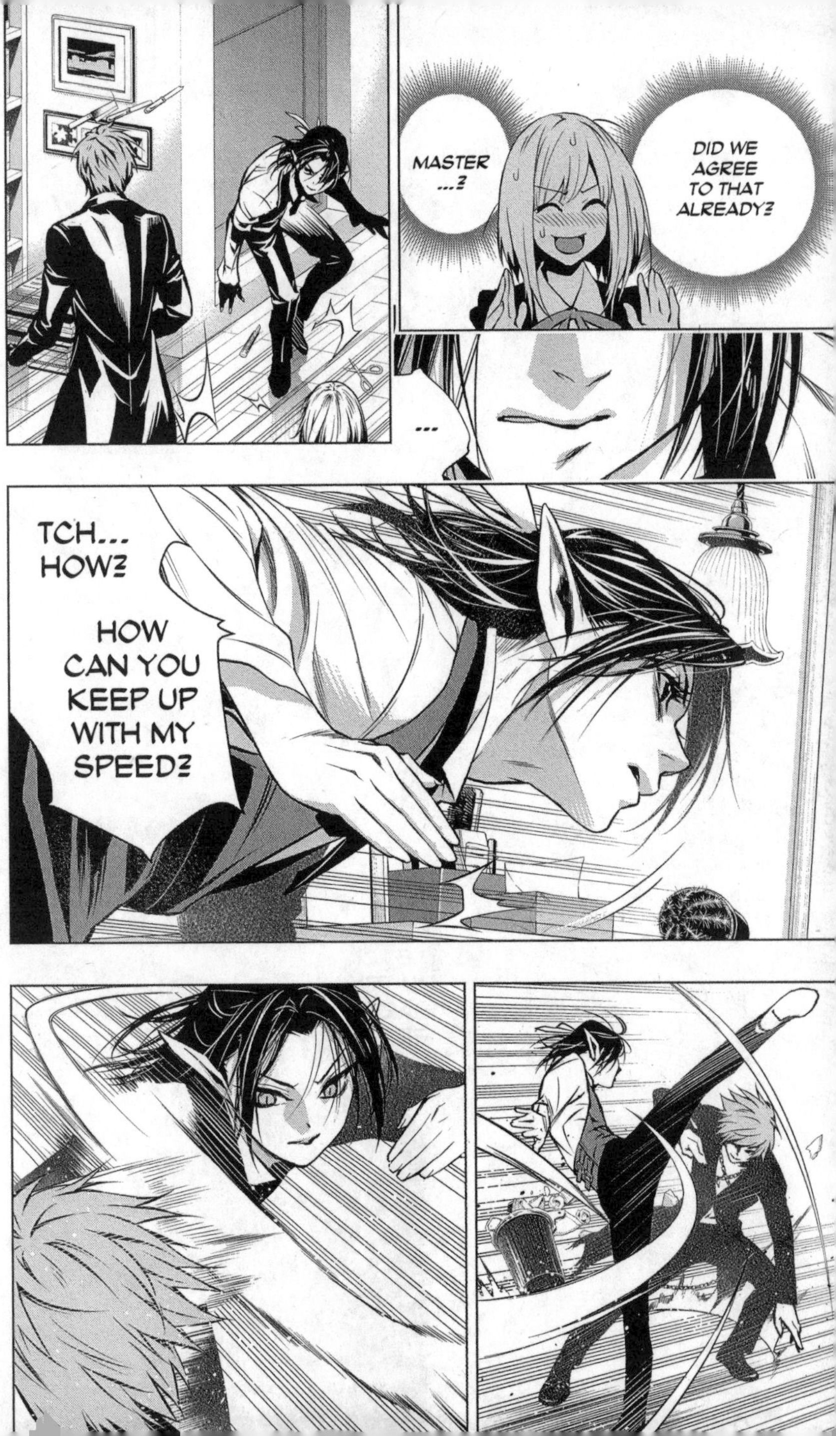
DID WE AGREE TO THAT ALREADY?
MASTER ...?
...
TCH... HOW?
HOW CAN YOU KEEP UP WITH MY SPEED?

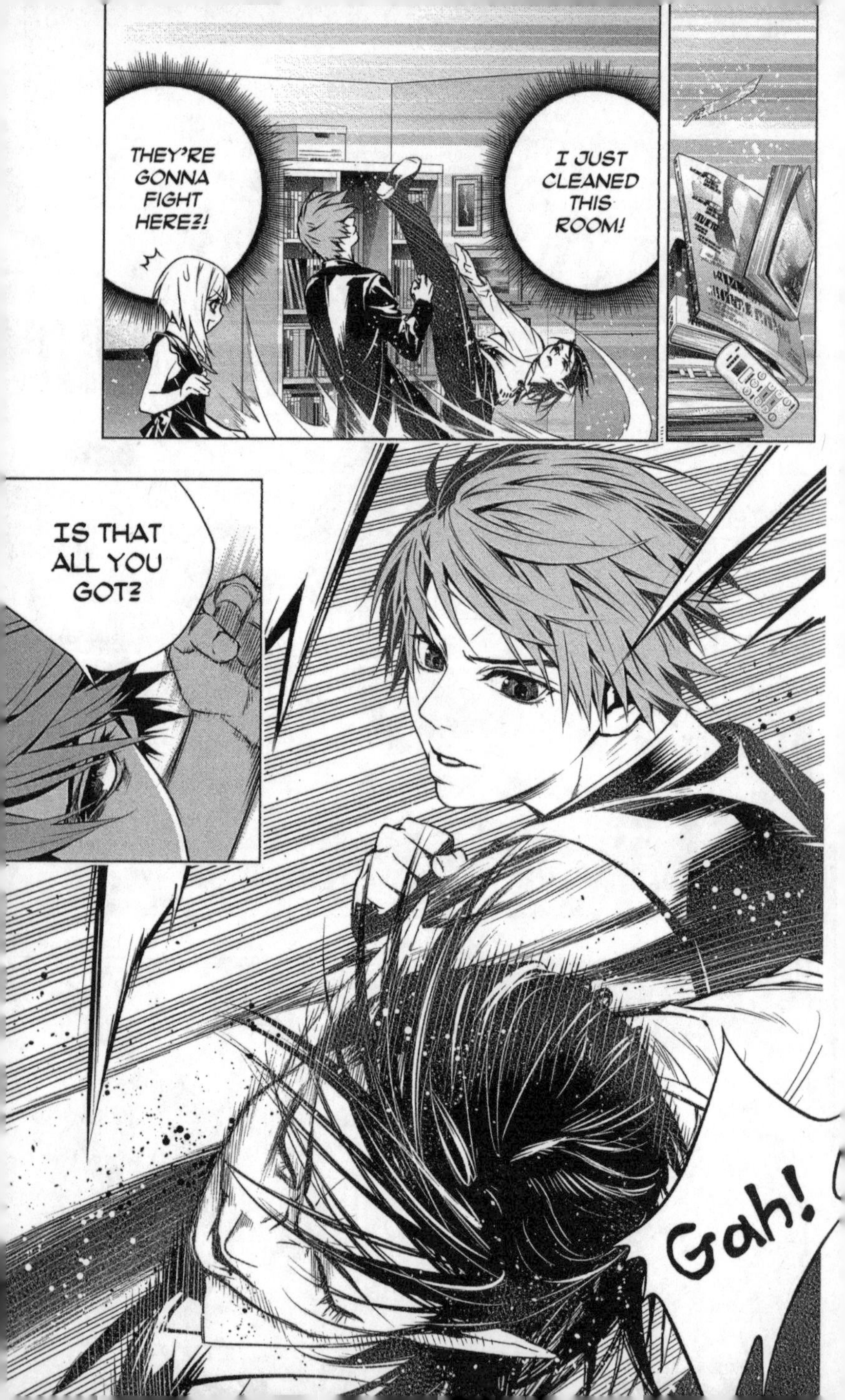
I JUST CLEANED THIS ROOM!
THEY'RE GONNA FIGHT HERE?!
IS THAT ALL YOU GOT?
Gah!

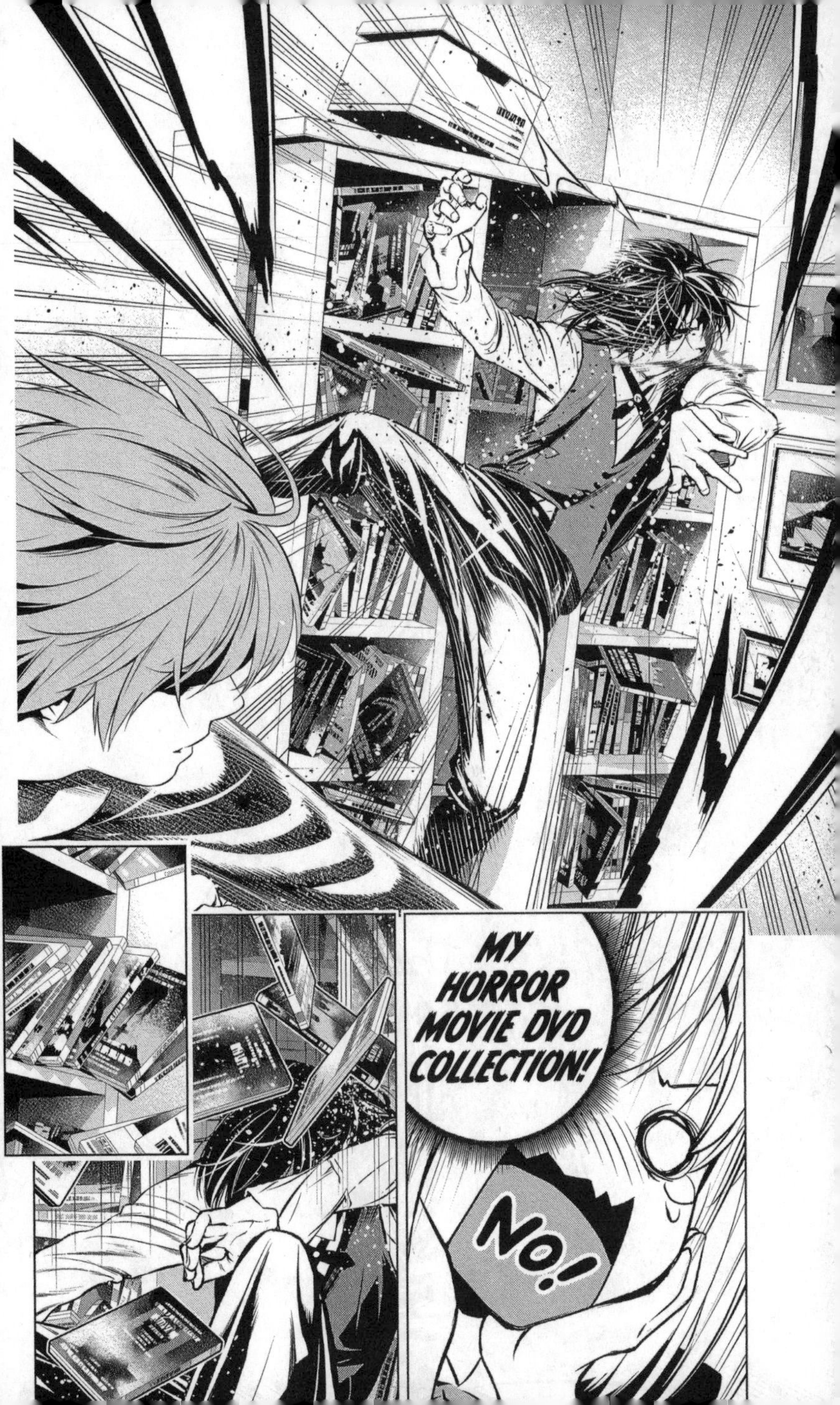
MY HORROR MOVIE DVD COLLECTION!
NO!

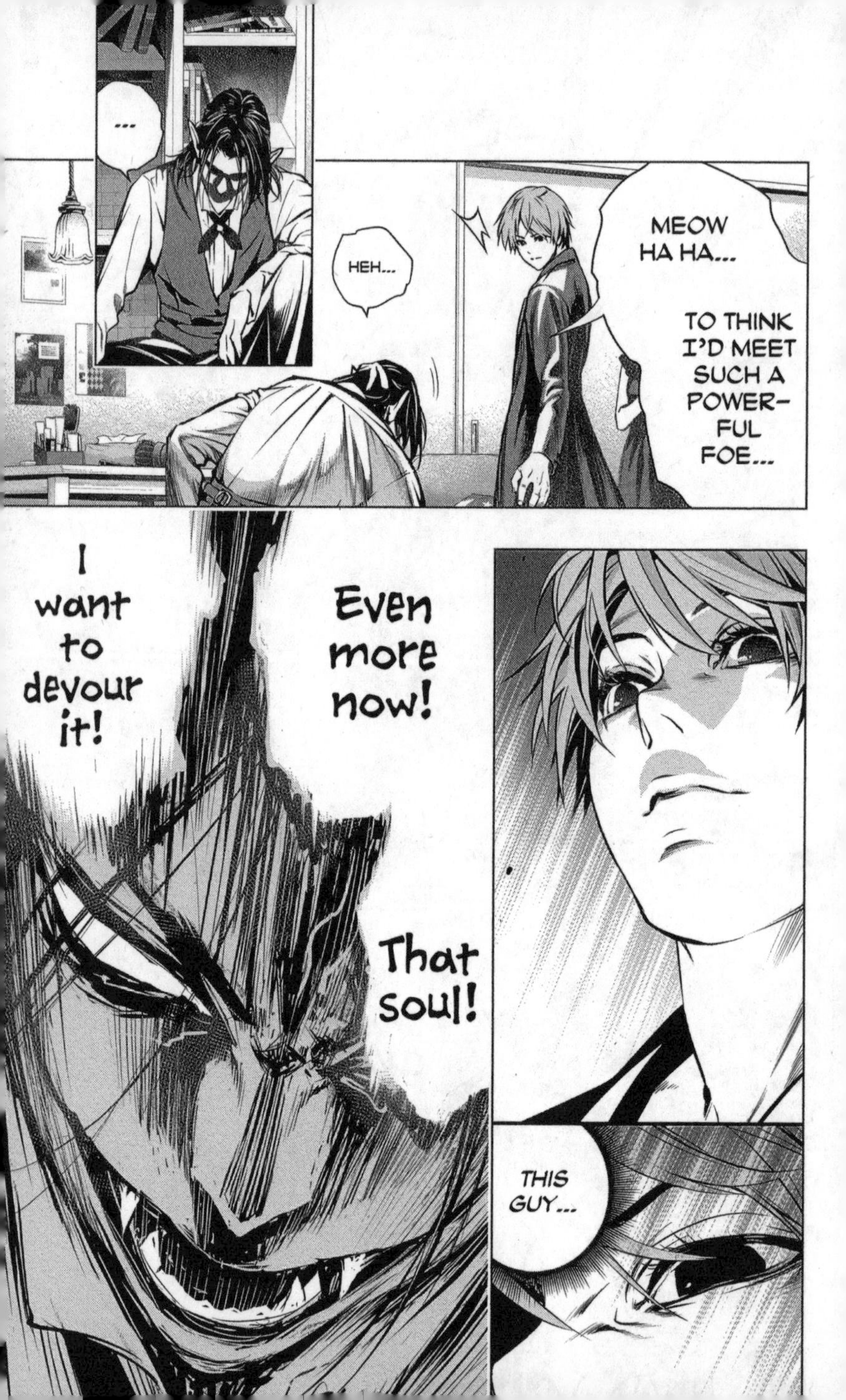
MEOW HA HA...
TO THINK I'D MEET SUCH A POWERFUL FOE...
HEH...
...
THIS GUY...
Even more now!
I want to devour it!
That soul!

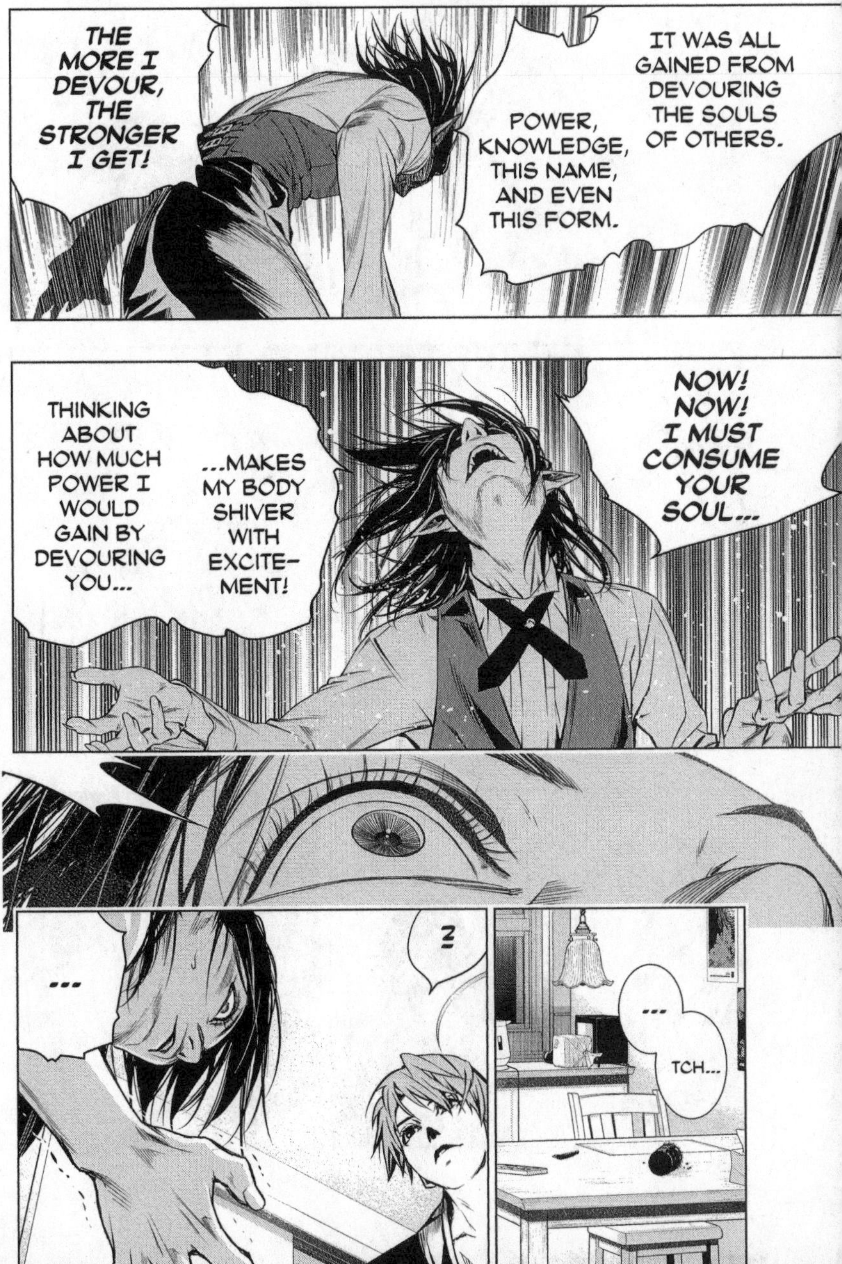
IT WAS ALL GAINED FROM DEVOURING THE SOULS OF OTHERS.
POWER, KNOWLEDGE, THIS NAME, AND EVEN THIS FORM.
THE MORE I DEVOUR, THE STRONGER I GET!
NOW! NOW! I MUST CONSUME YOUR SOUL...
THINKING ABOUT HOW MUCH POWER I WOULD GAIN BY DEVOURING YOU...
...MAKES MY BODY SHIVER WITH EXCITE-MENT!
...
TCH...
...

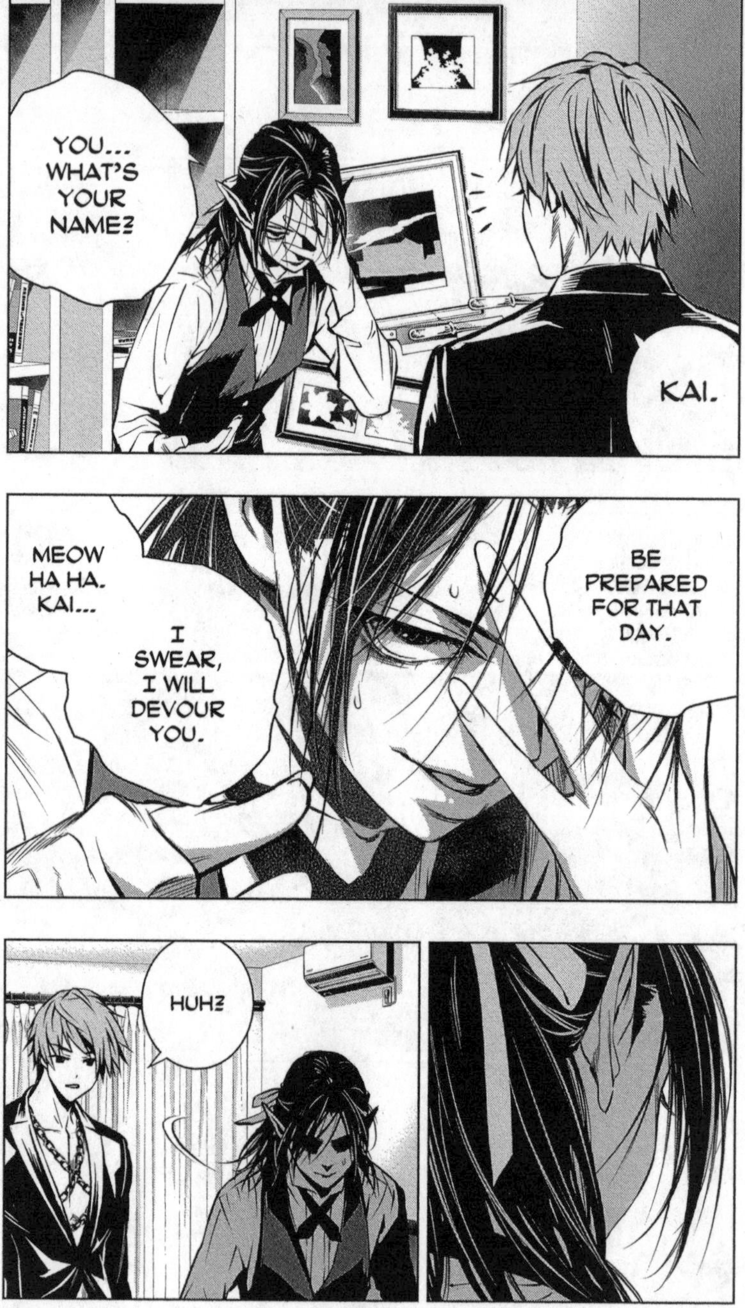
YOU... WHAT'S YOUR NAME?
KAI.
MEOW HA HA. KAI...
I SWEAR, I WILL DEVOUR YOU.
BE PREPARED FOR THAT DAY.
HUH?

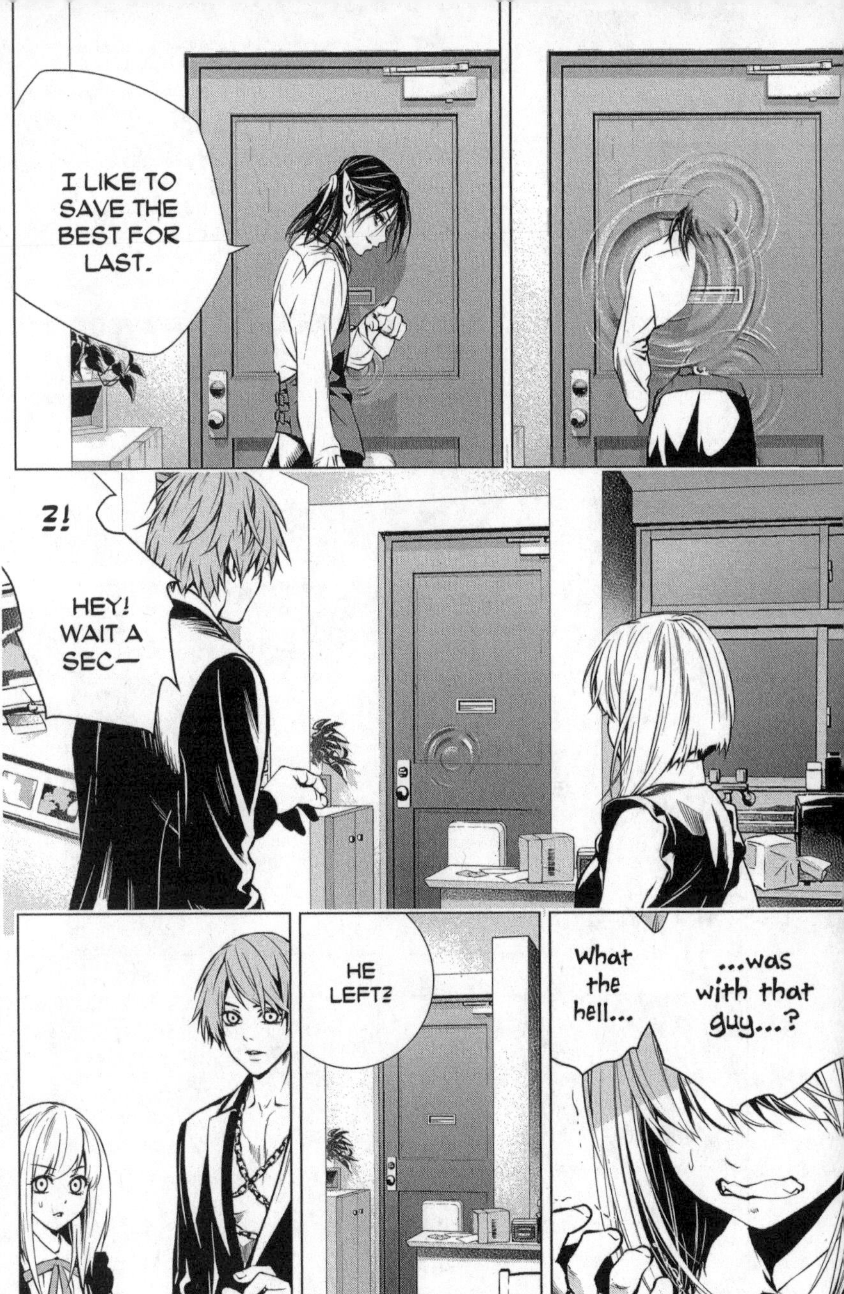
I LIKE TO SAVE THE BEST FOR LAST.
?!
HEY! WAIT A SEC—
What the hell...
...was with that guy...?
HE LEFT?

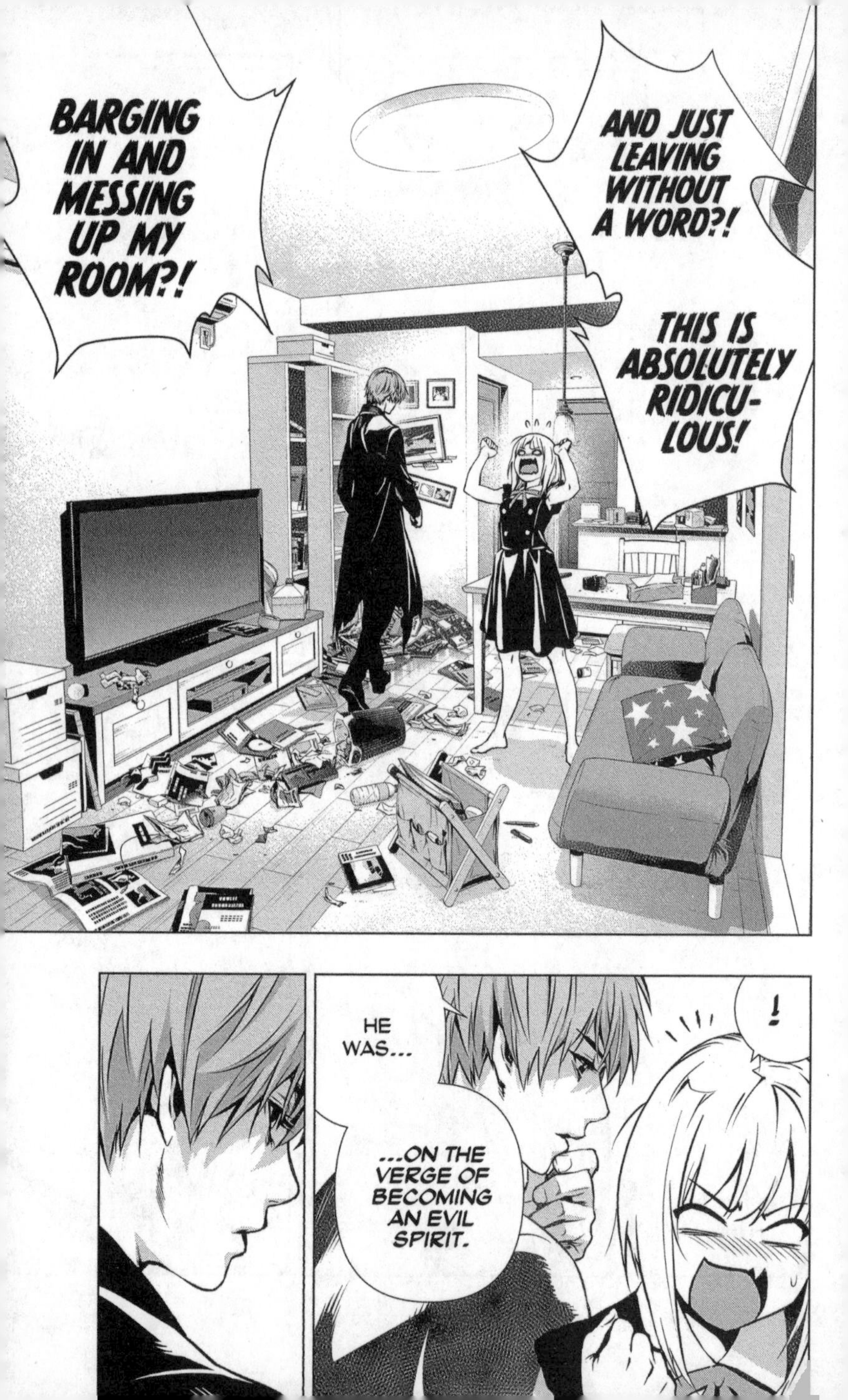
BARGING IN AND MESSING UP MY ROOM?!
AND JUST LEAVING WITHOUT A WORD?!
THIS IS ABSOLUTELY RIDICU-LOUS!
!
HE WAS...
...ON THE VERGE OF BECOMING AN EVIL SPIRIT.

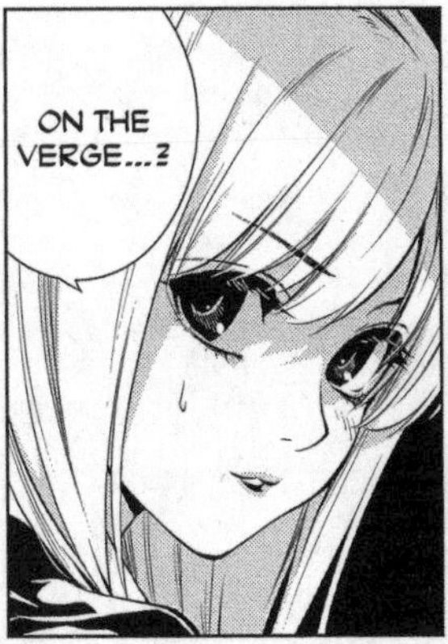
ON THE VERGE...?

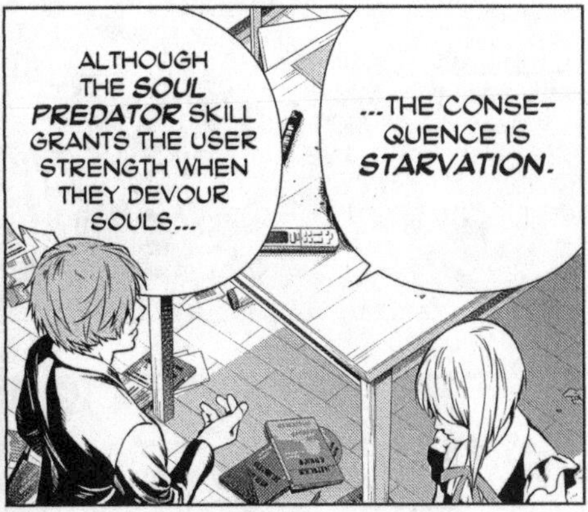
ALTHOUGH THE SOUL PREDATOR SKILL GRANTS THE USER STRENGTH WHEN THEY DEVOUR SOULS...
...THE CONSEQUENCE IS STARVATION.

AN ETERNAL STARVATION THAT CAN NEVER BE SATISFIED.

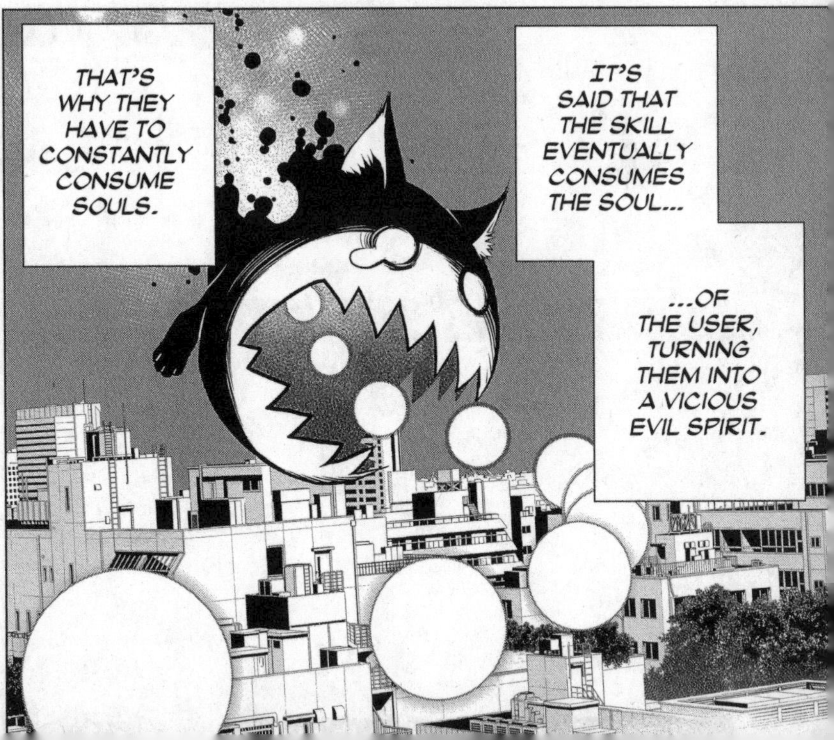
THAT'S WHY THEY HAVE TO CONSTANTLY CONSUME SOULS.
IT'S SAID THAT THE SKILL EVENTUALLY CONSUMES THE SOUL...
...OF THE USER, TURNING THEM INTO A VICIOUS EVIL SPIRIT.

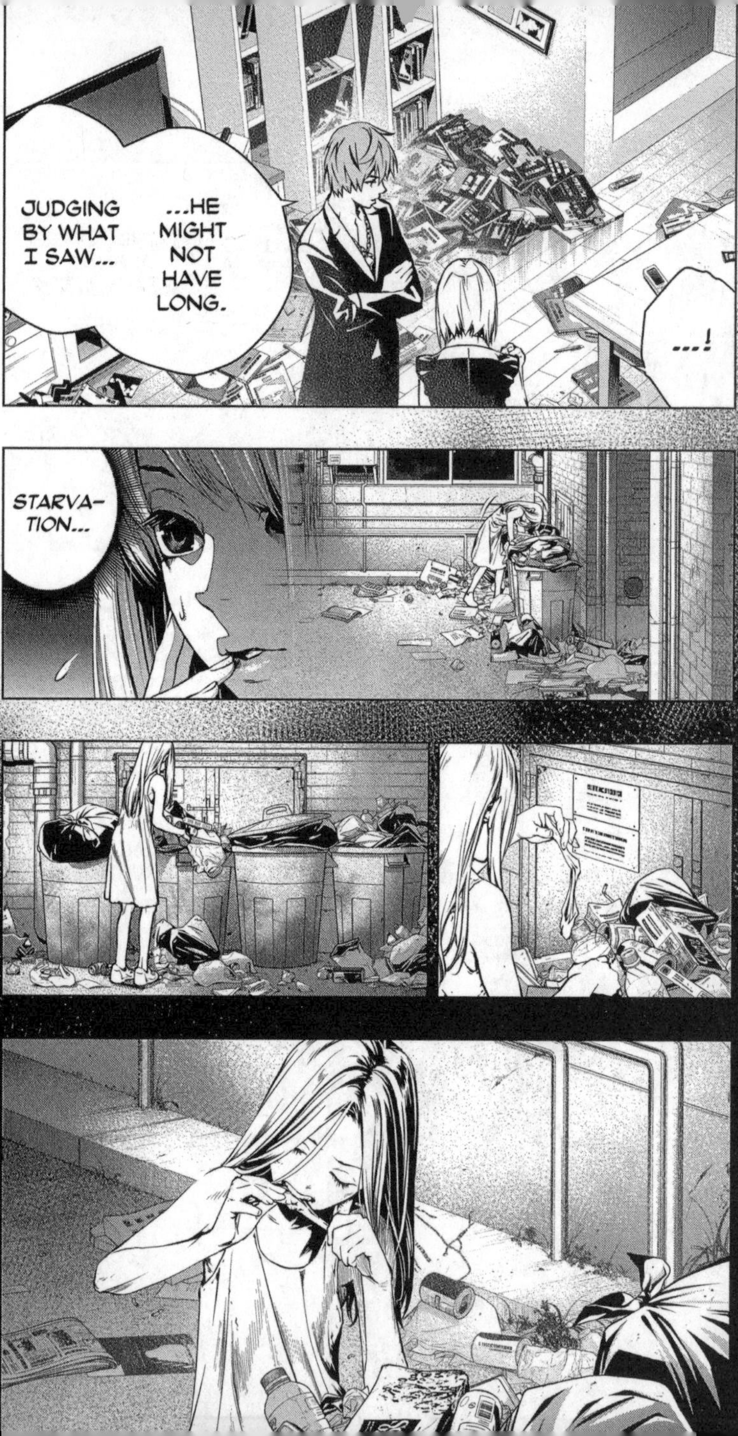
...!
JUDGING BY WHAT I SAW...
...HE MIGHT NOT HAVE LONG.
STARVATION...

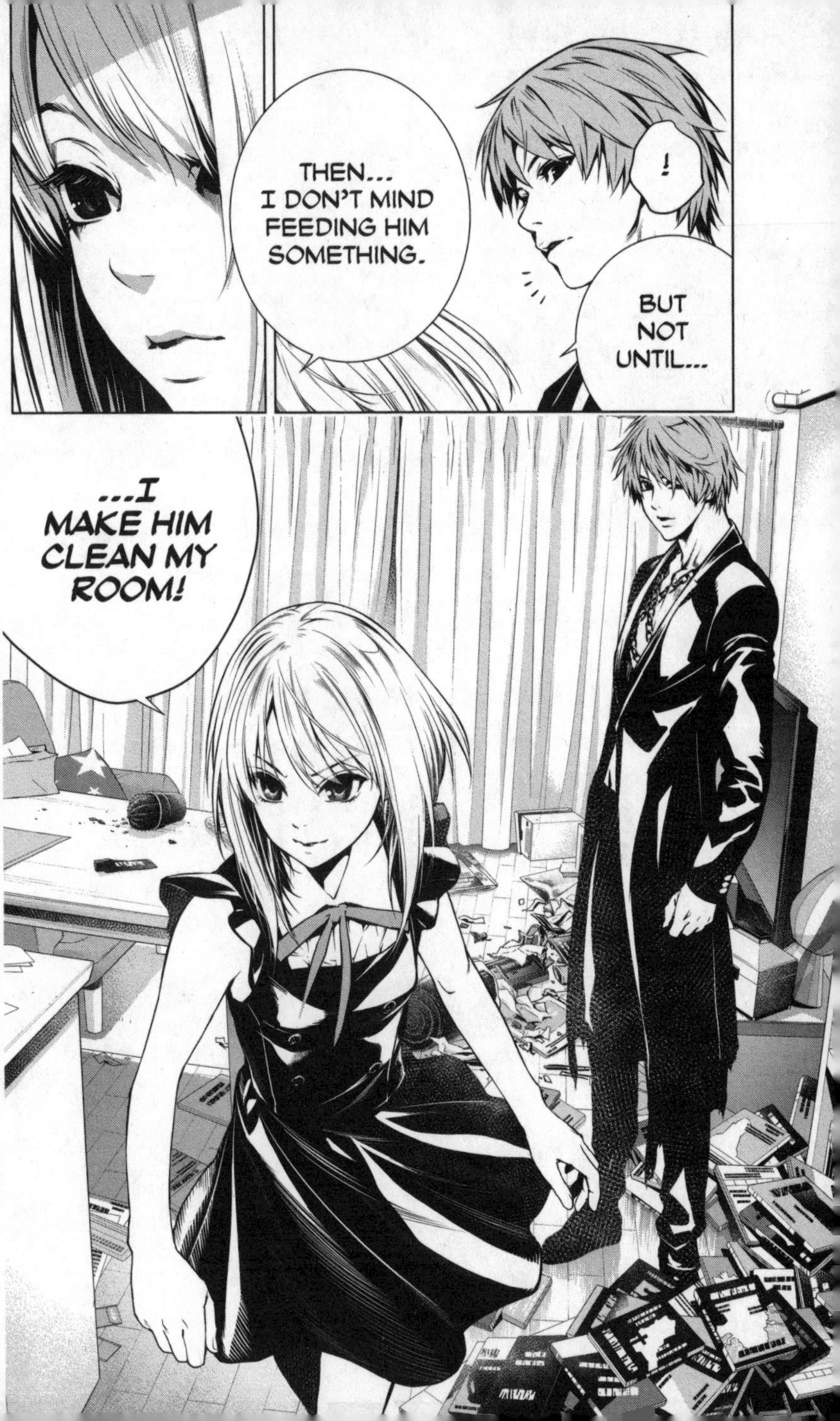
THEN... I DON'T MIND FEEDING HIM SOMETHING.
!
BUT NOT UNTIL...
...I MAKE HIM CLEAN MY ROOM!

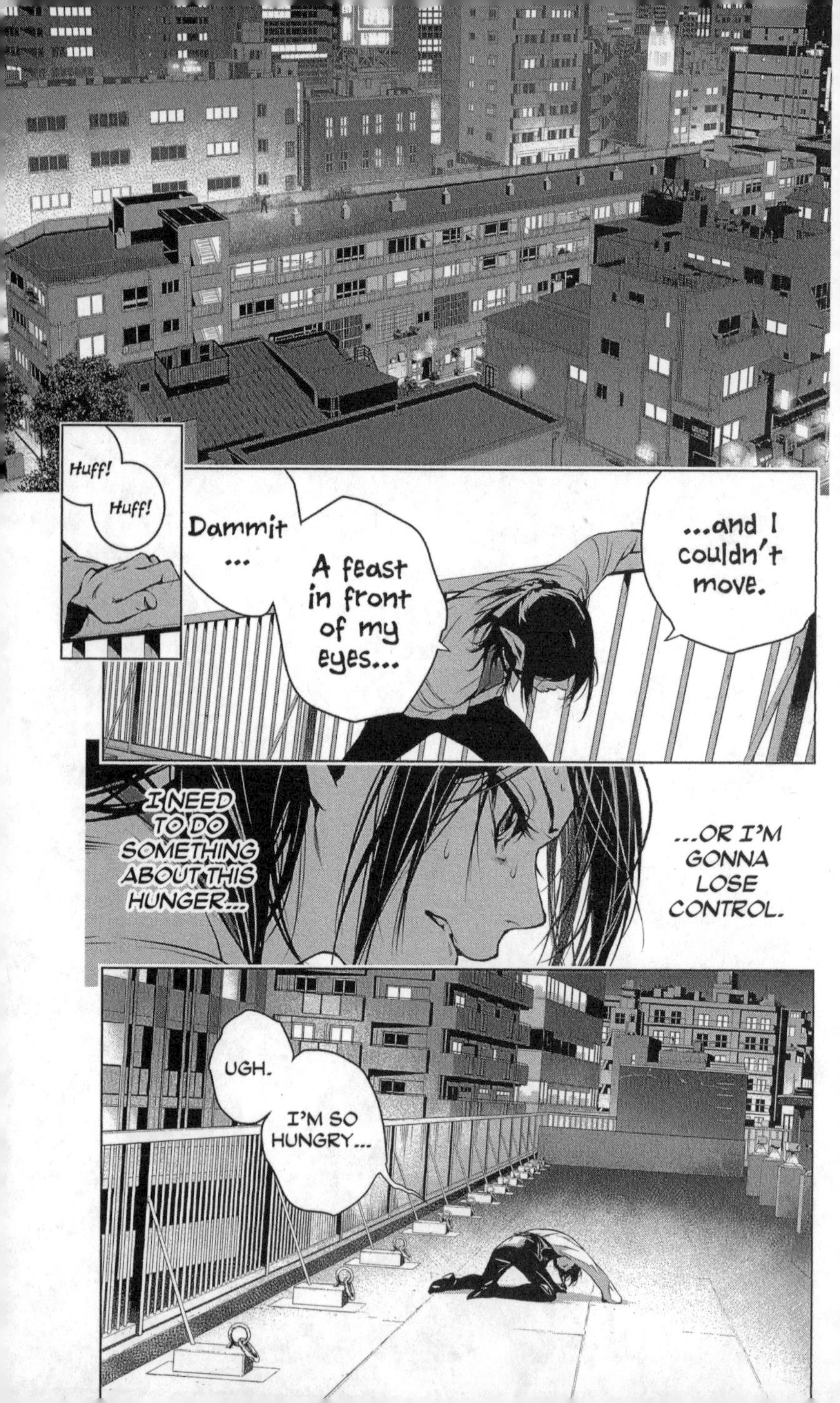

Huff!
Huff!
Dammit ...
A feast in front of my eyes...
...and I couldn't move.
I NEED TO DO SOMETHING ABOUT THIS HUNGER...
...OR I'M GONNA LOSE CONTROL.
UGH.
I'M SO HUNGRY...

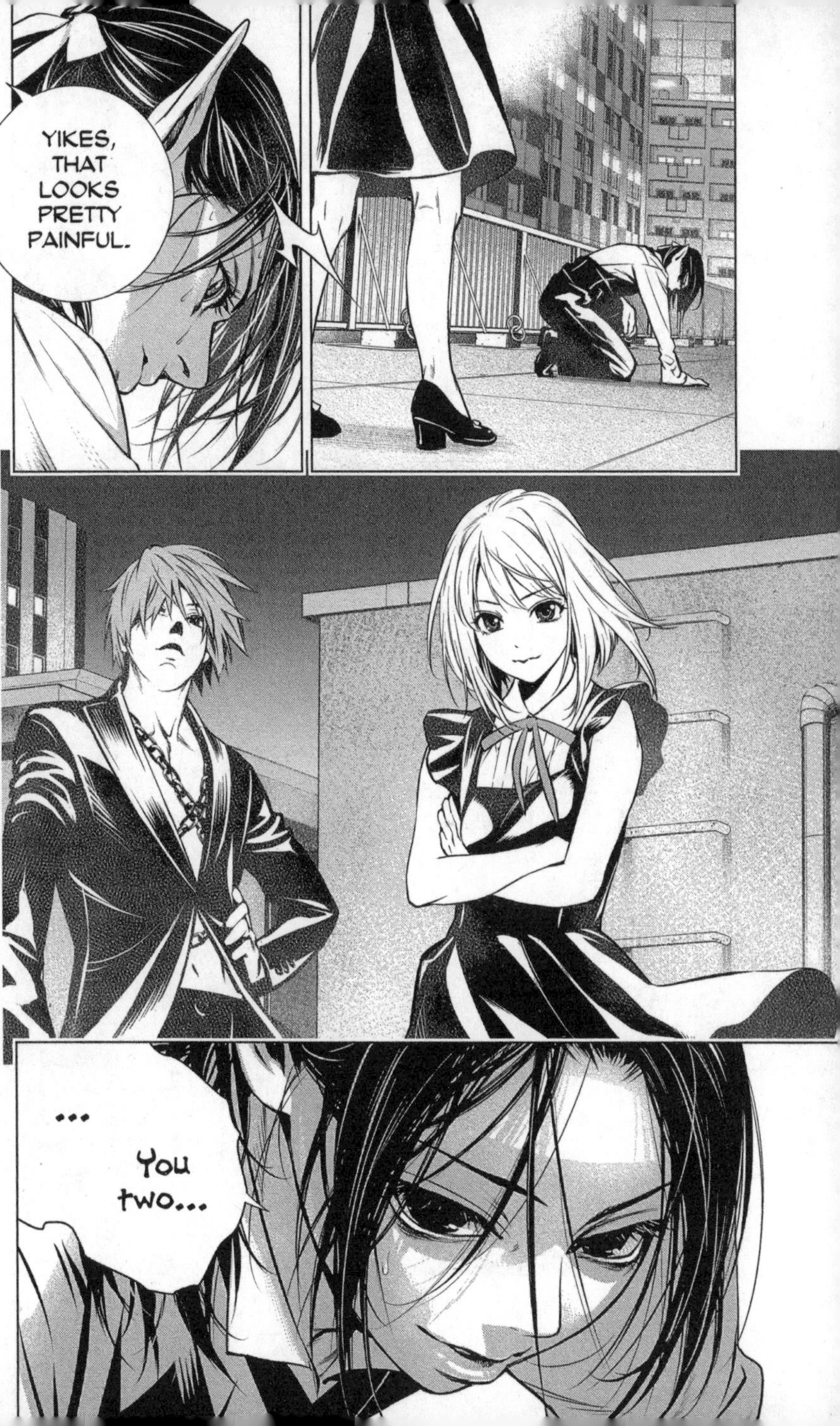
YIKES, THAT LOOKS PRETTY PAINFUL.
...
You two...

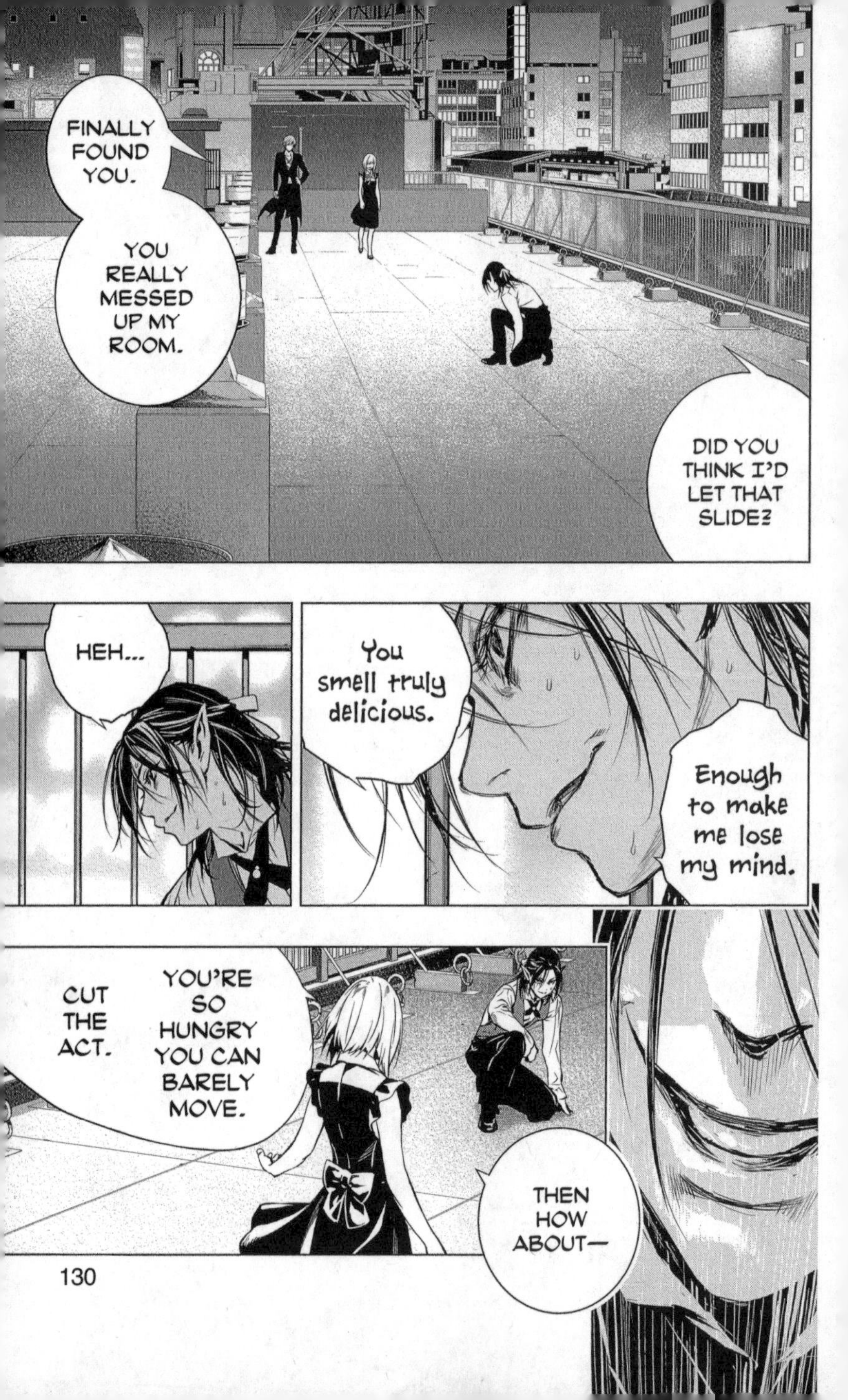
FINALLY FOUND YOU.
YOU REALLY MESSED UP MY ROOM.
DID YOU THINK I'D LET THAT SLIDE?
HEH...
You smell truly delicious.
Enough to make me lose my mind.
CUT THE ACT.
YOU'RE SO HUNGRY YOU CAN BARELY MOVE.
THEN HOW ABOUT—

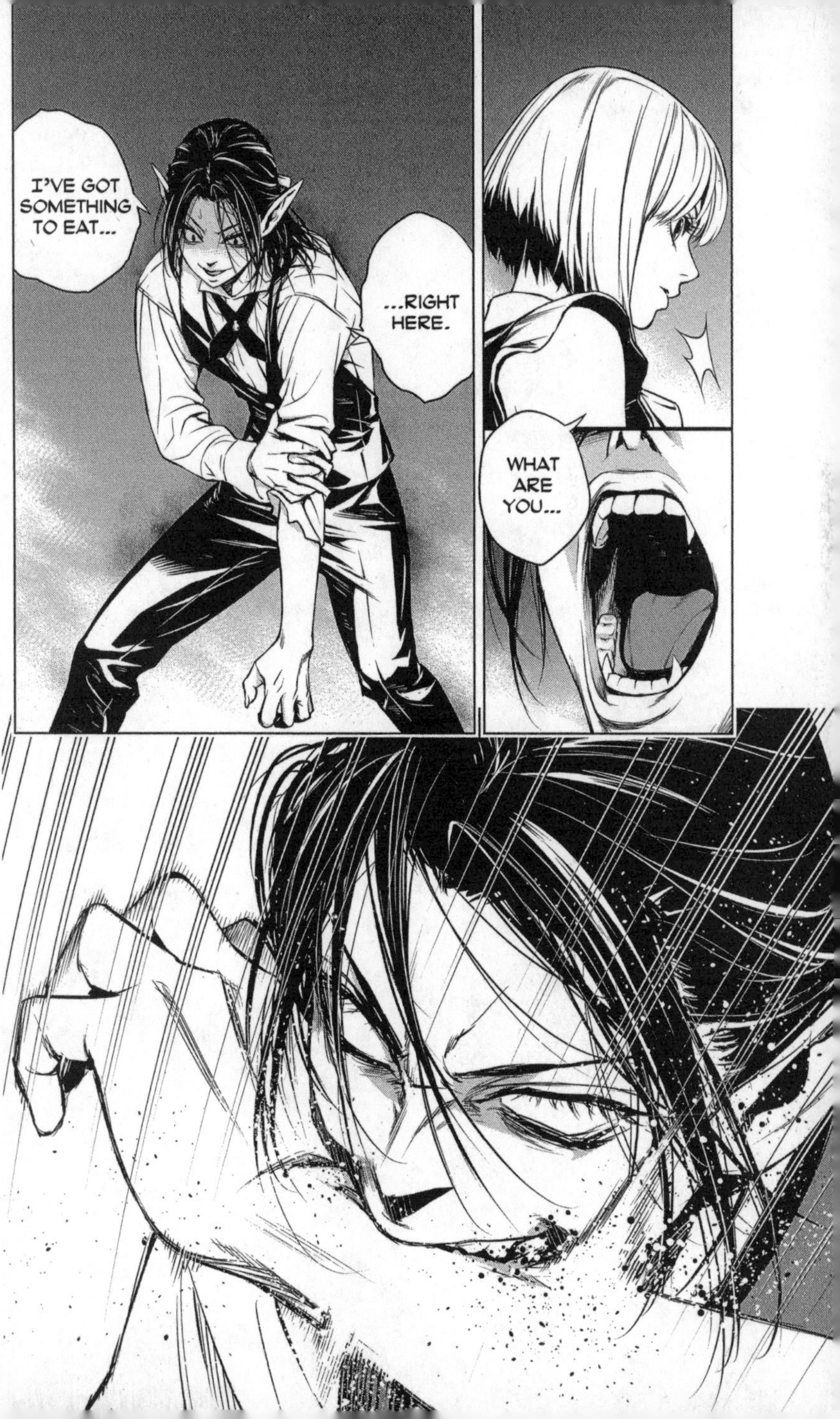
I'VE GOT SOMETHING TO EAT...
...RIGHT HERE.
WHAT ARE YOU...

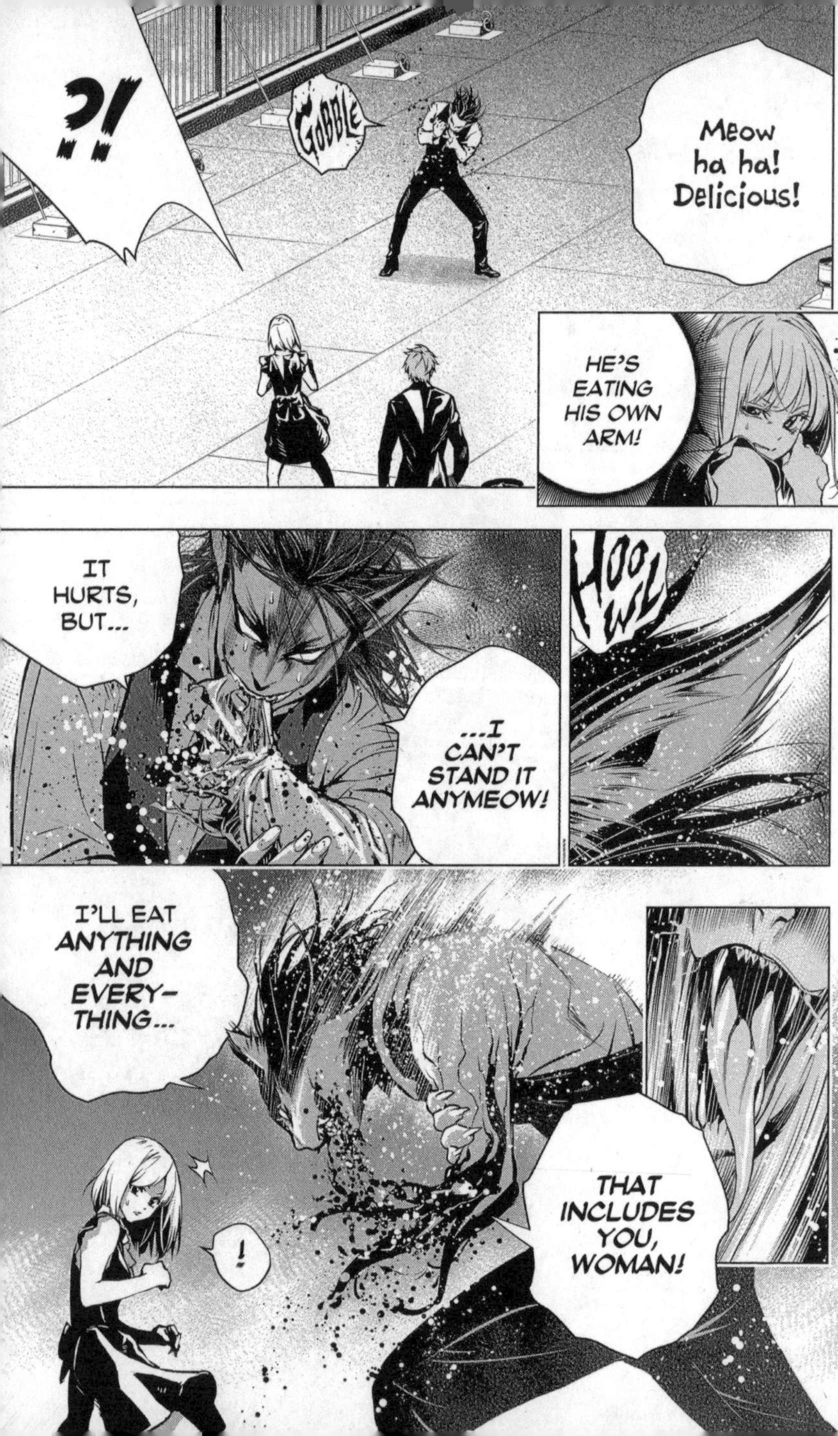
Meow ha ha! Delicious!
GOBBLE
?!
HE'S EATING HIS OWN ARM!
HOOWL
IT HURTS, BUT...
...I CAN'T STAND IT ANYMEOW!
I'LL EAT ANYTHING AND EVERY-THING...
THAT INCLUDES YOU, WOMAN!
!

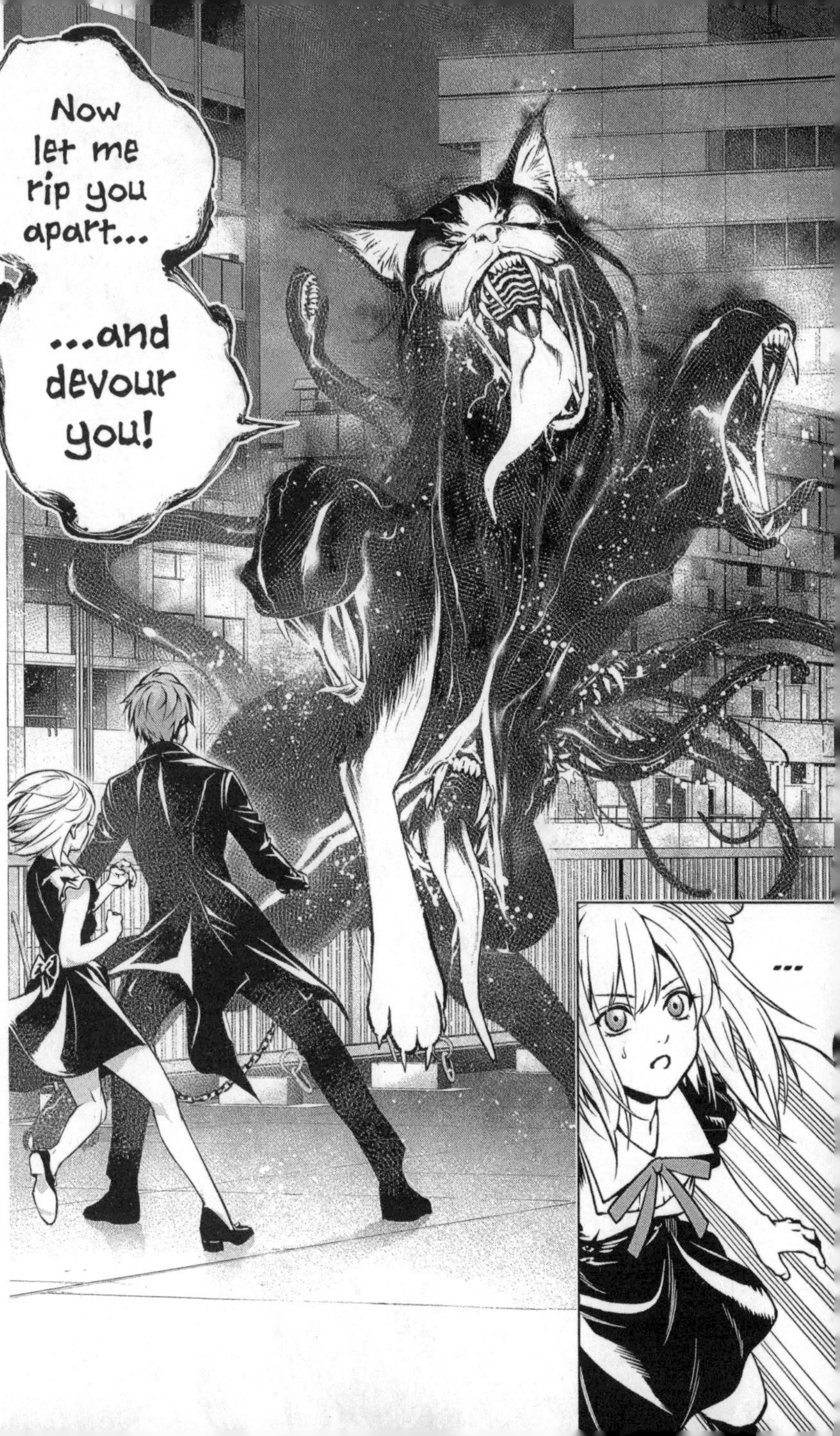
Now let me rip you apart...
...and devour you!
...

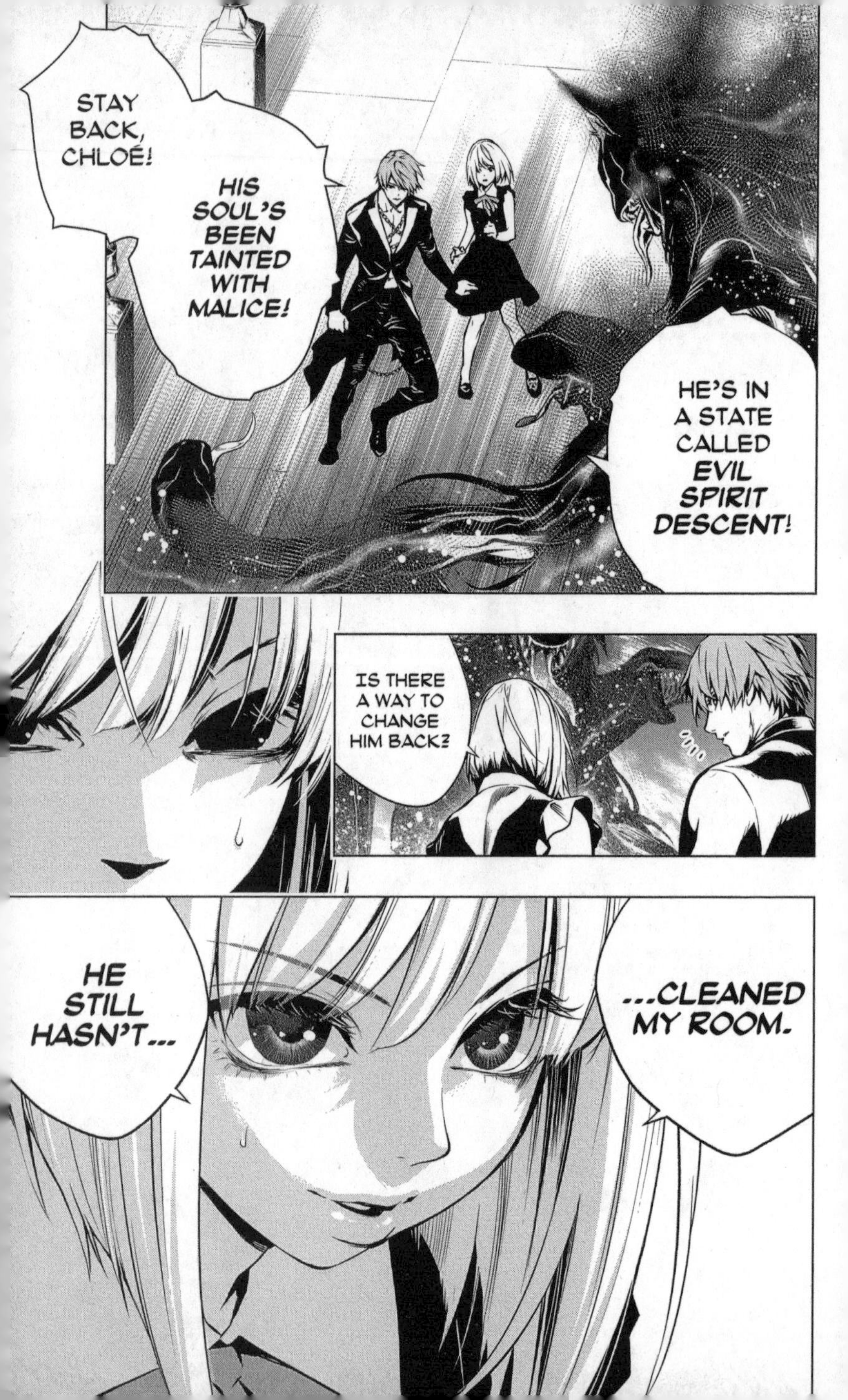
STAY BACK, CHLOÉ! HIS SOUL'S BEEN TAINTED WITH MALICE!
HE'S IN A STATE CALLED EVIL SPIRIT DESCENT!
IS THERE A WAY TO CHANGE HIM BACK?
HE STILL HASN'T...
...CLEANED MY ROOM.

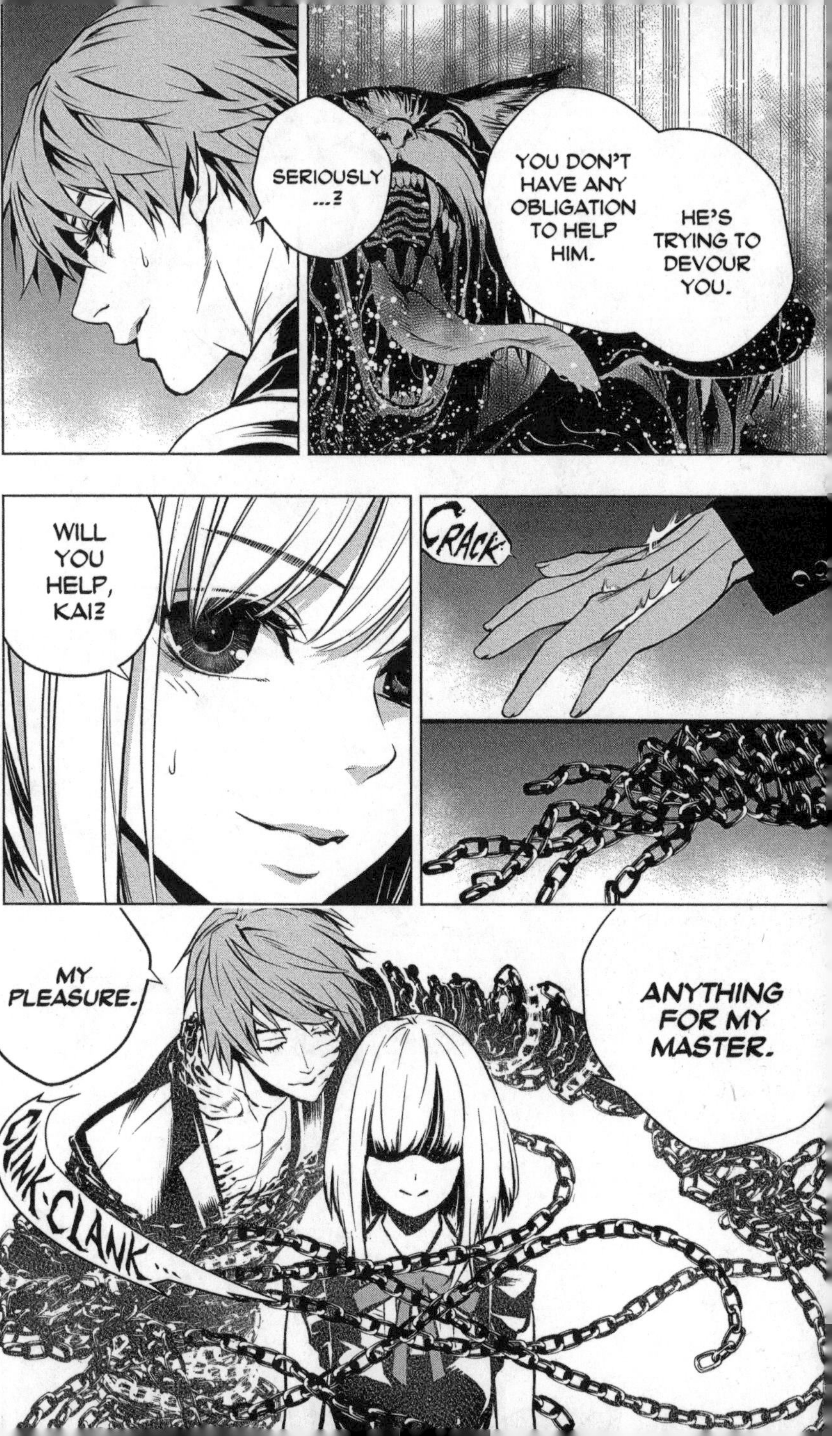
HE'S TRYING TO DEVOUR YOU.
YOU DON'T HAVE ANY OBLIGATION TO HELP HIM.
SERIOUSLY ...?
CRACK
WILL YOU HELP, KAI?
ANYTHING FOR MY MASTER.
MY PLEASURE.
CLINK-CLANK...

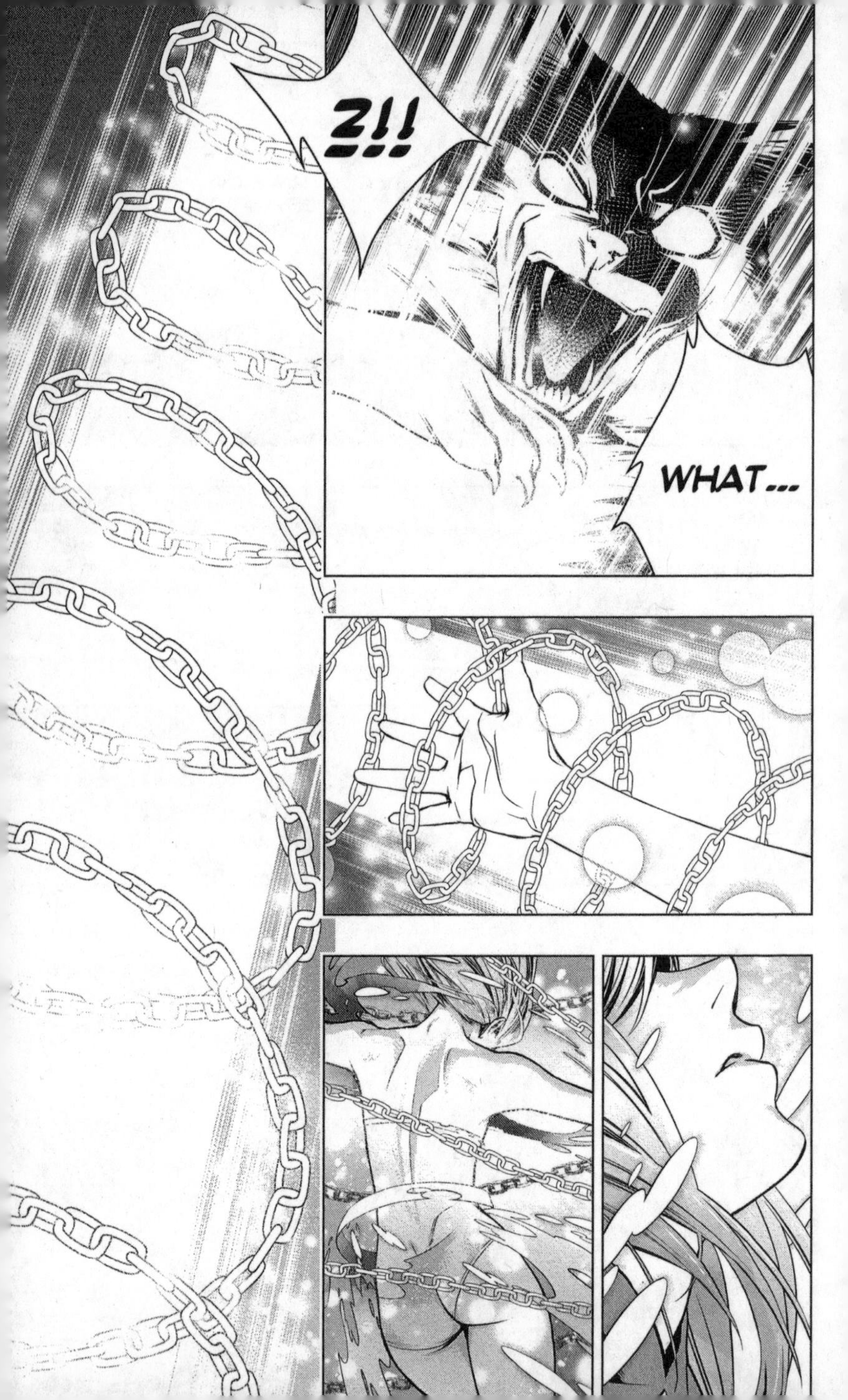

?!!
WHAT...

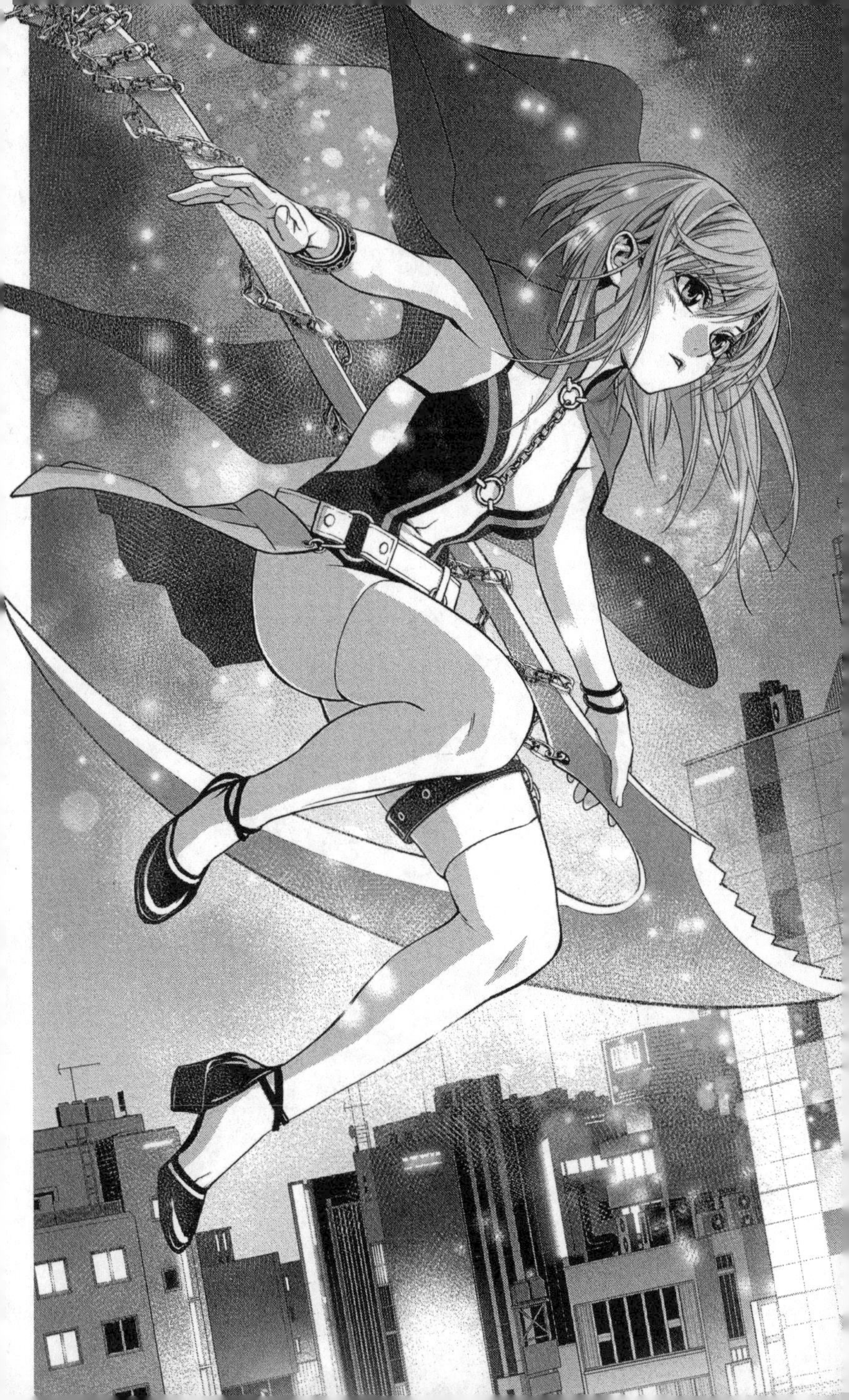

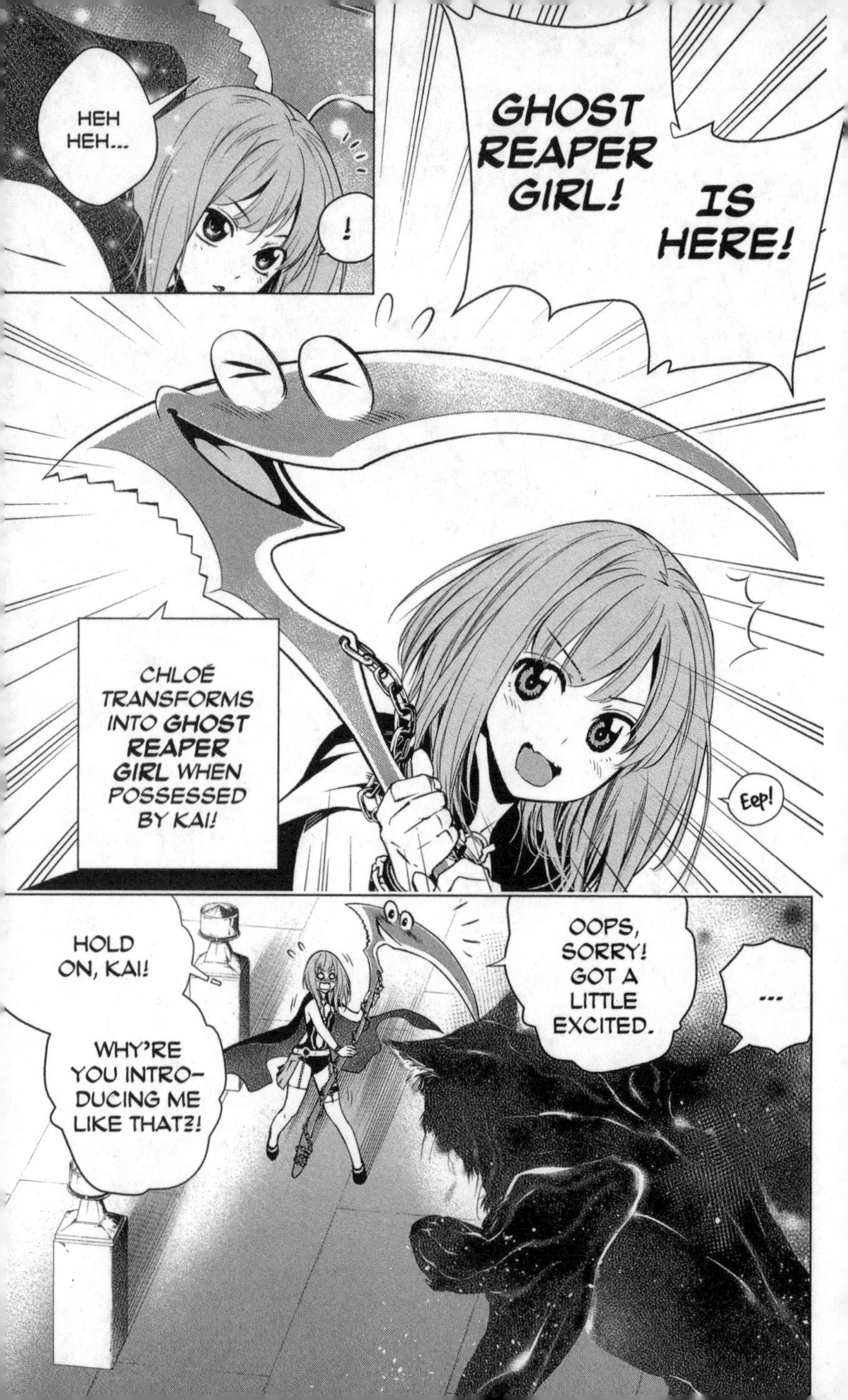
HEH HEH...
!
GHOST REAPER GIRL!
IS HERE!
CHLOÉ TRANSFORMS INTO GHOST REAPER GIRL WHEN POSSESSED BY KAI!
Eep!
HOLD ON, KAI!
WHY'RE YOU INTRO-DUCING ME LIKE THAT?!
OOPS, SORRY! GOT A LITTLE EXCITED.
...

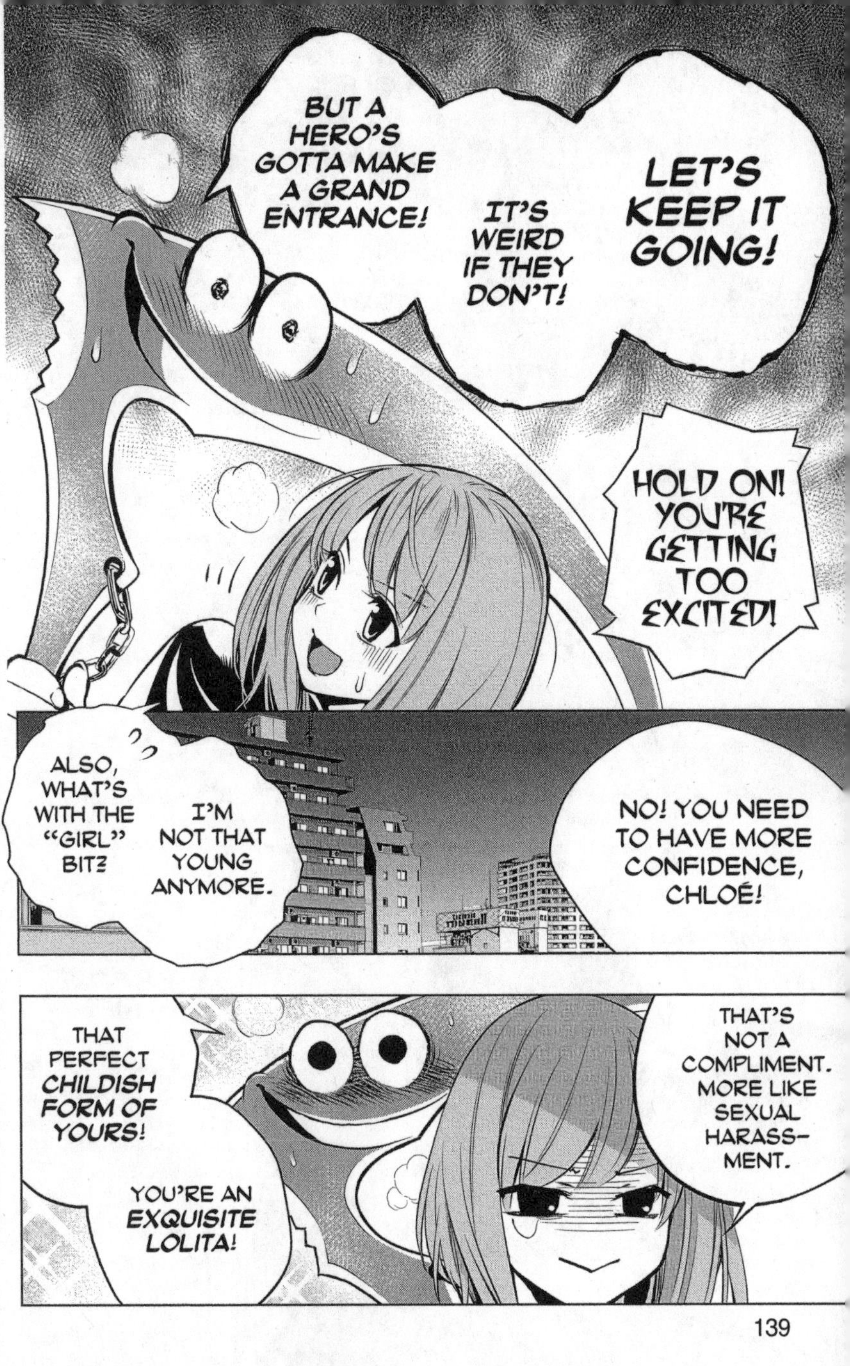
BUT A HERO'S GOTTA MAKE A GRAND ENTRANCE!
IT'S WEIRD IF THEY DON'T!
LET'S KEEP IT GOING!
HOLD ON! YOU'RE GETTING TOO EXCITED!
NO! YOU NEED TO HAVE MORE CONFIDENCE, CHLOÉ!
ALSO, WHAT'S WITH THE "GIRL" BIT?
I'M NOT THAT YOUNG ANYMORE.
THAT PERFECT CHILDISH FORM OF YOURS!
YOU'RE AN EXQUISITE LOLITA!
THAT'S NOT A COMPLIMENT. MORE LIKE SEXUAL HARASS-MENT.

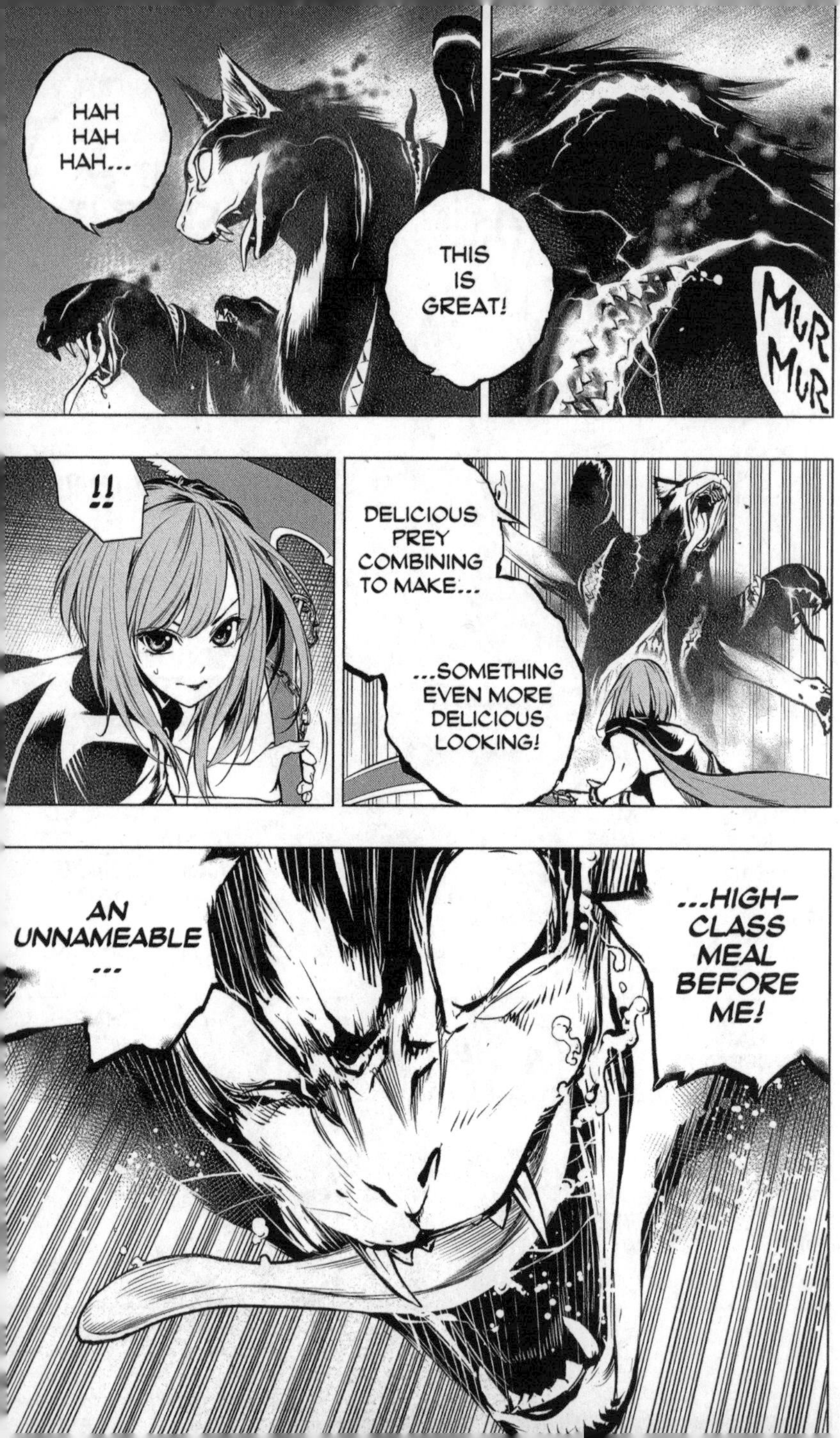
HAH HAH HAH...
THIS IS GREAT!
MUR MUR
!!
DELICIOUS PREY COMBINING TO MAKE...
...SOMETHING EVEN MORE DELICIOUS LOOKING!
AN UNNAMEABLE...
...HIGH-CLASS MEAL BEFORE ME!

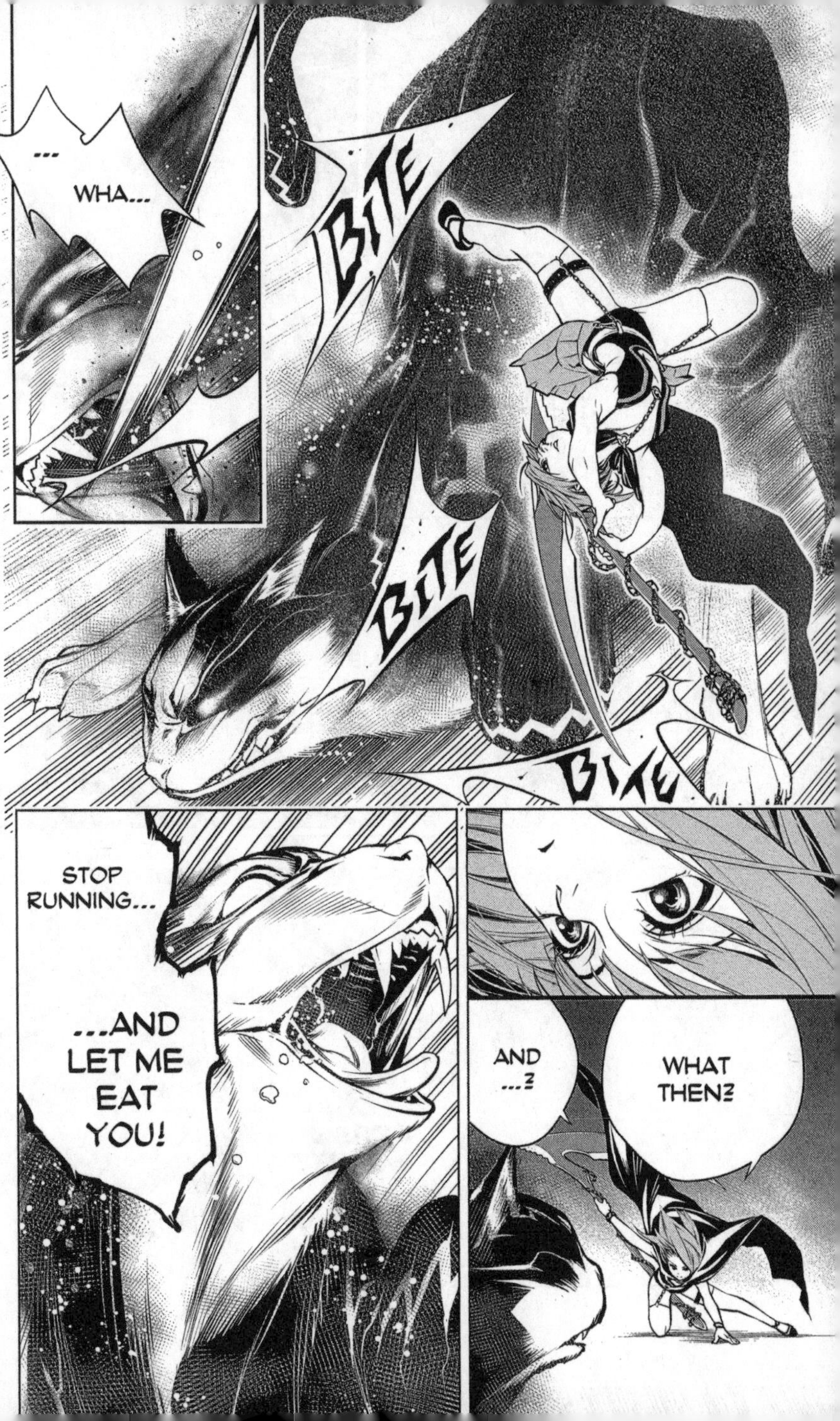
BITE
...
WHA...
BITE
BITE
STOP RUNNING...
...AND LET ME EAT YOU!
WHAT THEN?
AND ...?

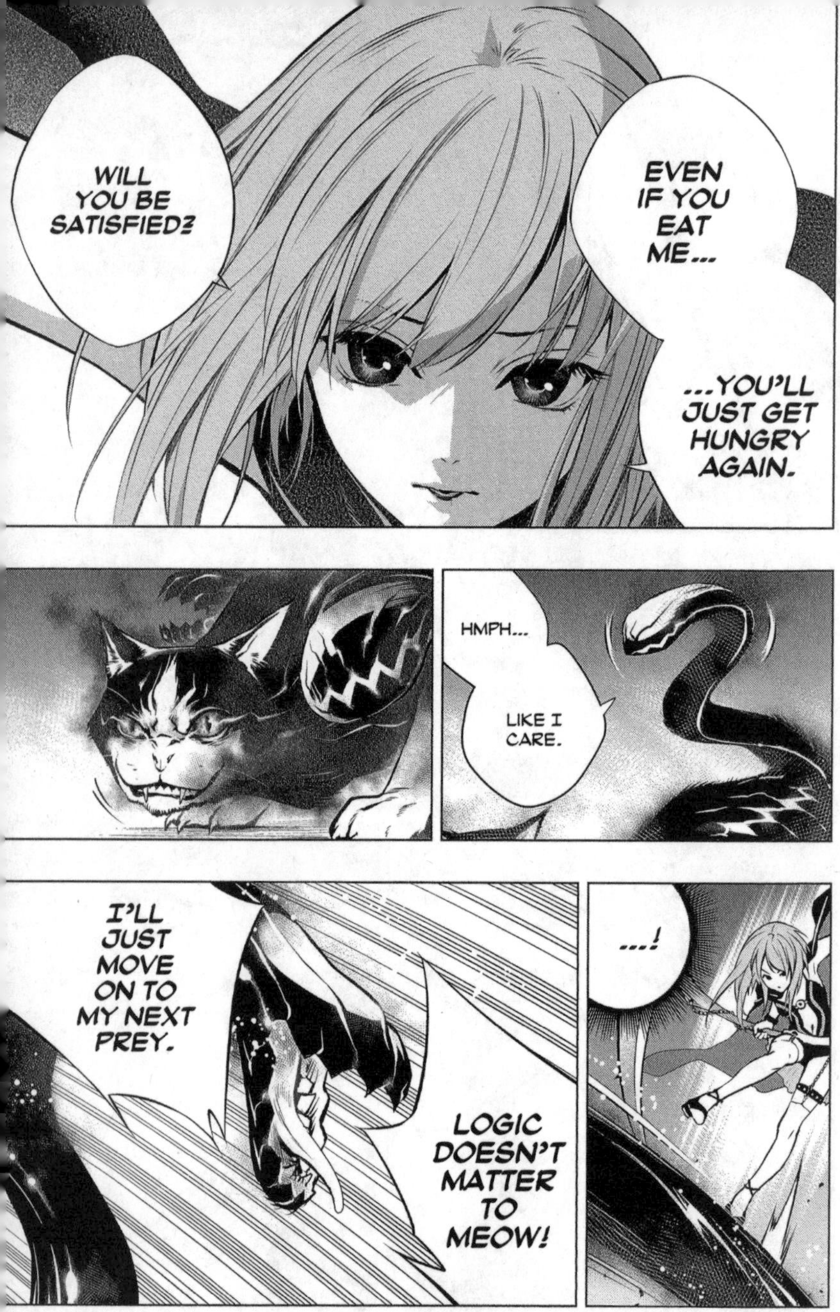
EVEN IF YOU EAT ME...
WILL YOU BE SATISFIED?
...YOU'LL JUST GET HUNGRY AGAIN.
HMPH...
LIKE I CARE.
...!
I'LL JUST MOVE ON TO MY NEXT PREY.
LOGIC DOESN'T MATTER TO MEOW!

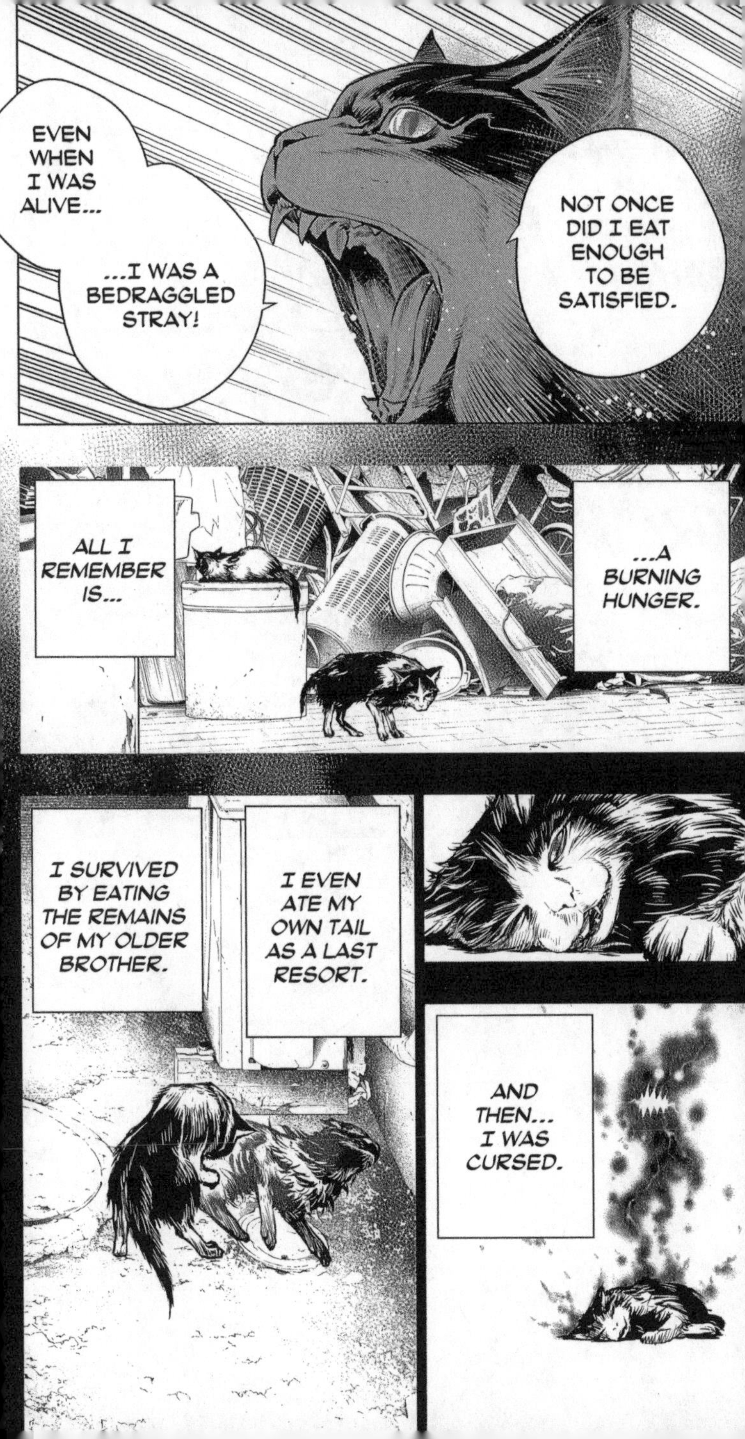
EVEN WHEN I WAS ALIVE...
...I WAS A BEDRAGGLED STRAY!
NOT ONCE DID I EAT ENOUGH TO BE SATISFIED.
ALL I REMEMBER IS...
...A BURNING HUNGER.
I SURVIVED BY EATING THE REMAINS OF MY OLDER BROTHER.
I EVEN ATE MY OWN TAIL AS A LAST RESORT.
AND THEN... I WAS CURSED.

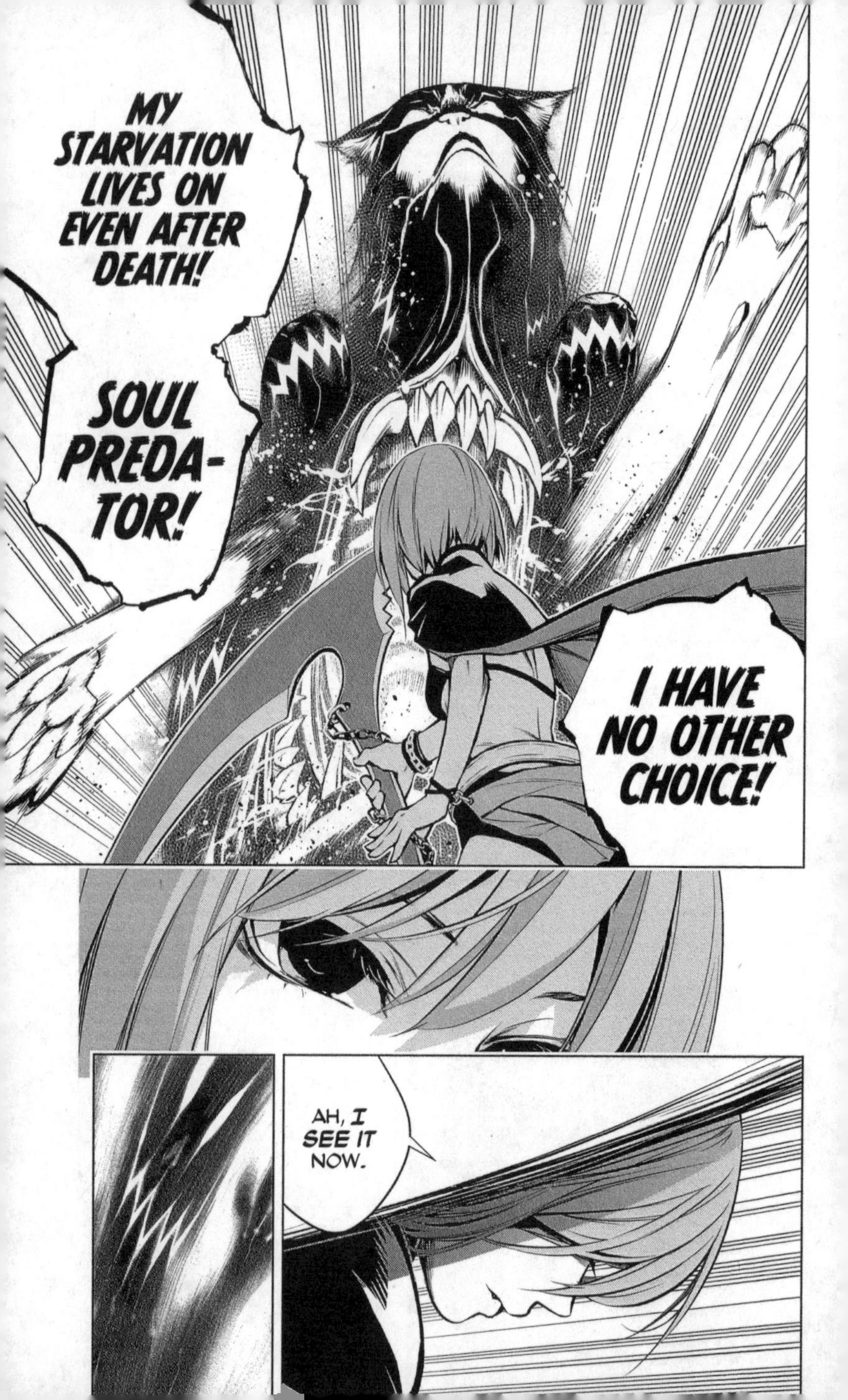
MY STARVATION LIVES ON EVEN AFTER DEATH!
SOUL PREDA-TOR!
I HAVE NO OTHER CHOICE!
AH, I SEE IT NOW.

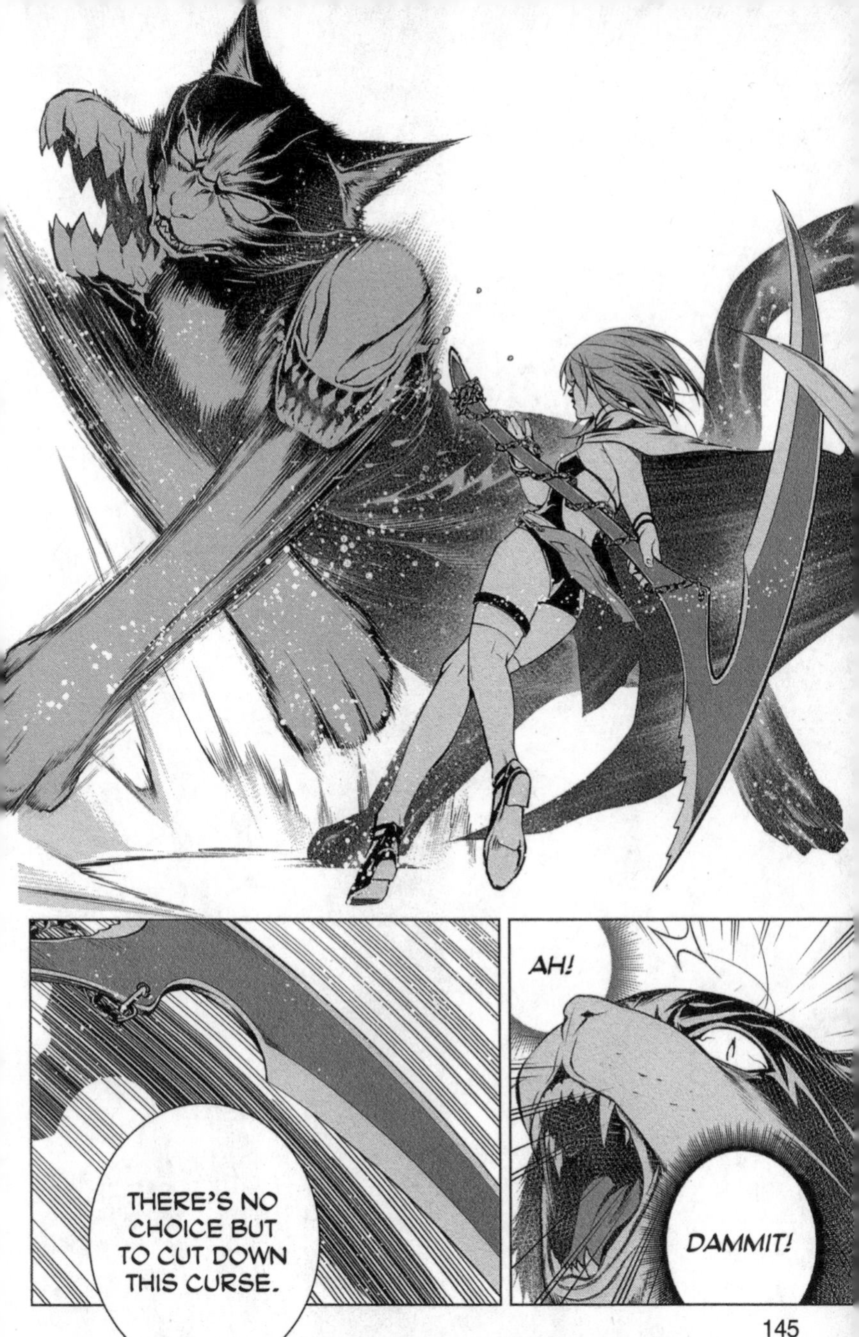
AH!
DAMMIT!
THERE'S NO CHOICE BUT TO CUT DOWN THIS CURSE.

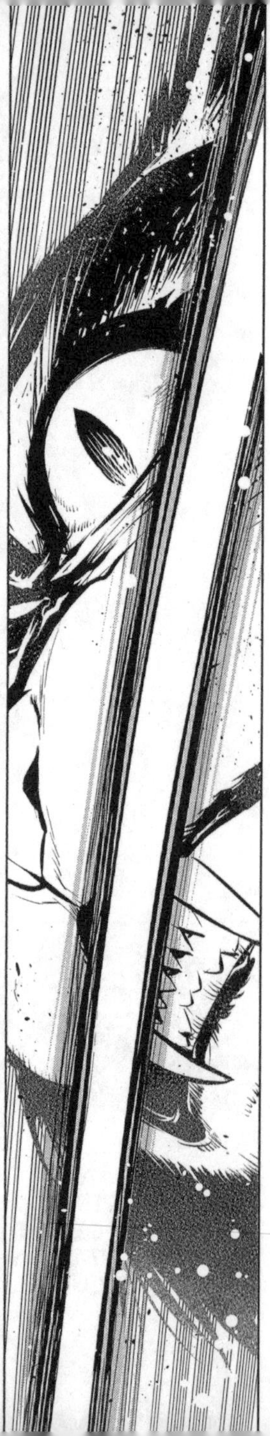
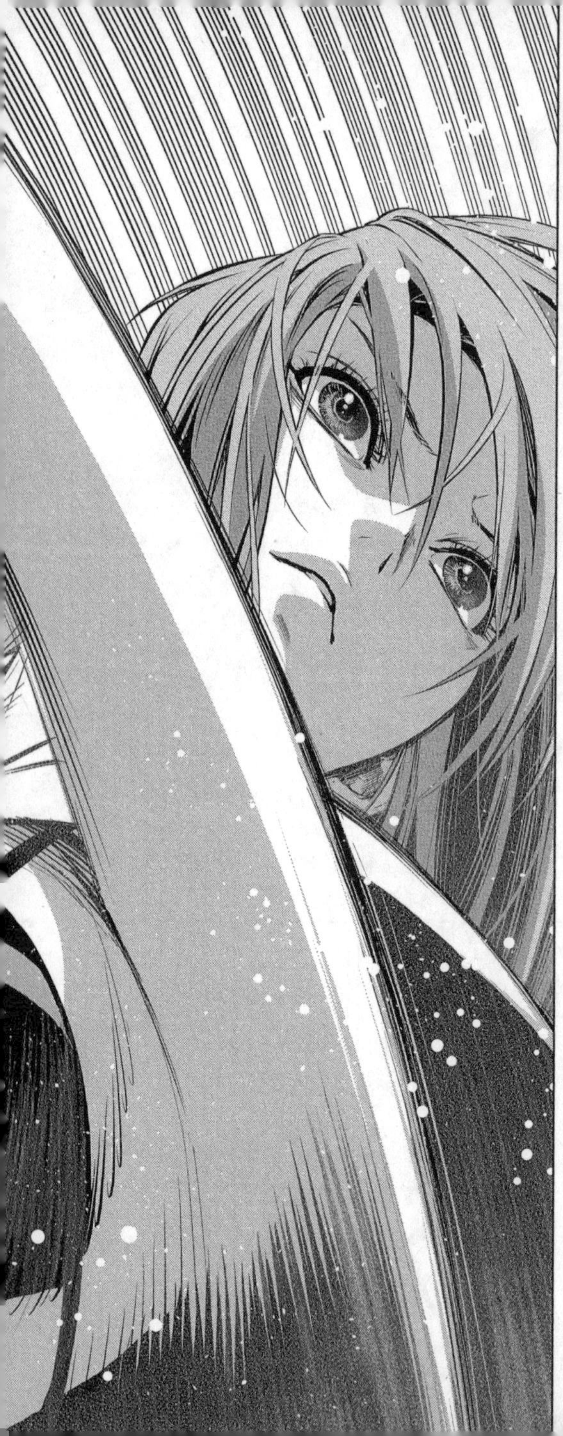

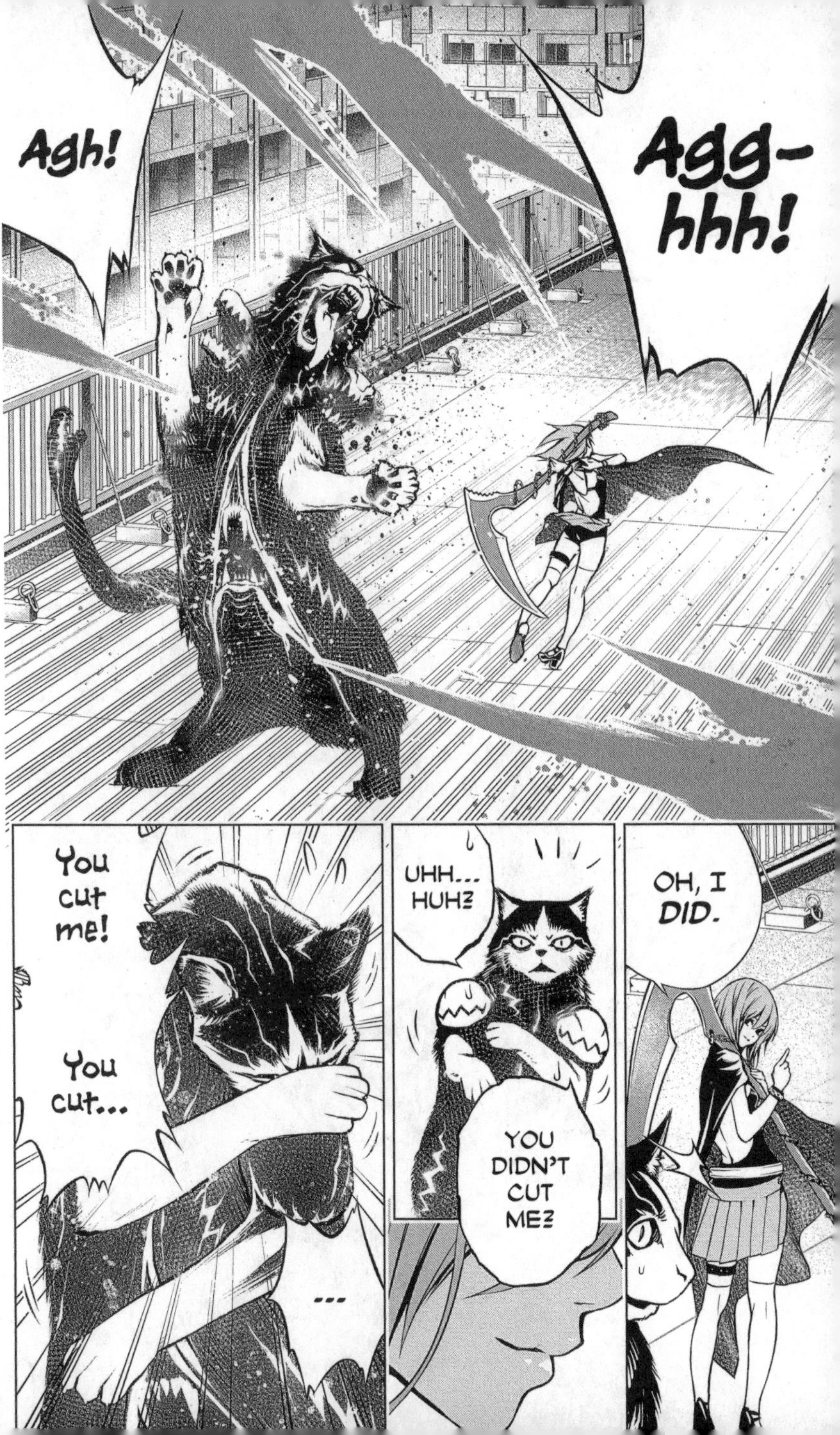
Agg-hhh!
Agh!
OH, I DID.
UHH... HUH?
YOU DIDN'T CUT ME?
You cut me!
You cut...
...

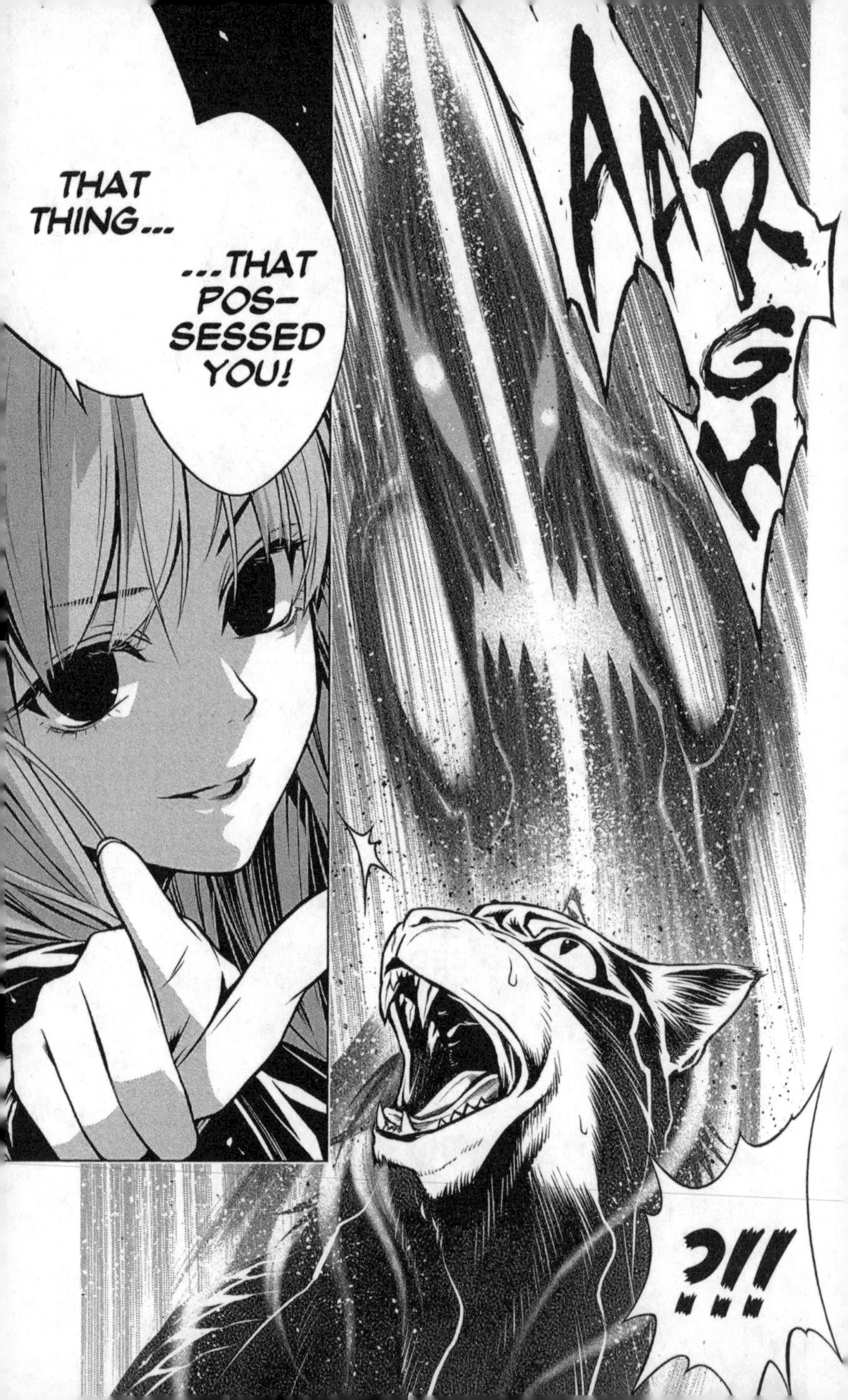
THAT THING...
...THAT POS-SESSED YOU!
AARGH
?!!

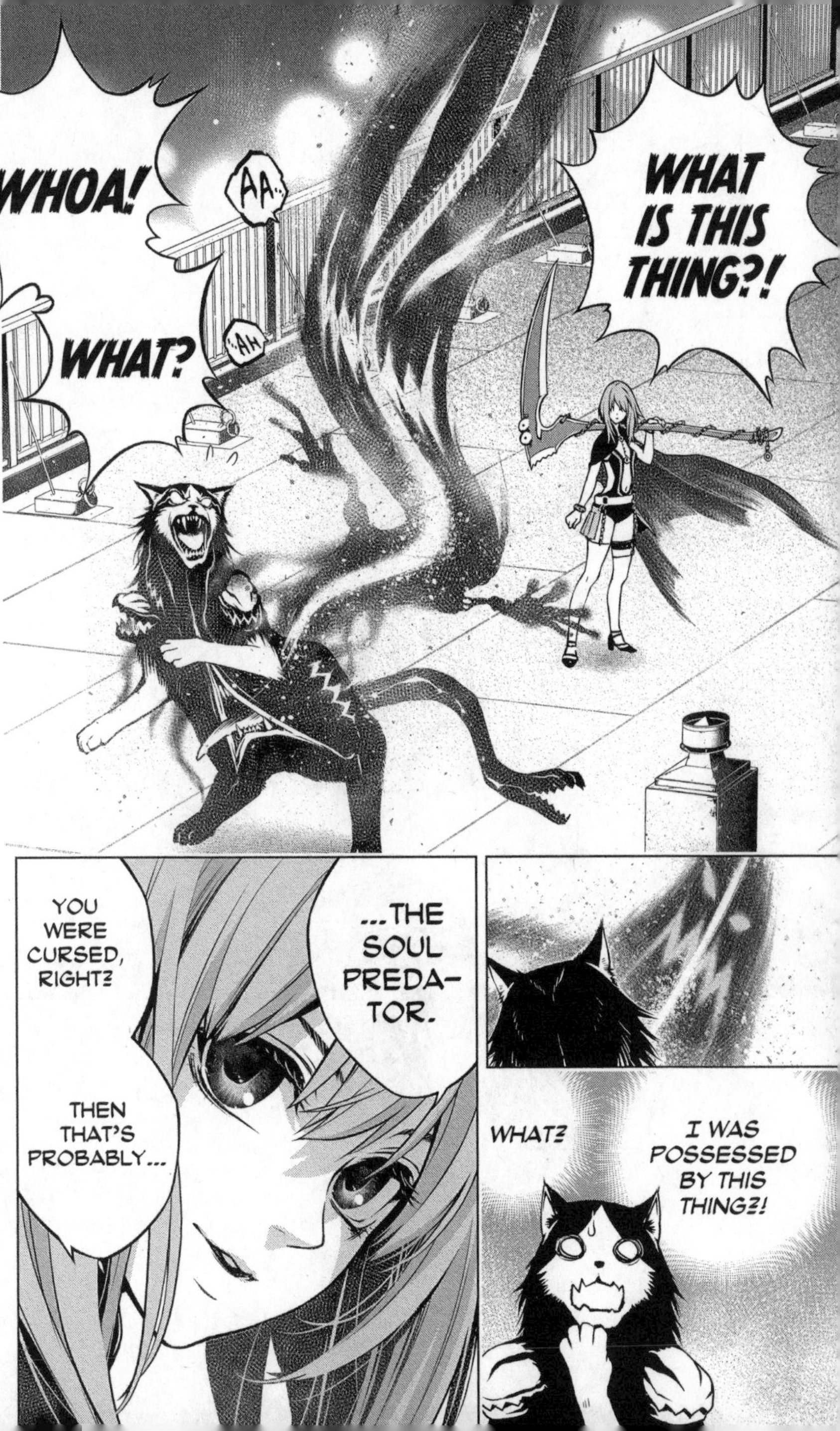
WHAT IS THIS THING?!
WHOA!
AA..
WHAT?
..AH
WHAT?
I WAS POSSESSED BY THIS THING?!
YOU WERE CURSED, RIGHT?
THEN THAT'S PROBABLY...
...THE SOUL PREDATOR.

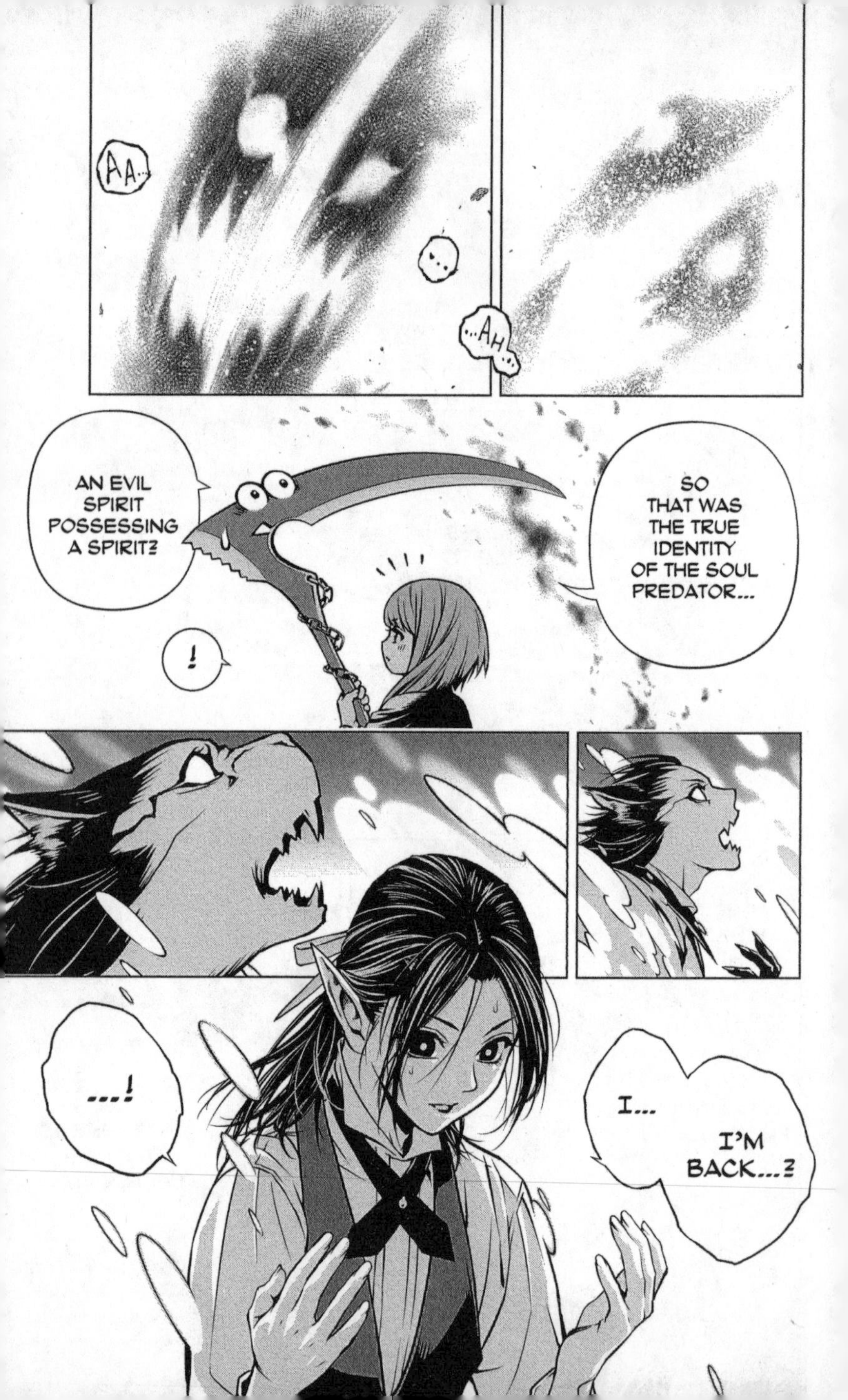
AA...
...AH...
SO THAT WAS THE TRUE IDENTITY OF THE SOUL PREDATOR...
AN EVIL SPIRIT POSSESSING A SPIRIT?
!
I... I'M BACK...?
...!

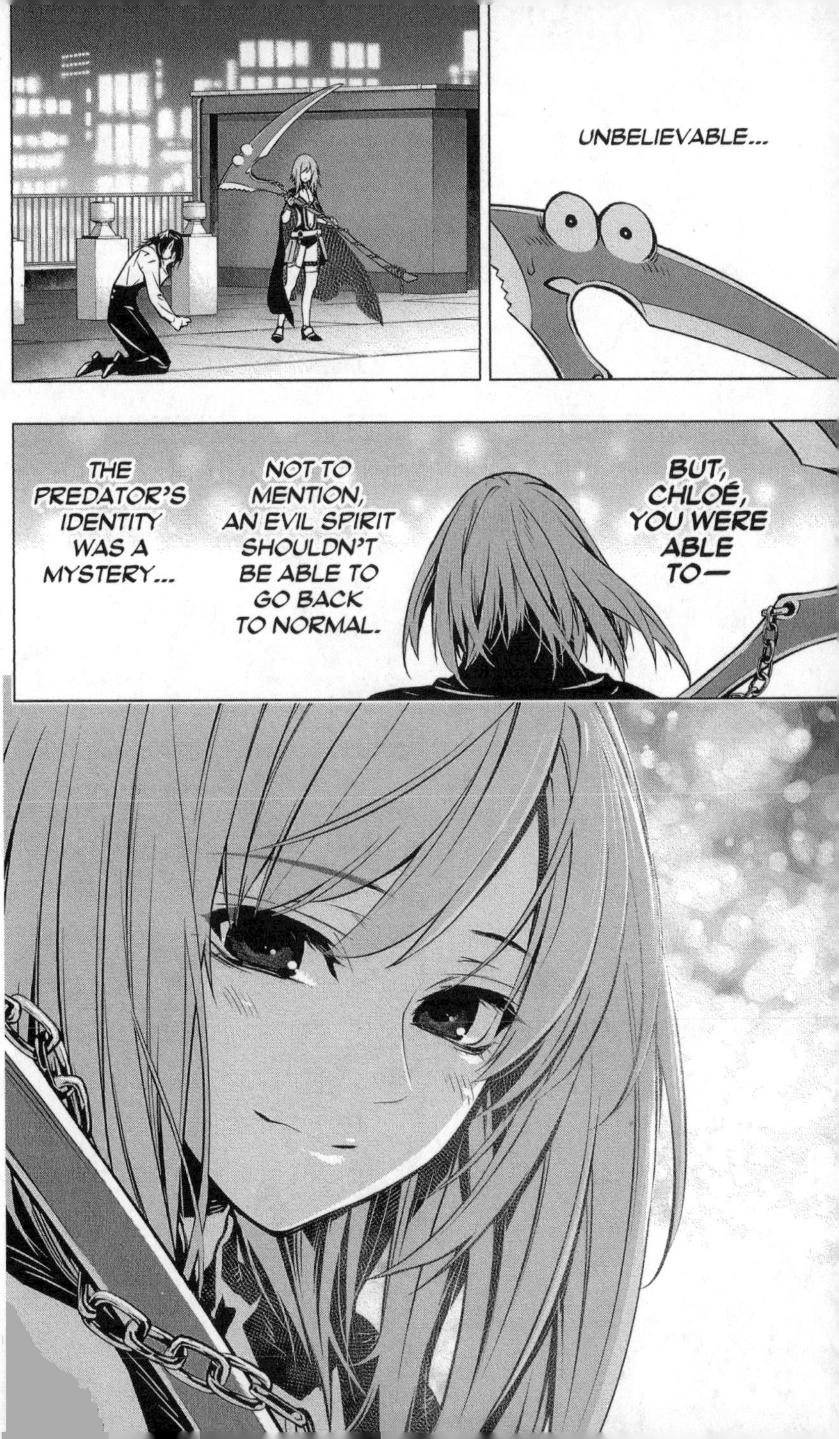
UNBELIEVABLE...
BUT, CHLOÉ, YOU WERE ABLE TO—
NOT TO MENTION, AN EVIL SPIRIT SHOULDN'T BE ABLE TO GO BACK TO NORMAL.
THE PREDATOR'S IDENTITY WAS A MYSTERY...

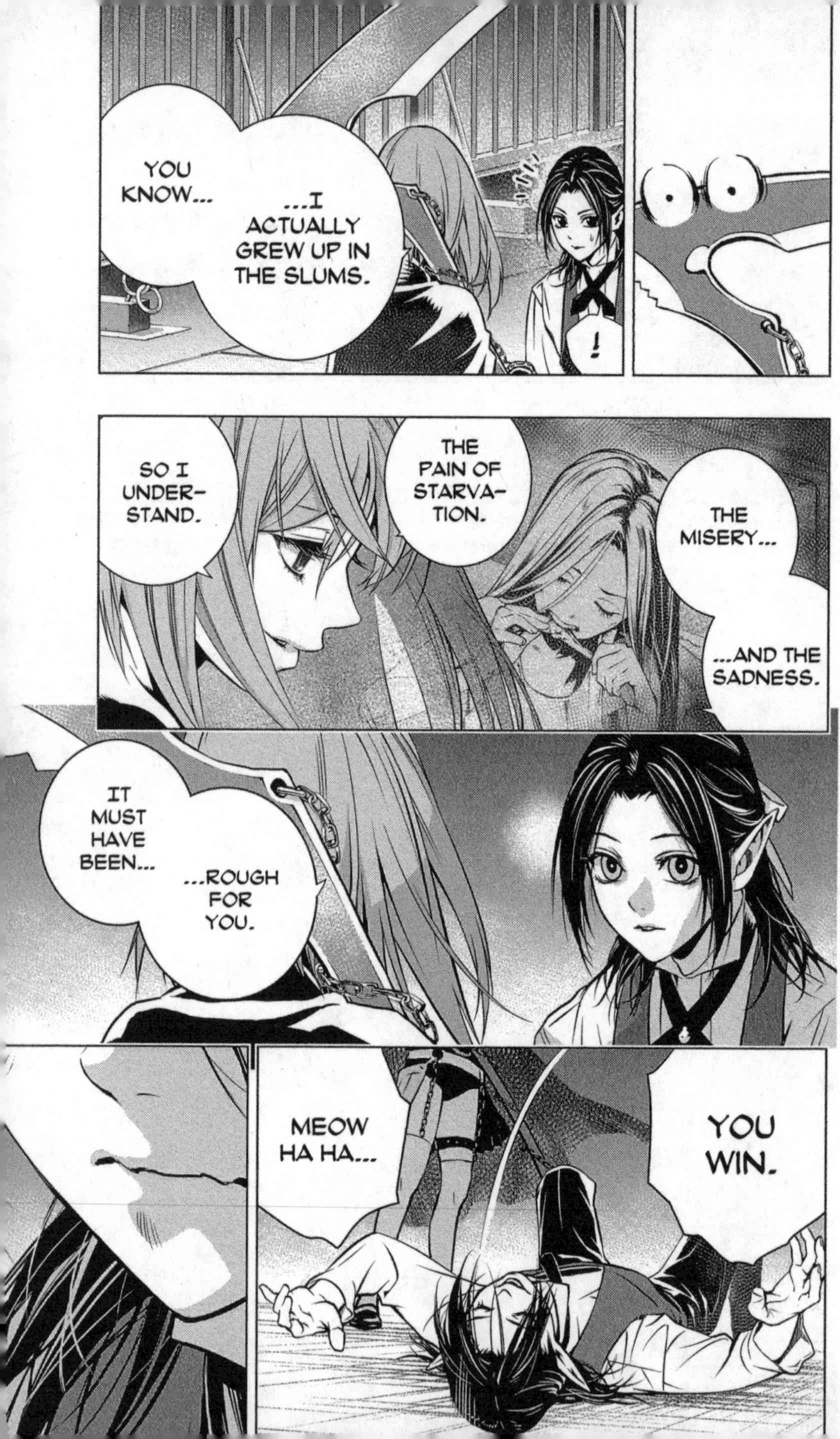
YOU KNOW...
...I ACTUALLY GREW UP IN THE SLUMS.
!
THE MISERY...
...AND THE SADNESS.
THE PAIN OF STARVATION.
SO I UNDERSTAND.
IT MUST HAVE BEEN...
...ROUGH FOR YOU.
YOU WIN.
MEOW HA HA...

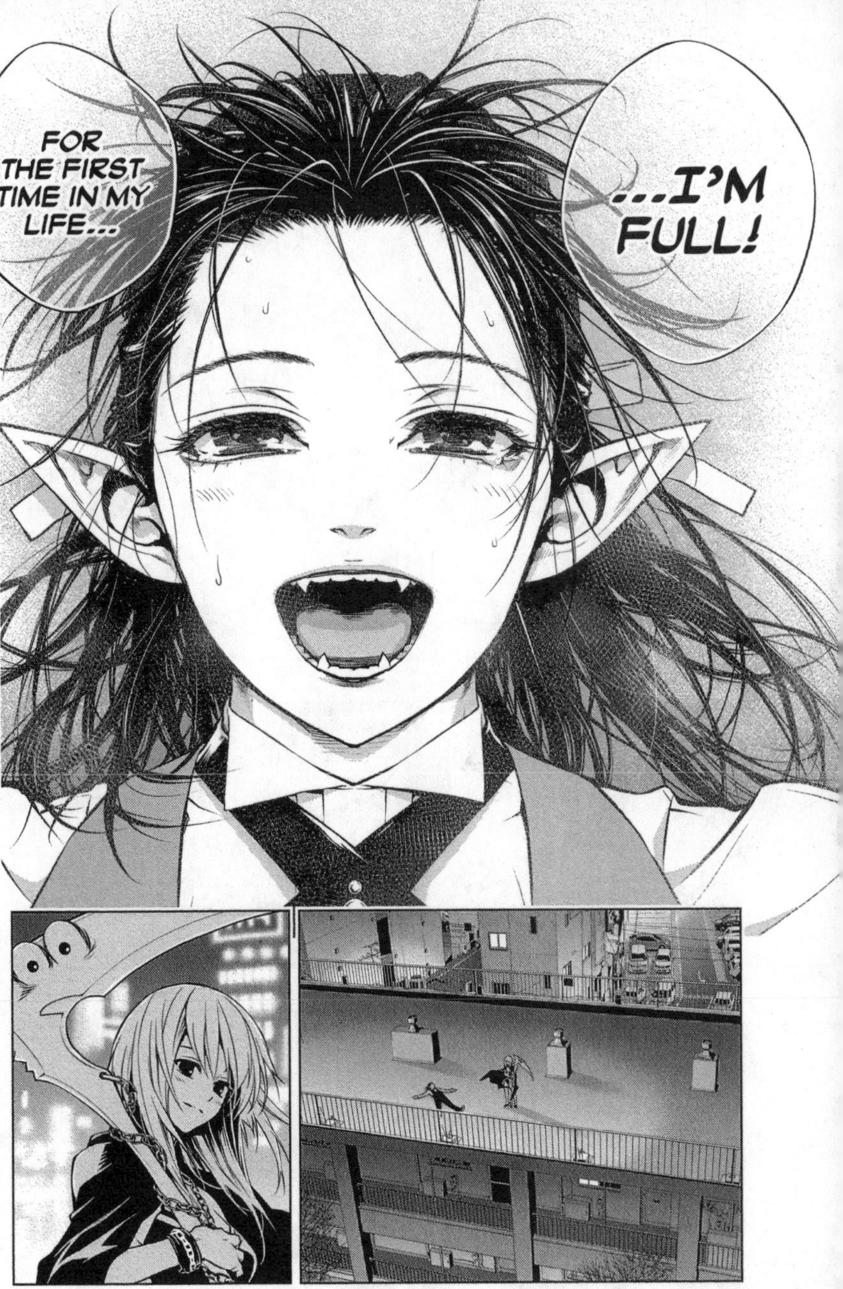
...I'M FULL!
FOR THE FIRST TIME IN MY LIFE...

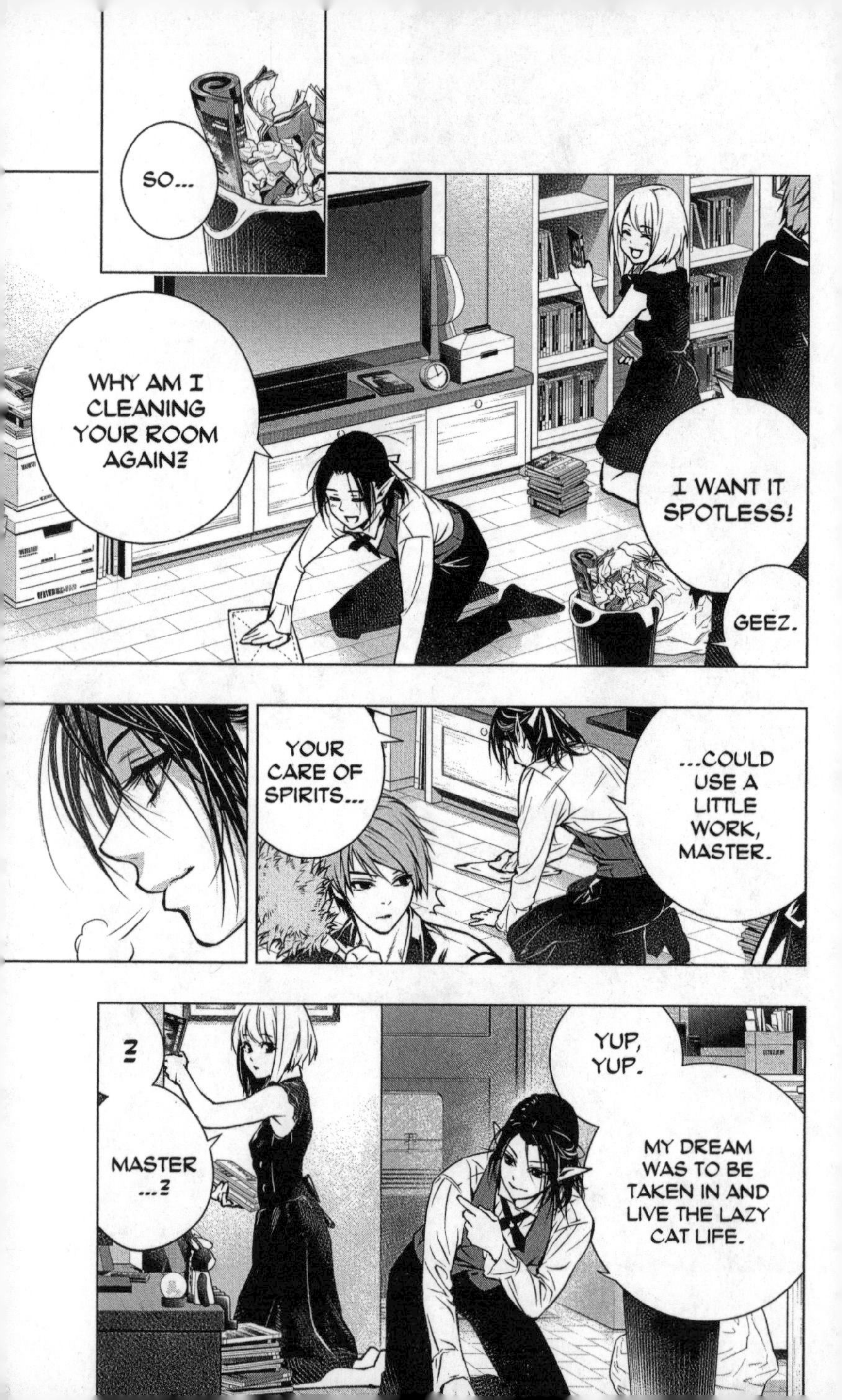
SO...
WHY AM I CLEANING YOUR ROOM AGAIN?
I WANT IT SPOTLESS!
GEEZ.
YOUR CARE OF SPIRITS...
...COULD USE A LITTLE WORK, MASTER.
YUP, YUP.
MY DREAM WAS TO BE TAKEN IN AND LIVE THE LAZY CAT LIFE.
?
MASTER ...?

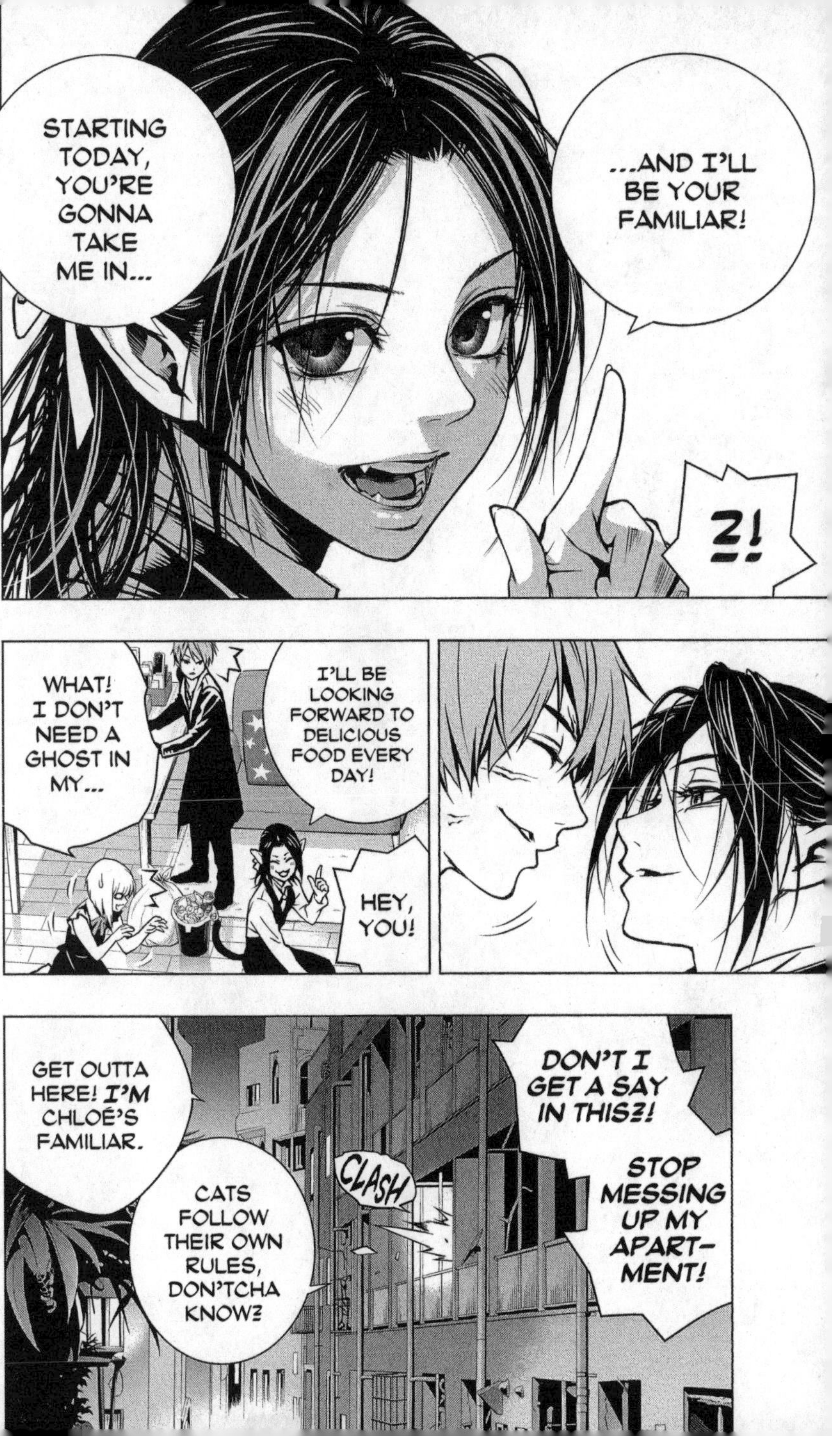
STARTING TODAY, YOU'RE GONNA TAKE ME IN...
...AND I'LL BE YOUR FAMILIAR!
?!
WHAT! I DON'T NEED A GHOST IN MY...
I'LL BE LOOKING FORWARD TO DELICIOUS FOOD EVERY DAY!
HEY, YOU!
GET OUTTA HERE! I'M CHLOÉ'S FAMILIAR.
CATS FOLLOW THEIR OWN RULES, DON'TCHA KNOW?
DON'T I GET A SAY IN THIS?!
CLASH
STOP MESSING UP MY APARTMENT!

GHOST REAPER GIRL

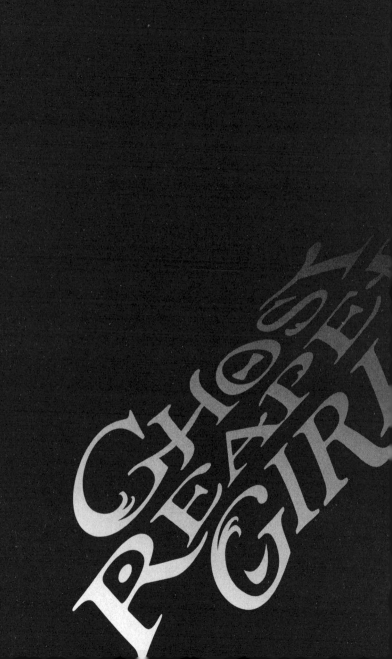

#3: Arkham Bullet

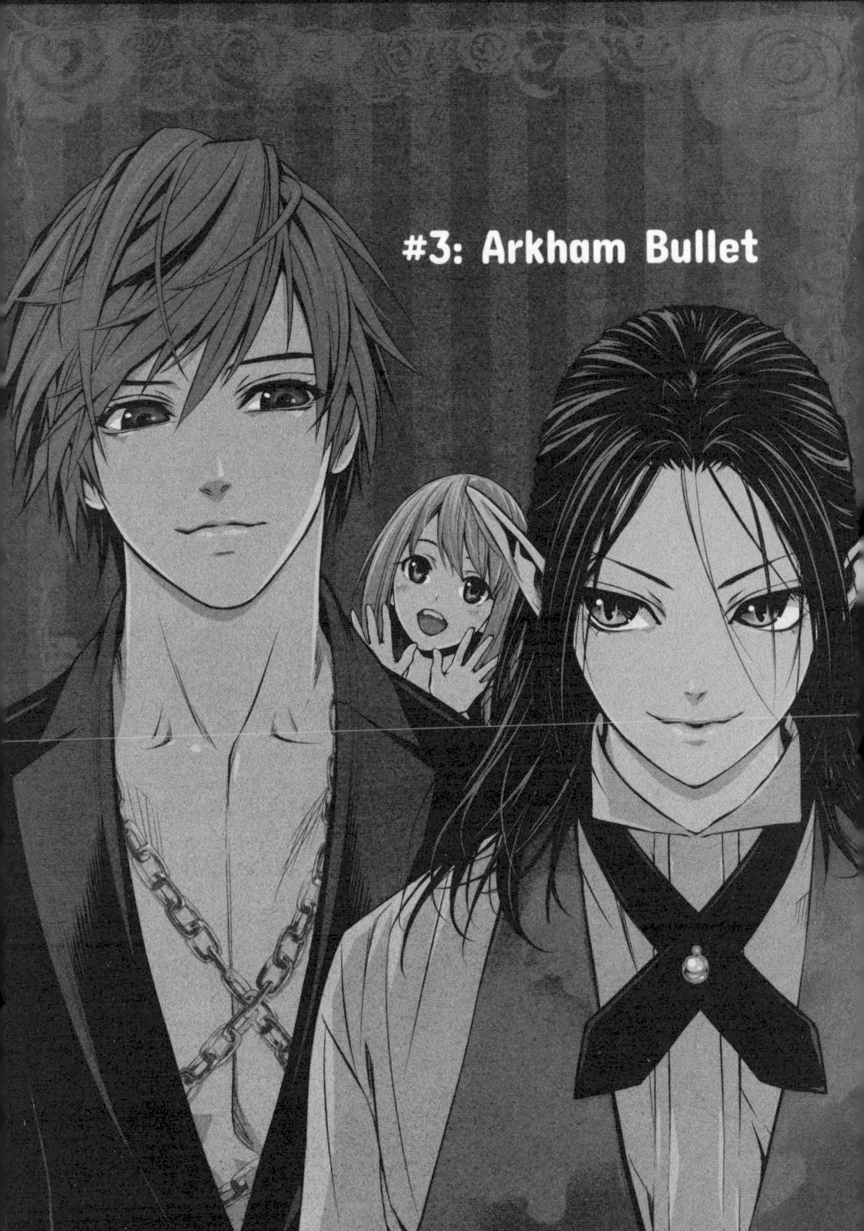

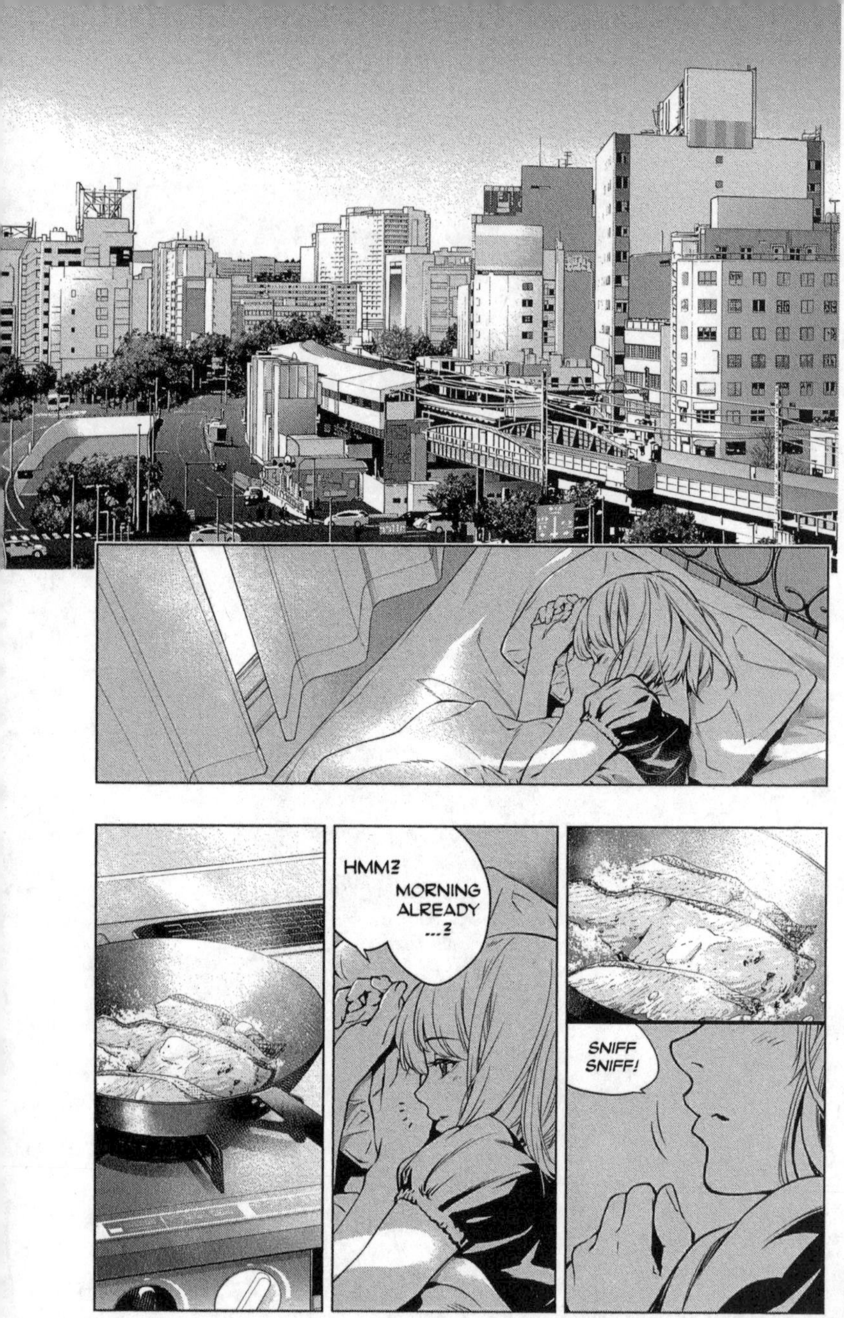
SNIFF SNIFF!
HMM? MORNING ALREADY ...?

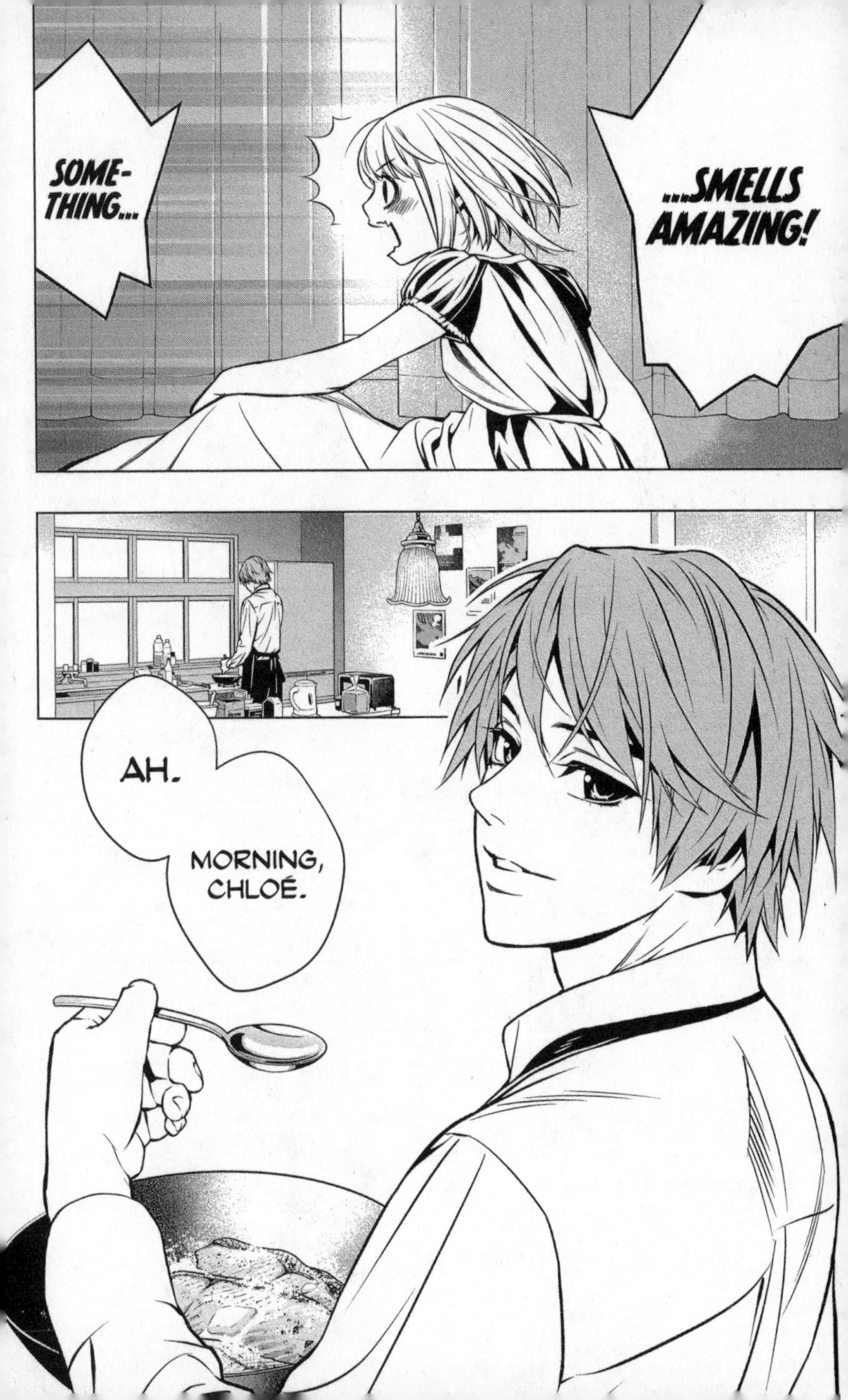
SOME-THING...
...SMELLS AMAZING!
AH.
MORNING, CHLOÉ.

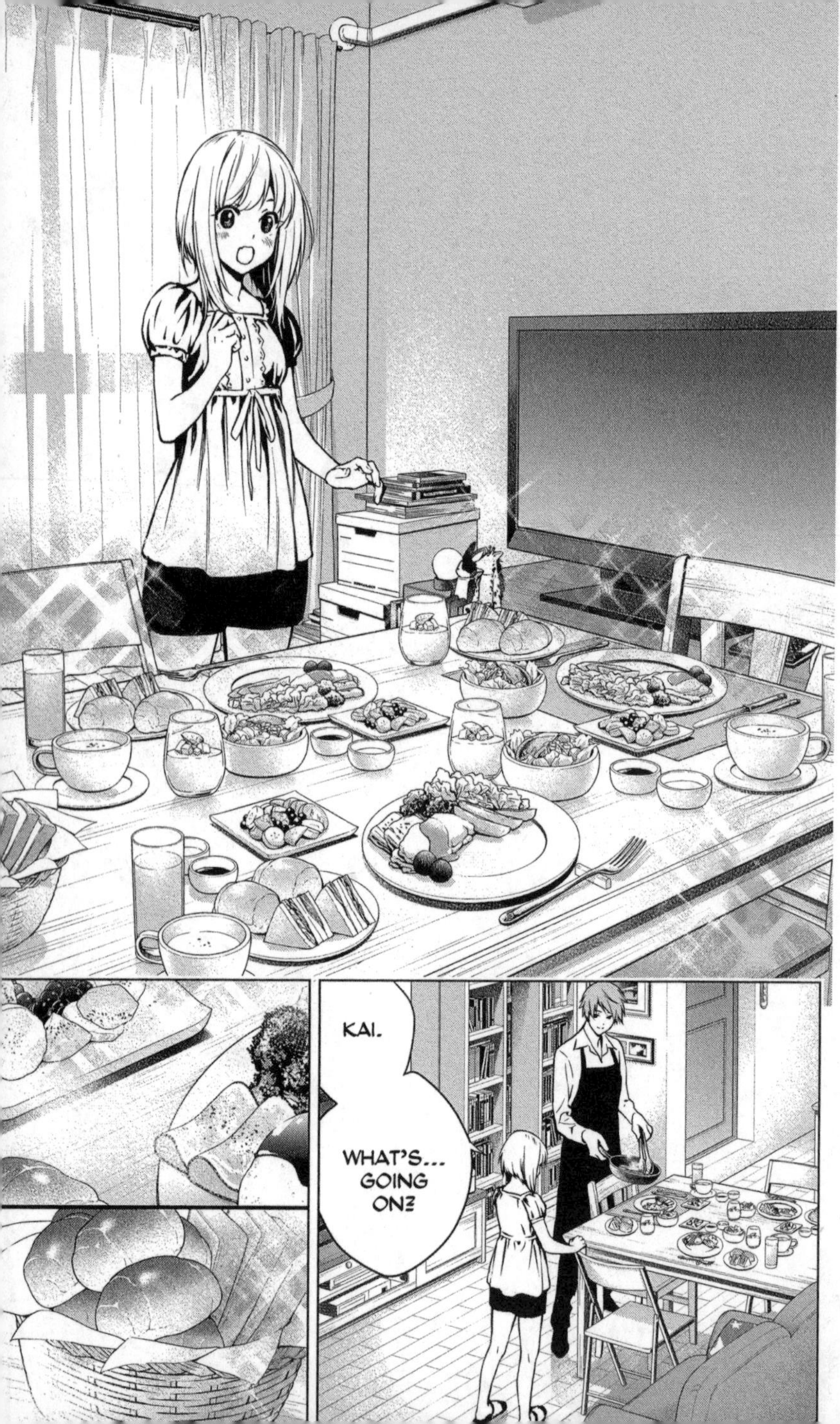
KAI.
WHAT'S... GOING ON?

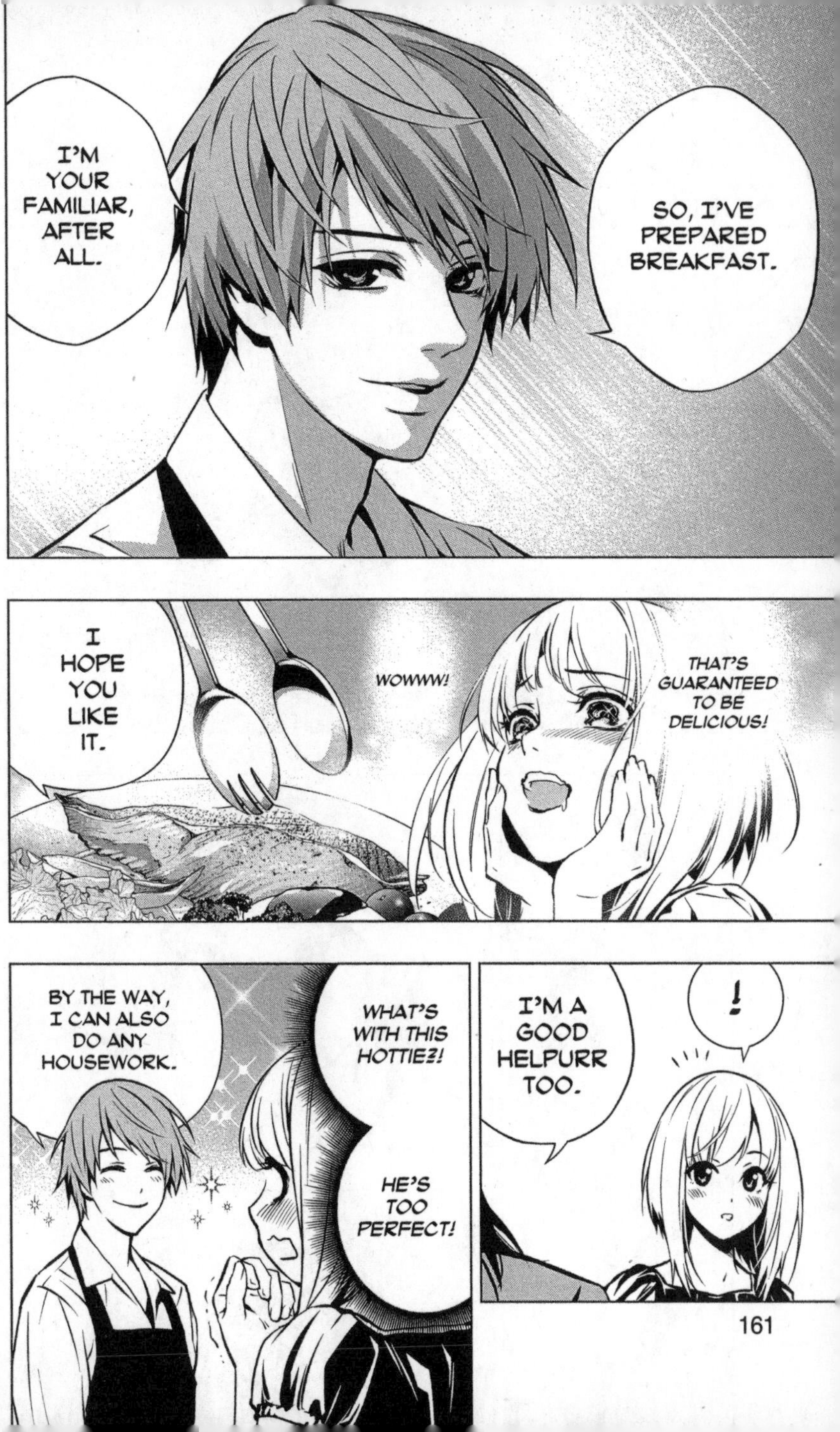
SO, I'VE PREPARED BREAKFAST.
I'M YOUR FAMILIAR, AFTER ALL.
THAT'S GUARANTEED TO BE DELICIOUS!
WOWWW!
I HOPE YOU LIKE IT.
!
I'M A GOOD HELPURR TOO.
BY THE WAY, I CAN ALSO DO ANY HOUSEWORK.
WHAT'S WITH THIS HOTTIE?!
HE'S TOO PERFECT!

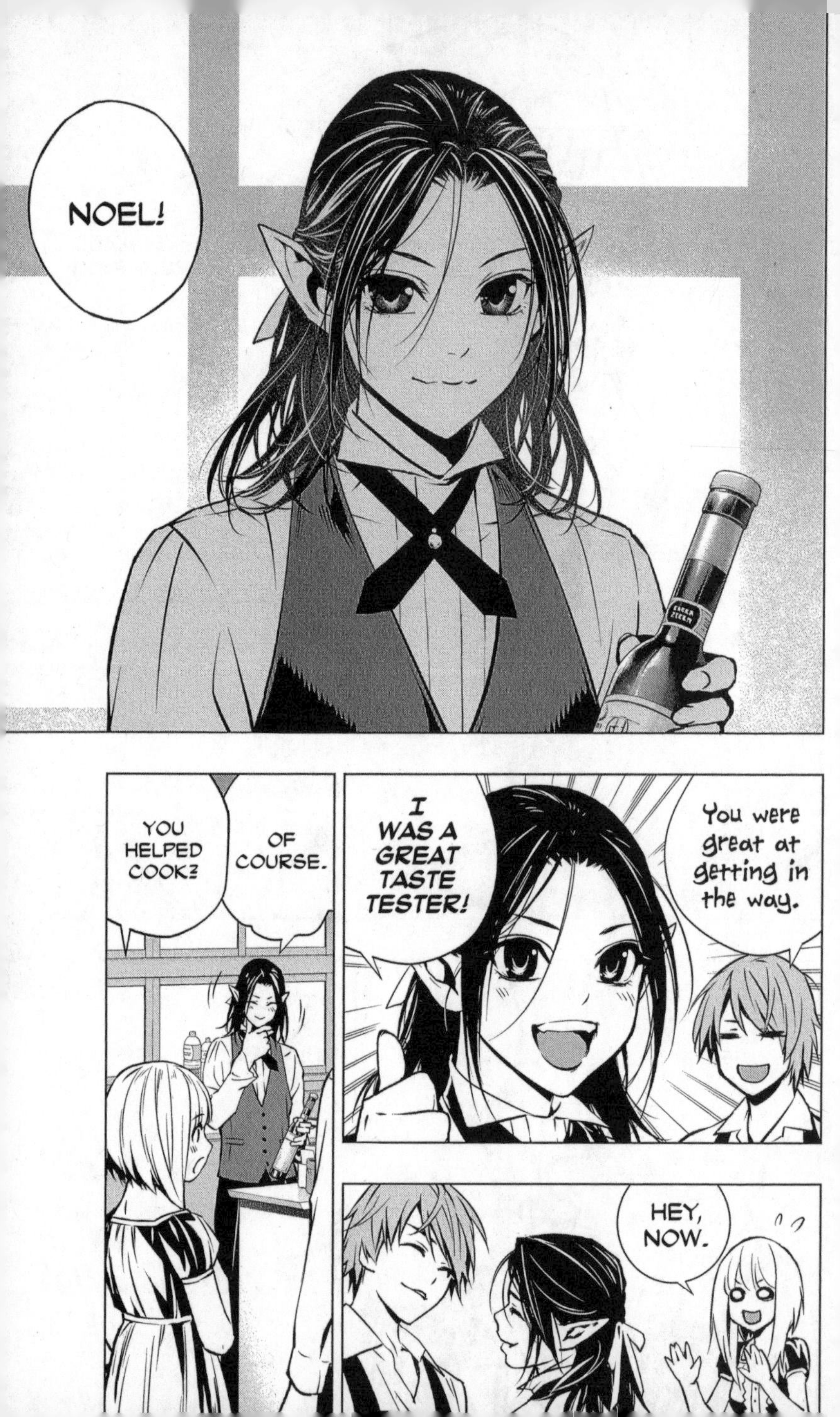
NOEL!
YOU HELPED COOK?
OF COURSE.
I WAS A GREAT TASTE TESTER!
You were great at getting in the way.
HEY, NOW.

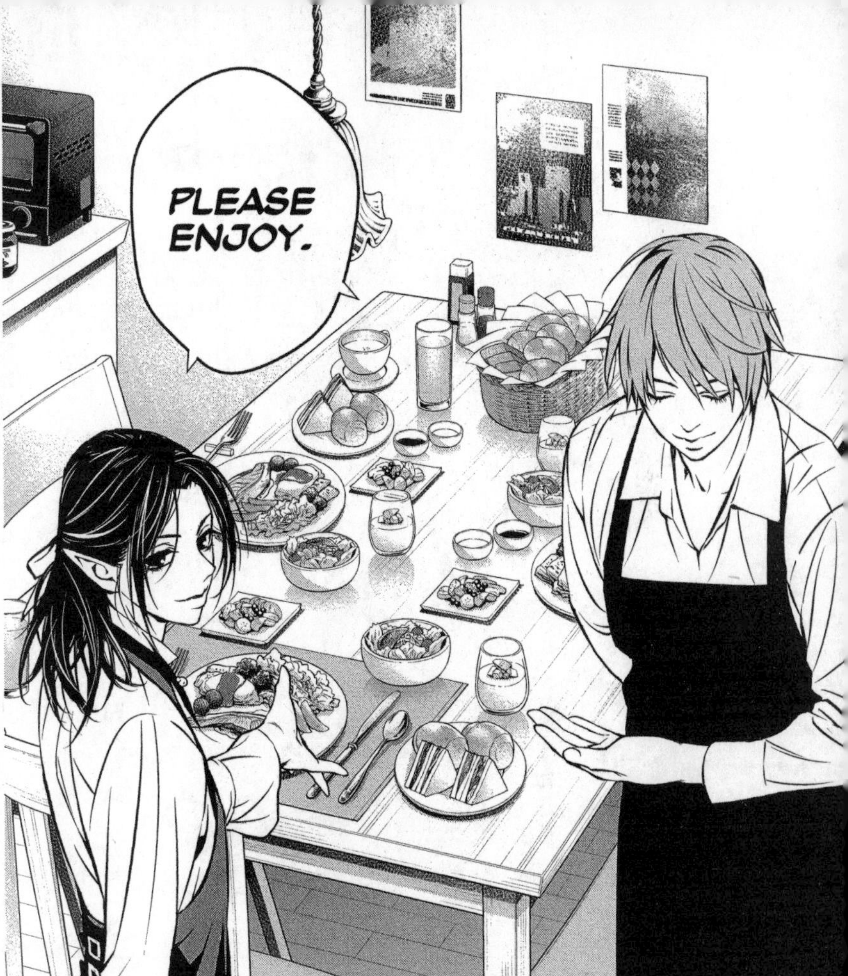
PLEASE ENJOY.

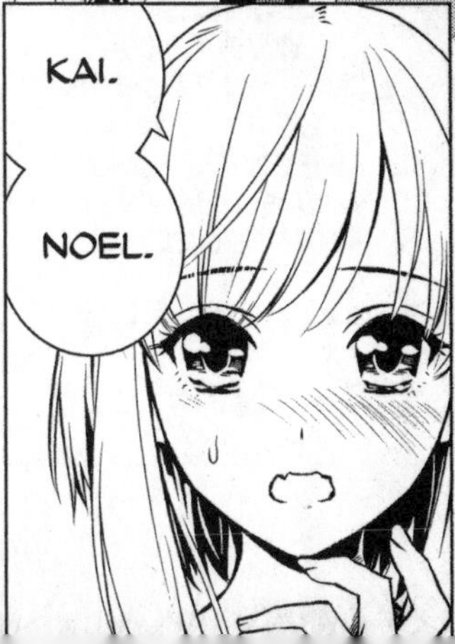
KAI.
NOEL.

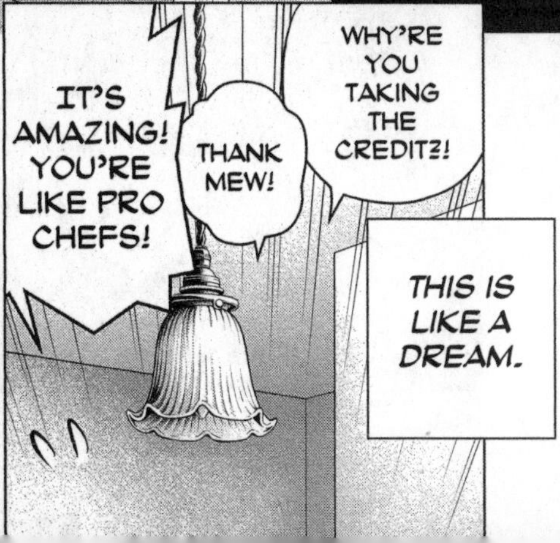
IT'S AMAZING! YOU'RE LIKE PRO CHEFS!
THANK MEW!
WHY'RE YOU TAKING THE CREDIT?!
THIS IS LIKE A DREAM.

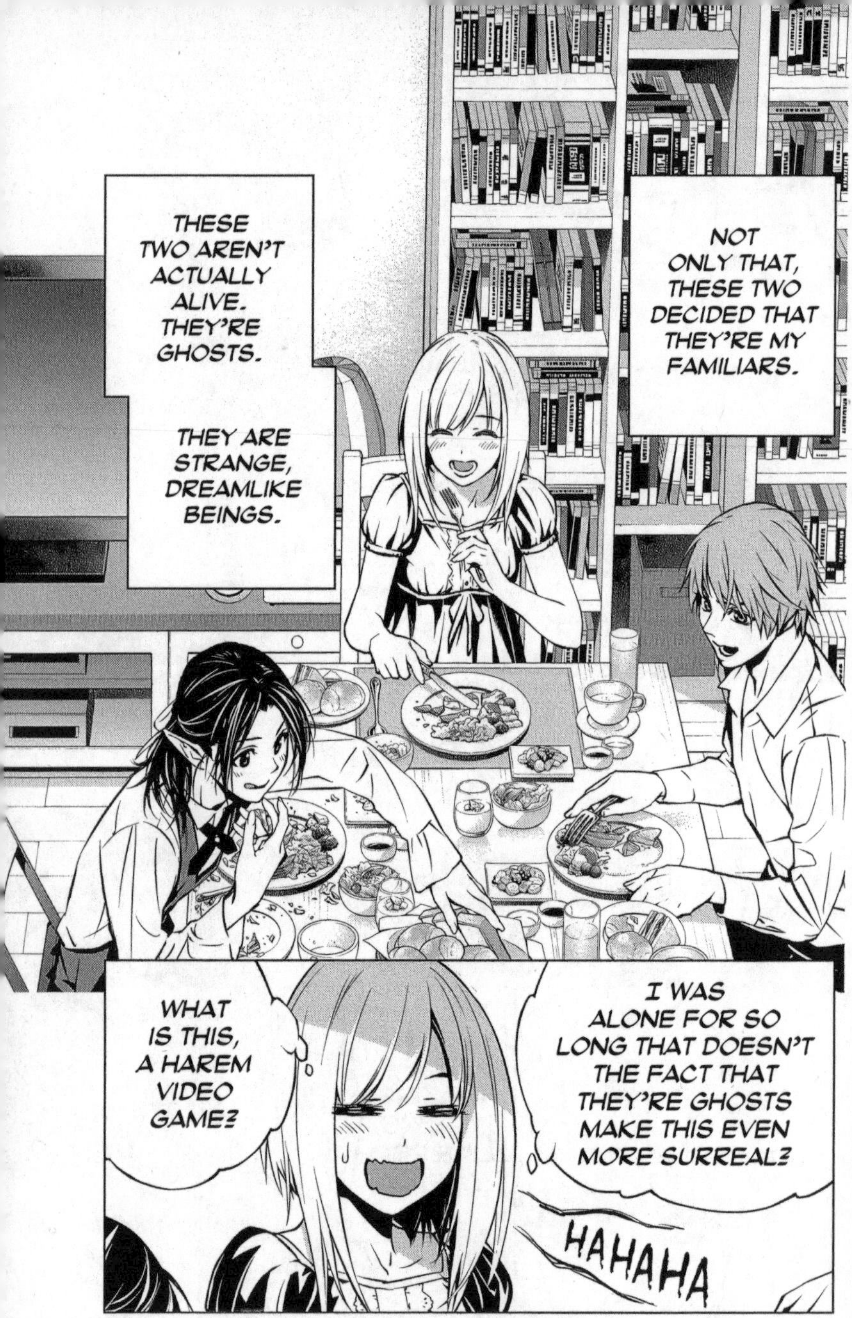
THESE TWO AREN'T ACTUALLY ALIVE. THEY'RE GHOSTS.
THEY ARE STRANGE, DREAMLIKE BEINGS.
NOT ONLY THAT, THESE TWO DECIDED THAT THEY'RE MY FAMILIARS.
WHAT IS THIS, A HAREM VIDEO GAME?
I WAS ALONE FOR SO LONG THAT DOESN'T THE FACT THAT THEY'RE GHOSTS MAKE THIS EVEN MORE SURREAL?
HAHAHA

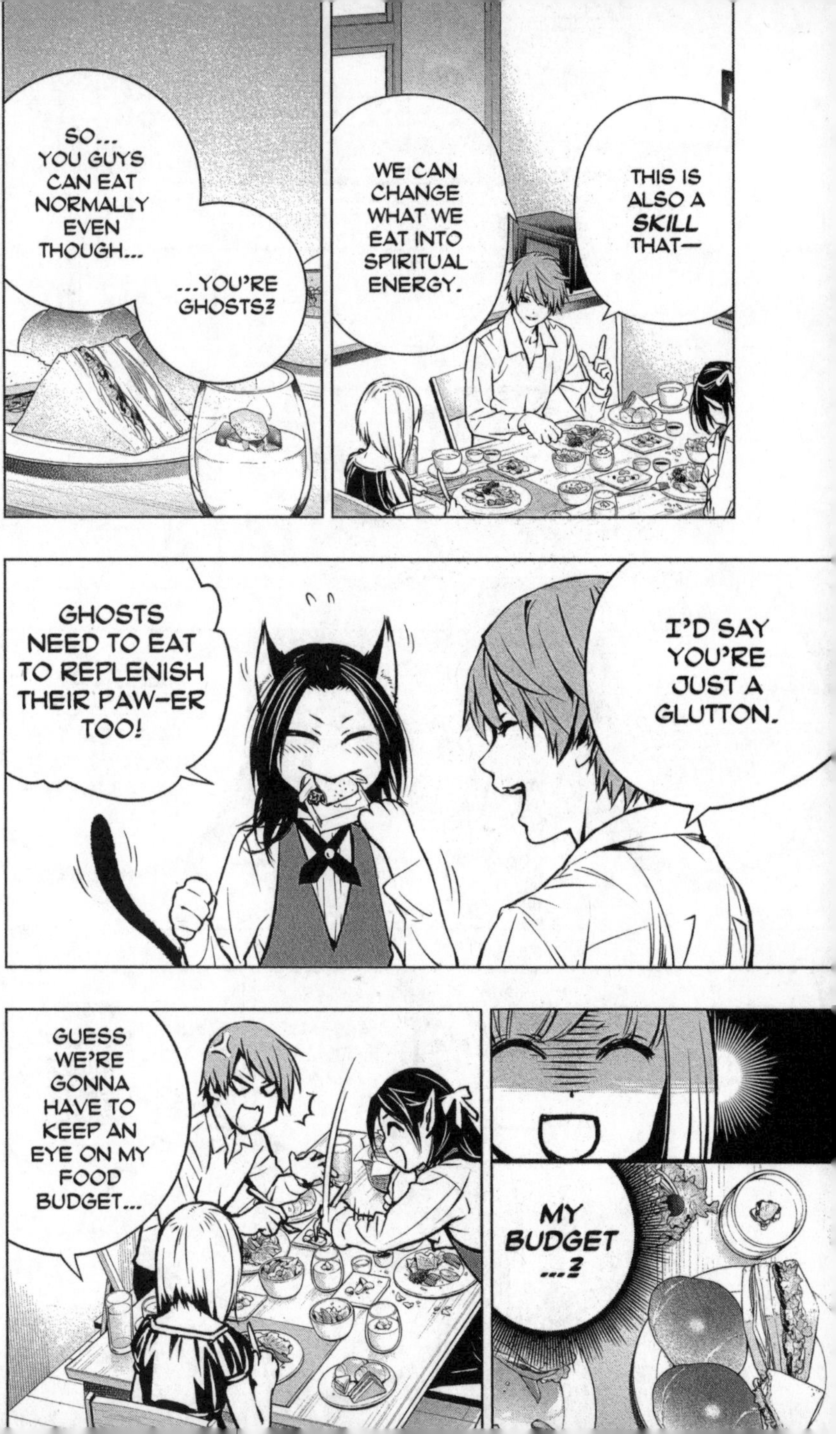
SO... YOU GUYS CAN EAT NORMALLY EVEN THOUGH...
...YOU'RE GHOSTS?
WE CAN CHANGE WHAT WE EAT INTO SPIRITUAL ENERGY.
THIS IS ALSO A *SKILL* THAT—
GHOSTS NEED TO EAT TO REPLENISH THEIR PAW-ER TOO!
I'D SAY YOU'RE JUST A GLUTTON.
GUESS WE'RE GONNA HAVE TO KEEP AN EYE ON MY FOOD BUDGET...
MY BUDGET ...?

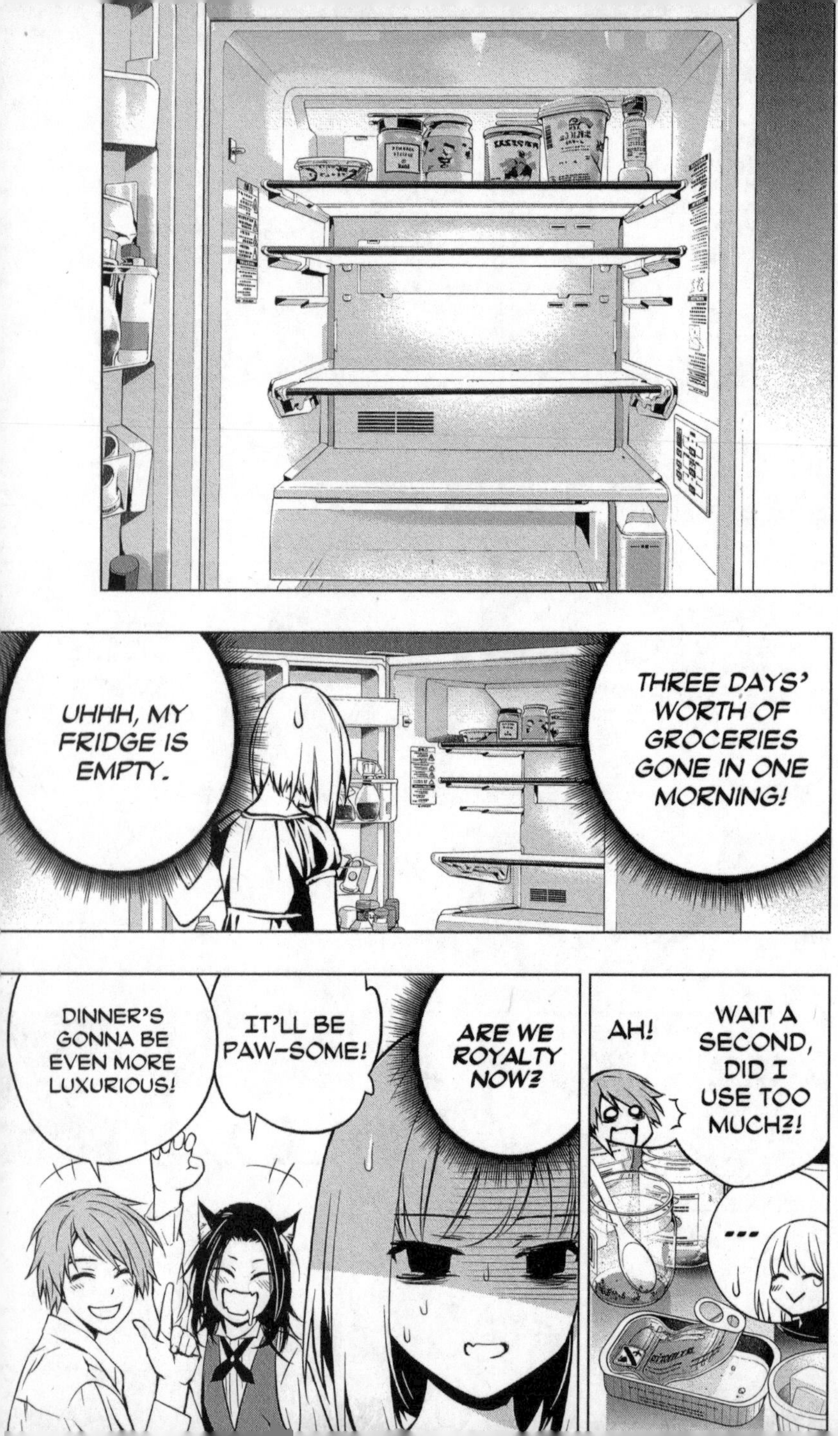
THREE DAYS' WORTH OF GROCERIES GONE IN ONE MORNING!
UHHH, MY FRIDGE IS EMPTY.
AH!
WAIT A SECOND, DID I USE TOO MUCH?!
...
ARE WE ROYALTY NOW?
IT'LL BE PAW-SOME!
DINNER'S GONNA BE EVEN MORE LUXURIOUS!

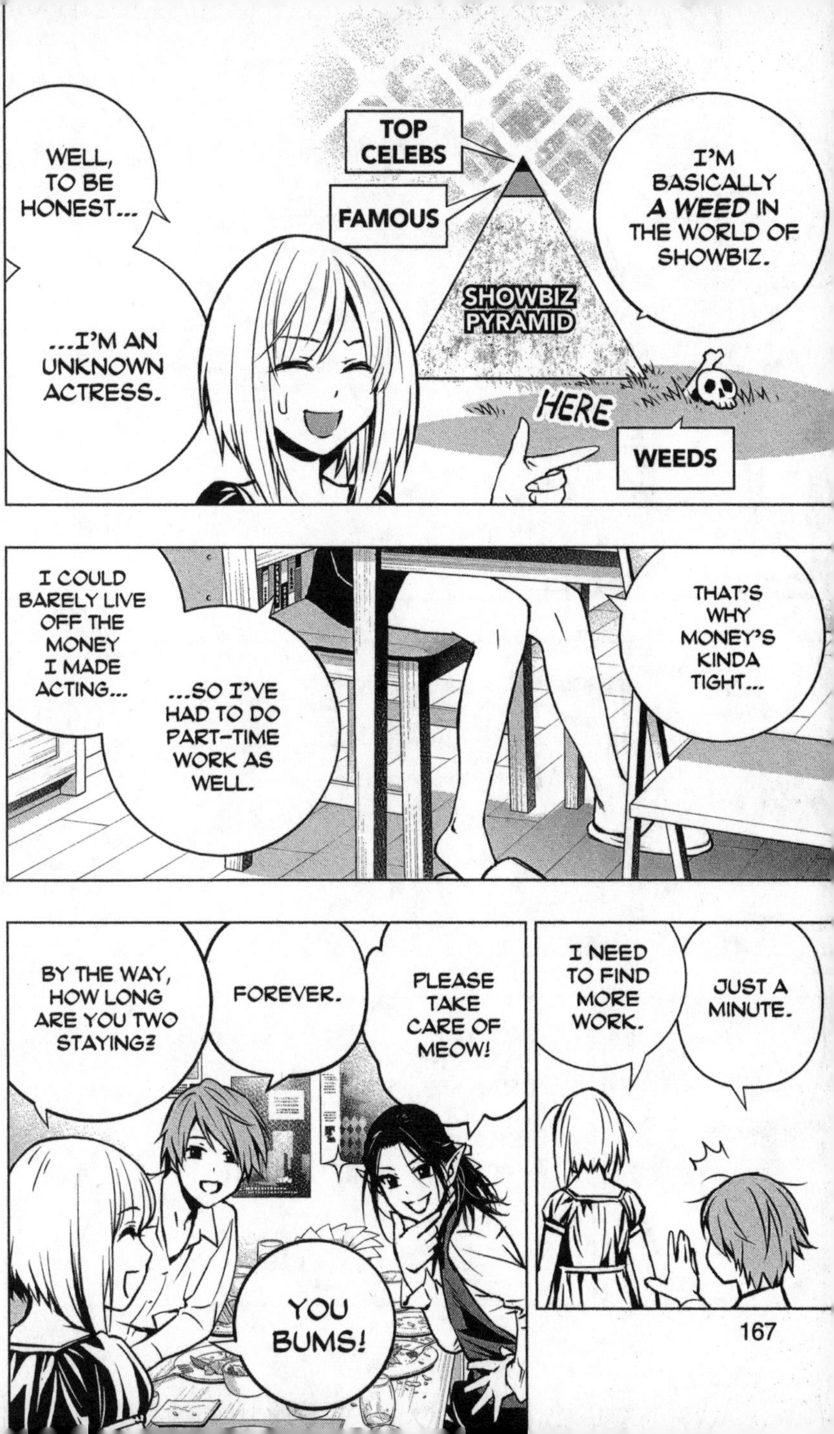
WELL, TO BE HONEST...
...I'M AN UNKNOWN ACTRESS.
TOP CELEBS
FAMOUS
SHOWBIZ PYRAMID
HERE
WEEDS
I'M BASICALLY **A *WEED*** IN THE WORLD OF SHOWBIZ.
I COULD BARELY LIVE OFF THE MONEY I MADE ACTING...
...SO I'VE HAD TO DO PART-TIME WORK AS WELL.
THAT'S WHY MONEY'S KINDA TIGHT...
BY THE WAY, HOW LONG ARE YOU TWO STAYING?
FOREVER.
PLEASE TAKE CARE OF MEOW!
YOU BUMS!
I NEED TO FIND MORE WORK.
JUST A MINUTE.

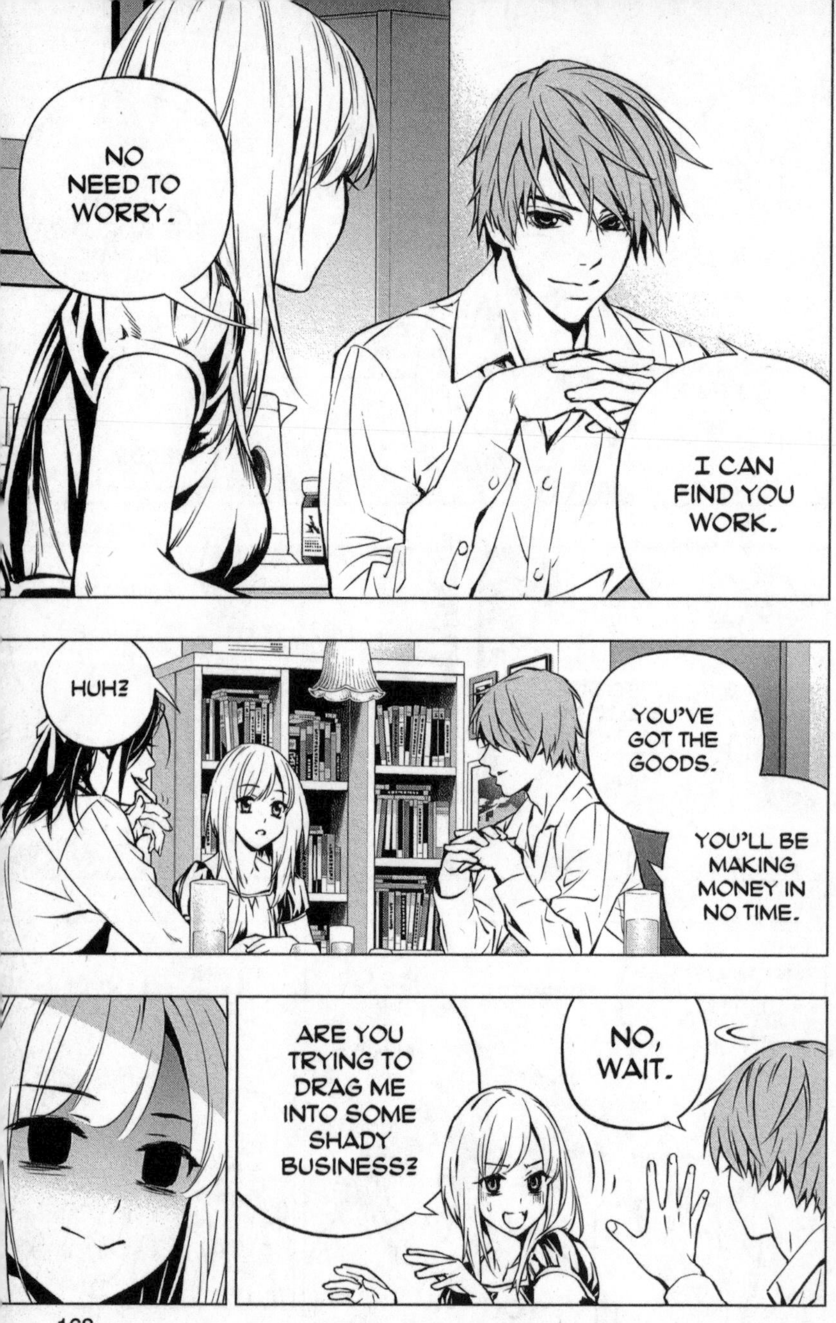
NO NEED TO WORRY.
I CAN FIND YOU WORK.
YOU'VE GOT THE GOODS.
YOU'LL BE MAKING MONEY IN NO TIME.
HUH?
ARE YOU TRYING TO DRAG ME INTO SOME SHADY BUSINESS?
NO, WAIT.

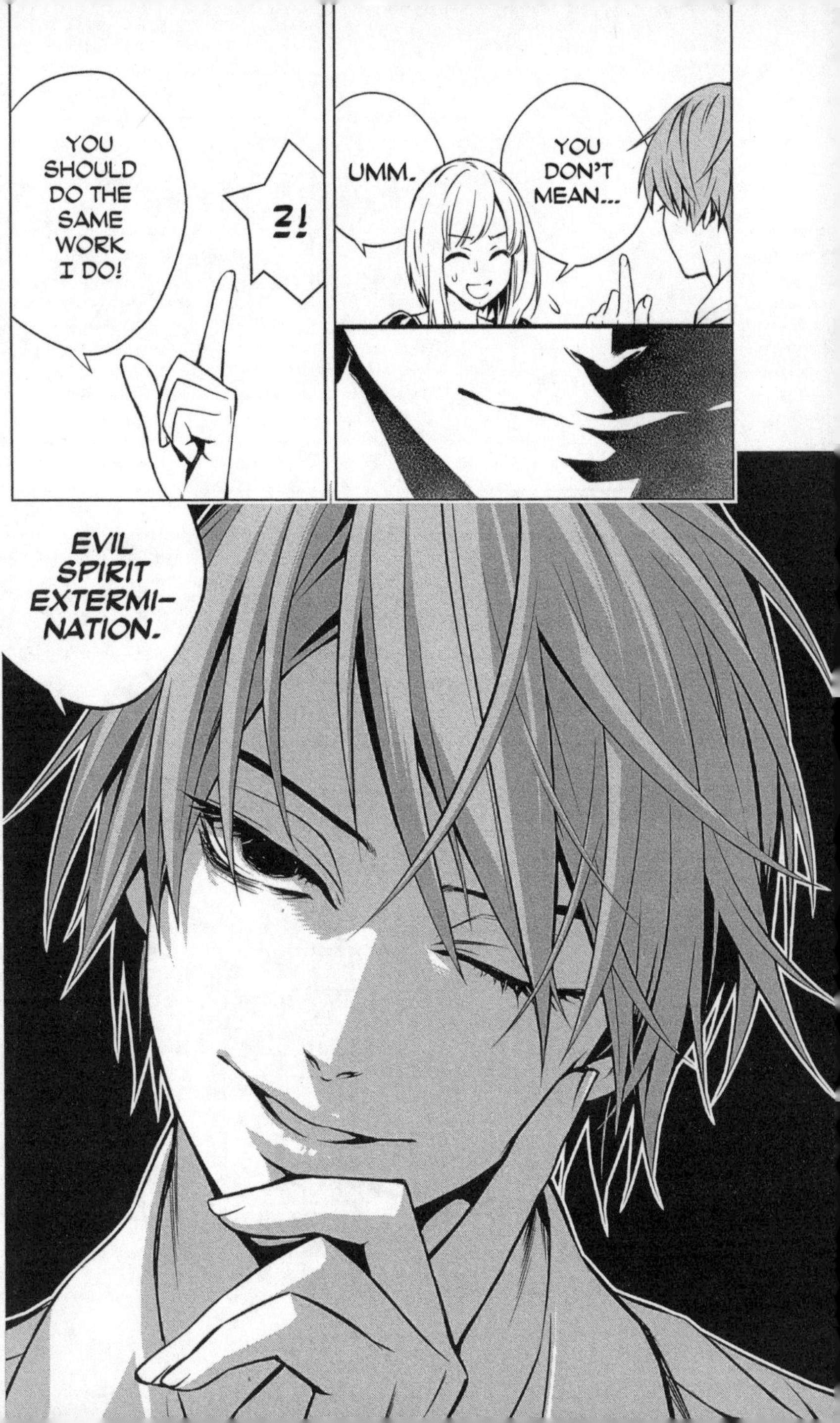
YOU SHOULD DO THE SAME WORK I DO!
?!
UMM.
YOU DON'T MEAN...
EVIL SPIRIT EXTERMI-NATION.

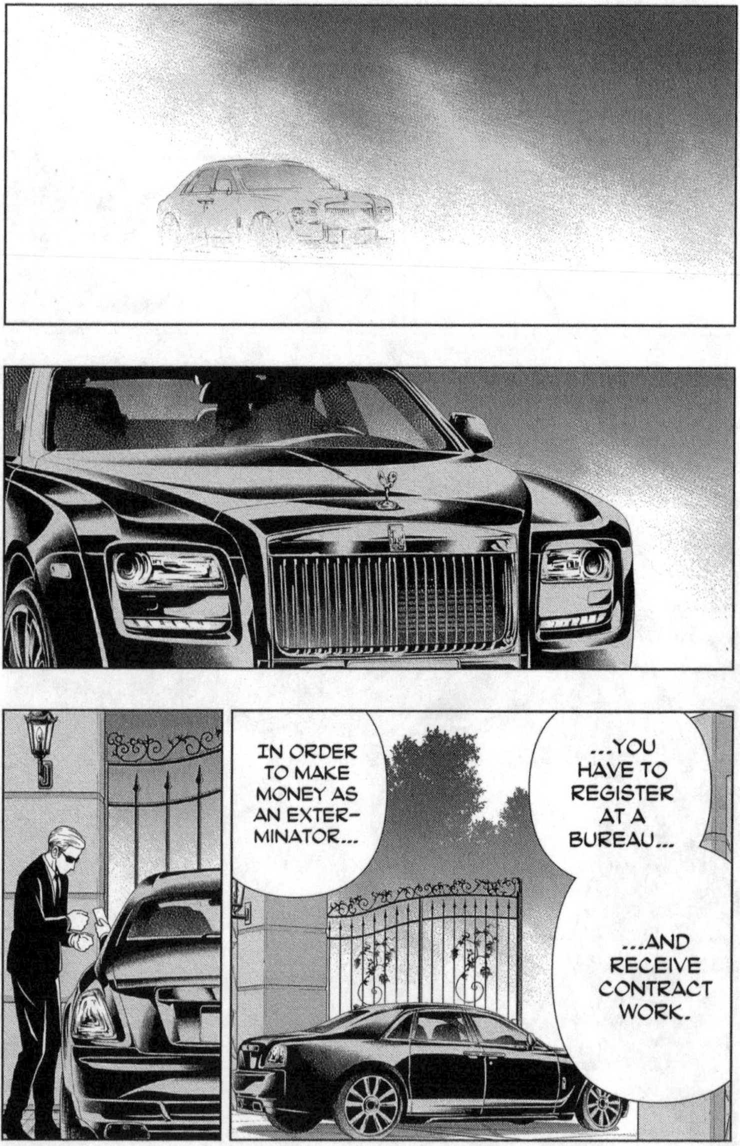
IN ORDER TO MAKE MONEY AS AN EXTER-MINATOR...
...YOU HAVE TO REGISTER AT A BUREAU...
...AND RECEIVE CONTRACT WORK.

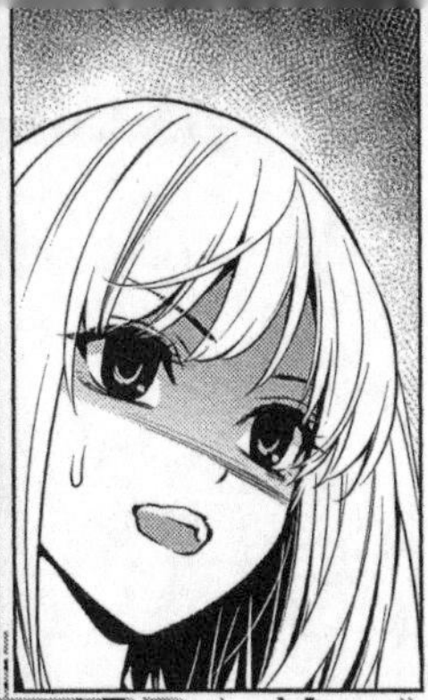
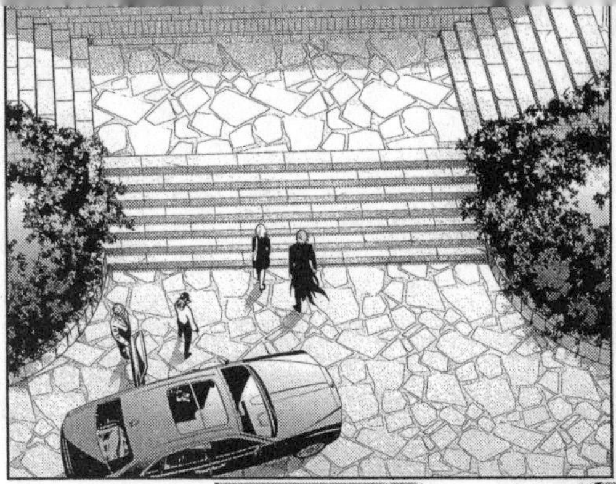
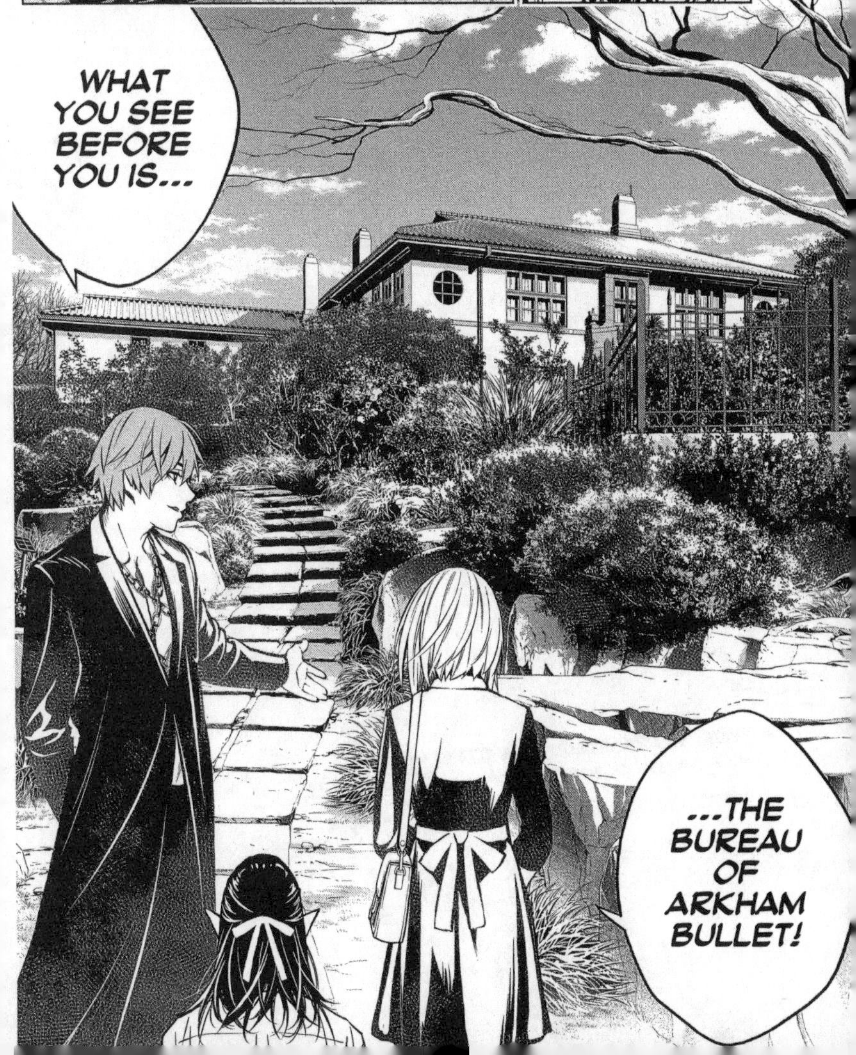
WHAT YOU SEE BEFORE YOU IS...
...THE BUREAU OF ARKHAM BULLET!

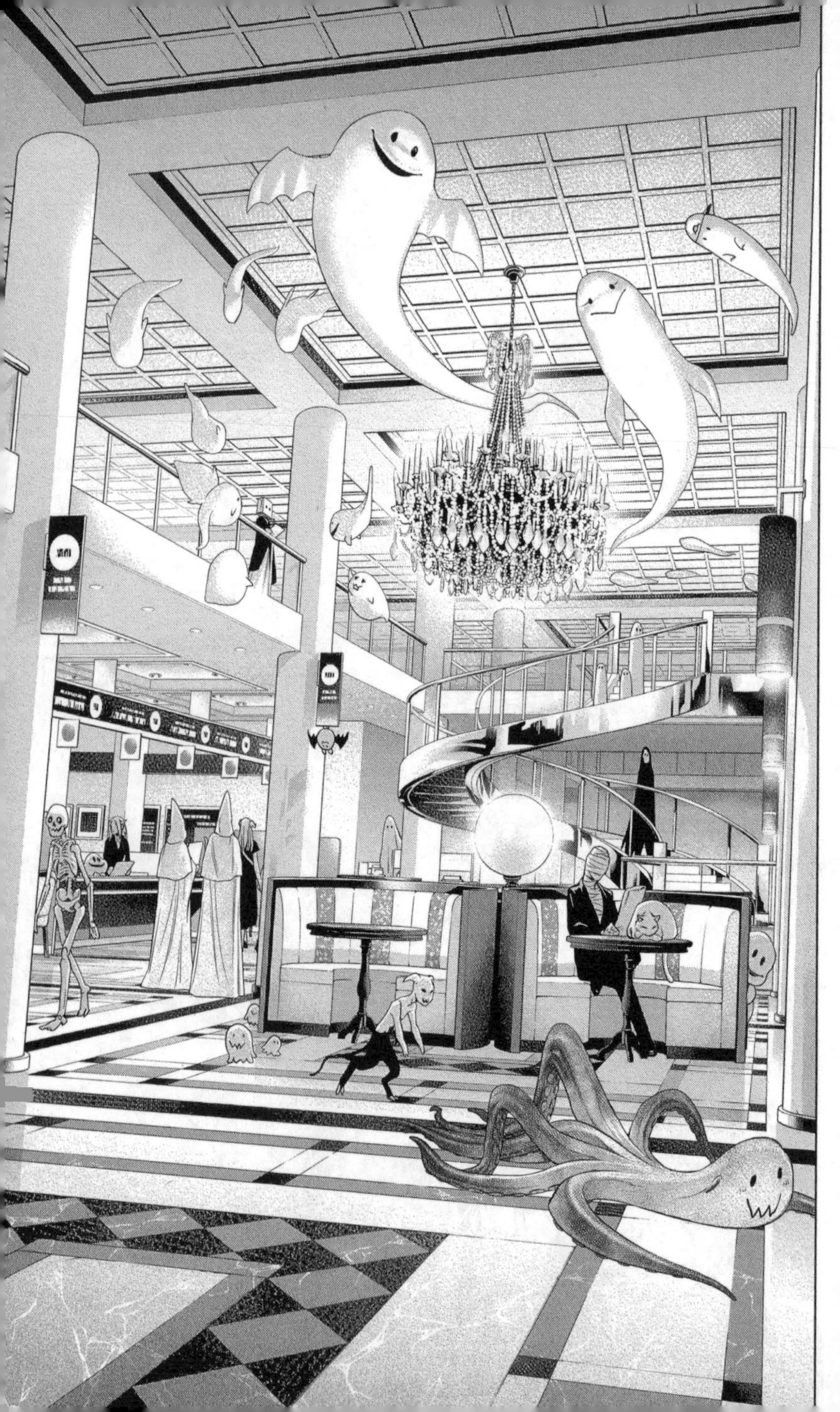

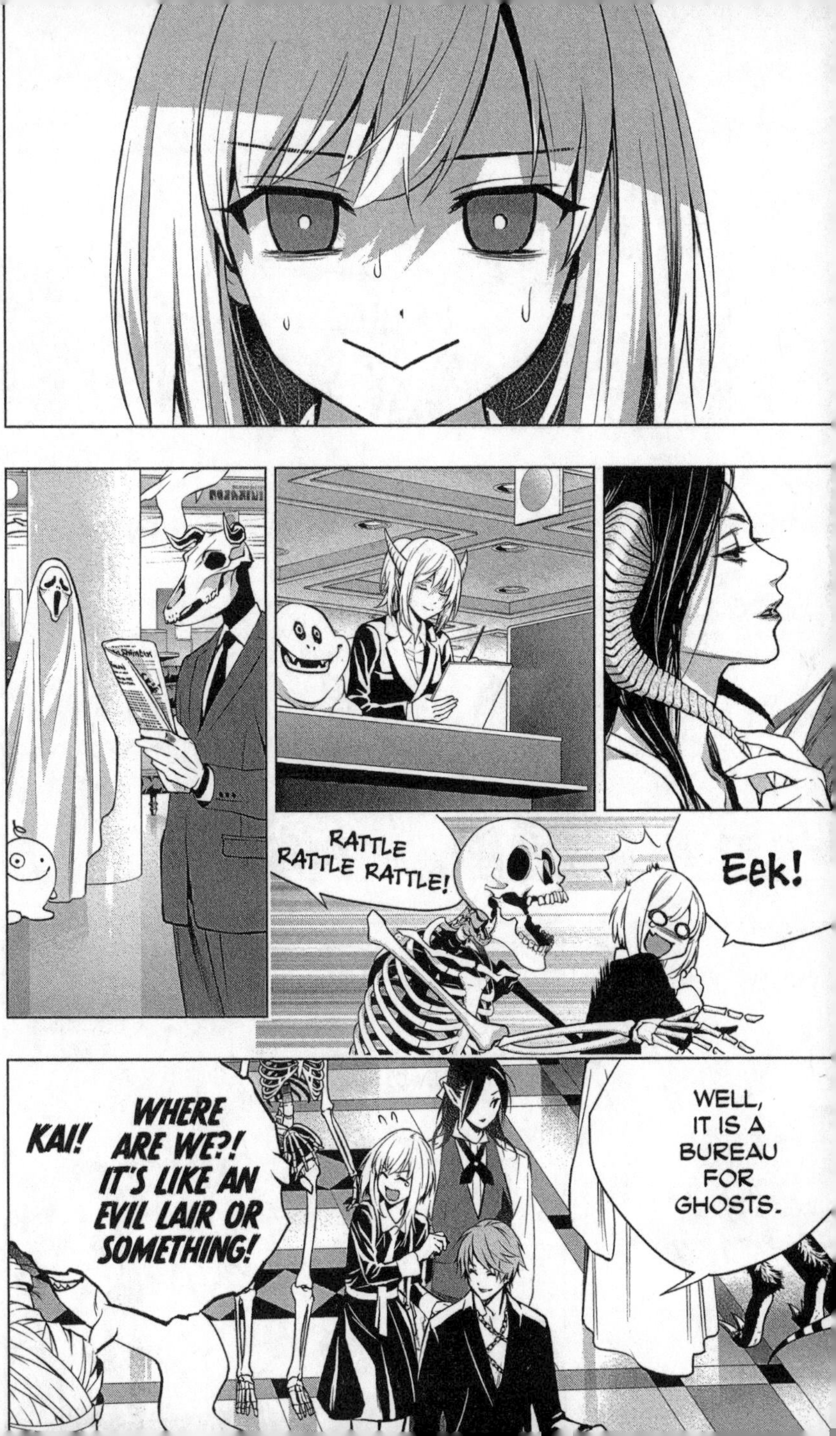
Eek!
RATTLE RATTLE RATTLE!
WELL, IT IS A BUREAU FOR GHOSTS.
WHERE ARE WE?! IT'S LIKE AN EVIL LAIR OR SOMETHING!
KAI!

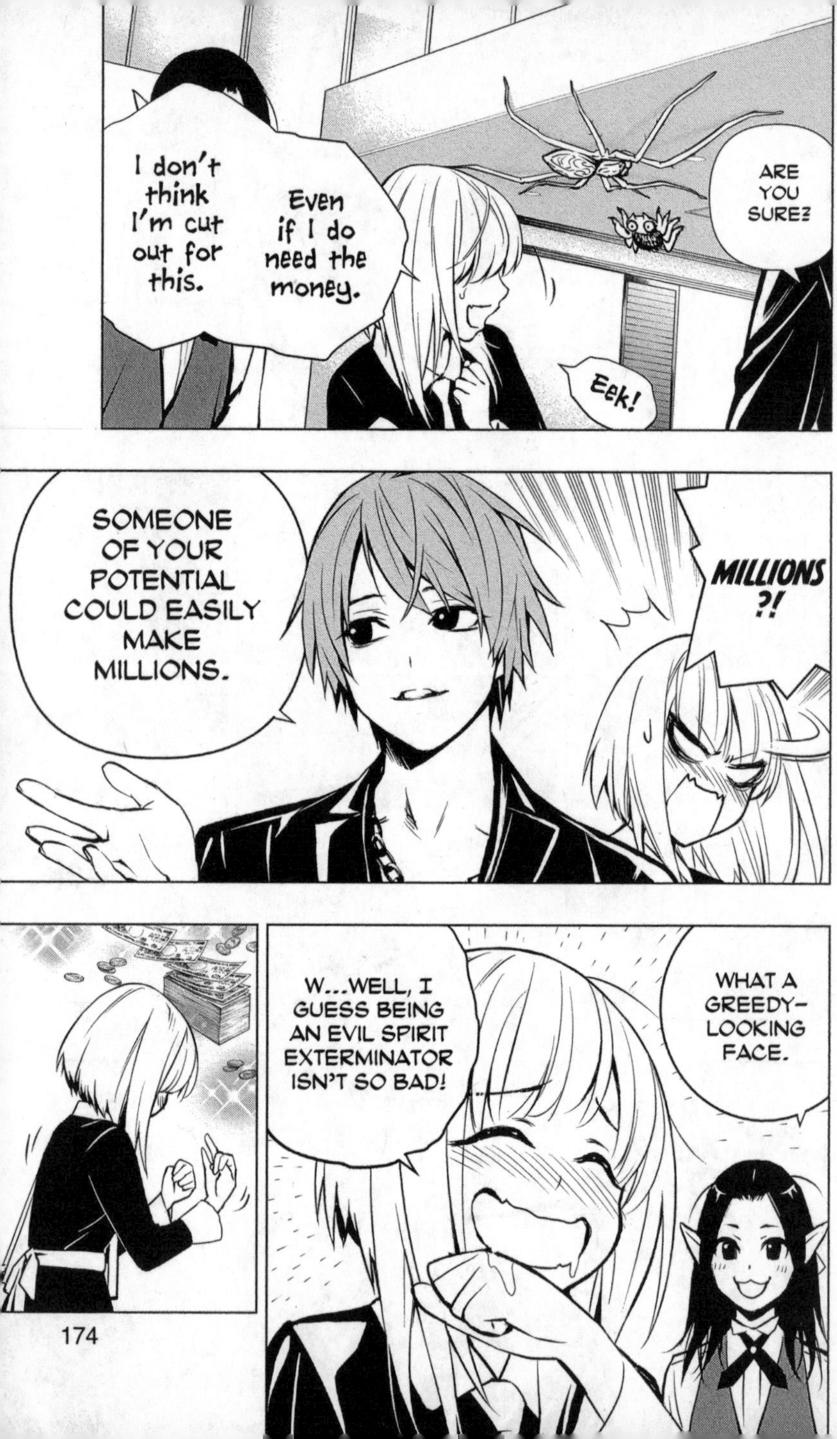
I don't think I'm cut out for this.
Even if I do need the money.
Eek!
ARE YOU SURE?
SOMEONE OF YOUR POTENTIAL COULD EASILY MAKE MILLIONS.
MILLIONS ?!
W...WELL, I GUESS BEING AN EVIL SPIRIT EXTERMINATOR ISN'T SO BAD!
WHAT A GREEDY-LOOKING FACE.

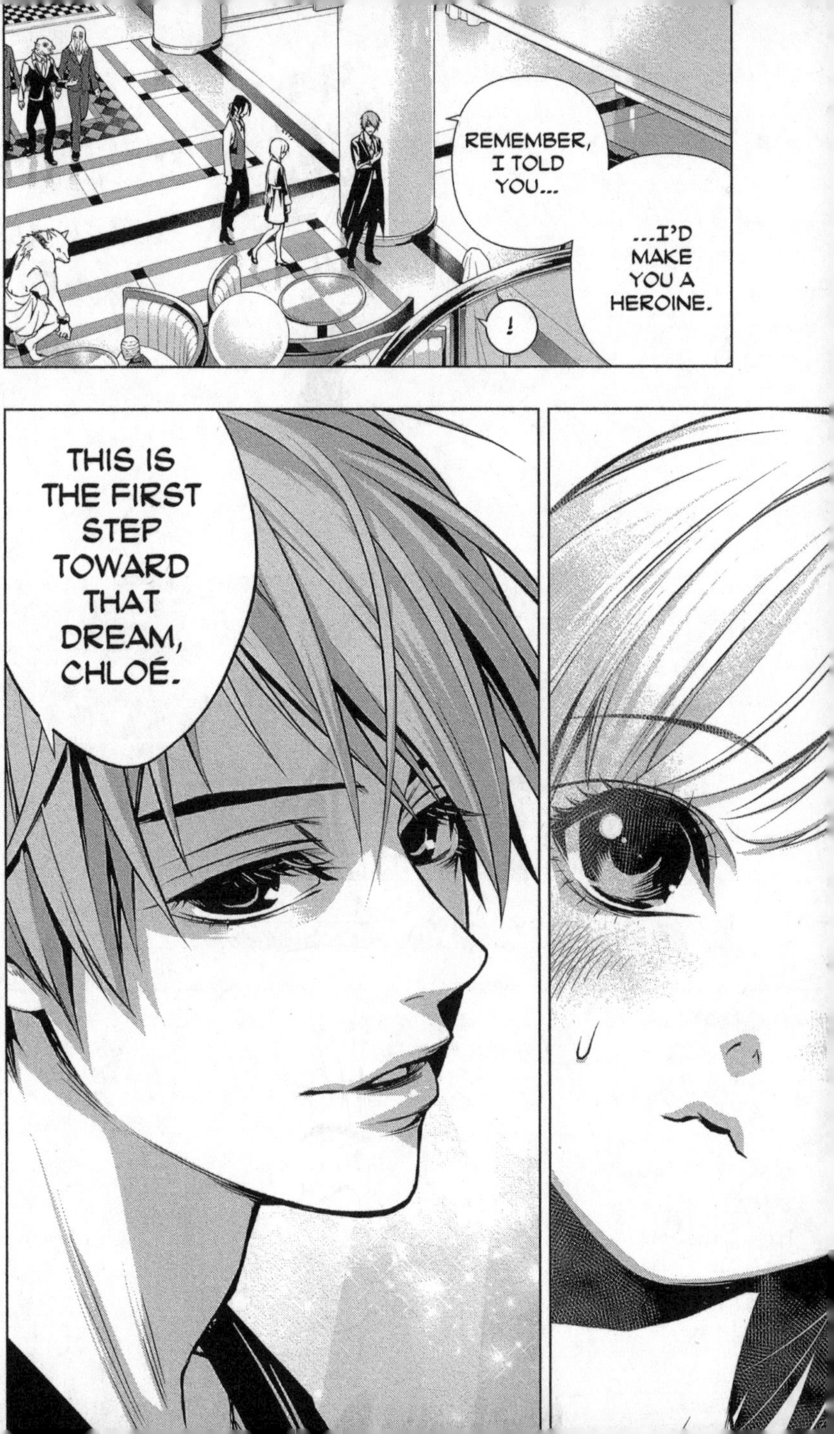
REMEMBER, I TOLD YOU...
...I'D MAKE YOU A HEROINE.
!
THIS IS THE FIRST STEP TOWARD THAT DREAM, CHLOÉ.

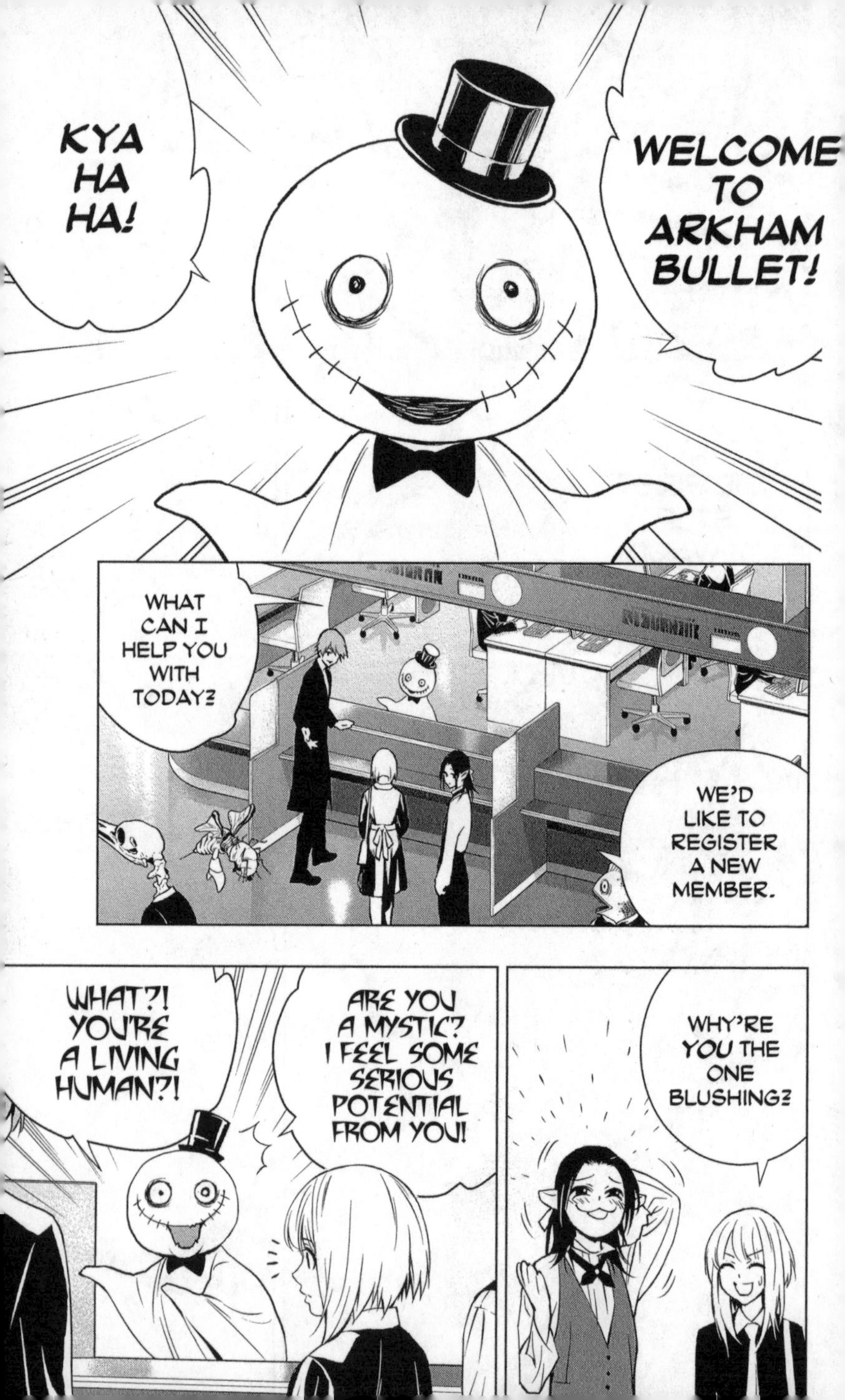
KYA HA HA!
WELCOME TO ARKHAM BULLET!
WHAT CAN I HELP YOU WITH TODAY?
WE'D LIKE TO REGISTER A NEW MEMBER.
WHAT?! YOU'RE A LIVING HUMAN?!
ARE YOU A MYSTIC? I FEEL SOME SERIOUS POTENTIAL FROM YOU!
WHY'RE YOU THE ONE BLUSHING?

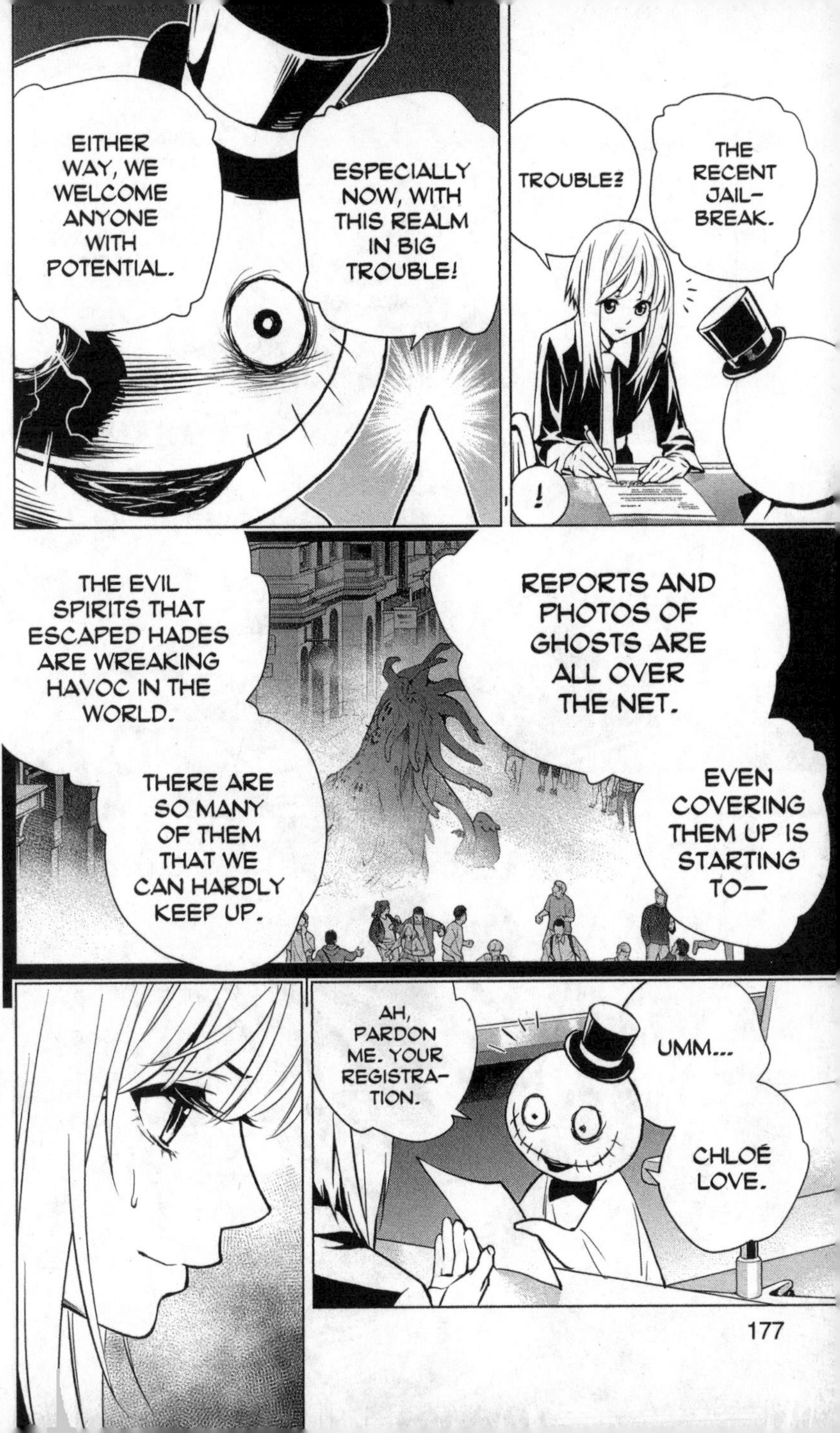
EITHER WAY, WE WELCOME ANYONE WITH POTENTIAL.
ESPECIALLY NOW, WITH THIS REALM IN BIG TROUBLE!
TROUBLE?
THE RECENT JAIL-BREAK.
!
THE EVIL SPIRITS THAT ESCAPED HADES ARE WREAKING HAVOC IN THE WORLD.
REPORTS AND PHOTOS OF GHOSTS ARE ALL OVER THE NET.
THERE ARE SO MANY OF THEM THAT WE CAN HARDLY KEEP UP.
EVEN COVERING THEM UP IS STARTING TO—
AH, PARDON ME. YOUR REGISTRATION.
UMM...
CHLOÉ LOVE.

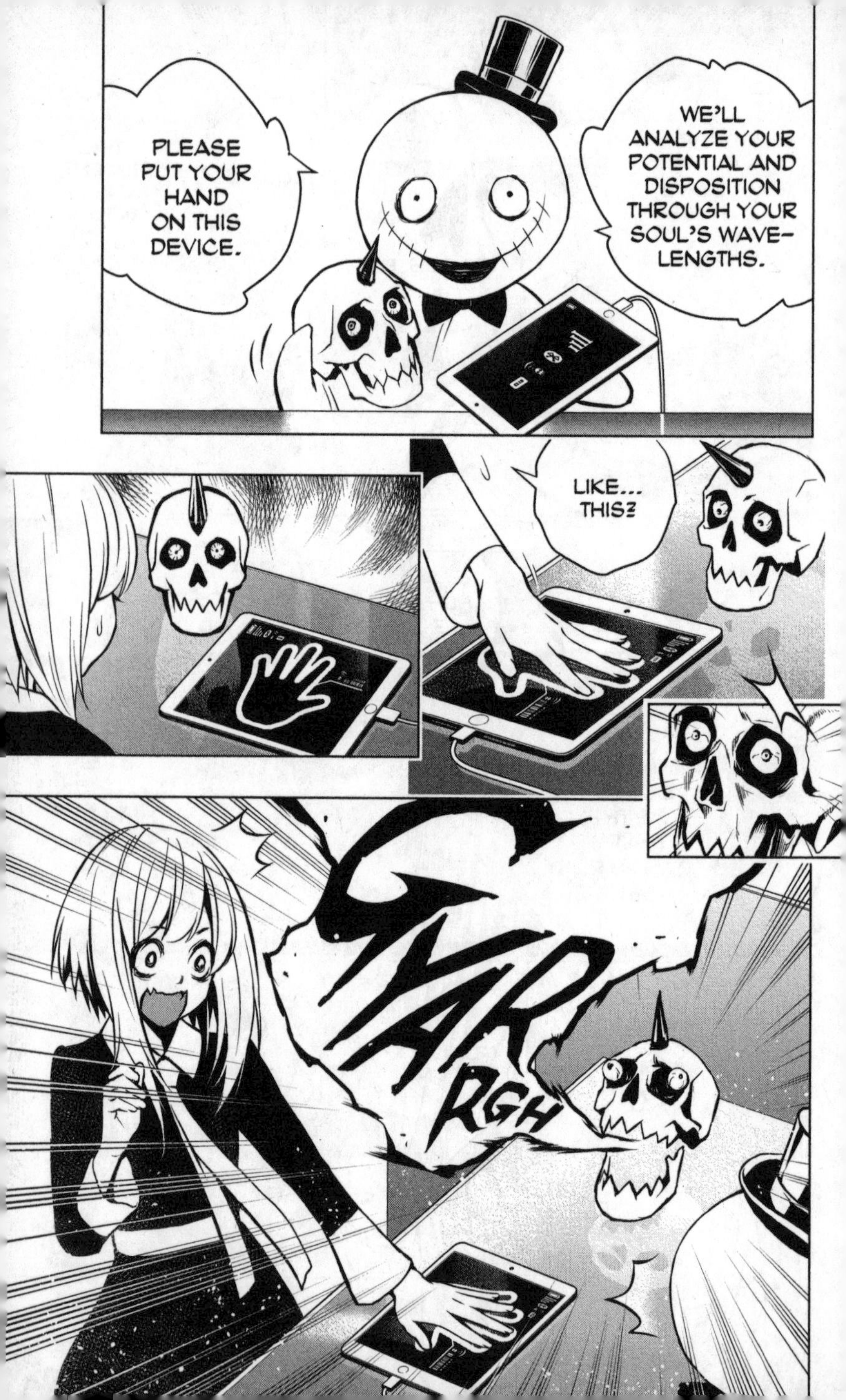
WE'LL ANALYZE YOUR POTENTIAL AND DISPOSITION THROUGH YOUR SOUL'S WAVE-LENGTHS.
PLEASE PUT YOUR HAND ON THIS DEVICE.
LIKE... THIS?
GWARRGH

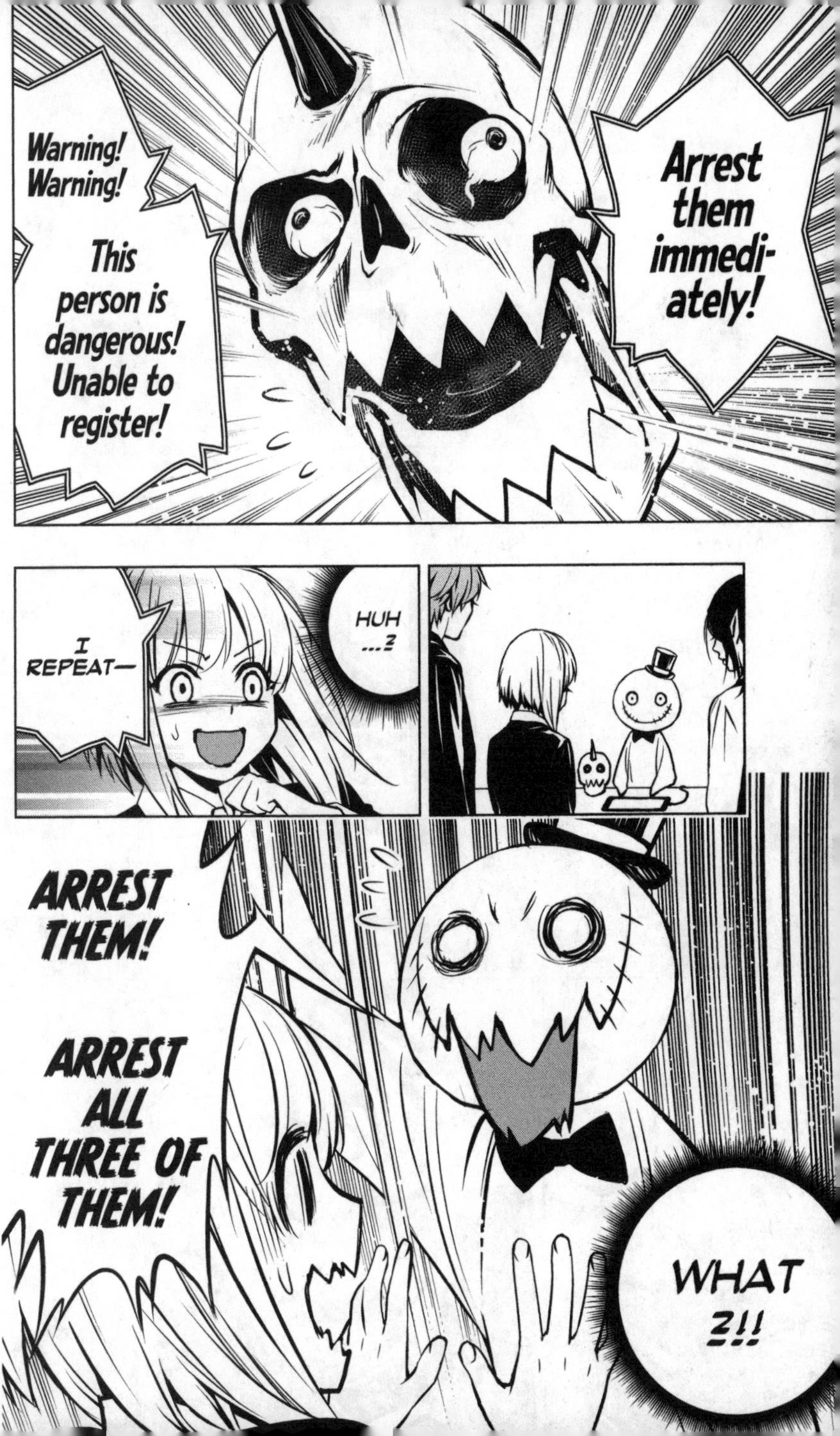
Arrest them immedi-ately!
Warning! Warning!
This person is dangerous! Unable to register!
HUH ...?
I REPEAT—
ARREST THEM!
ARREST ALL THREE OF THEM!
WHAT ?!!

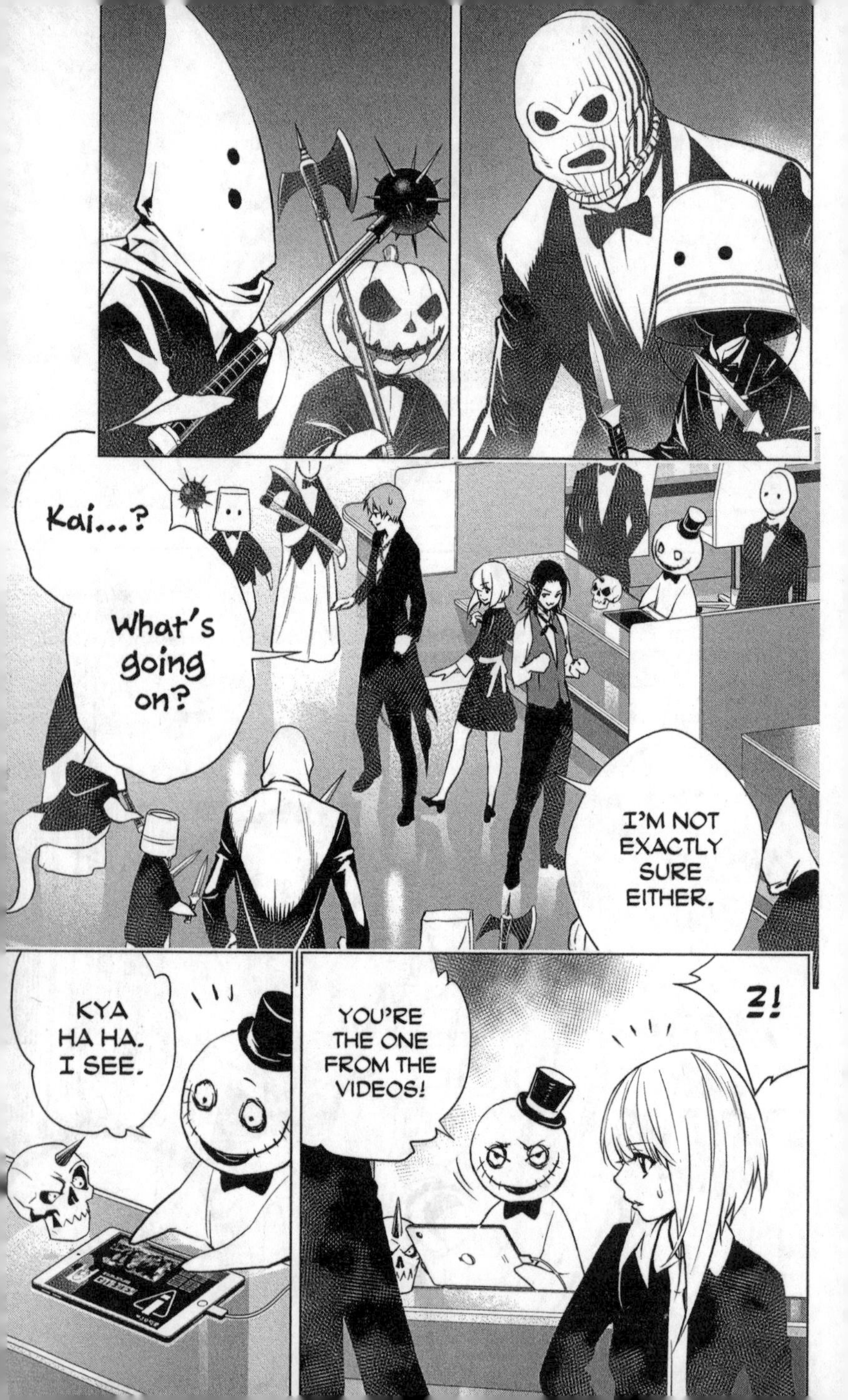
Kai...?
What's going on?
I'M NOT EXACTLY SURE EITHER.
YOU'RE THE ONE FROM THE VIDEOS!
?!
KYA HA HA. I SEE.

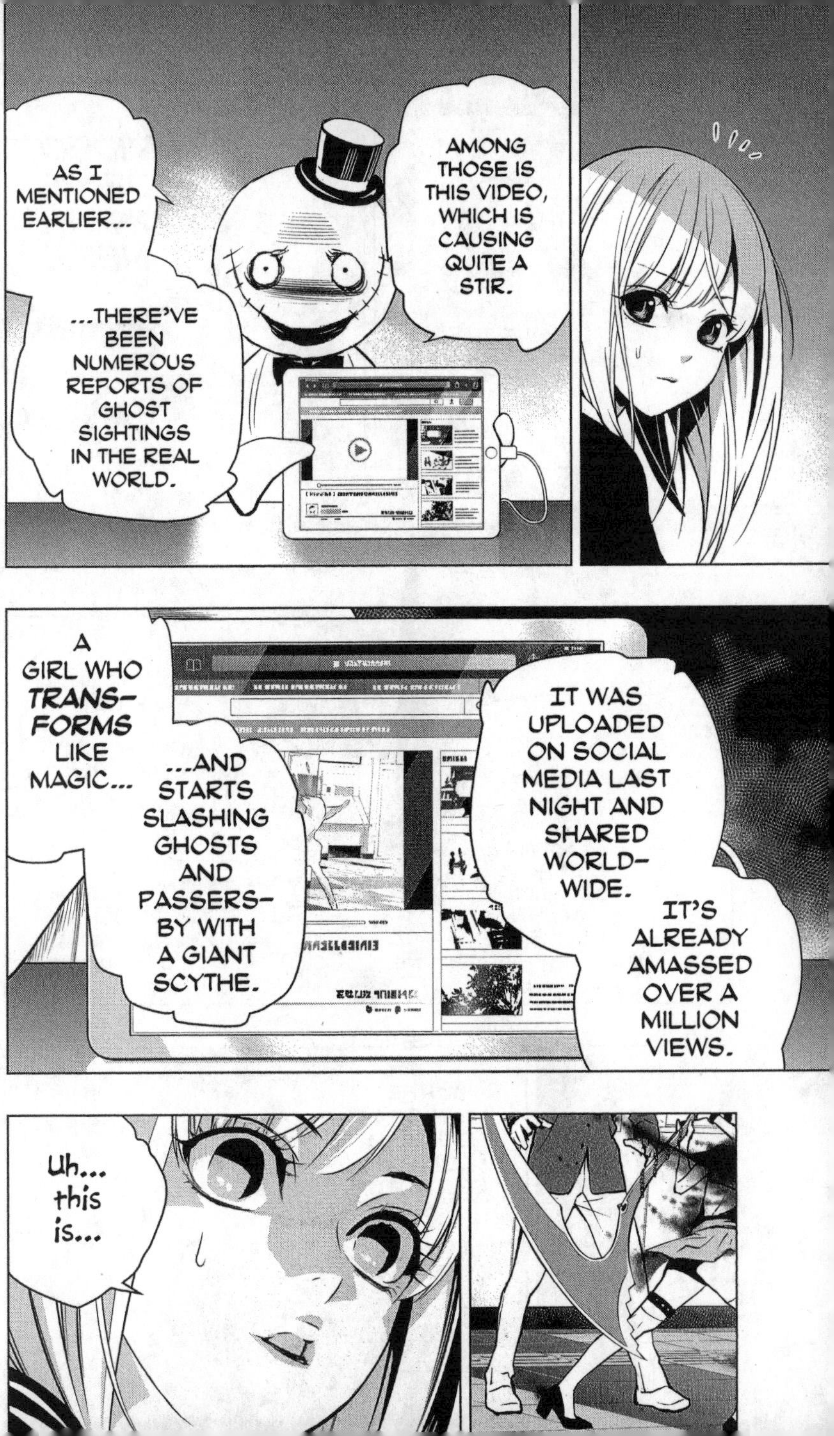
AS I MENTIONED EARLIER...
...THERE'VE BEEN NUMEROUS REPORTS OF GHOST SIGHTINGS IN THE REAL WORLD.
AMONG THOSE IS THIS VIDEO, WHICH IS CAUSING QUITE A STIR.
A GIRL WHO *TRANSFORMS* LIKE MAGIC...
...AND STARTS SLASHING GHOSTS AND PASSERS-BY WITH A GIANT SCYTHE.
IT WAS UPLOADED ON SOCIAL MEDIA LAST NIGHT AND SHARED WORLD-WIDE.
IT'S ALREADY AMASSED OVER A MILLION VIEWS.
Uh... this is...

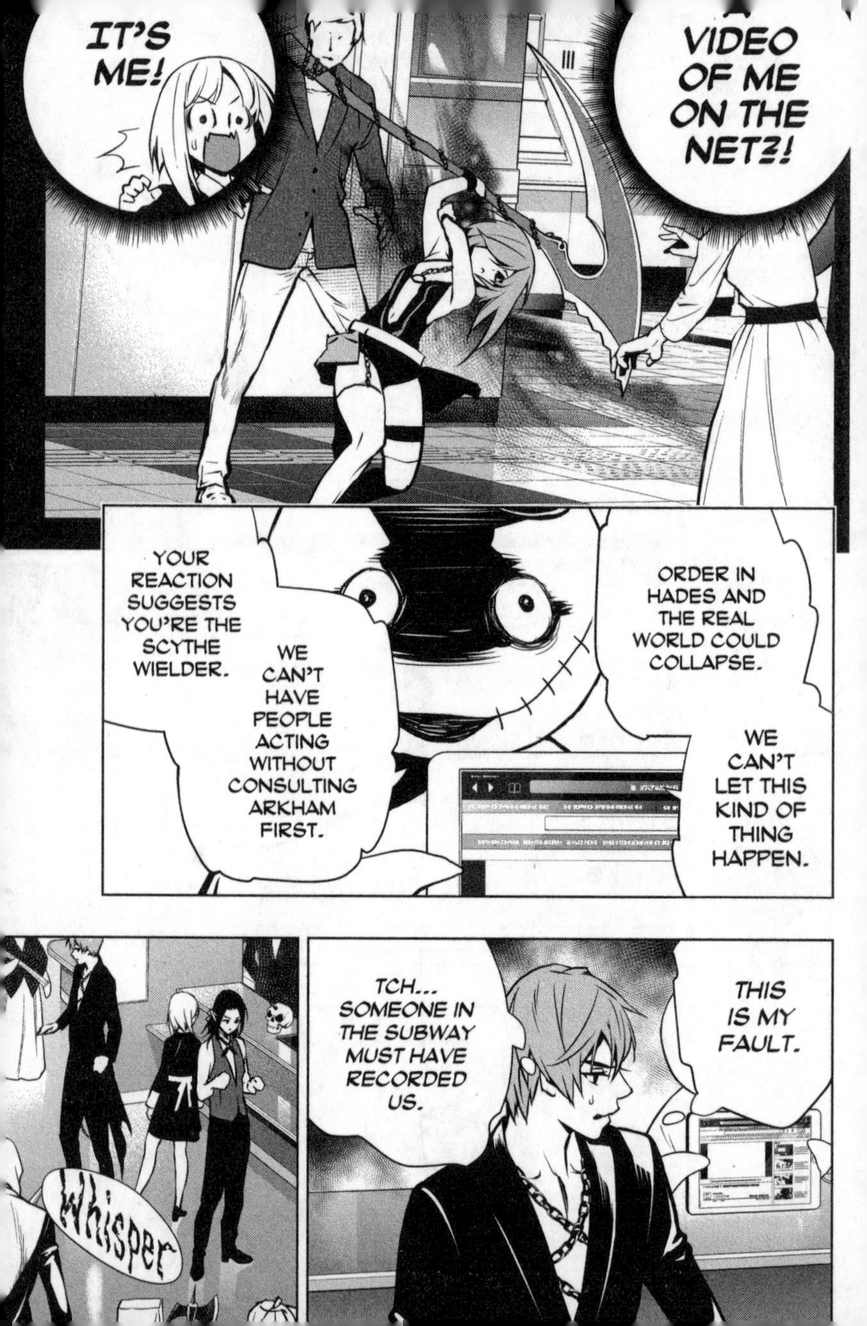
VIDEO OF ME ON THE NET?!
IT'S ME!
ORDER IN HADES AND THE REAL WORLD COULD COLLAPSE.
WE CAN'T LET THIS KIND OF THING HAPPEN.
YOUR REACTION SUGGESTS YOU'RE THE SCYTHE WIELDER.
WE CAN'T HAVE PEOPLE ACTING WITHOUT CONSULTING ARKHAM FIRST.
THIS IS MY FAULT.
TCH... SOMEONE IN THE SUBWAY MUST HAVE RECORDED US.
Whisper

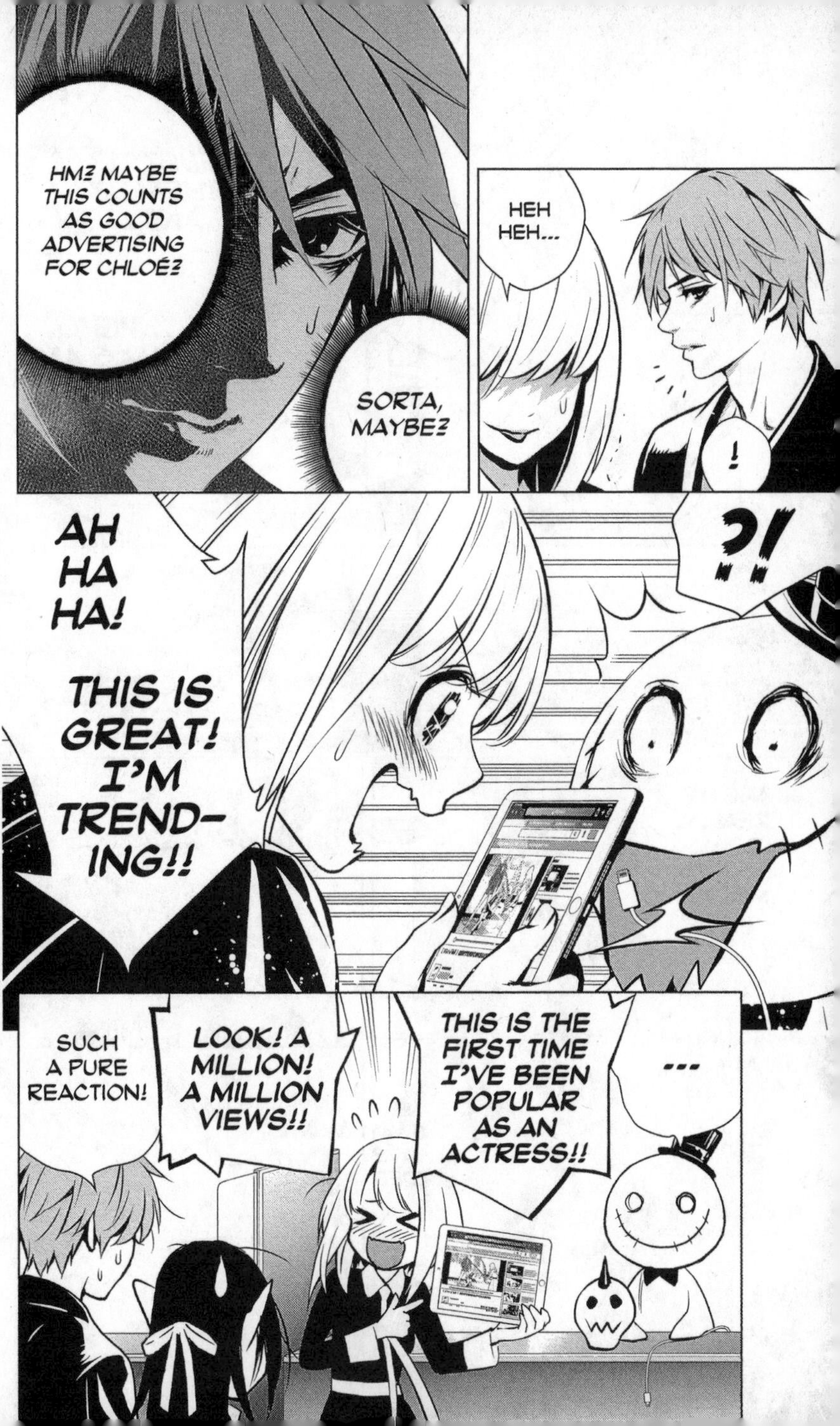
HEH HEH...
!
HM? MAYBE THIS COUNTS AS GOOD ADVERTISING FOR CHLOÉ?
SORTA, MAYBE?
?!
AH HA HA!
THIS IS GREAT! I'M TRENDING!!
...
THIS IS THE FIRST TIME I'VE BEEN POPULAR AS AN ACTRESS!!
LOOK! A MILLION! A MILLION VIEWS!!
SUCH A PURE REACTION!

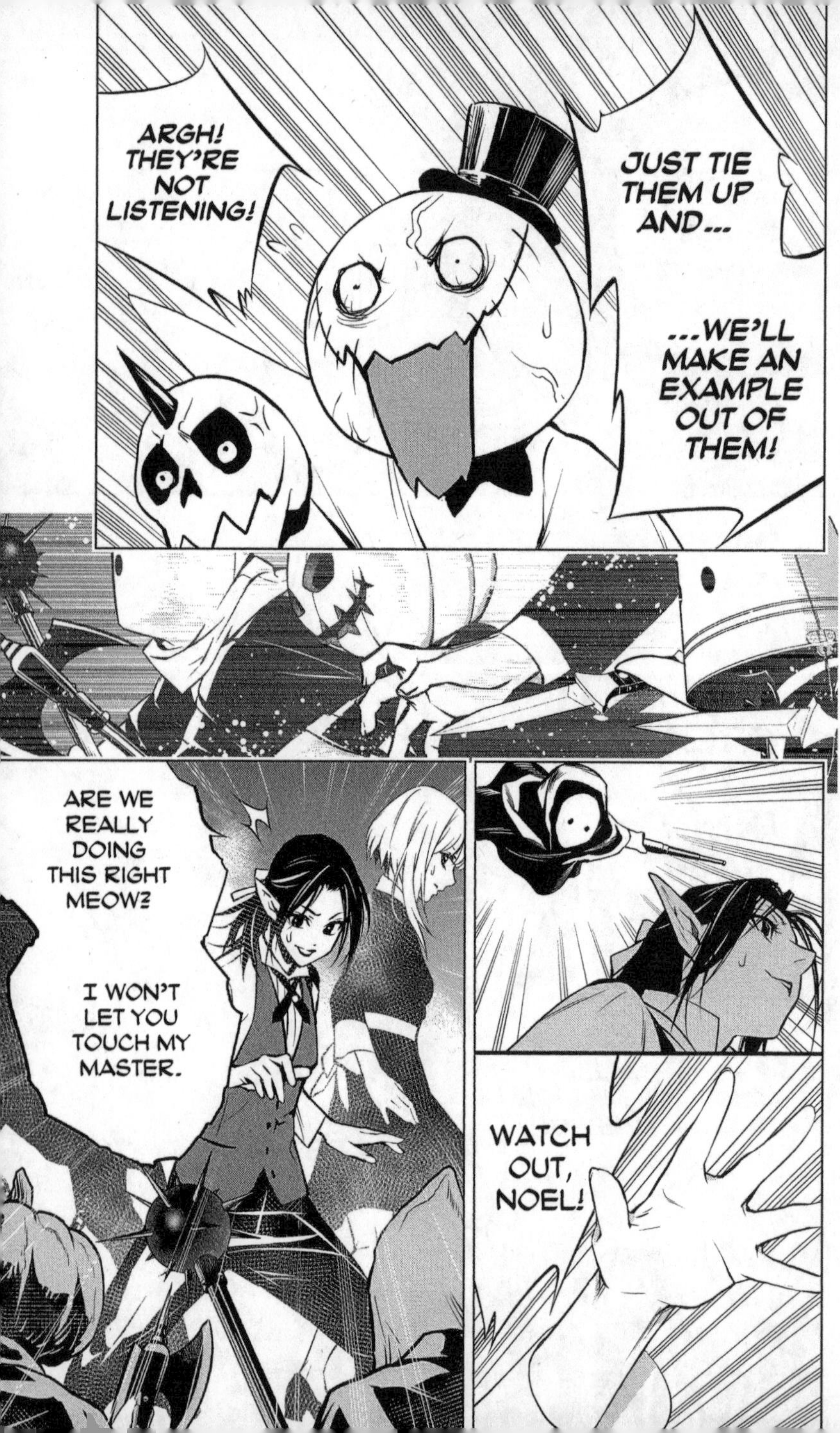
JUST TIE THEM UP AND...
...WE'LL MAKE AN EXAMPLE OUT OF THEM!
ARGH! THEY'RE NOT LISTENING!
WATCH OUT, NOEL!
ARE WE REALLY DOING THIS RIGHT MEOW?
I WON'T LET YOU TOUCH MY MASTER.

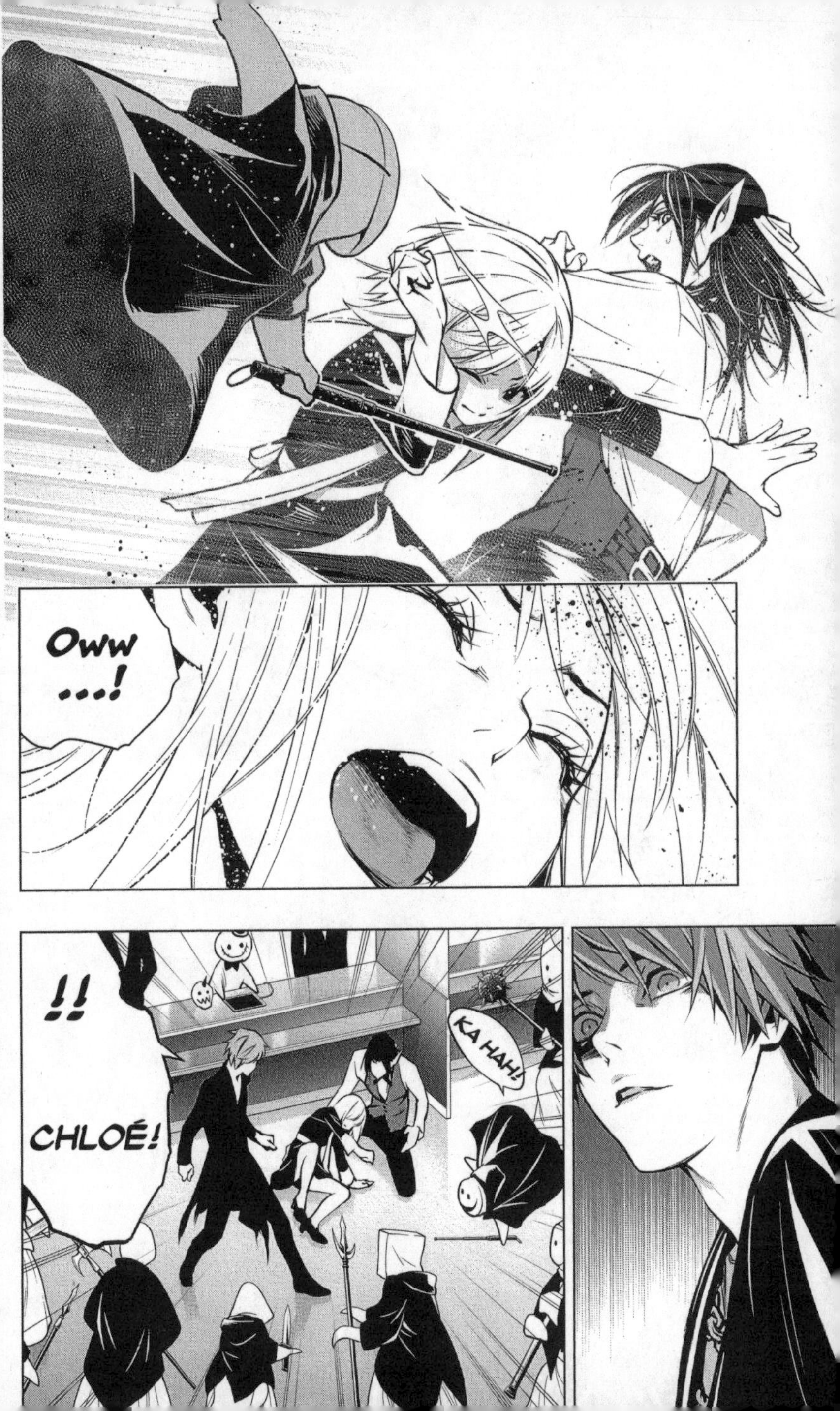
Oww ...!
!!
CHLOÉ!
KA HAH!

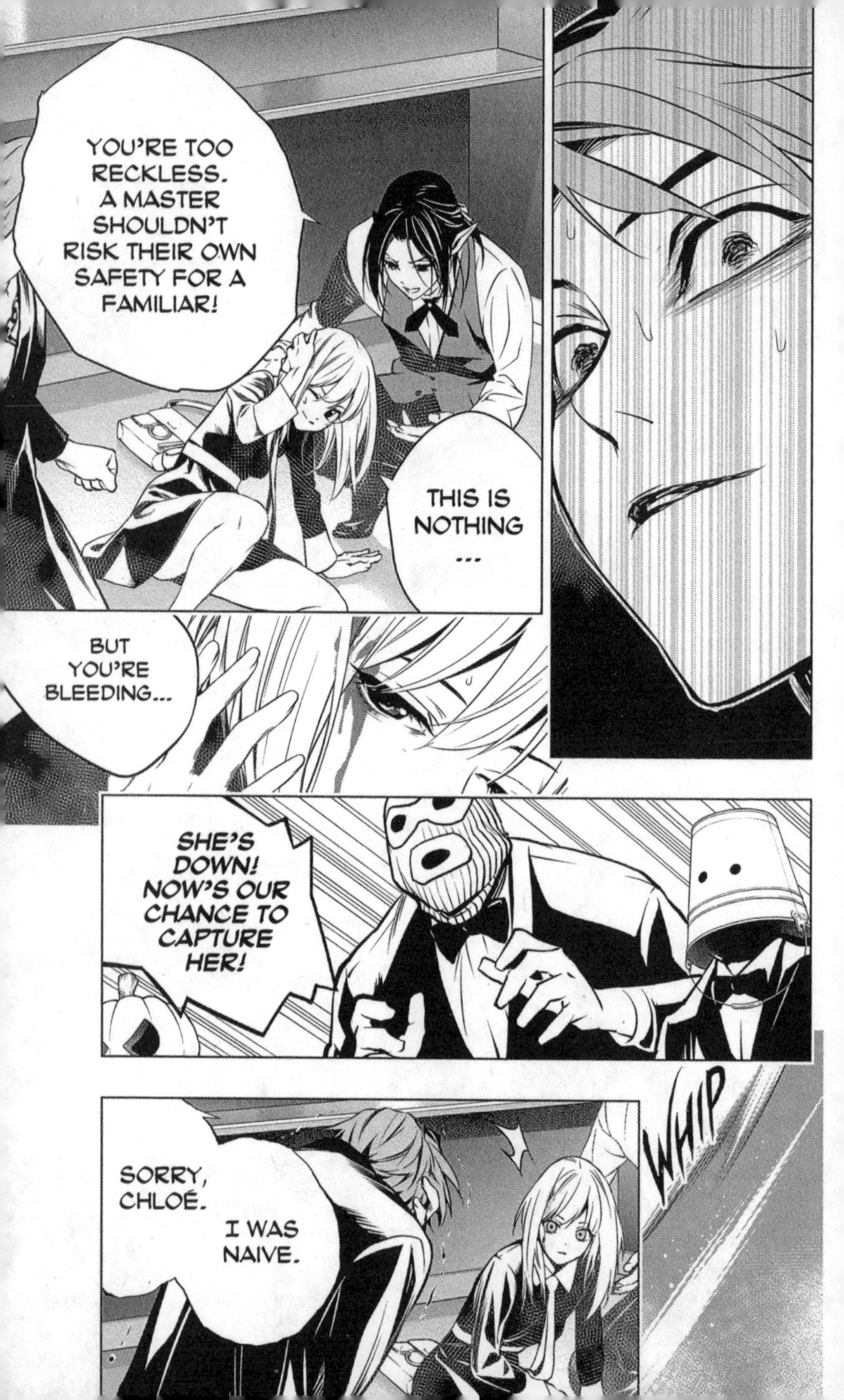
YOU'RE TOO RECKLESS. A MASTER SHOULDN'T RISK THEIR OWN SAFETY FOR A FAMILIAR!
THIS IS NOTHING ...
BUT YOU'RE BLEEDING...
SHE'S DOWN! NOW'S OUR CHANCE TO CAPTURE HER!
WHIP
SORRY, CHLOÉ.
I WAS NAIVE.

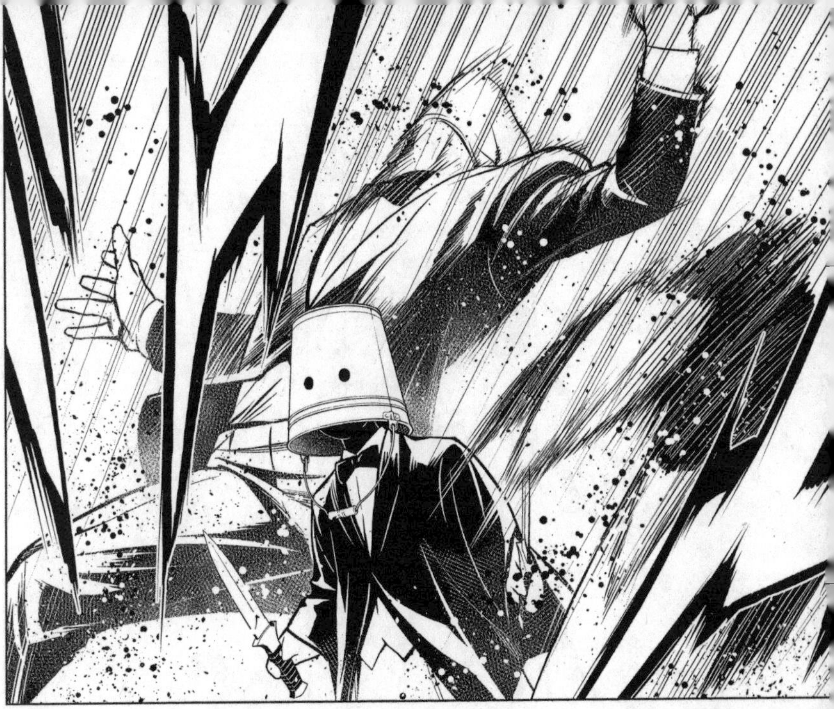

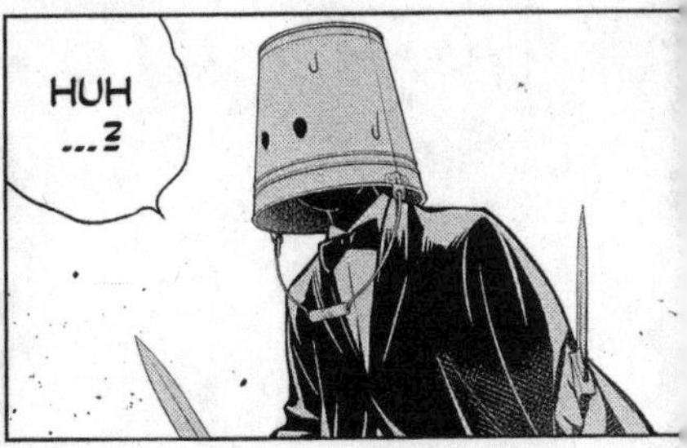
HUH ...?

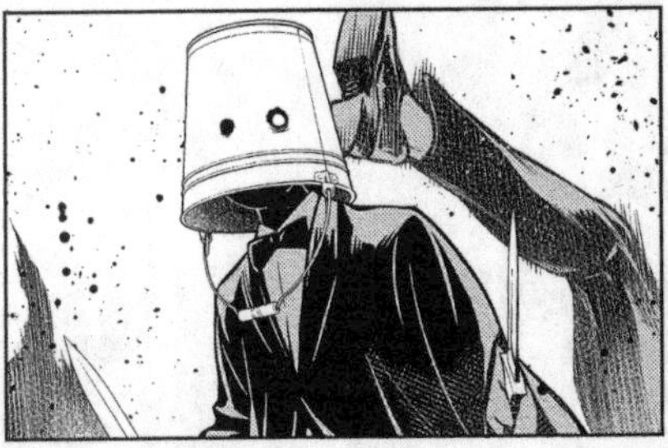

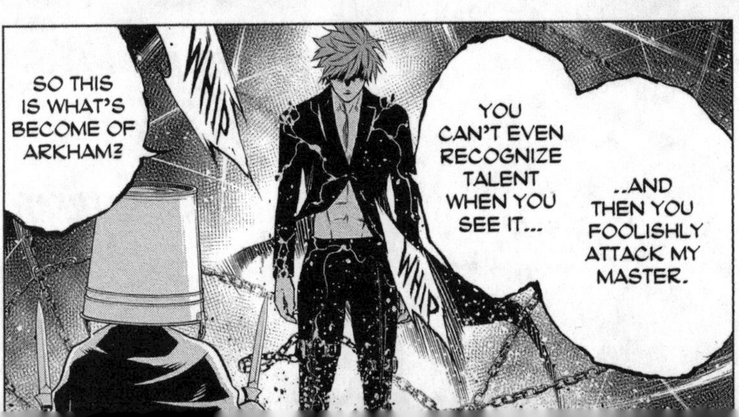
YOU CAN'T EVEN RECOGNIZE TALENT WHEN YOU SEE IT...
..AND THEN YOU FOOLISHLY ATTACK MY MASTER.
WHIP
WHIP
SO THIS IS WHAT'S BECOME OF ARKHAM?

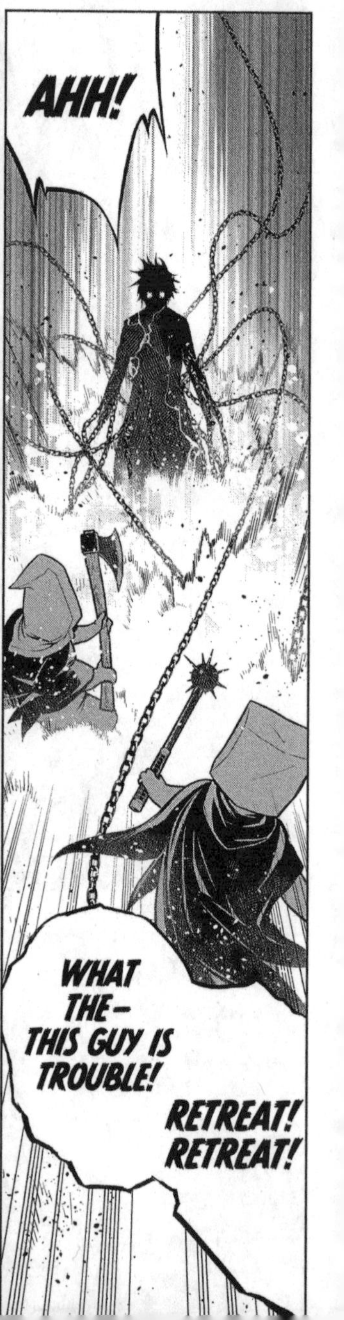
AHH!
WHAT THE— THIS GUY IS TROUBLE!
RETREAT! RETREAT!
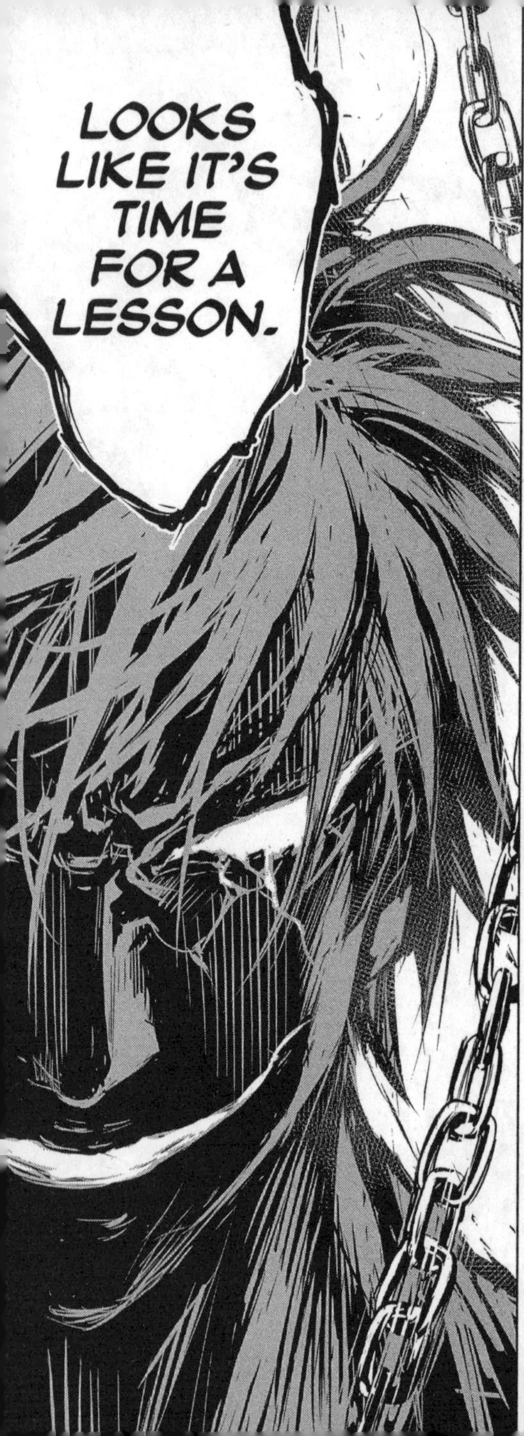
LOOKS LIKE IT'S TIME FOR A LESSON.

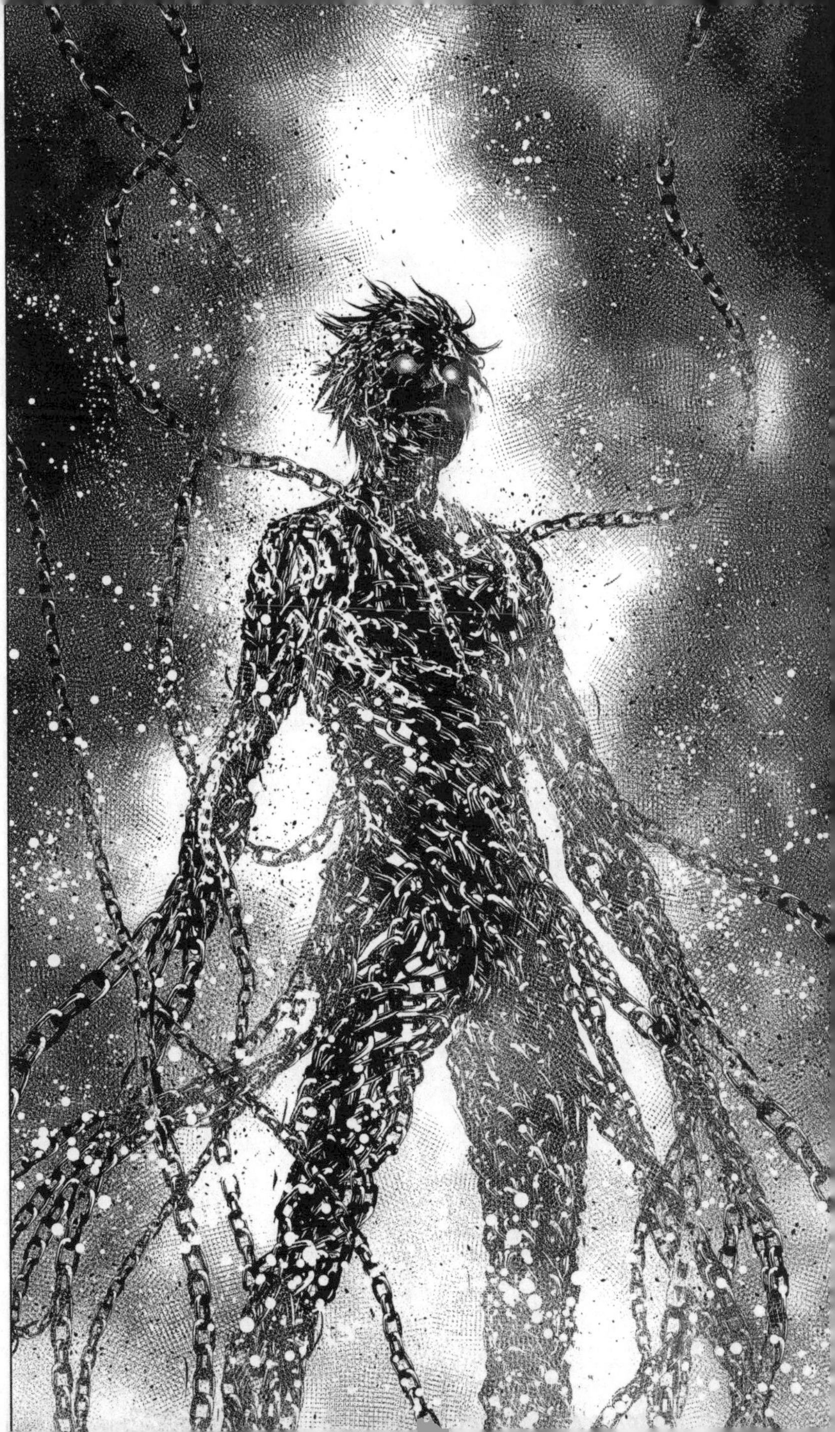

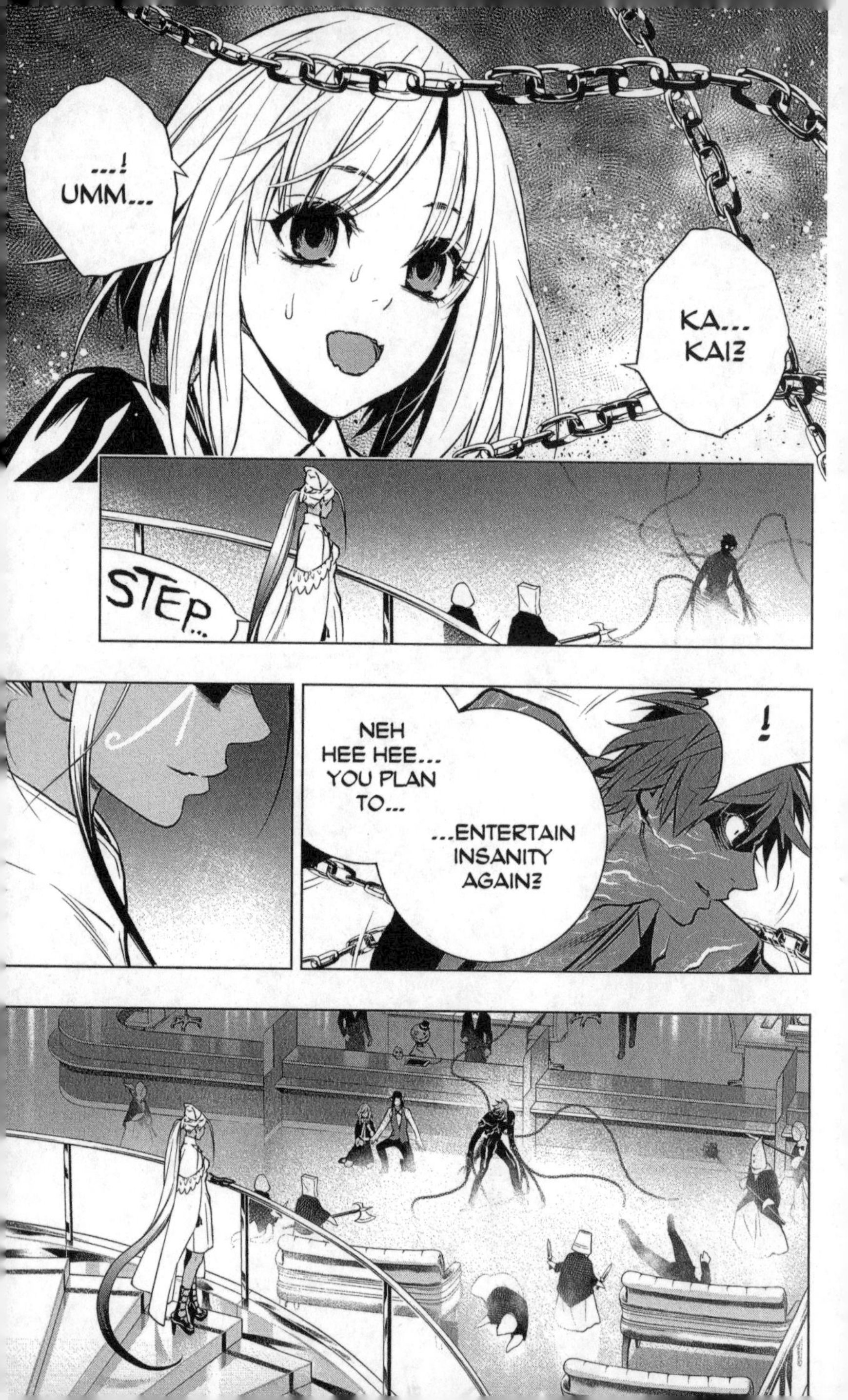
...! UMM...
KA... KAI?
STEP...
!
NEH HEE HEE... YOU PLAN TO...
...ENTERTAIN INSANITY AGAIN?

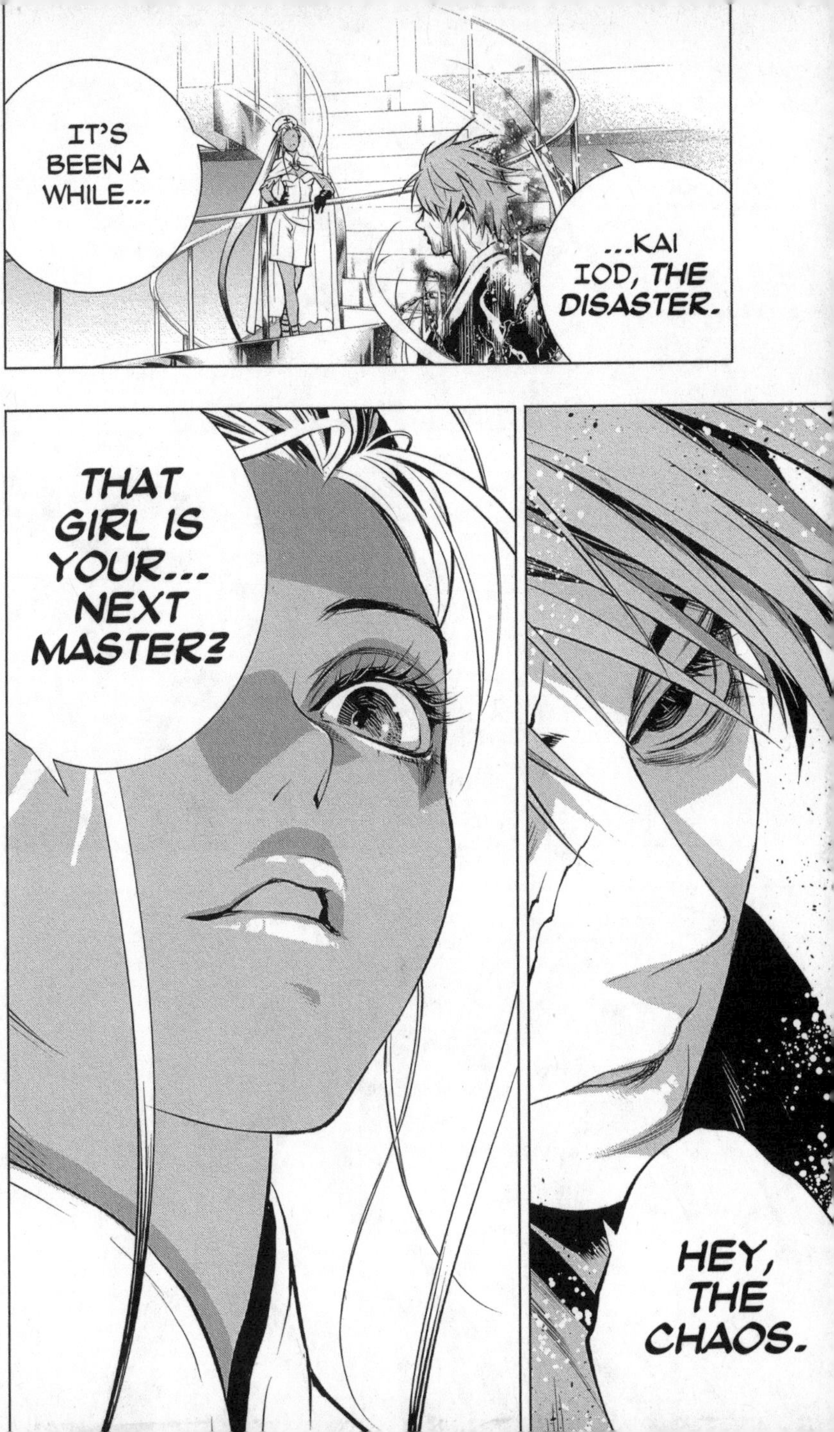
...KAI IOD, THE DISASTER.
IT'S BEEN A WHILE...
HEY, THE CHAOS.
THAT GIRL IS YOUR... NEXT MASTER?

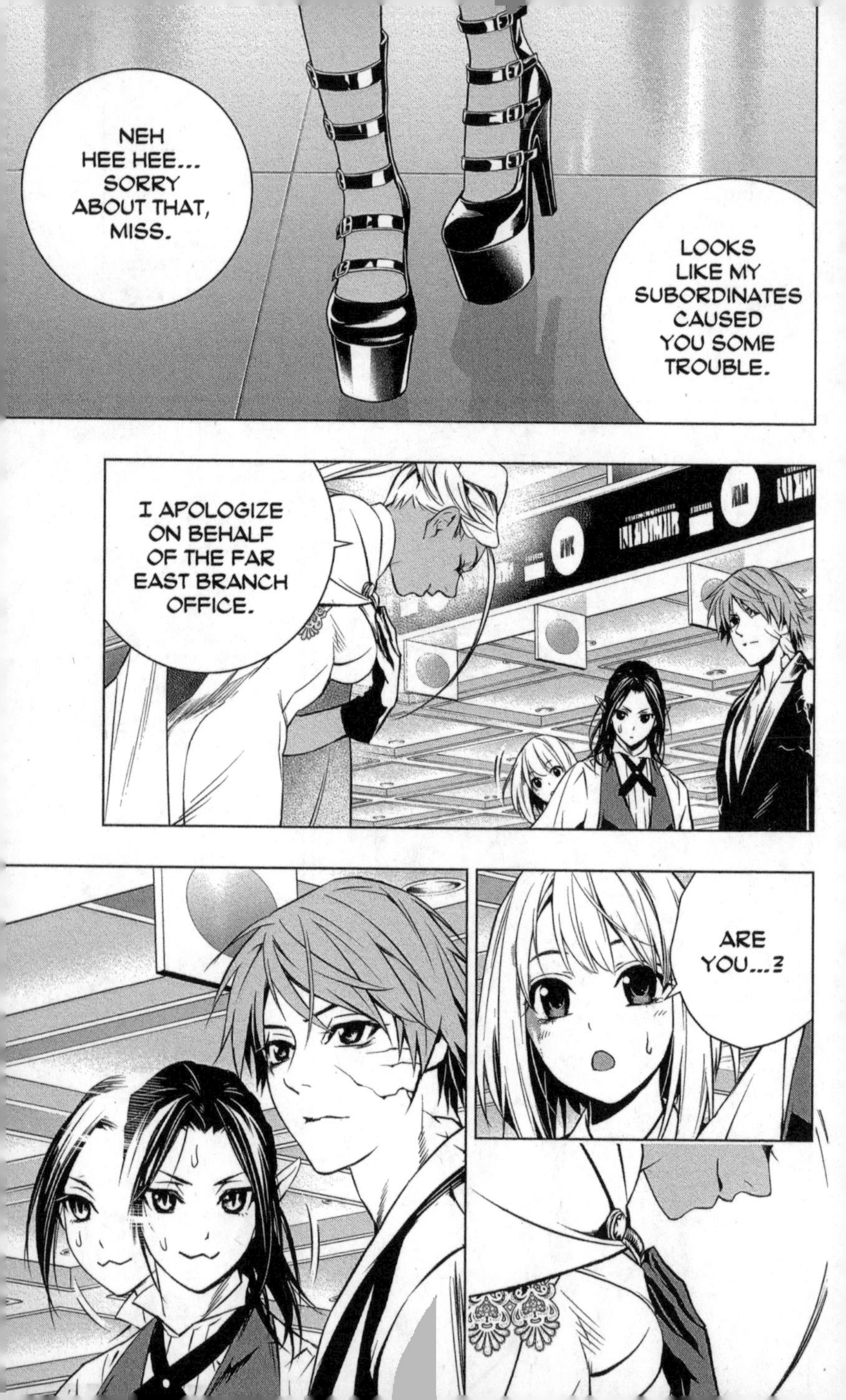
LOOKS LIKE MY SUBORDINATES CAUSED YOU SOME TROUBLE.
NEH HEE HEE... SORRY ABOUT THAT, MISS.
I APOLOGIZE ON BEHALF OF THE FAR EAST BRANCH OFFICE.
ARE YOU...?

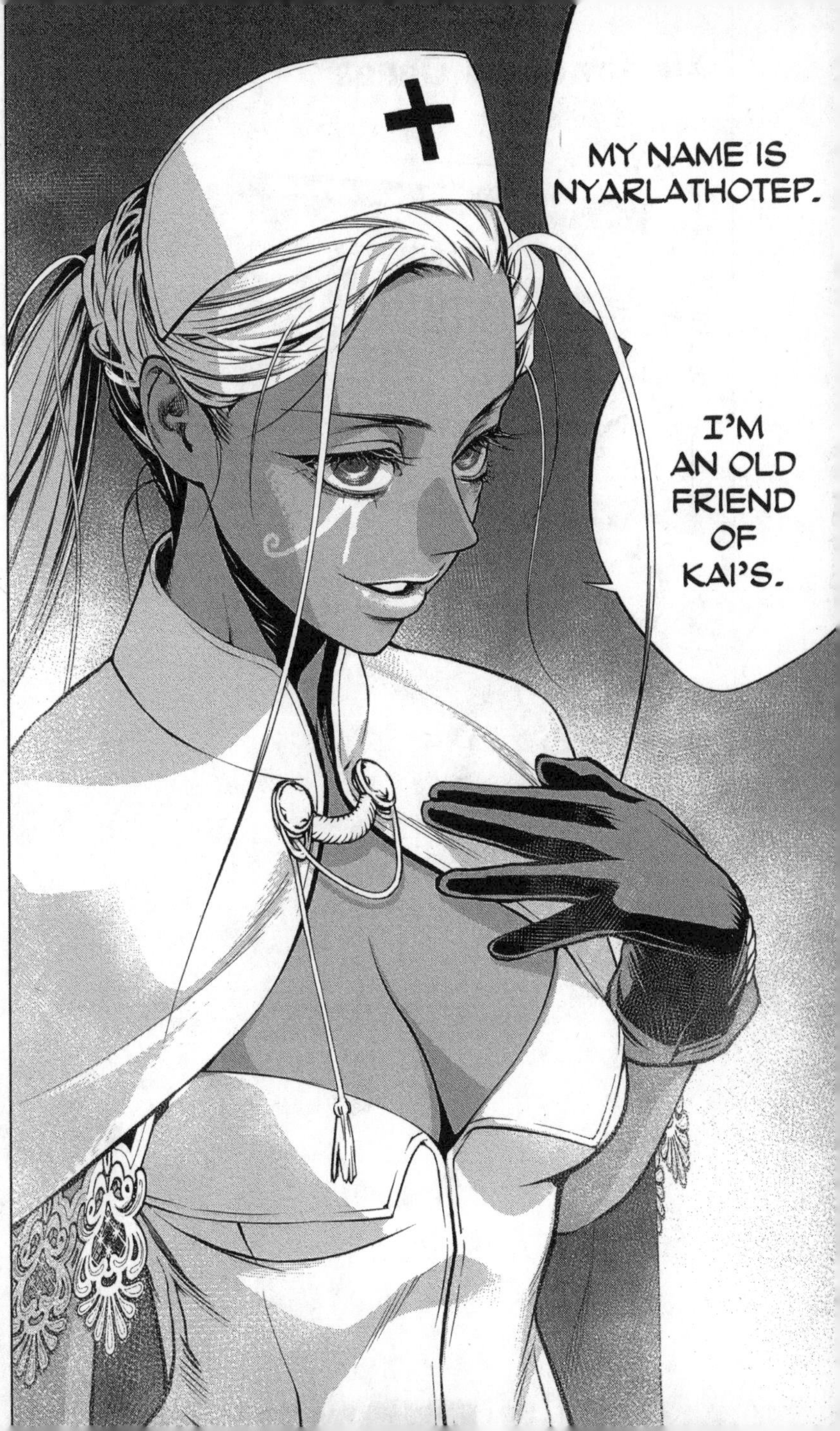
MY NAME IS NYARLATHOTEP.
I'M AN OLD FRIEND OF KAI'S.

#4: Crawling Chaos

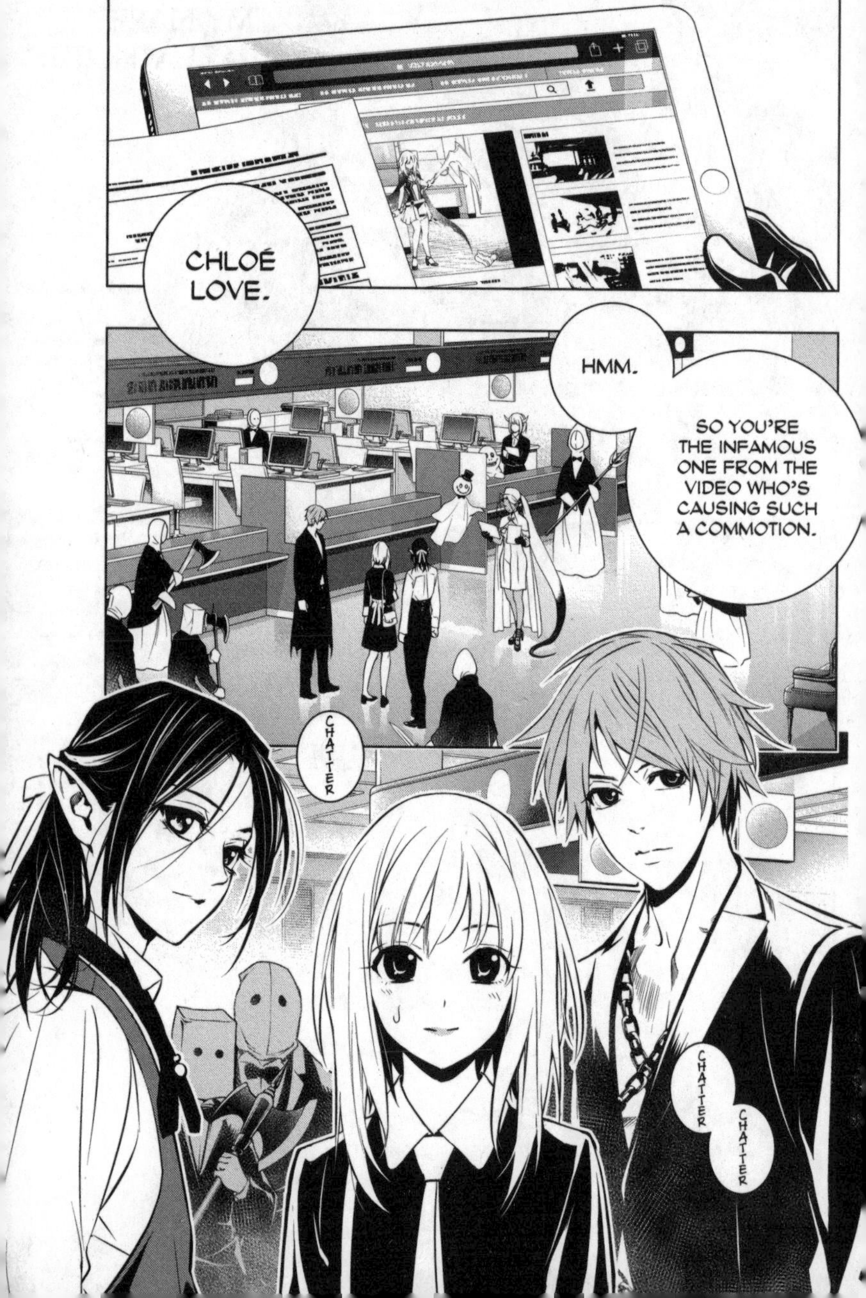
CHLOÉ LOVE.
HMM.
SO YOU'RE THE INFAMOUS ONE FROM THE VIDEO WHO'S CAUSING SUCH A COMMOTION.
CHATTER
CHATTER
CHATTER

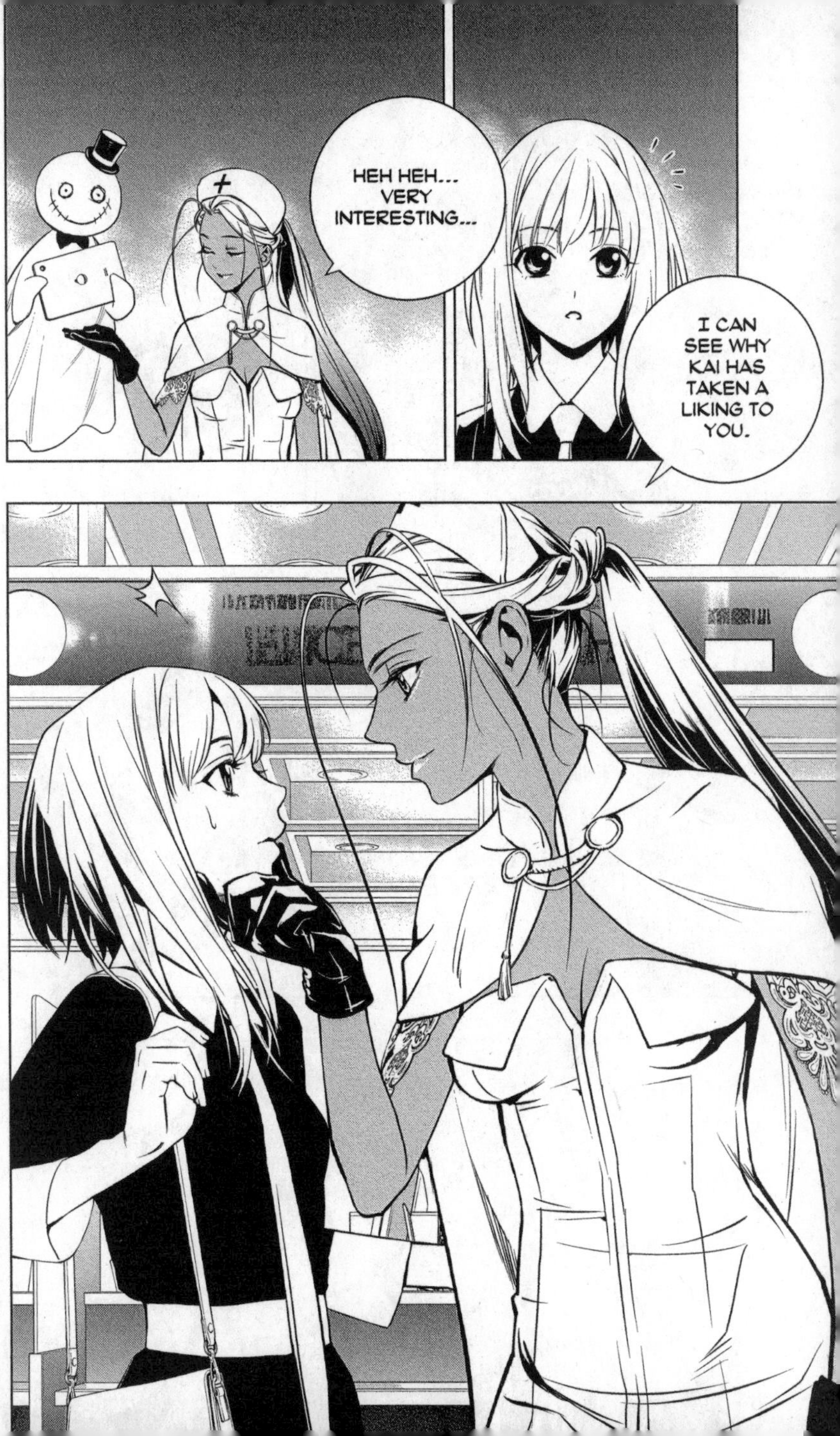
HEH HEH... VERY INTERESTING...
I CAN SEE WHY KAI HAS TAKEN A LIKING TO YOU.

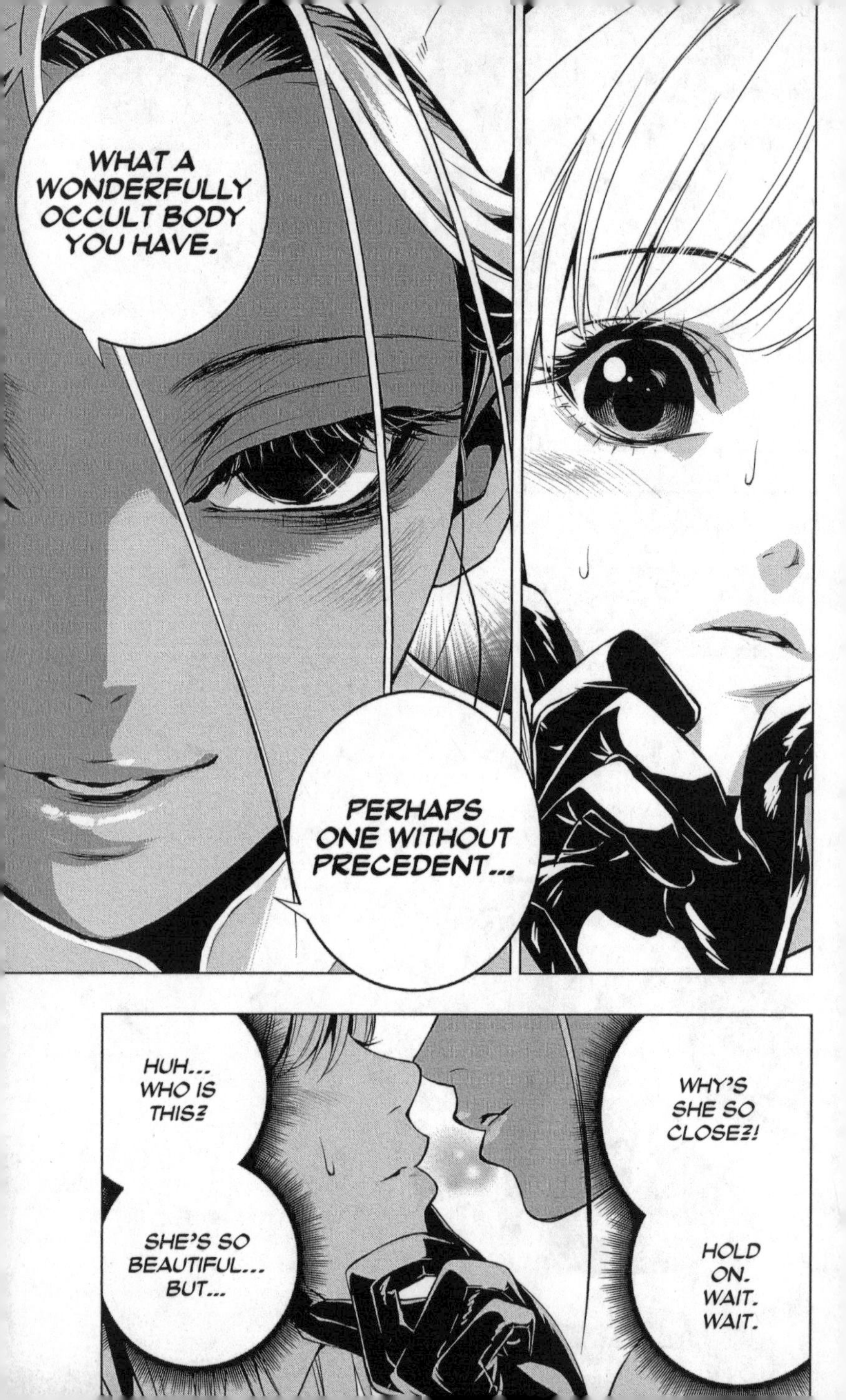
WHAT A WONDERFULLY OCCULT BODY YOU HAVE.
PERHAPS ONE WITHOUT PRECEDENT...
HUH... WHO IS THIS?
SHE'S SO BEAUTIFUL... BUT...
WHY'S SHE SO CLOSE?!
HOLD ON. WAIT. WAIT.

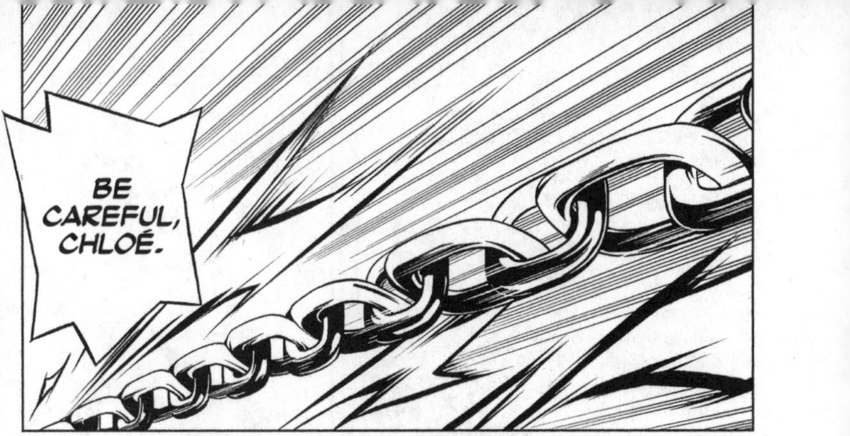
BE CAREFUL, CHLOÉ.

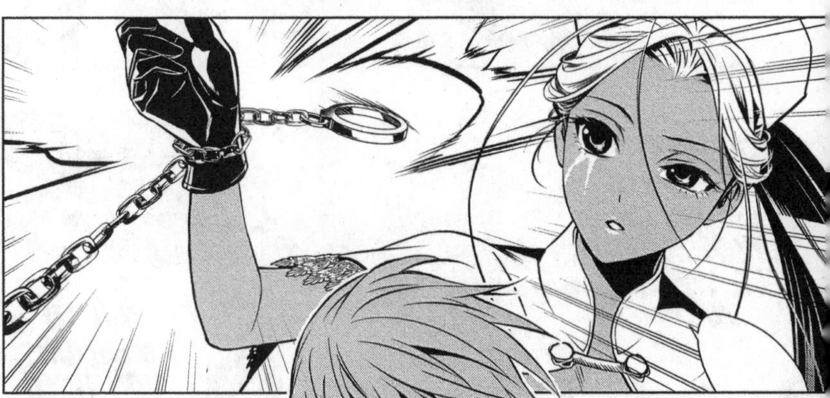

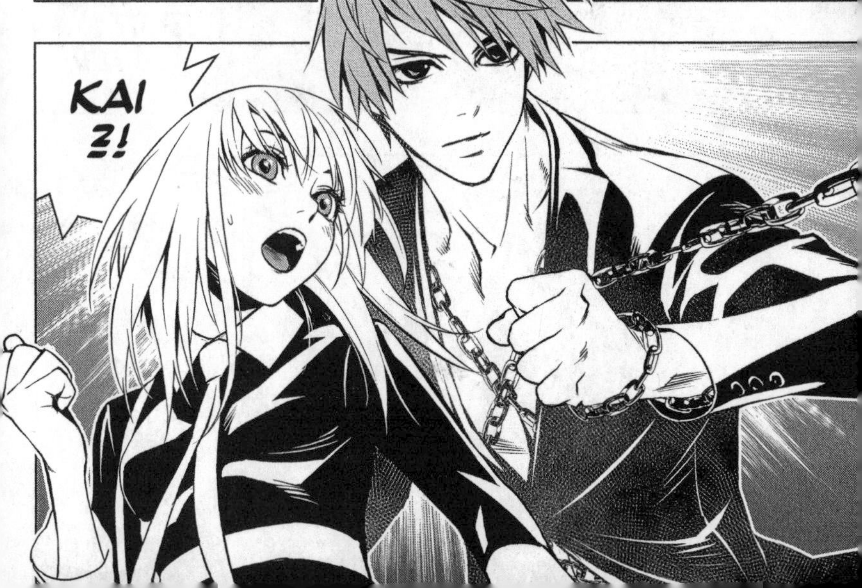
KAI ?!

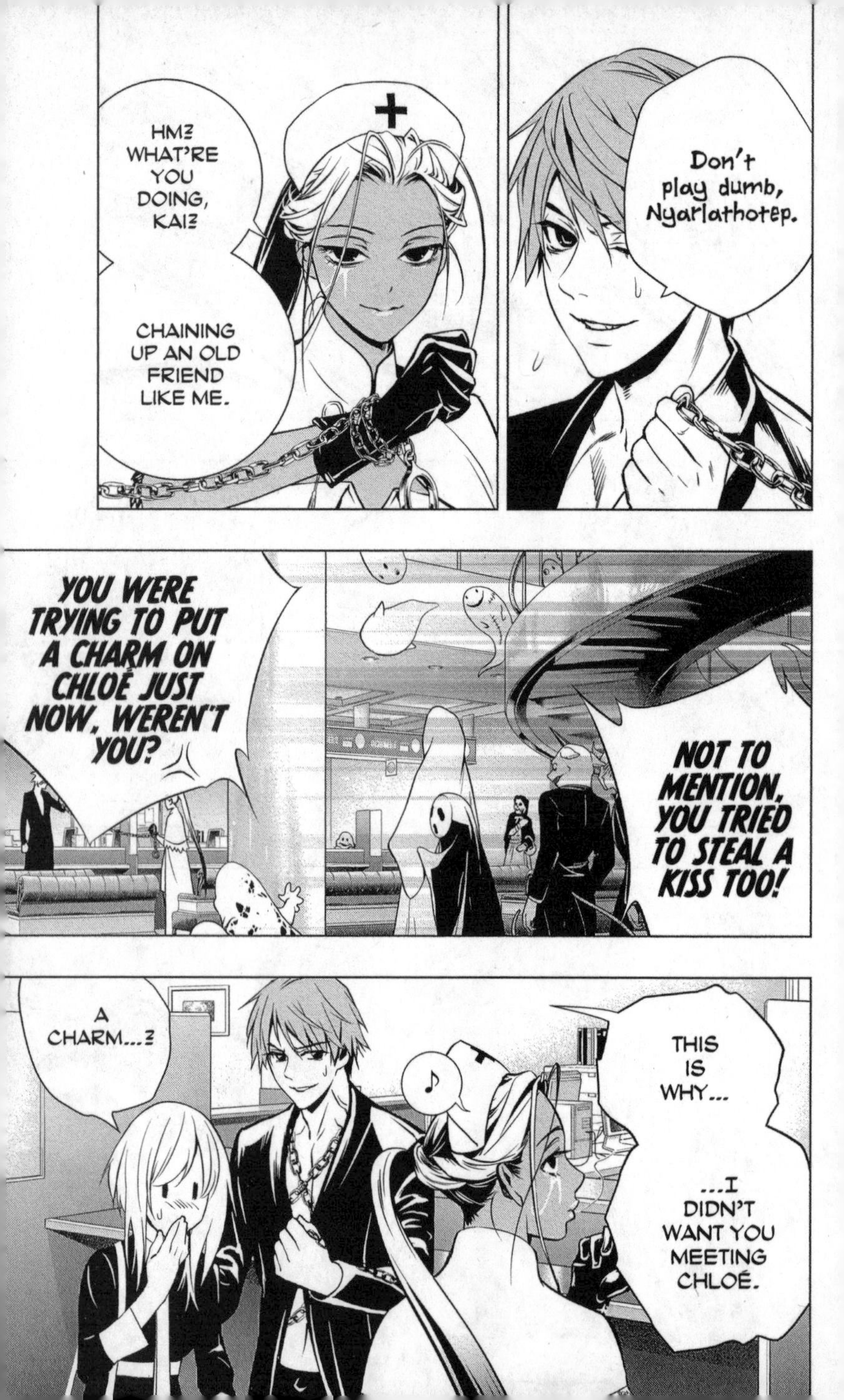
HM? WHAT'RE YOU DOING, KAI?
CHAINING UP AN OLD FRIEND LIKE ME.
Don't play dumb, Nyarlathotep.
YOU WERE TRYING TO PUT A CHARM ON CHLOÉ JUST NOW, WEREN'T YOU?
NOT TO MENTION, YOU TRIED TO STEAL A KISS TOO!
A CHARM...?
♪
THIS IS WHY...
...I DIDN'T WANT YOU MEETING CHLOÉ.

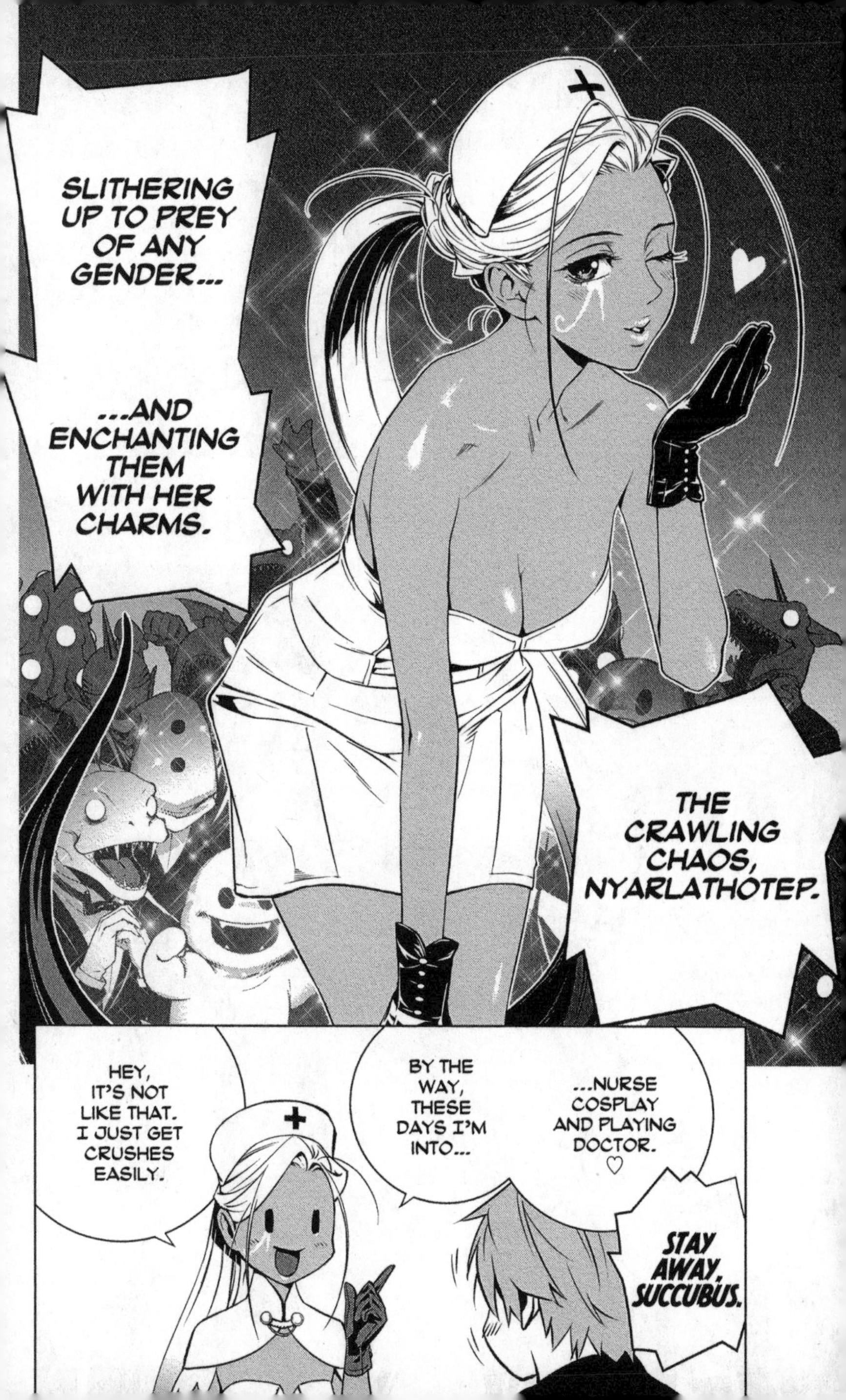
SLITHERING UP TO PREY OF ANY GENDER...
...AND ENCHANTING THEM WITH HER CHARMS.
THE CRAWLING CHAOS, NYARLATHOTEP.
HEY, IT'S NOT LIKE THAT. I JUST GET CRUSHES EASILY.
BY THE WAY, THESE DAYS I'M INTO...
...NURSE COSPLAY AND PLAYING DOCTOR. ♡
STAY AWAY, SUCCUBUS.

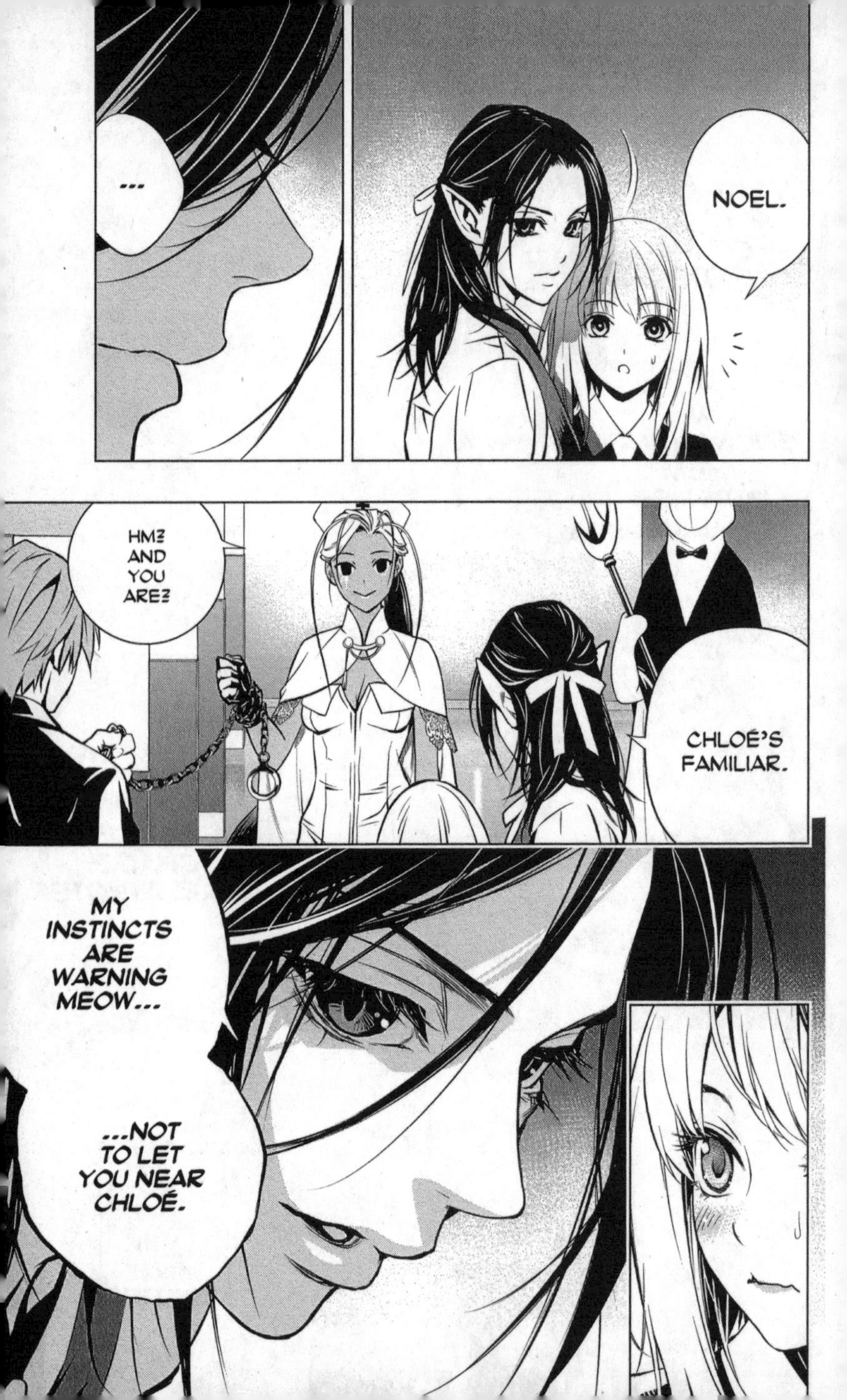
NOEL.
...
HM? AND YOU ARE?
CHLOÉ'S FAMILIAR.
MY INSTINCTS ARE WARNING MEOW...
...NOT TO LET YOU NEAR CHLOÉ.

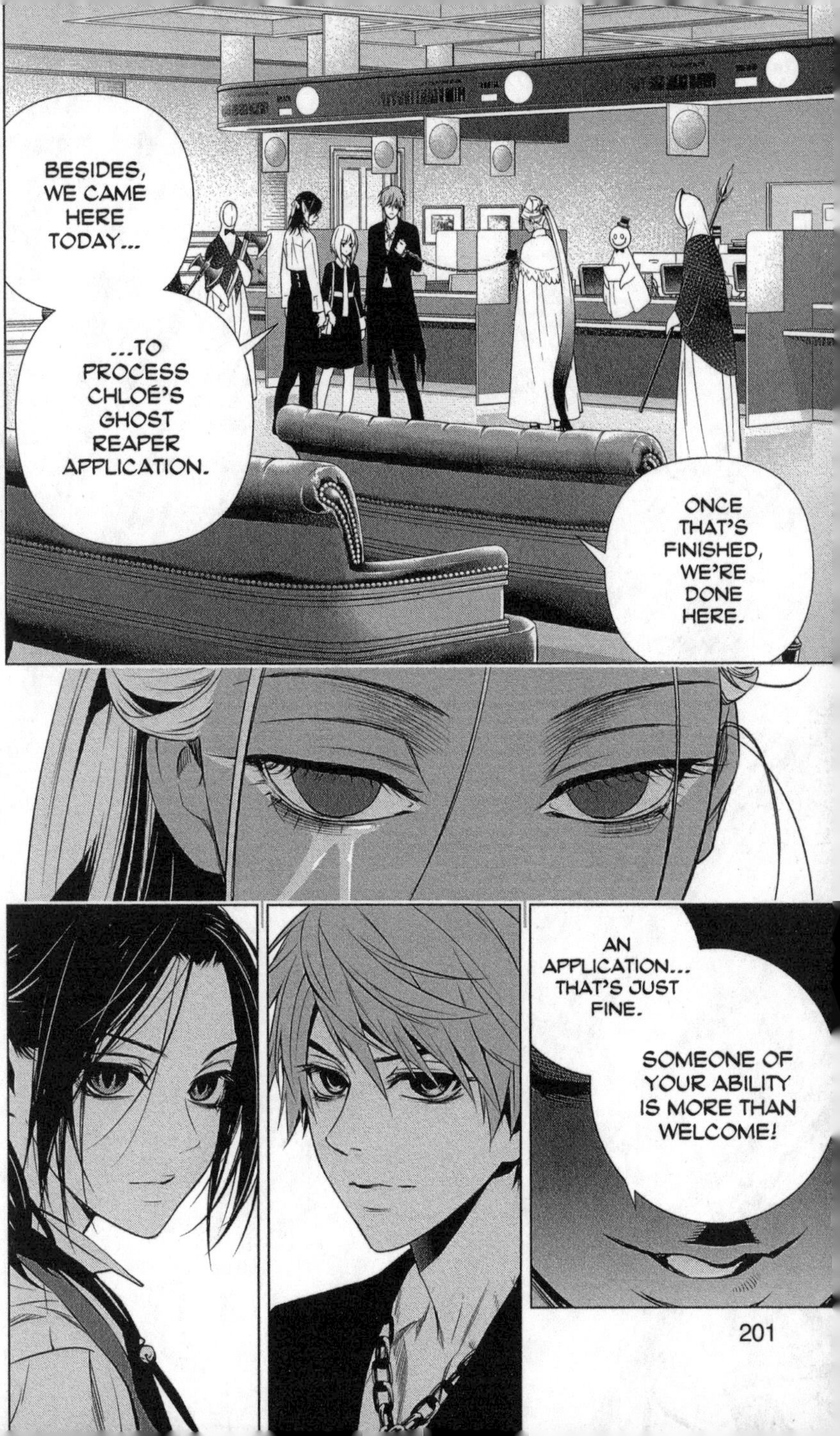
BESIDES, WE CAME HERE TODAY...
...TO PROCESS CHLOÉ'S GHOST REAPER APPLICATION.
ONCE THAT'S FINISHED, WE'RE DONE HERE.
AN APPLICATION... THAT'S JUST FINE.
SOMEONE OF YOUR ABILITY IS MORE THAN WELCOME!

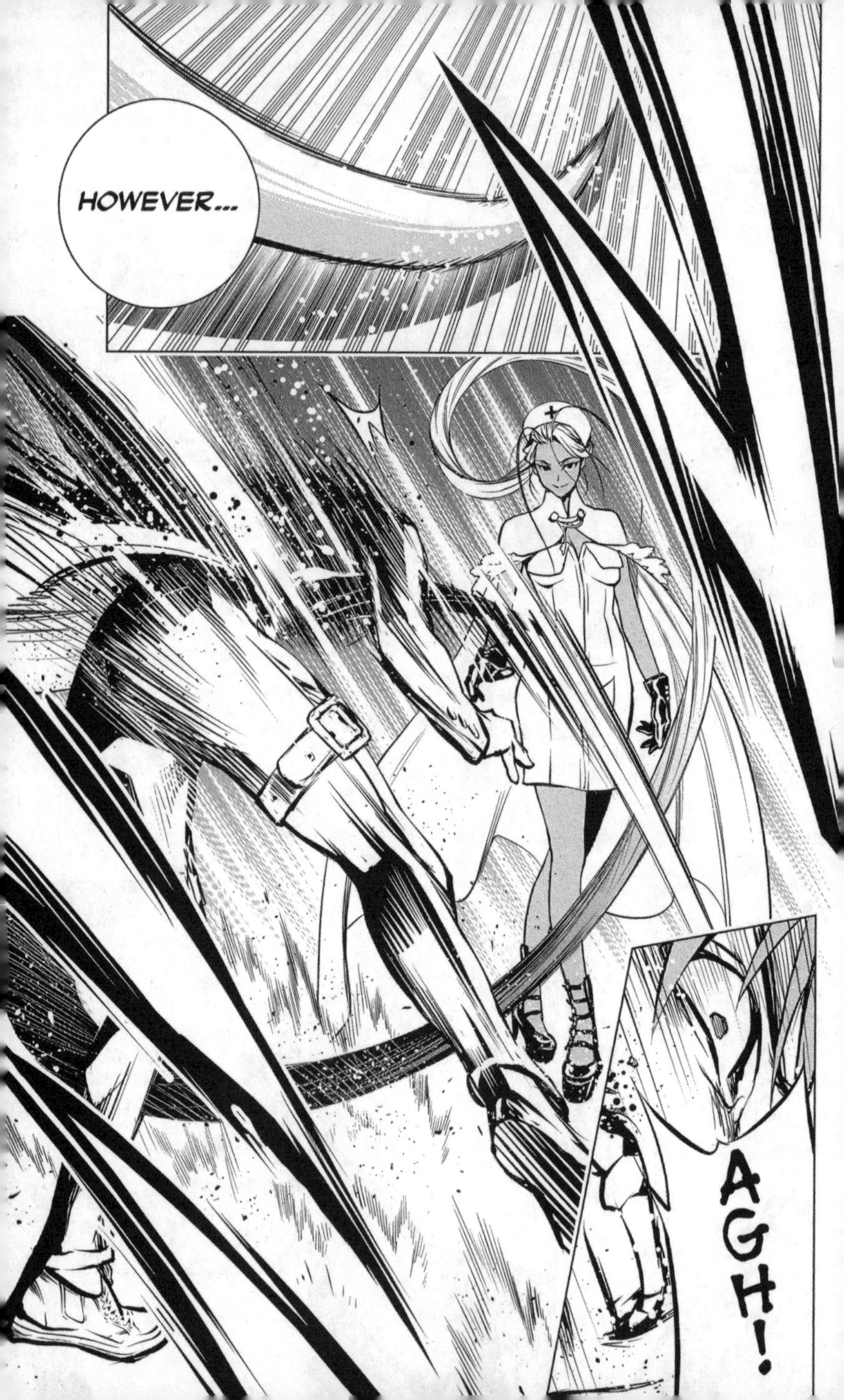
HOWEVER...
AGH!

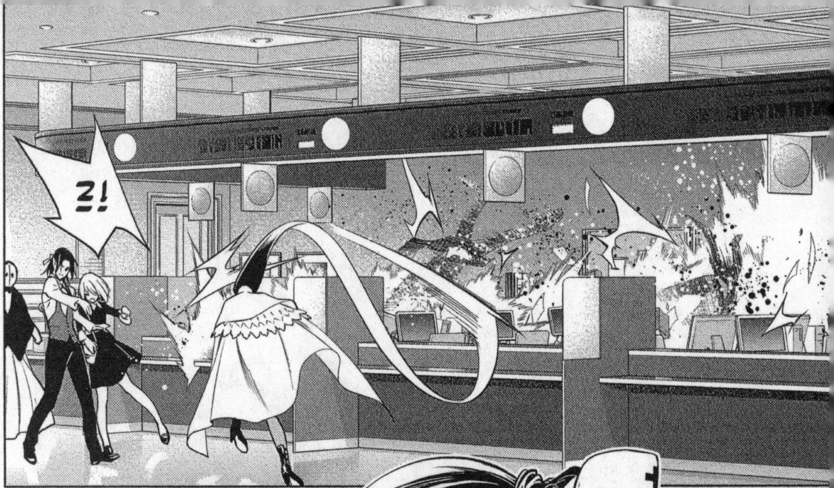
?!

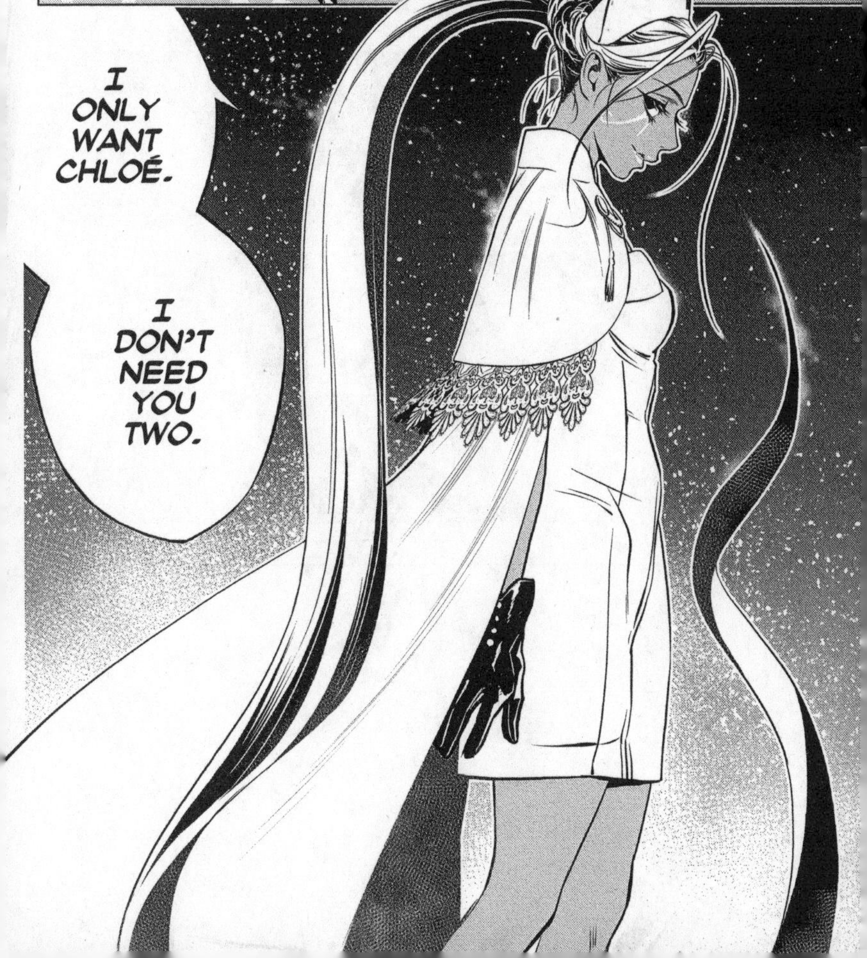
I ONLY WANT CHLOÉ.
I DON'T NEED YOU TWO.

KAI ?!

HE'LL BE FINE.

!

HE MAY BE IN A WEAKENED FORM RIGHT NOW...

...BUT EVEN SO, THAT ATTACK'S STILL NOT ENOUGH FOR HIM TO BITE THE DUST.

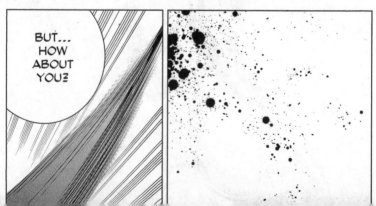

BUT... HOW ABOUT YOU?

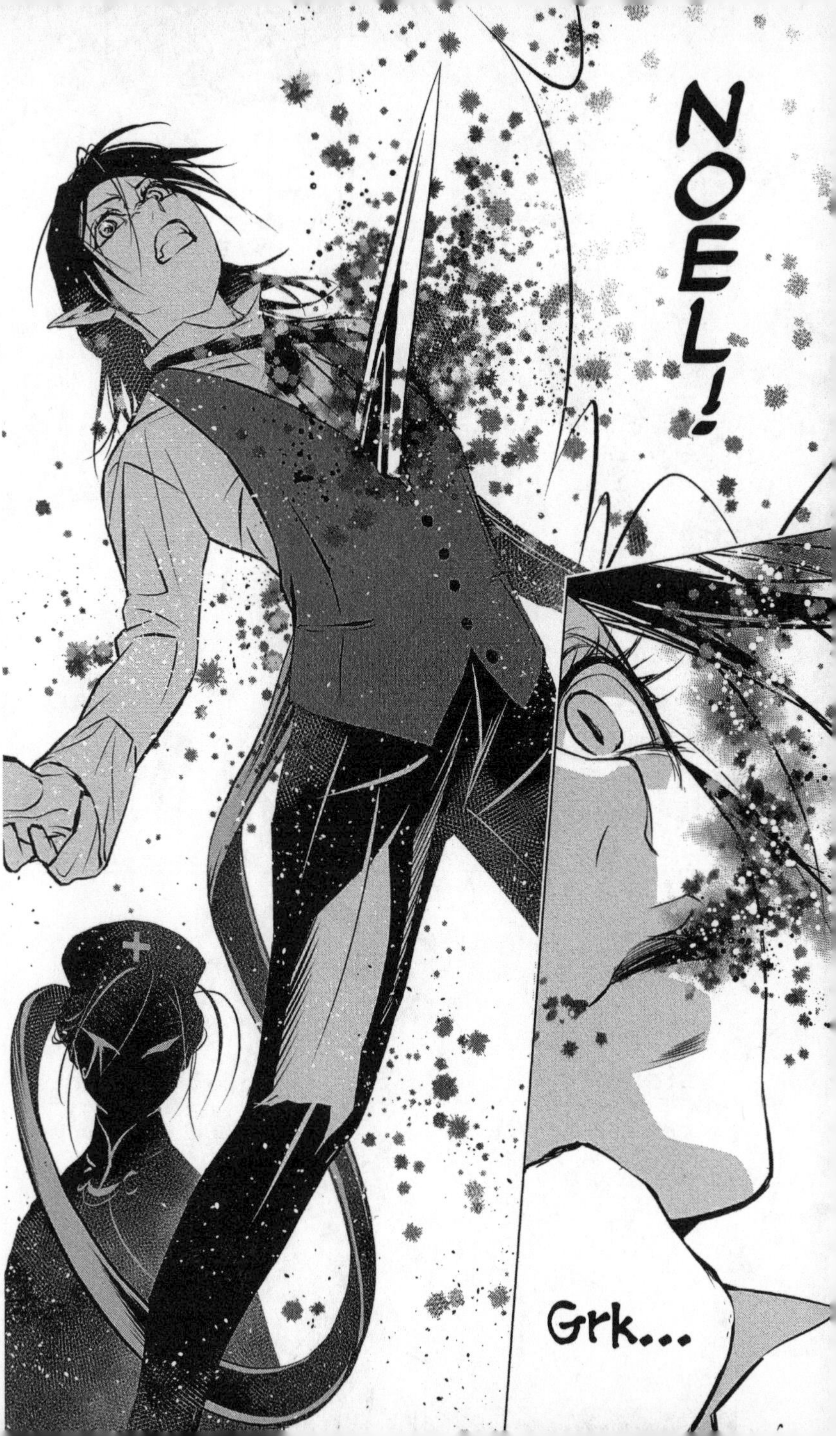
NOEL!!
Grk...

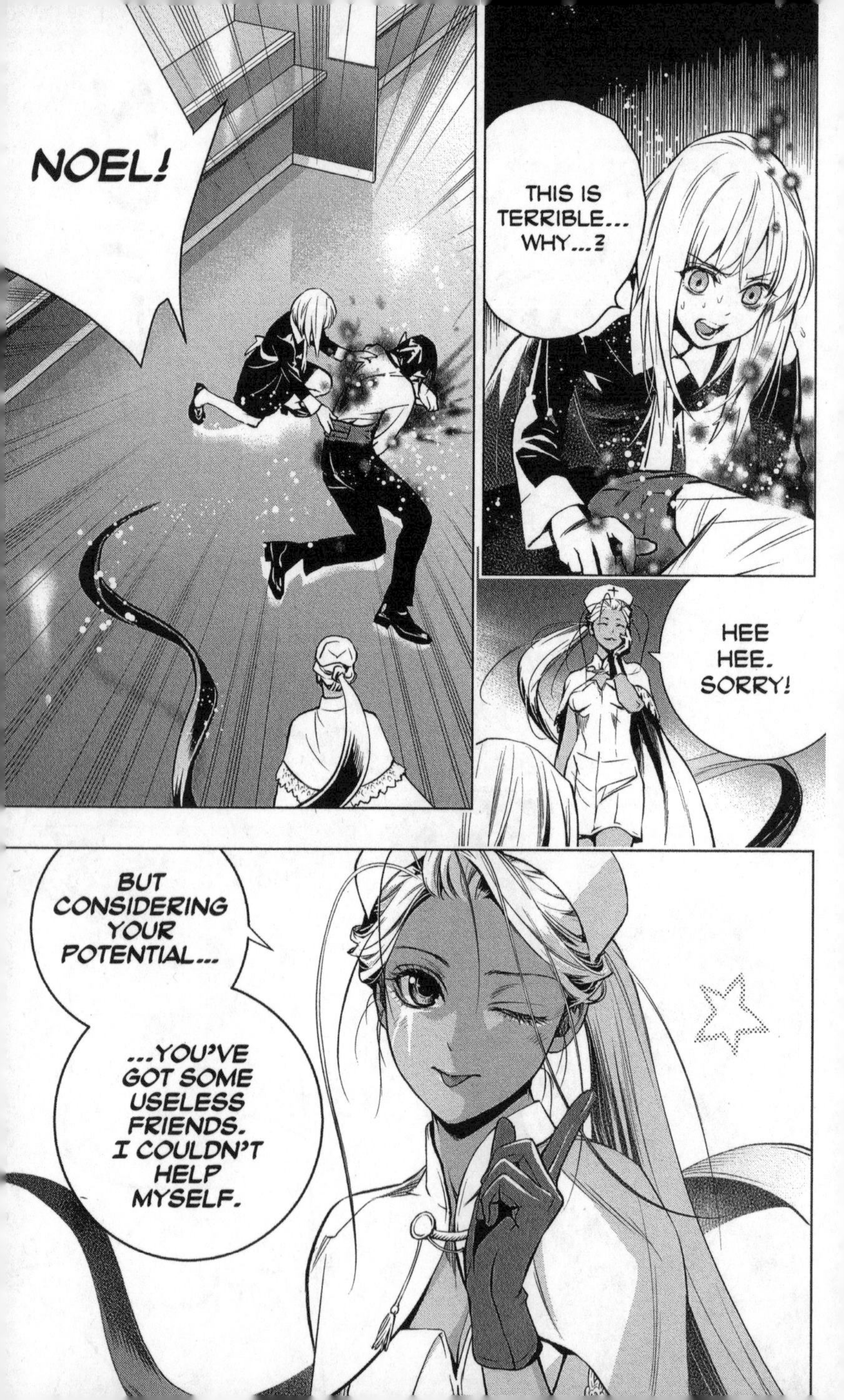
THIS IS TERRIBLE... WHY...?
HEE HEE. SORRY!
NOEL!
BUT CONSIDERING YOUR POTENTIAL...
...YOU'VE GOT SOME USELESS FRIENDS. I COULDN'T HELP MYSELF.

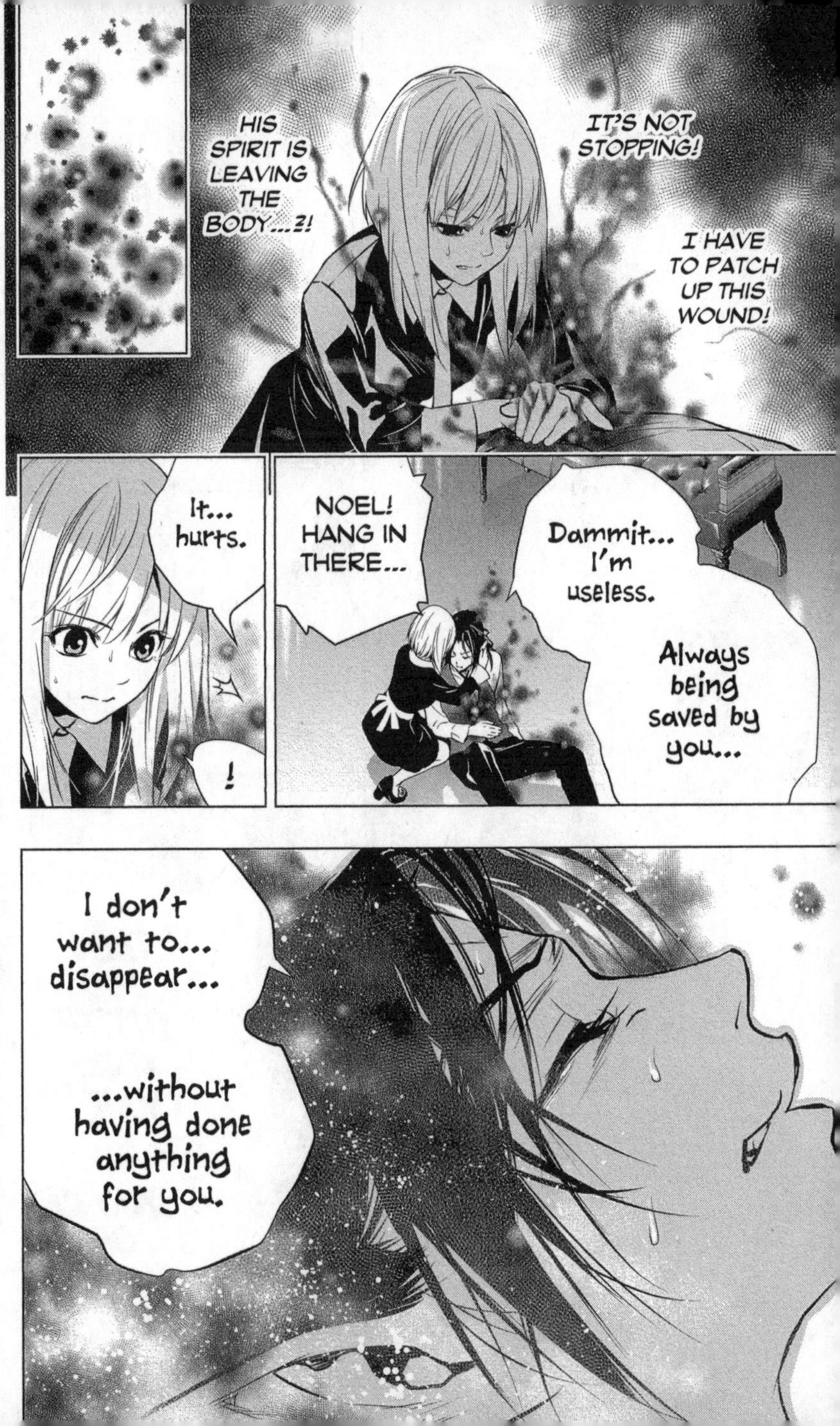
IT'S NOT STOPPING!
HIS SPIRIT IS LEAVING THE BODY...?!
I HAVE TO PATCH UP THIS WOUND!
Dammit... I'm useless.
Always being saved by you...
NOEL! HANG IN THERE...
It... hurts.
!
I don't want to... disappear...
...without having done anything for you.

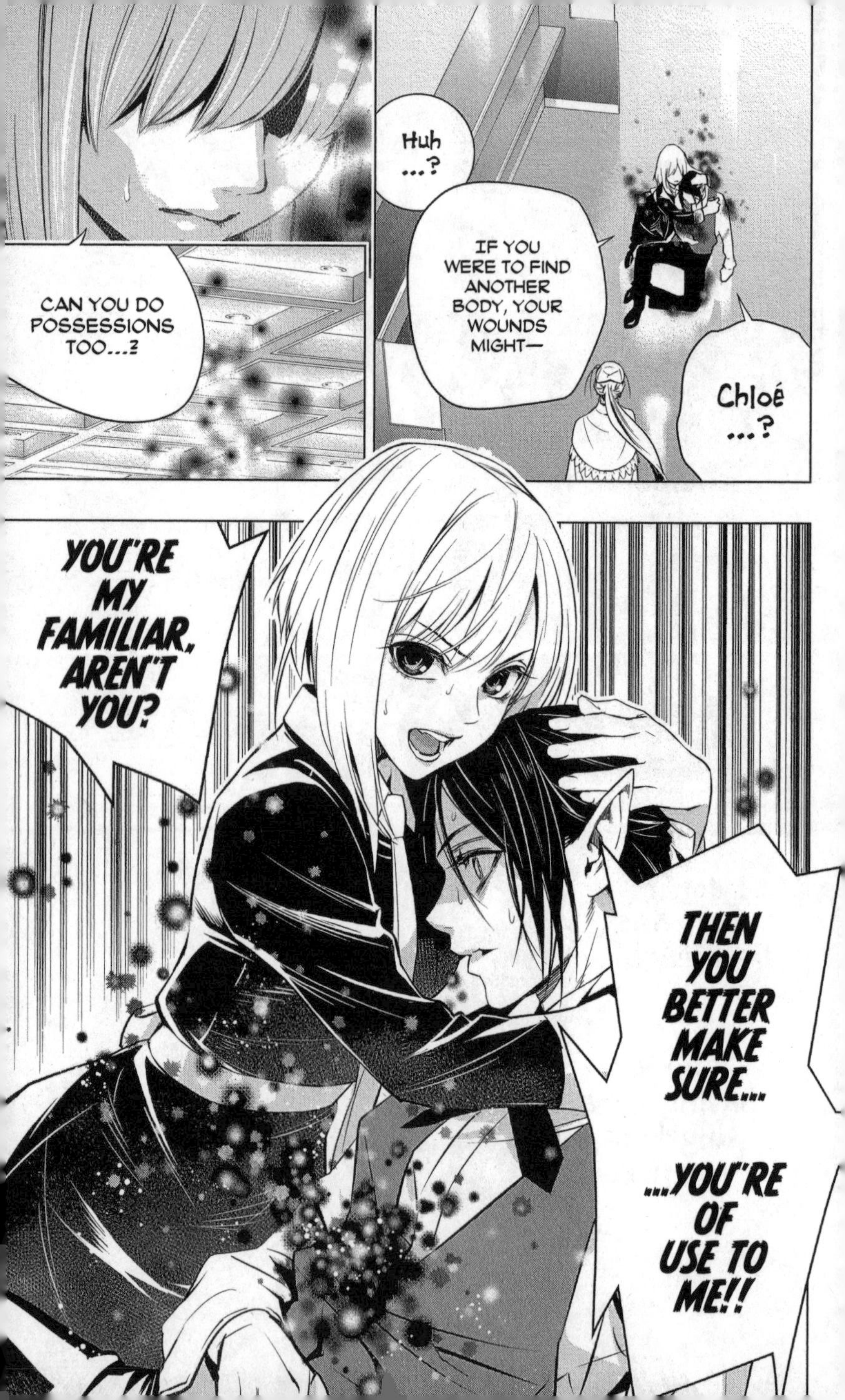
Huh ...?
IF YOU WERE TO FIND ANOTHER BODY, YOUR WOUNDS MIGHT—
Chloé ...?
CAN YOU DO POSSESSIONS TOO...?
YOU'RE MY FAMILIAR, AREN'T YOU?
THEN YOU BETTER MAKE SURE...
...YOU'RE OF USE TO ME!!

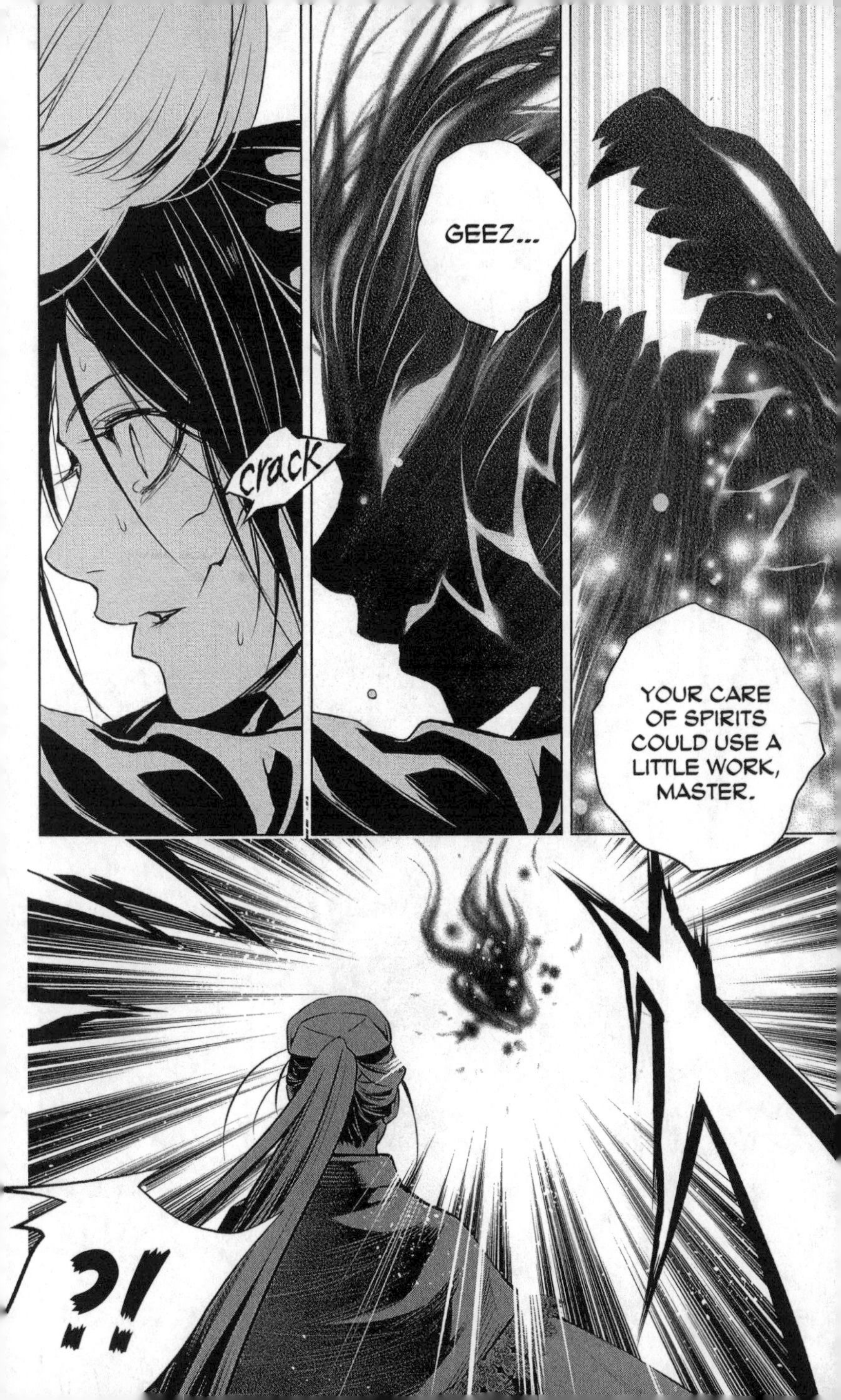
YOUR CARE OF SPIRITS COULD USE A LITTLE WORK, MASTER.
GEEZ...
crack
?!

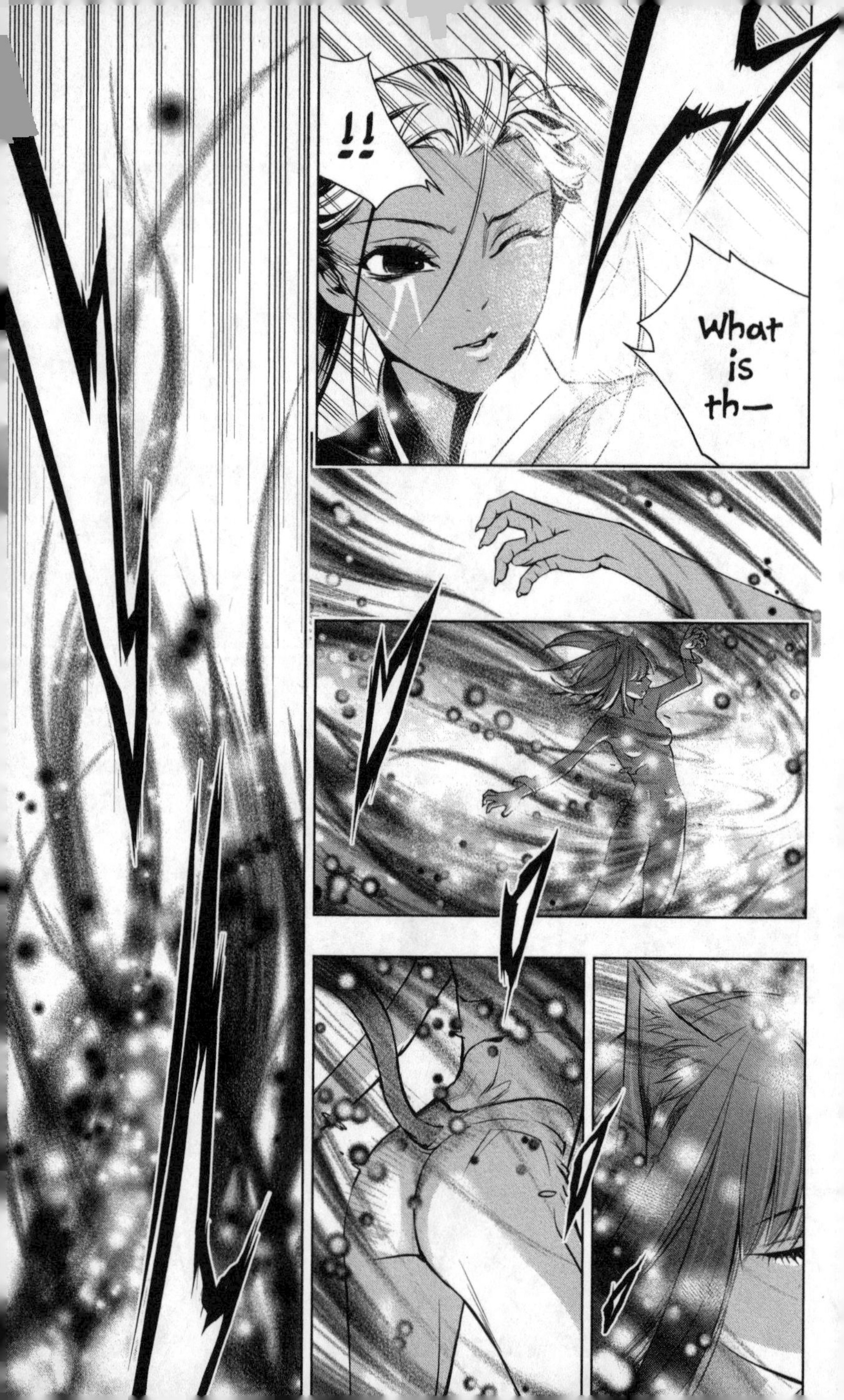
!!
What is th—

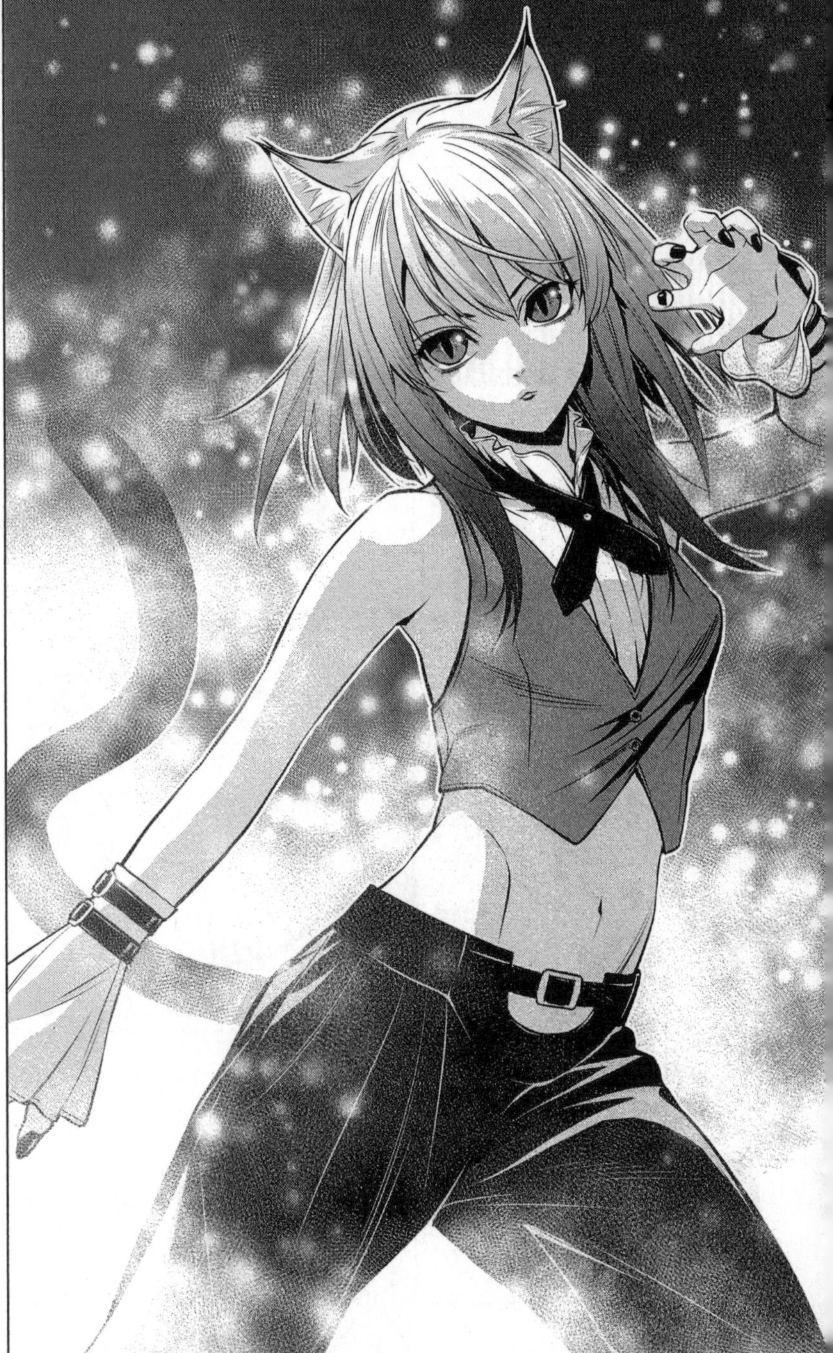

Ghost Reaper Girl Vol. 1 / End

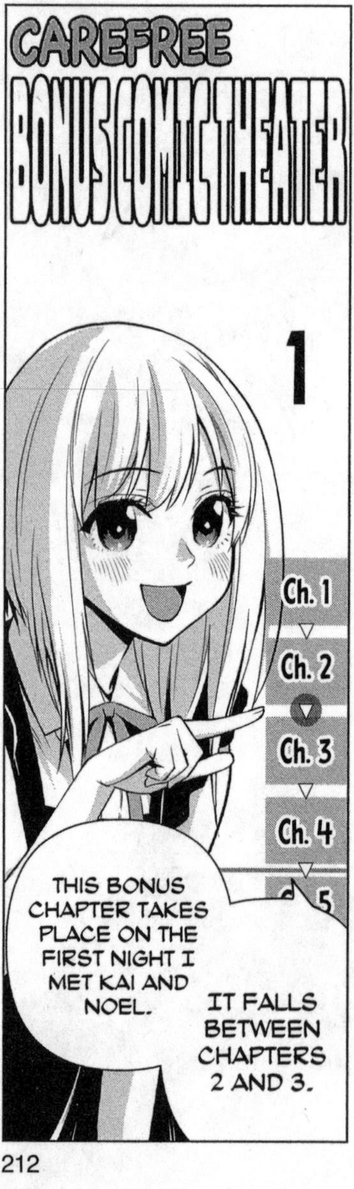
CAREFREE
BONUS COMIC THEATER
1
Ch. 1
Ch. 2
Ch. 3
Ch. 4
THIS BONUS CHAPTER TAKES PLACE ON THE FIRST NIGHT I MET KAI AND NOEL.
IT FALLS BETWEEN CHAPTERS 2 AND 3.

False Expectations

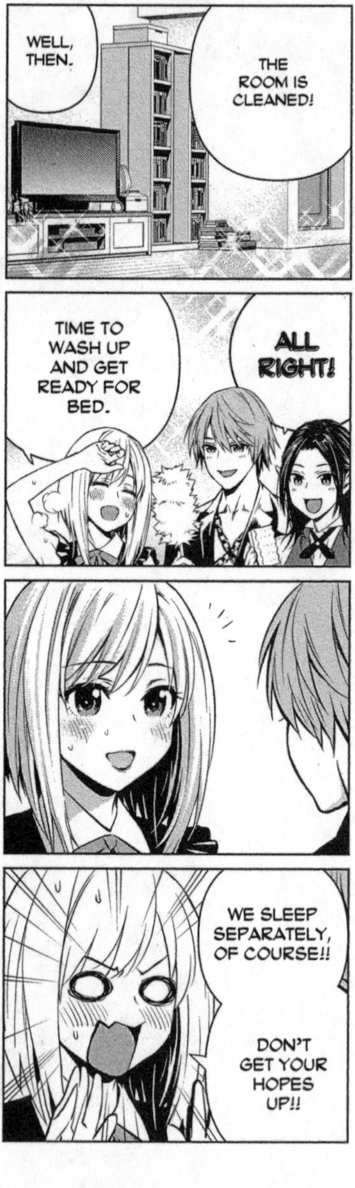
WELL, THEN.
THE ROOM IS CLEANED!
TIME TO WASH UP AND GET READY FOR BED.
ALL RIGHT!
WE SLEEP SEPARATELY, OF COURSE!!
DON'T GET YOUR HOPES UP!!

Strange Self-Consciousness

SO, I'M GONNA TAKE A SHOWER.

DON'T EVEN THINK...

...ABOUT TAKING A PEEK.

THAT'S NOT SOME...

...ROUND-ABOUT INVITATION, BY THE WAY.

Abundant Self-Consciousness

I CAN'T BELIEVE THIS.

MY HEART'S RACING!

TAKING A SHOWER WHILE TWO HOTTIES ARE IN MY APARTMENT?

WHAT AM I THINK-ING?!

AH! WAIT A SEC!

CAN THEY MOVE THROUGH WALLS?!

Watches Them All

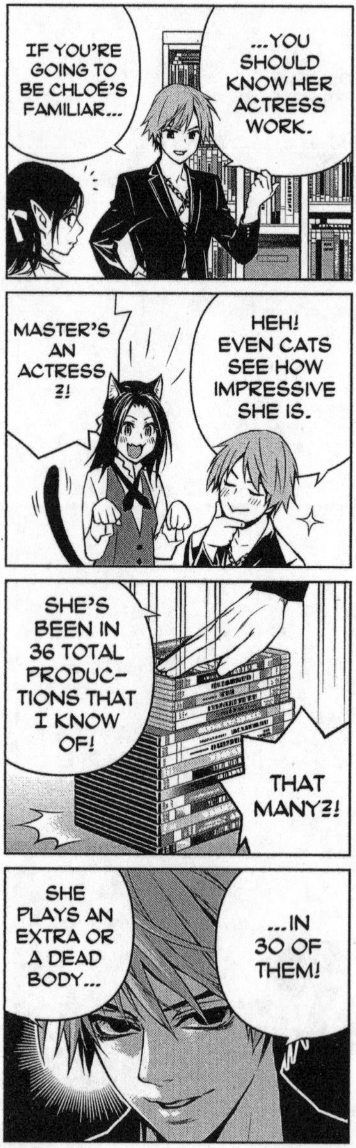
IF YOU'RE GOING TO BE CHLOÉ'S FAMILIAR...
...YOU SHOULD KNOW HER ACTRESS WORK.
MASTER'S AN ACTRESS?!
HEH! EVEN CATS SEE HOW IMPRESSIVE SHE IS.
SHE'S BEEN IN 36 TOTAL PRODUC-TIONS THAT I KNOW OF!
THAT MANY?!
SHE PLAYS AN EXTRA OR A DEAD BODY...
...IN 30 OF THEM!

Top-Notch Acting

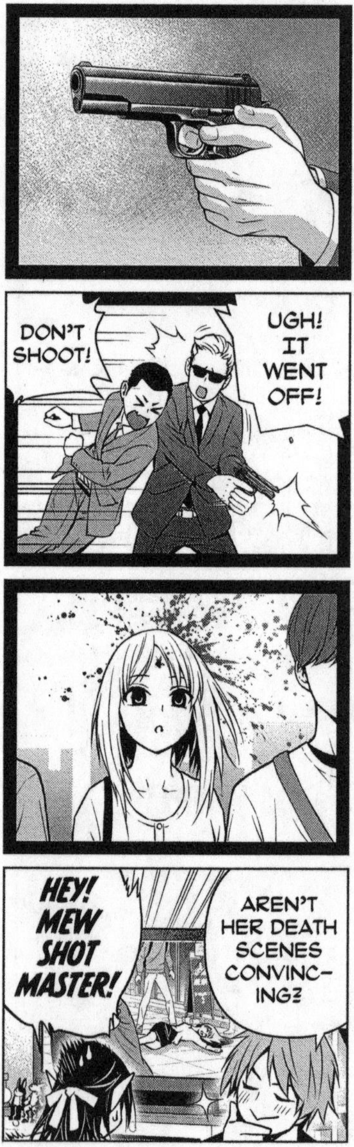
DON'T SHOOT!
UGH! IT WENT OFF!
HEY! MEW SHOT MASTER!
AREN'T HER DEATH SCENES CONVINC-ING?

Unsatisfied

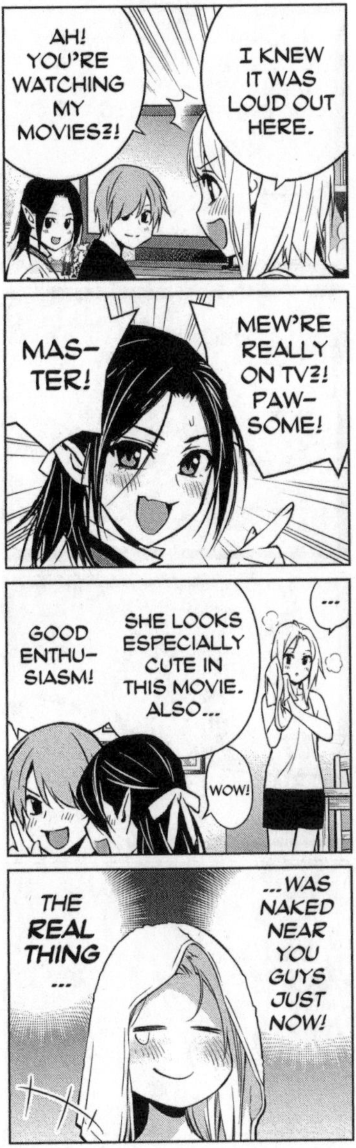
AH! YOU'RE WATCHING MY MOVIES?!
I KNEW IT WAS LOUD OUT HERE.
MAS-TER!
MEW'RE REALLY ON TV?! PAW-SOME!
GOOD ENTHU-SIASM!
SHE LOOKS ESPECIALLY CUTE IN THIS MOVIE. ALSO...
...
WOW!
THE REAL THING...
...WAS NAKED NEAR YOU GUYS JUST NOW!

The Gentleman and the Lady

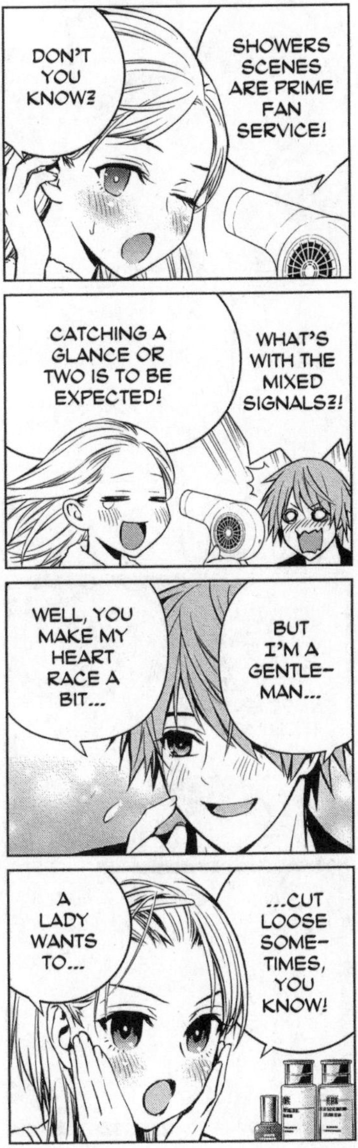
DON'T YOU KNOW?
SHOWERS SCENES ARE PRIME FAN SERVICE!
CATCHING A GLANCE OR TWO IS TO BE EXPECTED!
WHAT'S WITH THE MIXED SIGNALS?!
WELL, YOU MAKE MY HEART RACE A BIT...
BUT I'M A GENTLE-MAN...
A LADY WANTS TO...
...CUT LOOSE SOME-TIMES, YOU KNOW!

Bad Experiences

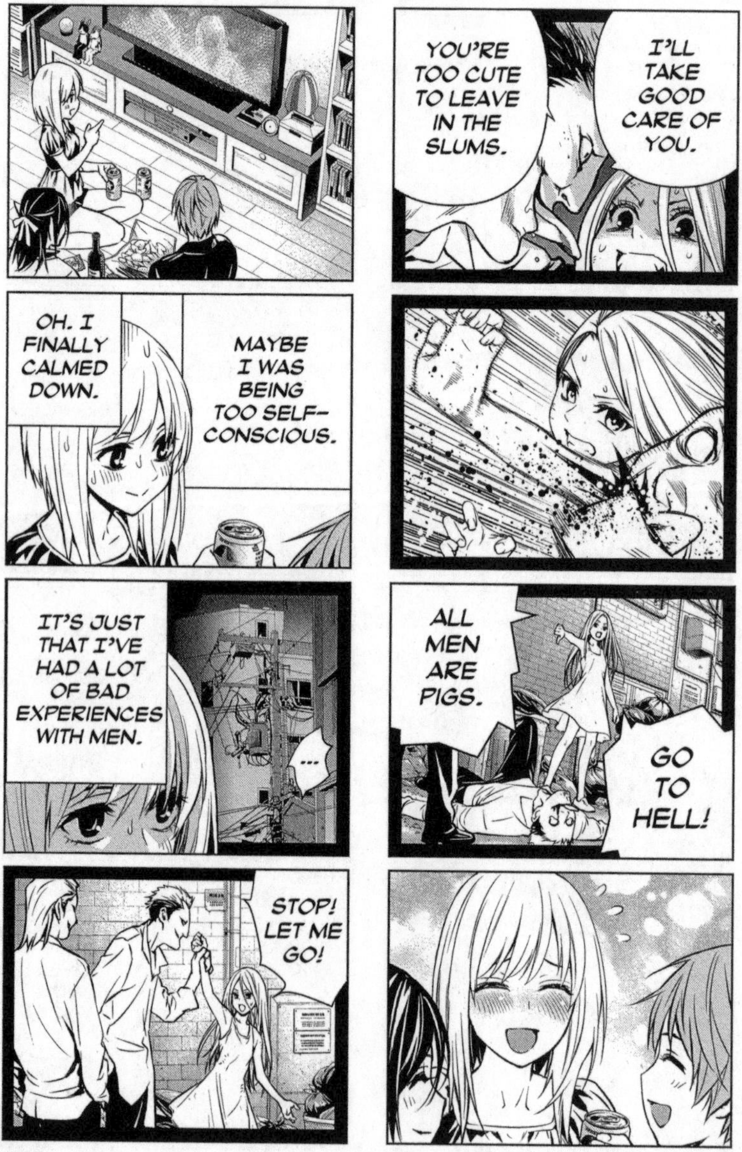
OH. I FINALLY CALMED DOWN.
MAYBE I WAS BEING TOO SELF-CONSCIOUS.
IT'S JUST THAT I'VE HAD A LOT OF BAD EXPERIENCES WITH MEN.
...
STOP! LET ME GO!
YOU'RE TOO CUTE TO LEAVE IN THE SLUMS.
I'LL TAKE GOOD CARE OF YOU.
ALL MEN ARE PIGS.
GO TO HELL!

The Night is Young

WHEW, I'M DRUNK. I'M GOING TO BED.

OH, GOOD NIGHT.

MY BEDROOM IS OFF-LIMITS, BY THE WAY!

AS FOR ME...

...THINK I'LL PREP FOR BREAK-FAST.

YOU SHOULD WATCH CHLOÉ'S MAGNUM OPUS.

MAGNUM OPUS?

THAT'S RIGHT.

IT'S CALLED GHOST REAPER GIRL!

GHOST REAPER GIRL

Akissa Saiké
Rika Shirota
Hashimoto
Shu Nagata

Editors
Ryota Kasai
Satoshi Watanabe

Designer
Daiju Asami

SEE YOU IN VOLUME 2!

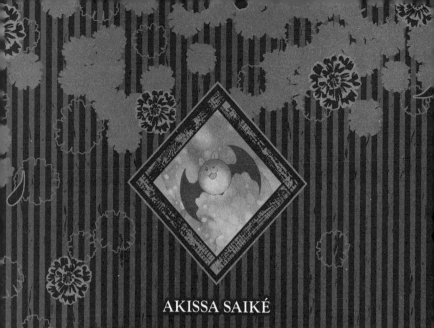

AKISSA SAIKÉ

Your late twenties and early thirties—what a great age to be! It's when you have the perfect balance of youthful exuberance and life experience. I think this period is one of life's peaks.

This story's heroine is 28 years old. A female protagonist who's almost 30! My editor joked that she's a very unusual main character for a shonen publication...

But if you think about it, doesn't shonen manga entrust battles over the fate of the world to minors a bit too often?

Akissa Saiké began working professionally as a manga artist with the four-volume magical-warrior fantasy series *Kiruto* in 2002, which was serialized in *Monthly Shonen Jump*. *Rosario+Vampire* began serialization in *Monthly Shonen Jump* in March of 2004 and continued in *Jump SQ* as *Rosario+Vampire: Season II*. In 2020, he changed his pen name from Akihisa Ikeda and launched *Ghost Reaper Girl* on the Jump+ platform.

GHOST REAPER GIRL

Volume 1
SHONEN JUMP Edition

STORY AND ART BY **Akissa Saiké**

GRAPHIC NOVEL TRANSLATION **Amanda Haley**
TOUCH-UP ART & LETTERING **Annaliese "Ace" Christman**
DESIGN **Joy Zhang**
EDITOR **Alexis Kirsch**

Printed in the U.S.A.

Published by VIZ Media, LLC
P.O. Box 77010
San Francisco, CA 94107

10 9 8 7 6 5 4 3 2 1
First printing, June 2022

viz.com

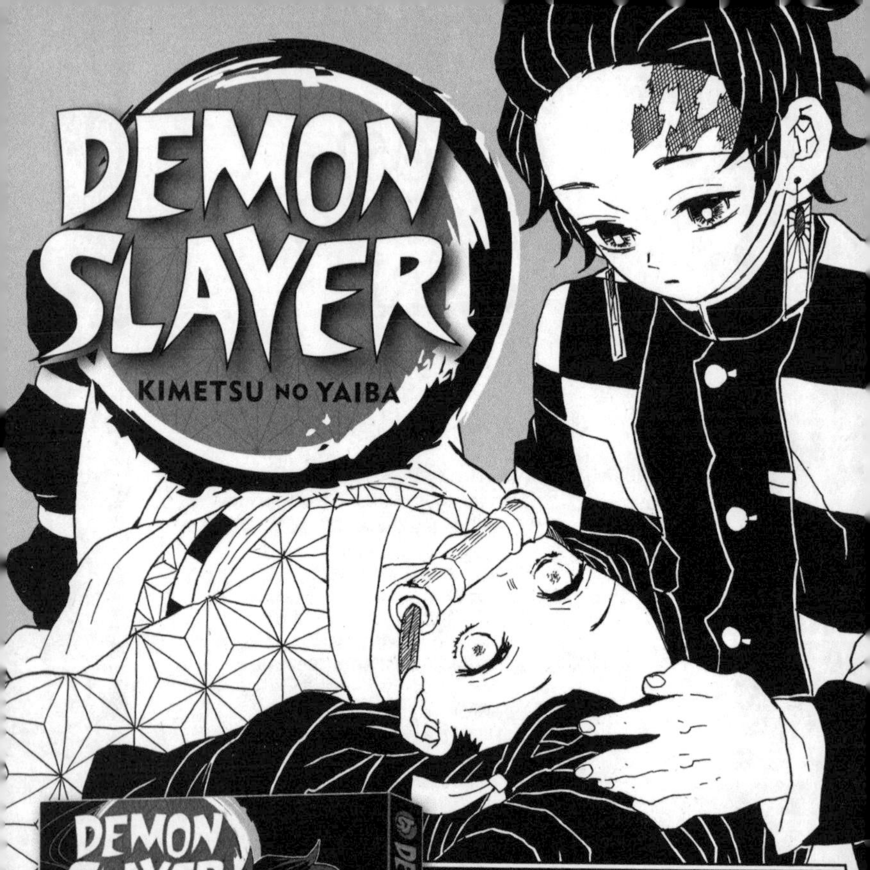
DEMON SLAYER
KIMETSU NO YAIBA

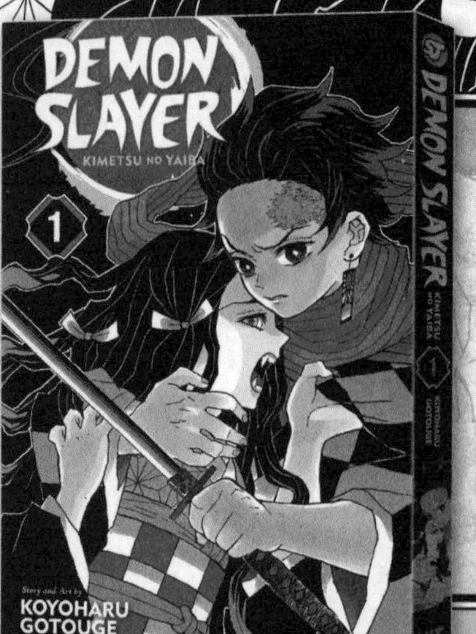
DEMON SLAYER
KIMETSU NO YAIBA
1
Story and Art by
KOYOHARU GOTOUGE

Story and Art by

KOYOHARU GOTOUGE

In Taisho-era Japan, kindhearted Tanjiro Kamado makes a living selling charcoal. But his peaceful life is shattered when a demon slaughters his entire family. His little sister Nezuko is the only survivor, but she has been transformed into a demon herself! Tanjiro sets out on a dangerous journey to find a way to return his sister to normal and destroy the demon who ruined his life.

RATED T TEEN

VIZ

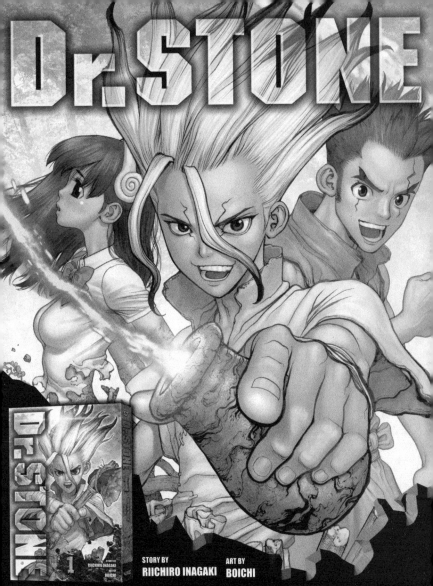

Dr. STONE

STORY BY
RIICHIRO INAGAKI

ART BY
BOICHI

One fateful day, all of humanity turned to stone. Many millennia later, Taiju frees himself from petrification and finds himself surrounded by statues. The situation looks grim—until he runs into his science-loving friend Senku! Together they plan to restart civilization with the power of science!

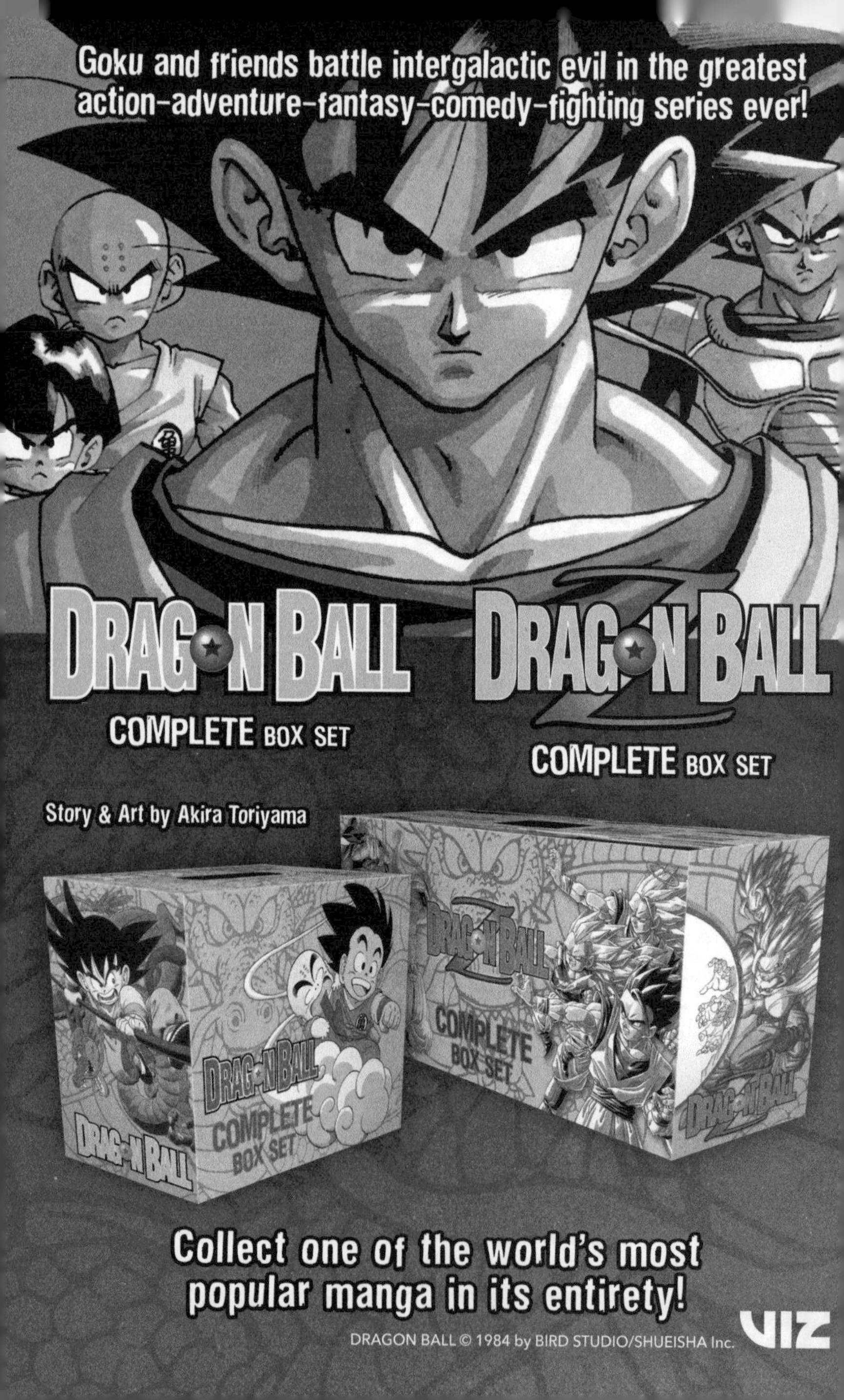

Goku and friends battle intergalactic evil in the greatest action-adventure-fantasy-comedy-fighting series ever!

DRAG★N BALL
COMPLETE BOX SET

DRAG★N BALL Z
COMPLETE BOX SET

Story & Art by Akira Toriyama

Collect one of the world's most popular manga in its entirety!

VIZ

Black ✤ Clover

STORY & ART BY YŪKI TABATA

Asta is a young boy who dreams of becoming the greatest mage in the kingdom. Only one problem—he can't use any magic! Luckily for Asta, he receives the incredibly rare five-leaf clover grimoire that gives him the power of anti-magic. Can someone who can't use magic really become the Wizard King? One thing's for sure—Asta will never give up!

SHONEN JUMP

VIZ media
www.viz.com

YOU'RE READING THE
WRONG WAY!

Have evil spirits taken over this manga?!
How can this be the wrong way?

Unlike most manga, *Ghost Reaper Girl*
reads left to right in traditional English
order, as requested by Akissa Saiké,
creator of the series.